Your

GUIDE
to
METABOLIC
HEALTH

D0879015

Dr. Gina Honeyman-Lowe
Dr. John C. Lowe

Editor: Jackie Yellin
Associate Editor: Gail Arnold
Proofreaders: Michael Yellin, Sue Wood
Cover artwork: Karenna LaMonica
Cover design: Gina Honeyman-Lowe
               Karenna LaMonica
               John C. Lowe

The information in *Your Guide to Metabolic Health* is for educational purposes only. It is not meant to be directions for the treatment of any individual patient, and it is not intended to substitute for care by a qualified, licensed, and competent health care professional. Care by such a professional may be necessary to meet the unique needs of an individual. The authors, publisher, and others involved in the production and publication of this book do not recommend that readers alter treatment programs devised for them by health care professionals without individualized guidance by those professionals or others. Neither the authors, publisher, nor any other parties who have been involved in the preparation or publication of this book warrant that the information contained herein is indicated, applicable, effective, or safe in any individual case. The authors, publisher, and others involved in the production and publication of this book also disclaim any liability resulting directly or indirectly from the use of the information contained in the book. Health care professionals should supervise readers in any matters pertinent to their physical or mental health.

Library of Congress Cataloging-in-Publication Data
Honeyman-Lowe, G., Lowe, John C.
       Your guide to metabolic health/Gina Honeyman-Lowe, John C. Lowe
       Includes bibliographical references and index
       1. Metabolism 2. Hypothyroidism 3. Fibromyalgia

ISBN 0-9741238-0-3

Printed in the United States of America

McDowell Health-Science Books, LLC
Boulder, Colorado

To the patients whose improvement or recovery with metabolic rehabilitation inspires us to continue our work on behalf of the millions who still suffer from poor metabolic health.

And, to the patient advocates and alternative doctors who diligently and courageously work to relieve human suffering by correcting conventional doctors' false beliefs.

Acknowledgments

Dr. Broda Barnes, for his colossal contribution to our understanding of hypothyroidism.

Dr. Leon Chaitow, for helping educate patients and health care practitioners by generously describing our work in his widely-read books.

Dr. Barry Durrant-Peatfield, for serving as an exemplary model for the practice of clinical medicine, for his courageous opposition to the political tyranny of conventional endocrinology, and for his generous hospitality toward us when we were in the United Kingdom.

Dr. William McK. Jefferies, for his immense contribution to our understanding of hypofunction of the adrenal cortex.

Jane, Karl, Josh, and Rachel Jones, for their generous and enthusiastic support of the Fibromyalgia Research Foundation, and for their friendship.

Dr. Steven Langer, for his gigantic contributions, along with James F. Scheer, to educating the public about hypothyroidism and thyroid hormone resistance.

Lyn Mynott (Chairperson), Eileen Elks (Secretary/Treasurer), and the other volunteers at Thyroid UK, for their steadfast commitment to helping patients recover from chronic illness caused by lack of treatment or under-treatment for hypothyroidism and thyroid hormone resistance.

Diane Patterson, our Office Manager (a.k.a. Office Goddess), for proofreading chapters of the book, for being a constant support, and for keeping our lives in order.

James F. Scheer, for helping educate the public about hypothyroidism and poor metabolic health in general through clear and prolific writing, and for his friendship.

Mary Shomon, for her support and encouragement, and for her continuing work to educate the public and health care professionals about hypothyroidism.

Dr. Devin Starlanyl, for contributing to the public understanding of the roles hypothyroidism and thyroid hormone resistance play in fibromyalgia, and for her and Justine Jeffrey's studies on the use of transdermal T_3 by fibromyalgia patients.

Paul Stein, for enriching conversations about health care and other matters, and for reading and commenting on *Chapter 8*.

Barry Thipthorp, for his support of Linda Thipthorp in her assistance to patients with poor metabolic health, for his valiant efforts to inform others of the need for effective metabolic treatment, and for his friendship.

Linda Thipthorp, for her suggestions on the content of this book, for her extraordinary devotion to helping relieve the suffering of patients the world over, and for her friendship.

Peter Warmingham, for serving as an example of exceptional rationality in the field of fibromyalgia, and for his clear and accurate reports of our work for patients and doctors in the United Kingdom.

Jackie and Michael Yellin, for their fraternal involvment in our work, for their family-like loyalty and support, and for their enduring friendship.

Contents

Foreword

MANAGING A DAILY SCHEDULE WAS my biggest challenge in life. Like most fibromyalgia sufferers, I had no idea which symptoms were going to flare and to what degree. I had severe morning stiffness, swollen and painful ankles, upper back and neck pain, fatigue, water retention, difficulty breathing, loss of muscle tone, and skin painful to the touch. I spent eleven years trying to find the cause of my debilitating symptoms. Simple household chores such as sweeping or taking clothes out of the washer were exhausting and painful. I gave up my life's ambition of training horses and teaching horsemanship. I didn't have enough strength to lift a saddle or mount a horse.

I had been to several doctors. Some, I refused to see again, and some told me to stay away. Each gave me the standard treatment for fibromyalgia: a multitude of prescription drugs such as anti-inflammatories, antidepressants, muscle relaxants, narcotics, diuretics, and the list goes on. I got no relief from the drugs and ended up with more symptoms. I reviewed the side effects of the drugs and found them to be dangerous. Concerned, I refused to take them because the prescription drug treatment made no sense. To my surprise, when I refused to take the prescribed drugs, my doctor got angry. I was told I didn't want to get well and was fired as a patient! Shocked, I remember sitting in my car for hours overwhelmed, devastated, humiliated, guilt-ridden, and terrified. I was so sick and needed help now more than ever, and a doctor was my only hope, I thought. After hours of despair and turmoil, I was afraid that I would never find out the cause of my symptoms.

Two years later, under the guidance of a new doctor, I changed my diet to whole foods and started taking vitamin supplements. I looked for food allergies, realized my physical limitations, and made some great lifestyle changes. Still, though, I had debilitating symptoms, and this aggravated my fears.

My doctor put me through a multitude of tests, including a thyroid function test. When my test result came back slightly abnormal, I thought my problems were solved. I was given a very small replacement dose of Synthroid, but my symptoms remained. I was confused because my thyroid function test result now appeared normal, yet my symptoms were those of hypothyroidism. My doctor kept assuring me that my thyroid was fine. I trusted and depended on him to know about all the latest research and treatment for fibromyalgia.

When my family purchased a personal computer, I began researching web sites on fibromyalgia. Most of the web sites focused on the latest expensive drugs or supplements I had tried. When I came across Dr. Lowe's and Dr. Honeyman-Lowe's web site, I was intrigued. I learned that fibromyalgia sufferers were improving or recovering with the use of the thyroid hormone T_3 and a well-rounded plan of nutritional supplements, wholesome diet, and exercise.

Inspired, I took the information to my doctor with great anticipation. His reaction floored me! He said, "You don't want to do this; it's experimental; *you could have a heart attack and die!*"

I left his office confused and devastated. I felt like a punctured tire—deflated, depressed, no air left to continue. This doctor had always worked with me to find alternatives to prescription drugs. I trusted him to keep me safe and to give me the best possible health care available. I certainly wanted to do nothing dangerous, but I refused to ignore Dr. Lowe's and Dr. Honeyman-Lowe's research.

A few weeks later, as I walked up the dreaded stairs, I gasped for breath. I felt so much pain; I felt that I was likely to have a heart attack and die even without taking T_3. If I tried this new and supposedly dangerous protocol, I'd have nothing to lose. My doctor's opposition convinced me that I first had to take responsibility for my own health care. I read the studies by Dr. Lowe and his research team to find out how people improved or recovered, despite the apparent risk involved. The more I read, the more Dr. Lowe's approach made sense. I wanted to follow the protocol exactly and needed some questions answered, so I wrote to him. He graciously took the time to respond. He gave me the information, confidence, and encouragement I needed. Most of all, I learned that he genuinely cares about people.

After gathering all the information I could, I was convinced I could be helped by his protocol, even though my doctor told me of its danger. I evaluated my present situation: I was eating a whole food diet, I took vitamin supplements, and abstained from using prescription medications. Exercise was out of the question. In no way, without tremendous pain and fatigue, could I exercise. My next step would be to use T_3, for which I needed a prescription. Now, I'd need to find another doctor.

On my first visit with my new doctor, I brought with me a notebook containing information about Dr. Lowe's and Dr. Honeyman-Lowe's protocol, my correspondence with Dr. Lowe, and the latest information on the thyroid function test. When we discussed the results of the thyroid function test I had taken the week before, he informed me that it was normal. We talked about what else could cause my symptoms. He agreed not to focus on what the thyroid function test can reveal but to focus on my symptoms, which indicated hypothyroidism. He looked over the information in the notebook and wanted to know the bottom line. This is it, I thought, the moment of truth; I'm going to ask for what is, according to my last doctor, a very dangerous treatment—T_3. I kept my composure and asked for the prescription. I braced myself for the expected opposing reaction. When he said, "That won't hurt you," I thought, Wow! What a contradiction! I thought T_3 was this harmful, "You-can-have-a-heart-attack-and-die" drug.

I read all the information I could about T_3. I read it several times in disbelief because I could find no dangerous side effects. When I discovered that it was safer than any of the drugs ever prescribed for fibromyalgia, I was furious. I realized my previous doctor of eight years, who did a lot for me and whom I trusted, lied to me! What motive could he have for keeping a treatment option from me? Though puzzled by his unknown motivation, I began to plan my recovery.

With the results of my research on Dr. Lowe's and Dr. Honeyman-Lowe's protocol, and my new doctor's willingness to prescribe T_3, I began to focus on getting well. According to Dr. Lowe's advice, I began by keeping a journal. I kept track of my diet, vitamins, and medication. I used charts and graphs to record the intensity of my symptoms and the changes in my ability to exercise (see Chapter 3). Also, I kept a copy of every thyroid function test result. Whenever I saw my doctor, I could show him my monthly progress, instead of just how I felt that particular day. The charts and graphs made clear to my doctor and me that the intensity of my symptoms had decreased, and my exercise/activity level had increased.

I had some small flare-ups along the way, but I kept progressing. Within four months of starting the protocol, my symptoms had improved. I was maintaining a regular walking schedule, and I was regaining my muscle tone through exercise. Within six months of starting the protocol, I felt like a normal person. I was enjoying the benefits of a full recovery! After my recovery, I returned to school and am now a licensed massage practitioner in Washington.

I've thought a lot about my fellow fibromyalgia sufferers who could improve or recover as I did. But because doctors ignore hypothyroid symptoms and treat each symptom individually with prescription drugs that give no relief, fibromyalgia patients don't have a chance to improve or recover. In my opinion, fibromyalgia patients are the people most *undiagnosed*, *misdiagnosed*, *untreated*, *undertreated*, and most outrageously *mistreated* by the medical community. To get past this and improve or recover, you must take responsibility for your own health care. You must research and learn all your options so that you can make informed decisions, and then accept only the treatment options that are best for you. *Your Guide to Metabolic Health* can help you accomplish this.

I want to thank all the people who have supported Dr. Honeyman-Lowe's and Dr. Lowe's research, and I want to thank the doctors for their remarkable work that has solved the puzzle of fibromyalgia. Through them and their research, I got the information and encouragement I needed to achieve full recovery! I become very emotional when I think of how their dedicated work and tremendous compassion for people who are needlessly suffering have impacted my family, my friends, my community, and me. I thank God that Dr. Lowe and Dr. Honeyman-Lowe cared enough to write this book for you and me. And I pray that the book will serve as the resource and guide that enables you to recover as I did.

Vicky Massey
Former Fibromyalgia Sufferer
Licensed Massage Practitioner
Puyallup, WA 98373
Phone: 253-445-5193
Fax: 253-537-6072
E-mail: Victrail@aol.com

Introduction

Poor metabolic health is a worldwide problem, and it has been for some thirty years. Commonly today, doctors of patients with poor metabolic health give them a diagnosis that's a label for their set of symptoms. (For a list of the most common symptoms, see Table 2 in *Chapter 1*.) The most common labels are fibromyalgia, chronic fatigue syndrome, and myalgic encephalomyelitis. These labels suggest that the patients suffer from mysterious "new diseases." But as we explain in *Chapter 1*, the patients' various symptoms are caused by the same basic mechanism—abnormally slow metabolism.

Through many years of clinical practice and experimental research, we developed and refined a treatment program, called "metabolic rehabilitation" (metabolic rehab) to relieve patients' suffering. The treatment frees some 85% of patients from their symptoms. As we explain in *Your Guide to Metabolic Health*, when patients go through metabolic rehab and recover, relief from their symptoms lasts—as long as the patients continue the lifestyle practices and treatments they need to maintain good metabolic health.

In the chapters of this book, we explain how most patients can use a simplified version of metabolic rehab to improve their metabolic health. Most patients will need at least minimal cooperation from one or more health care practitioners. For example, most patients with poor metabolic health have either hypothyroidism or thyroid hormone resistance. For them to fully recover from their symptoms, effective thyroid hormone therapy is essential. In *Chapter 7*, we explain what "effective thyroid hormone therapy" is and how to get it. Most of the methods patients must use to improve or recover, however, are lifestyle practices they can begin using without help from a clinician. We explain what these practices are.

We also explain how to use the backbone of metabolic rehab— systematic monitoring and graphing of patients' symptoms. Building an individual program of metabolic rehab around this backbone is essential to achieving metabolic health, and it increases the chance that patients will recover from their symptoms of slow metabolism.

In the rest of this introduction to *Your Guide to Metabolic Health*, we explain how best to use this book. Reading the introduction is important—it will give you the proper orientation for getting started with an individualized program of metabolic rehab. We can't overemphasize the importance of a proper orientation. It provides patients the greatest chance of achieving optimal metabolic health. And optimal metabolic health is what we sincerely desire for every patient whose metabolism is presently too slow. It's for that purpose that we've written this book.

READERS IN ONE OF THREE CIRCUMSTANCES

We've designed this book for patients to use in one of three circumstances: working without a doctor's help, working with a minimally cooperative doctor, and working with a fully collaborative doctor.

Working Without a Doctor's Help

You may be working without the help of a doctor and not using thyroid hormone or other prescription medications. If so, you may be able to markedly improve your metabolic health using other methods we describe in this book.

Wholesome diet, nutritional supplements, and exercise to tolerance haven't been a part of many patients' lifestyles. For some of these patients, the absence of these practices from their lifestyles is the main cause of their symptoms of abnormally slow metabolism. Our research shows that 90% of fibromyalgia patients have some form of inadequate thyroid hormone regulation and must take thyroid hormone to completely recover. But if you do not have fibromyalgia or thyroid disease, or if you fall within the 10% of fibromyalgia patients who do not need thyroid hormone, then the other metabolism-stimulating practices we describe in this book may be sufficient for you. If you're one of these patients, you may improve, or even recover, by making these practices part of your life.

Keep in mind, though, that for *all* patients, self-monitoring and graphing regularly (see *Chapter 3*) can be the difference between success or failure. Most likely, you'll improve some if you merely use the methods we describe to speed up your metabolism and reduce your metabolic demand. But you stand a far greater chance of improving or getting completely well if you use those methods *and* systematically monitor and graph changes in your health status over time. Also, by systematically monitoring and graphing, you'll gain knowledge of which metabolism-regulating methods most improve your health. You can use this knowledge to gradually improve your health even more, and you can use it to recover your health should it slip at times in the future.

Working With a Minimally Cooperative Doctor

You may be under the care of a doctor who'll prescribe thyroid hormone and other medications you may need. If so, that's good. Chances are, though, the doctor won't cooperate in using our method of monitoring and graphing your health status. If your doctor works within managed care or socialized medicine, he probably can't cooperate even if he'd like to. Without the monitoring and graphing, the chance of you succeeding at achieving metabolic health is much smaller. But you can markedly increase your chance of improving or recovering by doing the monitoring and graphing yourself.

Working With a Collaborative Doctor

You may have a cooperative doctor who'll work collaboratively with you. This is the best of possible circumstances. Our patients use *Your Guide to Metabolic Health* to aid them in working collaboratively with us. You should use it the same way in working with your doctor.

We regularly monitor our patients' metabolic health status. Then we post to line graphs the scores from the measures we take.

Patients gain an advantage by also doing their own monitoring, and by posting their scores to the line graph we've included in the *Forms* section. Doing their own monitoring and graphing, as we describe in *Chapter 3*, involves them more deeply in their own rehab process.

Our patients use *Your Guide to Metabolic Health* as a quick reference to the essentials of metabolic rehab. When we work with patients at the Center for Metabolic Health, we discuss with them far too much for them to remember at home. The book serves as an easy reminder for what they don't recall.

MAKING *YOUR GUIDE TO METABOLIC HEALTH* UNDERSTANDABLE

Many patients who'll use *Your Guide to Metabolic Health* have poor memory and concentration. Because of this, we've used every writing device we know to make the book understandable.

We've used contractions, short sentences, and short paragraphs. The text contains the simplest words and fewest technical terms possible. We've also chosen to be politically incorrect in the United States and refer to "the doctor" with the masculine pronoun "he." We believe statements such as "he or she" and "his or hers" are awkward and cumbersome. Such statements would needlessly make the book tough reading for many patients. We've used "she," however, to refer to the patient. Our reason is that the majority of patients who'll use this book are women.

HOW BEST TO USE THIS BOOK

We recommend that you read *Your Guide to Metabolic Health* cover-to-cover, and then refer back to chapters of special interest to you. If you're to understand why we make various recommendations, it's essential that you look at the overall picture of metabolic rehab. Metabolic rehab is a comprehensive, holistic program to improve your metabolic health. You must understand it as such if it is to work well for you. What doesn't work well is a piecemeal approach—choosing the practices that are easy or most convenient for you and neglecting other features of the comprehensive, holistic program. You'll understand best the approach we recommend by a thorough reading of the book. This won't be a daunting task for most patients since we've made the book a snugly condensed presentation of metabolic rehab.

Be sure to check the *Index* when you're looking for a topic of interest to you. The *Table of Contents* will point you in the right direction, but it can be frustrating to scan an entire chapter looking for just that topic you want to read about at the moment. We made the *Index* of the book extensive so that you can find the information you want as easily as possible.

When you come across terms you're not familiar with, look in the *Glossary* for the definitions. Understanding new material is much easier when you aren't guessing at the meanings of words. We've also included a section named *Resources*. It contains a list of books and websites that can expand your knowledge of matters related to metabolic health.

We also *strongly* encourage you to copy the blank graph from the *Forms* section, and use it for monitoring changes in your symptoms of poor metabolic health. Knowing which symptoms have changed, and how much, is essential to discerning whether you're on the right track or not. It's easy for most of us to lose sight of where we began and how far we've progressed over time. But you can keep accurate sight of your progress by using the graph. In the *Foreword*, Vicky Massey describes how this method was helpful in her recovery.

THE ULTIMATE REFERENCE BOOK—
THE METABOLIC TREATMENT OF FIBROMYALGIA

We *strongly* recommend that your doctor or therapist and you get copies of *The Metabolic Treatment of Fibromyalgia*.[1] The book is the ultimate resource on what we call fibromyalgia. It's also a comprehensive book on metabolism, thyroid hormone, and thyroid diseases. We know of no other book that more comprehensively covers hypothyroidism and thyroid hormone resistance and their proper treatment. The book contains practically anything your doctor or therapist and you might want to know about these subjects. Many patients have told us that their doctors have been far more cooperative after reading parts of the book and seeing, by its extensive documentation, how heavily grounded in science our approach is.

If you have the bigger book to refer to, you can become better informed and increase your chances of getting well. *Your Guide to Metabolic Health* is the pure essence and reminder of what most patients must know to achieve and optimize their metabolic health. Throughout this book, we'll refer to the sections of *The Metabolic Treatment of Fibromyalgia* where you can read details we lack space to include here. *The Metabolic Treatment of Fibromyalgia* contains more than 6,000 references to support our research findings.

The Metabolic Treatment of Fibromyalgia is available through: <www.McDowellPublishing.com> If you wish, you can instead have your local bookstore special order the book.

SECTION I
UNDERSTANDING
METABOLIC HEALTH

Chapter 1

Slow Metabolism:
Cause of the "New Diseases"

OVER THE PAST TEN YEARS, our treatment for patients whose metabolism is too slow—that is, patients who are "hypometabolic"—has received worldwide attention. There are two main reasons for the attention. First, many patients and doctors have told us that unlike other explanations of patients' symptoms, ours makes perfect sense. Second, patients who've fully recovered with our treatment have let others know, especially over the Internet.

The widespread attention has let us know something important: The beliefs to which our research and clinical experience have brought us are on target: Our work is meaningful and helpful to many patients and their doctors. This has encouraged us to continue our research and clinical care of patients.

These sweet aspects of the attention, however, are offset a bit by a slightly bitter one. The bitter aspect involves hearing many people's misconceptions about our work. In fact, we more commonly hear inaccurate descriptions of our work than we do accurate ones.

COMMON MISCONCEPTIONS ABOUT OUR WORK

Several misconceptions of our work are common. One is pervasive on Internet news groups and among medical writers. The misconception is that our treatment involves nothing more than the use of the thyroid hormone T_3. This is grossly inaccurate as we'll make clear in this book.

Some of our critics repeatedly state that we believe all fibromyalgia patients have subclinical hypothyroidism. At the same time, some of our supporters report that we believe thyroid hormone resistance underlies all patients' fibromyalgia. The critics and the supporters are wrong.

23

Recently, in a popular book on the holistic treatment of fibromyalgia and chronic fatigue syndrome, the author incorrectly explained our treatment to his readers.[287,p.46] He wrote that our patients use sustained- or timed-release T_3, which, as we'll make clear in this book, is never the case.

On a website that provides information about the conventional medical approach to hypothyroidism, the authors incorrectly characterized our treatment. They wrote that it is virtually the same as the "Wilson treatment program." Actually, the only similarity between Dr. Dennis Wilson's approach and ours is that he recommends that patients use T_3. However, he advises that all patients use the hormone, while only a percentage of our patients use it. Moreover, Wilson encourages the use of sustained- or timed-release T_3 in divided daily doses. In contrast, our protocol calls for the use of plain T_3 in a single daily dose. Other than Wilson's treatment and ours involving T_3, the protocols are *completely* different. In fact, the similarity between the two treatments is literally as tiny as the microscopic T_3 molecule itself.

The most erroneous description of our treatment comes from some rheumatologists who study fibromyalgia. They've stated that we use T_4 replacement therapy. Why they believe this baffles us. We firmly believe and have widely publicized that mainstream doctors' use of T_4 replacement is a cause of worldwide human misery and premature death. In fact, if we are to blame one cause for the rise of the so-called "new diseases," such as fibromyalgia and chronic fatigue syndrome, it would be the use of T_4 replacement therapy within mainstream medicine.[83][222] Rather than using T_4 replacement therapy, we believe it should be abandoned as one of the worst disasters in modern medicine.

WHY OUR WORK IS MISUNDERSTOOD

Over the years, we've learned several reasons for the widespread misconceptions about our work. First, our approach is based on complicated research, and it's tough even for us to state it simply. For that reason, it's understandable that many people don't grasp it.

Second, many patients interested in our work have poor memory and concentration due to their medical condition. It's often hard for them to hold onto the meaning of the most basic information. But even patients with good memory and concentration sometimes have trouble fully understanding our work.

Third, the maddening pace of modern life limits most patients to learning only snippets of information about our work—too little to fully comprehend it. They pass along their fragmented understanding to other patients who are equally rushed and busy. In turn, these people give the fragments of information only a fleeting glance. Then they pass on to others an even more inaccurate version. So, even if the description of our work was accurate to start with, it becomes less so in passing from person to person.

We find it fascinating, though, that despite their poor memory and concentration and their rushed lives, far more patients than doctors accurately understand our work. The main reason patients are more knowledgeable is their stronger motivation. It is they who are ill, and they who want to recover their health. So, they more often invest the time and effort to gain accurate knowledge. As a result, patients often teach their open-minded and collaborative doctors about our work. Or, on the other hand, they irritate and alienate closed-minded doctors who want to dictate and have patients obey.

But like patients, doctors and researchers today are victims of the accelerated pace of life. These professionals are rushed, harried, and overwhelmed with the deluge of new information in their own specialties. It's distressing for them to have to take the time and effort to revise their long-held beliefs based on new information from fields that overlap their own. So they cling to outdated beliefs they learned in school and fall further behind many patients' more current knowledge.

Fourth, even though our treatment isn't complicated or esoteric, it's not what many patients and doctors are used to. Most patients are accustomed to seeing a doctor who gives them a prescription and asks them to report back in a few weeks. Many patients get physical treatment from chiropractic physicians or therapists in clinics and, at intervals, return for more. Patients and doctors are less accustomed to *rehabilitative* treatment (see *Chapter 3*), in which the patient and doctor closely work together over a period of months. The goal of this collaboration is for the patient to recover her health by gradually and systematically eliminating health-impairing obstacles. Patients and doctors don't readily absorb details of this type of treatment into their memory banks and pass it on to others. Not, of course, unless they themselves have gone through rehab.

For several reasons, then, people commonly misconceive our clinical approach and the scientific beliefs it's based on. So, to set the record straight, we accurately explain in Table 1 what our research and clinical experience have taught us, and in *Chapter 2*, we describe our treatment.

WHY YOU SHOULD UNDERSTAND FIBROMYALGIA—EVEN IF YOU DON'T SUFFER FROM IT

As you read this book, you'll note that we write a lot about fibromyalgia. In fact, fibromyalgia is our point of reference within the field of slow metabolism and its effects on health. If you've never been diagnosed as having fibromyalgia, you might think that this book doesn't concern your health problems. However, it's important that you take a few moments to understand fibromyalgia, even if you don't suffer from it. If you do, you'll see the relevance of the entire book to you, even if your major symptom is chronic fatigue, depression, painful menstruation, or any of a wide array of other symptoms caused by slow metabolism.

Fibromyalgia is the clinical problem that led us to the more general subject of poor health from slow metabolism. The fibromyalgia patient's major symptoms are chronic widespread pain and tenderness. The patient perceives that it's her muscles that are painful. Her muscles, however, aren't the underlying source of the pain and tenderness. Instead, too little thyroid hormone regulation of cells in the patient's brain stem and spinal cord cause her to be extremely sensitive to pain.

As chiropractic physicians, we are trained to diagnose and treat patients for muscle pain. Naturally, many fibromyalgia patients seek out chiropractic physicians. In fact, the types of health care professionals fibromyalgia patients most prefer are chiropractic physicians and massage therapists.[139]

Fibromyalgia patients, however, don't suffer only from pain and tenderness. Most also have other symptoms, such as stiffness and fatigue, although these other symptoms are less severe than their pain. In caring for our fibromyalgia patients, we were determined to figure out the cause of their pain and other symptoms. We learned that their symptoms are caused by one or more metabolism-slowing factors. The most common factors are:

1) inadequate thyroid hormone regulation
2) poor diet, usually one that causes irregular blood sugar levels and low energy in cells
3) multiple nutritional deficiencies
4) low physical fitness
5) adrenal and sex hormone imbalances
6) the use of drugs that slow metabolism

We discuss each of these in detail in different chapters of *Your Guide to Metabolic Health.*

Learning that abnormally slow metabolism was the underlying cause of fibromyalgia patients' pain, tenderness, and other symptoms opened our eyes to something of vital importance to the health and well-being of millions of people. That something is: Slow metabolism is the underlying cause of a vast array of health problems other than fibromyalgia.

WHAT PATIENTS WITH DIFFERENT
DIAGNOSES HAVE IN COMMON

Many doctors (most notably Broda Barnes[185]) have long argued that thyroid blood test results don't reliably identify patients with hypothyroidism. Because the tests aren't reliable, these doctors argue that we should treat patients with thyroid hormone when they have hypothyroid-like symptoms.

Conventional endocrinologists disagree, arguing that doctors shouldn't treat patients based on symptoms. Their reason is that symptoms are "nonspecific." What they mean by nonspecific is that disorders other than hypothyroidism can cause symptoms similar to those of hypothyroidism. And treating patients because they have these symptoms may miss the mark; a disorder unrelated to thyroid hormone might be causing the symptoms.

The conventional endocrinologists are correct that conditions other than a thyroid hormone deficiency can cause hypothyroid-like symptoms. As *The Metabolic Treatment of Fibromyalgia*[1,pp.248-249] details, several conditions can cause hypothyroid-like symptoms: resistance to thyroid hormone; low physical fitness; cortisol deficiency; folic acid and vitamin B_1 deficiencies; beta-blocking drugs; and fasting, chronic low-calorie dieting, or starvation. The reason these conditions all cause hypothyroid-like symptoms is that they all decrease metabolism just as hypothyroidism does.

Recognizing that such conditions cause symptoms similar to those of hypothyroidism is important. It shows us the variety of conditions that can cause the subject of this book—poor metabolic health. Knowing what conditions to look for enables us to identify them when they're affecting a patient. And after identifying them, we can devise a therapeutic strategy to eliminate or control the conditions, enabling the patient to recover from her symptoms and achieve optimal metabolic health.

Table 1. What Our Studies and Clinical Experience Have Taught Us

● Fibromyalgia is a label for two symptoms, pain and tenderness. These symptoms are caused largely by impaired metabolism of cells in the spinal cord and brain stem that normally keep humans pain free.

● Many other patients' symptoms, diagnosed as different disorders, are caused by impaired metabolism of other body tissues.

● Of the fibromyalgia patients we tested, 12% had lab results consistent with primary hypothyroidism. About 44% had lab results consistent with central hypothyroidism. In total, about 56% of our patients were hypothyroid according to lab results.

● The remaining 44% of our fibromyalgia patients had lab results consistent with normal interaction of the pituitary gland and thyroid gland. Of this 44%, we have conclusive proof that some 75% have partial cell resistance to thyroid hormone.

● Both hypothyroidism and thyroid hormone resistance are forms of thyroid disease. Adding together our patients who have one or the other of these diseases shows that 90% of our fibromyalgia patients have thyroid disease.

● Most of the 90% of our patients with evidence of thyroid disease are, before treatment, also affected by one or more other metabolism-slowing factors. The most common factors are (1) poor diet (usually one that causes irregular blood sugar levels and energy abnormalities in cells), (2) nutritional deficiencies, (3) low physical fitness, (4) adrenal and sex hormone imbalances, and (5) the use of drugs that impair metabolism. These other factors compound the effects of hypothyroidism and thyroid hormone resistance in causing patients' symptoms of fibromyalgia.

● To become fully and lastingly well, fibromyalgia patients must undergo treatment with the proper form and dose of thyroid hormone. But the patients must also eliminate or control all other factors that contribute to their slow metabolism. Most patients can succeed using the principles of metabolic rehab—a systematic method of assessing changes in symptoms over time in response to a combination of metabolism-normalizing therapies. The cooperation of a clinician experienced at guiding patients to metabolic health is ideal. But as Vicky Massey did (see the *Foreword*), many patients working alone, or with a little cooperation from a clinician, can use metabolic rehab to systematically guide themselves to optimal metabolic health.

● Patients with other symptoms and diagnoses, such as chronic fatigue syndrome, also have impaired metabolism. The factors slowing their metabolism are the same as those affecting fibromyalgia patients. The other patients have different symptoms because the metabolism-slowing factors mainly affect different tissues than in fibromyalgia patients. These other patients benefit from metabolic rehab just as do most fibromyalgia patients.

We want to emphasize, however, that the answer to diagnosing the cause of a patient's hypothyroid-like symptoms doesn't depend exclusively on using thyroid blood test results. We don't rule out a thyroid problem even if the TSH is within its reference range. A TRH-stimulation test may suggest that a patient has central hypothyroidism. And if this test is also negative, the patient may still have "peripheral resistance to thyroid hormone." We use thyroid blood tests along with a wide range of others. But we also use what's traditionally been called "deductive differential diagnosis." This is an approach to diagnosis in which the doctor uses his or her intelligence in a process of rational judgment. This approach is largely absent from modern mainstream medicine, much to the detriment of millions of patients.

As we've said, patients usually receive diagnostic labels based on their *major* symptom, such as fatigue or pain. When patients with different diagnoses begin comparing notes, they find something intriguing. First, what is a major symptom for some patients is a minor one for others. When patients list all their symptoms, even minor ones, and they compare the lists, the symptoms of different patients notably overlap.

Second, what differs most among patients is only which symptom is the most severe one. And third, the patients get the distinct impression that the underlying cause of one list of symptoms is the same as the underlying cause of the other lists.

In short, the patients seem to have the same disease. And in fact, they do in the sense that the symptoms of all are caused by impaired metabolism. What's equally intriguing is that when the patients undergo metabolic rehab, the successful result confirms what caused the symptoms of each despite their differing diagnoses—slow metabolism of various body tissues due to one or more of the metabolism-impairing factors we describe in this book.

For convenience, Table 2 lists symptoms of hypometabolism, regardless of which metabolism-slowing factors cause them. We provide this list so that you can check off the symptoms you suffer from. You should use the symptoms you check to create your monitoring system that we explain in *Chapter 3*.

The assorted symptoms caused by impaired metabolism lead to different diagnoses. But regardless of the diagnosis, identifying and eliminating the factors impairing a patient's metabolism is a powerful approach to freeing patients from their symptoms.

WHY DIFFERENT SYMPTOMS
AND DIFFERENT DIAGNOSES

To understand how to achieve metabolic health, it will help to know why poor metabolic health has become a major public health problem. And knowing why will make it obvious that impaired metabolism can cause many different symptoms.

Mainstream medicine has taken a couple of odd routes over the last thirty years. Both of the routes involve a surrender of informed judgment. These routes have led to decades of disaster for millions of patients.

One route has been for doctors to base any and every clinical decision on the results of lab tests. The outcome of this extremist technological approach is absurd. A patient can have the classic symptoms and appearance of a disease. Yet if her lab results are "normal," the doctor denies that the patient has the disease and refuses to give her treatment. Doctors abide by this practice even though few lab tests reliably identify patients with the disease the test is intended to detect. Most conventional doctors have become so dependent on lab results that they've lost the ability to make intelligent decisions based on what they see, hear, and feel. In fact, the doctors have made themselves dispensable. They could easily be replaced by robots that print out prescriptions based on the results of automated tests of blood or urine that patients deposit into the robot. Functioning like such robots, conventional doctors bear a striking resemblance to soda or candy machines that respond to an item number or button choice by dispensing the appropriate product.

The other route conventional doctors have taken seems contra-dictory in view of their exclusive dependence on lab results. This route has been to invent new diagnostic labels that are really noth-ing more than synonyms for patients' main symptoms. They invent these labels when lab results—again, few of which are especially reliable—don't point to a particular disease. So if a patient has the classic symptoms of a specific disease, but lab results don't verify the disease, doctors invent a new diagnostic label. The new diag-nosis says nothing about an underlying cause of the symptoms. It's merely a label that succinctly says the patient has a particular set of symptoms.

Let's take an example, chronic fatigue syndrome. Conventional doctors falsely believe that most lab tests are *absolutely* failsafe in identifying patients with various diseases. When a patient has chronic fatigue, doctors order the tests that should identify the diseases known to involve chronic fatigue. Among such diseases is hypothyroidism. The test most conventional doctors mistakenly believe is guaranteed to identify hypothyroidism—the "Gold Stan-dard" for doing so—is the TSH.[134][222] Naturally, then, when pa-tients complain about chronic fatigue, most doctors include the TSH test among those they order.

Seldom do patients' TSH levels indicate hypothyroidism. (Our studies suggest the test result indicates hypothyroidism in only ab-out 12% of cases.[2][3]) Because patients' TSH levels are "normal," conventional doctors conclude that it's *impossible* that a problem with thyroid hormone could be related to the patient's fatigue. And since other test results are also usually within the "normal" range, the doctors conclude that the patient's fatigue must be caused by some mysterious "new disease"—a disease whose cause is yet un-discovered. And the cause *remains* undiscovered—in the case of fibromyalgia, for some 30 years!—because the "cause" of the new disease is in fact the mistaken thinking of conventional doctors and researchers: mistaken in the sense that they falsely believe in the perfection of their lab tests in identifying known diseases.

Table 2. Symptoms and Signs of Hypometabolism*

☐ Fatigue	☐ Dry skin	☐ Emotional instability
☐ Lethargy	☐ Dry mucous	☐ Choking sensation
☐ Low endurance	membranes	☐ Fineness of hair
☐ Slow speech	☐ Constipation	☐ Hair loss
☐ Slow thinking	☐ Weight gain with	☐ Blueness of skin
☐ Poor memory	little food intake	☐ Dry, thick, scaling skin
☐ Poor concentration	☐ Paleness of lips	☐ Dry, coarse, brittle
☐ Depression	☐ Shortness of breath	hair
☐ Nervousness	☐ Swelling	☐ Paleness of skin
☐ Anxiety	☐ Hoarseness	☐ Puffy skin
☐ Worrying	☐ Loss of appetite	☐ Puffy face or eyelids
☐ Easy emotional upset	☐ Prolonged or heavy	☐ Swelling of ankles
☐ Obsessive thinking	menstrual bleeding	☐ Coarse skin
☐ Low motivation	☐ Painful menstruation	☐ Brittle or thin nails
☐ Dizziness	☐ Low sex drive	☐ Dry ridges down nails
☐ Sensation of cold	☐ Impotence	☐ Difficulty swallowing
☐ Cold skin	☐ Hearing loss	☐ Weakness
☐ Decreased sweating	☐ Rapid heart rate	☐ Vague body aches
☐ Heat intolerance	☐ Pounding heart beat	& pains
☐ Non-restful sleep	☐ Slow pulse rate	☐ Muscle pain
☐ Insomnia	☐ Pain at front of chest	☐ Joint pain
☐ Thick tongue	☐ Poor vision	☐ Numbness or tingling
☐ Swelling of face	☐ Weight loss	☐ Protrusion of one
☐ Swelling of eyelids	☐ Wasting of tongue	or both eyeballs
		☐ Sparse eyebrows

*After L.J. DeGroot, P.R. Larsen, S. Refetoff, and J.B. Stanbury, *The Thyroid and Its Diseases*, 5th edition. New York, John Wiley & Sons, Inc., 1984, and Lowe, J.C.: *The Metabolic Treatment of Fibromyalgia*. McDowell Publishing Co., L.C., Boulder, 2000.

As we said, conventional doctors and researchers invented new terms for what's ailing the fatigued patients. In the United States, doctors made up the label "chronic fatigue syndrome." For the same fatigued patients, doctors in the United Kingdom came up with a label seemingly pregnant with meaning—"myalgic encephalomyelitis" or "ME."

We've treated many patients who met the criteria for chronic fatigue syndrome. As Dr. Jay Goldstein also reported,[223] these patients met the criteria for fibromyalgia as well as chronic fatigue syndrome. When we've treated the chronic fatigue syndrome patients with metabolic rehab, they've responded just as fibromyalgia patients do. Most fully recover and no longer meet the criteria for either chronic fatigue syndrome or fibromyalgia.

Essentially, our clinical experiences have shown that most of the patients, regardless of their diagnosis, get well with metabolic rehab involving thyroid hormone therapy. We've concluded from these clinical experiences that thyroid lab tests don't do what they're supposed to do: reliably identify patients who have too little thyroid hormone regulation of their tissues.

Patients with fibromyalgia symptoms have a history similar to that of chronic fatigue syndrome patients. It's well established that too little thyroid hormone regulation causes many patients to have chronic widespread pain. But in the 1970s, rheumatologists tested and found that some patients with widespread pain had thyroid test results that were within the so-called "normal" ranges. This led the rheumatologists to decide that it was impossible that the patients' pain was related to too little thyroid hormone regulation. So, the doctors invented a new label, fibromyalgia, as a synonym for the patients' widespread pain.

And patients with other major symptoms have undergone the same labeling. This is true of patients with high cholesterol ("hypercholesterolemia"), women with prolonged menstrual bleeding ("hypermenorrhea") or painful menstruation ("dysmenorrhea"), men with low sex drive and trouble maintaining an erection ("erectile dysfunction"), patients with dry skin and mucous membranes ("sicca syndrome"), depression unrelated to life events ("endogenous depression"), and so on—a new label for any symptom that lab results fail to indicate is part of a known disease. And for every new label, companies market one or more drugs for doctors to prescribe, reducing mainstream medical practice to the equivalent of painting by numbers.

These trends—exclusive dependence on lab results and inventing labels for patients' main symptoms—are part of the decay of modern medicine. The result is that doctors have become less competent at finding the underlying causes of patients' symptoms. The doctors simply apply the new label for the symptom and then prescribe drugs that corporations have concocted and marketed to control the symptoms.

None of the drugs, however, succeed at what they're intended to do—completely control the patient's main symptom. The reason is that the drugs don't correct the underlying cause of the symptom. Despite this, the practice of mainstream medicine today mostly involves providing patients with these ineffective drugs based on the new labels for their main symptom. As a result, patients under the care of conventional doctors continue to receive prescriptions for the drugs and yet continue to suffer from symptoms of slow metabolism. And tragically, the very drugs conventional doctors prescribe to try to control symptoms may actually worsen the symptoms by slowing the patients' metabolism even more (see *Chapter 15*).

Our approach is different, and our aim in writing this book is to teach you to use it. By doing so, you stand a far better chance of achieving metabolic health.

Chapter 2

Metabolic Rehabilitation

METABOLIC REHABILITATION (REHAB) IS A process in which a patient gets control of, or eliminates, all the factors that are impeding her metabolism. We want to emphasize, however, that the process is *not* haphazard; it's highly organized and systematic.

When we guide patients through metabolic rehab (as does any clinician who helps patients through a rehabilitation process), we take numerous measurements of the patients' metabolic status at fairly close intervals, say every one to two weeks. We post the patients' scores from the measures to line graphs. It's the graphs that give us power and precision in guiding the patients to full recovery. Without the measures, and without the graphs, we wouldn't be practicing rehabilitation.

An important measure we use with every patient is her estimate of the severity of her symptoms. In *Chapter 3*, we guide you through setting up your own system for monitoring your symptoms, and we show you how to create your own line graph. Unless you monitor a large number of symptoms, you can use a single graph. Figure 1 is an example of a patient's line graph.

When you choose the symptoms you want to free yourself from, and you create your monitoring system including a line graph, you'll be set to do your own simplified version of metabolic rehab. As you progress through your treatment, you should measure the severity of your symptoms, either weekly or biweekly, depending on the form of thyroid hormone you may be using. You should measure the symptoms at regular intervals, and each time, post your scores (one score for each symptom you're measuring) to your line graph. Post it as a small dot, triangle, square, or other such symbol. Or you can use different colors for the different symptom lines.

As the dots or other symbols accumulate on the line graph, draw a line through those that refer to the same symptom (as in

Figure 1). This will create what we call a "trend line." The trend lines on your graph will show you how your treatment is progressing. The lines are your most dependable source of information during your metabolic rehab process.

By using the lines, you'll know whether your treatment is working, and if so, how well it's working. With this information, you can make informed decisions about what you must do next to achieve your goal of optimal metabolic health. Your target is to be free from symptoms of hypometabolism. The trend lines will show you how far on or off target you are. If you're off target, you can readjust your aim, and by doing so, you can systematically guide yourself to the bull's-eye—being symptom free.

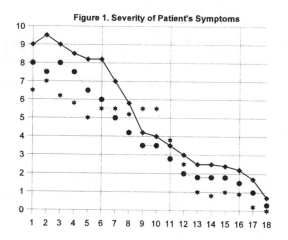

Figure 1. Severity of Patient's Symptoms

As we said, *Chapter 3* shows you how to set up and use a graph. In this chapter, though, we focus on two other things: selecting the symptoms you'll monitor, and the metabolism-slowing factors you may need to correct or control to achieve and maintain metabolic health.

WHAT YOU'RE TO MEASURE

Crucial to improving your metabolic health, as we explained in *Chapter 1*, is being clear on what symptoms of hypometabolism you suffer from. In Table 2 of *Chapter 1*, we list symptoms common to hypometabolic patients, especially those who are hypothyroid or thyroid hormone resistant. List the symptoms you have in the order of their severity. Place more severe symptoms highest on your list.

Be aware that the list in Table 2 of *Chapter 1* doesn't contain all possible symptoms of hypometabolism. You may have some rare symptom of sluggish metabolism that isn't in the list. Over the years, we've occasionally been surprised when patients going through metabolic rehab tell us about symptoms that improved for them—symptoms we had never imagined were caused by slow metabolism. For example, a patient of mine (JCL) told me that for years, he'd blinked so often that it was dangerous for him to drive a car. After he began improving during his metabolic rehab, the blinking ceased.

You can include any symptom you would like to be free of, but if you monitor too many, graphing the severity scores can be unwieldy. If you want to monitor more than four to six, you would best make two graphs and divide the symptoms between the graphs. For most patients, however, monitoring the most bothersome four to six symptoms works well. This is especially so if the symptoms are among the classic ones for hypothyroid or thyroid hormone resistant patients: fatigue, widespread pain, muscle stiffness, poor memory and concentration, depression, nonrestful sleep, exercise intolerance, abnormal coldness, bowel disturbance, dry skin and hair, hair loss, and inability to lose excess fat despite exercise and a wholesome diet.

When you have your list of symptoms, make a severity scale for each. To learn how to do this, read the first section in *Chapter 3*. Also make a line graph for your symptoms (see "Graphing Your Symptom Score" in *Chapter 3*). Before beginning your metabolic rehab program, estimate the severity of your symptoms using your symptom severity scales. Then post the "baseline" scores for each symptom to your line graph. At this point, you're ready to begin your program of metabolic rehab. During your rehab, monitor the severity of your symptoms at regular intervals. Each time, post the symptom scores to your graph. You'll then be actively engaged in the process of metabolic rehab.

Responses to Treatment That Health Care Practitioners Can Evaluate

Measuring improvements in your symptoms isn't the only way for you to evaluate your progress. Health care practitioners can assess some responses to your treatment. Practitioners can be especially helpful if part of your metabolic rehab is the use of thyroid hormone. See *Chapter 7*, section titled "Tissue Responses to Thyroid Hormone that Your Therapist or Doctor Can Monitor."

METABOLISM-SLOWING FACTORS: WHAT YOU MUST CHANGE TO IMPROVE YOUR SYMPTOMS

People have poor metabolic health because they are affected by one or more metabolism-slowing factors. To achieve optimal metabolic health, they must correct or control the factors. They can do so by undergoing various therapies and adopting several lifestyle practices. The therapies and lifestyle practices patients use in their individualized treatment programs have one aim: to correct or control the factors that are keeping their metabolism too slow.

In this section, we briefly describe the most common metabolism-slowing factors that cause or contribute to poor metabolic health. We've described them here to help you identify which factors may be keeping your metabolism too slow. If you're to achieve metabolic health, you must identify the factors and correct or control them, while systematically monitoring the effects on your symptoms.

Most patients can do most of the therapies and all of the life-style practices without professional help. Of course, to use some therapies (such as treatment for low adrenal function), you'll have to have the cooperation of a health care practitioner. If you decide that you need thyroid hormone therapy, you must find a coopera-tive doctor to work with you. In this case, the best thing you could do for both yourself and your doctor would be to obtain a copy of *The Metabolic Treatment of Fibromyalgia* (see *Resources*). The book will guide you through metabolic rehab and be your greatest tool for success with the use of thyroid hormone.

If you can't find a cooperative doctor in your area, you always have the option of consulting with us long distance or coming to our Center for Metabolic Health in Boulder, Colorado (see *Resour-ces*).

When you've identified the factors you believe are causing your hypometabolism, write a treatment plan that involves cor-recting or controlling the factors. Writing your plan is a way of clarifying what you must do in the way of therapies and lifestyle practices, and it's a way of committing to follow through with your plan. We can't overemphasize the importance of committing in writing that you'll follow through with your metabolic rehab (please read our final word in this book, *Chapter 17*). Your written plan might look something like the top of page 42.

In the remainder of this section, we briefly mention the most common metabolism-slowing factors. We also point you to the oth-er chapters where we explain how the various factors contribute to poor metabolic health and how to correct or control them. Reading the chapters should give you enough information to understand what you must do to free yourself from the influence of these fac-tors so that you move closer to metabolic health.

Here are the nine most common factors that cause hypometa-bolism. It's important to remember that the first one can cause or influence many of the others.

My Treatment Plan*

1. Eat no sugary foods. Instead, eat vegetables, fruits, lean meats, and only a small amount of grains. Also drink 8 glasses of purified water each day.

2. Walk vigorously for 20 minutes once every day. Before walking, do my stretching regimen for five minutes. When I return from walking, do each of my toning exercises.

3. Take all of my nutritional supplements each day.

4. Take my thyroid hormone dose every day when my stomach is empty.

5. Each Wednesday & Saturday, monitor my symptoms and post the scores to my graph.

6. If my symptoms aren't improving enough, find and correct or control any obstacles that are holding up my progress.

* I commit to following this treatment plan. The benefits of achieving optimal metabolic health are worth it!

Mary Connelly
October 6, 2002

1. Under-Regulation by Thyroid Hormone

The two most potent and common metabolism-slowing factors are hypothyroidism and thyroid hormone resistance. If one or both of these are causing your hypometabolism, you'll need to undergo safe and effective thyroid hormone therapy. (See *Chapter 7*.)

2. Too Little Cortisol

Having too little cortisol can cause symptoms that markedly overlap those of too little thyroid hormone regulation. The idea that cortisol and thyroid hormone deficiencies go hand-in-hand has been championed by eminent physicians such as Dr. William McK. Jefferies[104] in the U.S. and Dr. Barry Durrant-Peatfield in the U.K.[219] If your doctor isn't familiar with their point of view, we strongly recommend the books each has published that deal with the subject. In our experience, cortisol deficiency is common among hypothyroid and thyroid hormone resistant patients, and their full recovery depends on correcting the deficiency. (See *Chapter 8.*)

3. Sex Hormone Imbalance

Sex hormone imbalance can complicate the symptoms of hypometabolic patients. Thyroid hormone powerfully regulates sex hormones in men and women, and imbalances of the hormones are common in hypothyroidism and thyroid hormone resistance. Age-related changes, however, also alter the balance of sex hormones, and controlling the resulting symptoms can be important to metabolic health. (See *Chapter 9.*)

4. Nutritional Deficiencies

Nutritional deficiencies are also a common cause of hypometabolism. When a patient's symptoms are caused, or complicated, by these deficiencies, she must correct them before she can achieve optimal metabolic health. And, if the patient takes thyroid hormone, nutritional supplementation is necessary. (See *Chapter 5*, section titled "Vitamins and the Use of Thyroid Hormone.")

5. Unhealthy Diet

An unwholesome diet causes hypometabolism as commonly as do nutritional deficiencies. Consuming refined carbohydrates causes blood sugar irregularities in many people, and as a result, their energy metabolism is impaired. Fatigue and listlessness aren't the only results of the impaired energy metabolism; excess muscle tension and pain also commonly occur.

Some food constituents can worsen chronic aches and pain. Too high an amount of arachidonic acid in foods can do this; so can the artificial sweetener aspartame, and the flavor enhancer monosodium glutamate. (See *Chapter 4*.)

6. Chemical Contaminants

Chemical contaminants can be the major factor responsible for a patient's poor metabolic health. We mentioned above the sweetener aspartame and the flavoring agent glutamate. These are powerful nervous system stimulants that appear to have toxic effects on many of the millions of people who ingest them in massive amounts. We consider them chemical contaminants. Preliminary evidence suggests that some people's fibromyalgia remarkably improves by giving up these additives (see *Chapter 4*, section titled "Aspartame").

Most people can give up aspartame and glutamate, but all of us have trouble avoiding other chemical contaminants. Some tough ones to avoid that can impair thyroid function are chlorine, dioxins, and PCBs. The best we can do is reduce our intake of these contaminants to as low a level as possible. Doing so is crucial to achieving optimal metabolic health. (See *Chapter 12*.)

7. Low Physical Fitness

Ancient medical texts described the symptoms of hypometabolism suffered by people who were sedentary and had low physical fitness. Modern people are just as susceptible to hypometabolism from too little physical activity. (See *Chapter 10*.)

8. Untreated Physical Problems

Many people go about their lives tolerating physical problems that could be relieved with effective physical treatment. These physical problems can strongly contribute to hypometabolism. This is especially true of myofascial trigger points and spinal subluxations.

They contribute to hypometabolism mainly by the volleys of unpleasant nerve impulses they send into the spinal cord and up to the brain stem and brain. These impulses often disturb the patient's sleep and contribute to her chronic fatigue and low pain threshold.

Muscles with impaired energy metabolism often form pain-referring trigger points. If the patient is hypothyroid, and all her muscles are hypometabolic, trigger points may form in many of her muscles. Because of the slow muscle metabolism, her trigger points will be resistant to therapies that otherwise would quickly eliminate them. Often, after metabolic therapy normalizes the patient's muscle energy metabolism, trigger points in the muscles persist and continue to refer pain. They can be self-sustaining and don't spontaneously clear up. Only effective physical treatment will eliminate them. In such cases, then, getting physical treatment is a part of taking advantage of increased metabolic capacity (see section below).

We explained the importance of physical treatment for fibromyalgia patients in the *Journal of Bodywork and Movement Therapies*.[137] What we wrote there also applies to other hypometabolic patients, as we explain in *Chapter 13*.

9. Troublesome Drugs

It's unfortunate that some of the drugs intended to make life easier for people often make it harder by causing or contributing to hypometabolism. For many people, achieving metabolic health requires giving up some drugs that are impediments. (See *Chapter 15*, section titled "Troublesome Drugs.")

TAKING ADVANTAGE OF YOUR INCREASED METABOLIC CAPACITY: ESSENTIAL PARTS OF METABOLIC REHAB

If you're hypothyroid or thyroid hormone resistant, you'll most likely improve somewhat by merely taking a high-enough daily dose of an effective thyroid hormone product. But limiting your treatment regimen solely to the use of thyroid hormone would be a costly mistake.

Thyroid hormone is the most potent regulator of metabolism. But—and this "but" is crucial to understand if you're to enjoy even moderate metabolic health—it must work synergistically in the body with a host of other metabolism-regulating influences: constituents and effects of a wholesome diet, a wide array of nutrients, the effects on body and mind of vigorous physical activity, and practices that reduce the demands we place on our metabolism.

Because thyroid hormone benefits us most only when it acts synergistically with all these other influences, we often advise patients using thyroid hormone: Take advantage of the increased metabolic capacity the hormone provides, and doing so will bring the improvement in your health that you want.

Taking advantage of the increased metabolic capacity that thyroid hormone provides is largely a matter of engaging in several lifestyle practices. The practices include eating a wholesome diet (see *Chapter 4*); taking nutritional supplements (see *Chapter 5*); doing toning, stretching, and aerobic exercises to tolerance (see *Chapter 10*); taking time for recreation and relaxation; and abstaining from the use of metabolism-slowing drugs (see *Chapter 15*, section titled "Troublesome Drugs").

We mention these practices only briefly here because we've included information on them in different parts of the book. If you're having trouble practicing them, we encourage you to read the chapters that deal with each.

One shouldn't feel that the need to engage in these lifestyle practices is a liability uniquely imposed upon her. More accurately, one would feel that the practices are a tariff imposed on anyone who wants to enjoy optimal health. There's some price to pay regardless of choosing poor or optimal metabolic health. The formula is simple and straightforward: Those who don't regularly engage in the lifestyle practices don't enjoy optimal metabolic health— whether or not they take thyroid hormone.

The lifestyle practices, of course, interact and depend on each other. Consider nutritional supplements. If you haven't taken them before, you should immediately start. Doing so can increase your metabolic capacity enough for you perceive it! But you shouldn't stop there. Nutrients interact with other metabolism-regulating influences. Exercise to tolerance is an example. Nutritional supplements can enhance most people's ability to exercise, and by exercising, they capitalize on the increased metabolic capacity the supplements provide.

Patients Likely to Stay in Poor Metabolic Health

Through our years of practice, we've made some observations that are worth noting here. Some patients who've consulted us were doing everything wrong in terms of lifestyle. They ate the worst traditional American diet, took no nutritional supplements, were thoroughly sedentary, and used conventional prescription and over-the-counter drugs liberally. Those who wouldn't drastically change these lifestyle practices had completely unsuccessful results with metabolic rehab.

Eventually, we learned to quickly spot the people who decline to cooperate in their own care. Before we give up on them, we encourage them, nudge them, entice them, and then warn them of the disastrous results they face by refusing to adopt a health-inducing lifestyle. We regret to say that some simply won't do it.

So, after a lot of effort on our part, we terminate our professional relationship with these patients. We do so because we sympathize with the view of psychologist Andrew Salter. He wrote of such patients:

> I explain to them that my appointment book is like a life raft. There is room for only a limited number of people, and I do not intend to waste my time trying to convince any of the bobbing heads around me to get on board. There are others drowning who are only too happy to cooperate in their rescue.[399,p.69]

We lament eliminating even a single patient from our practice, and see it as a tragic loss of opportunity for another human being to come back to life from poor metabolic health. But we don't lock the door behind them on their way out. They're always welcome back when they commit to getting well.

Patients Likely to Fully Recover Rapidly

Other patients who come to us for treatment have been doing everything right in terms of lifestyle. In their quest for relief, they've stuck to a high quality, wholesome diet supplemented by most every vitamin, mineral, and trace element. They've exercised despite fatigue and pain, and take practically no drugs. Some have done this for as long as twenty years.

When these patients begin metabolic rehab, they add to their daily health regimen the proper form and dose of thyroid hormone. Almost always, they *rapidly* and *fully* recover their health. We love to meet these patients because we know they stand the best chance to quickly be completely well.

Getting Well Merely Through Lifestyle Practices

In our years of practice and research, we've encountered a few patients who recovered solely through making lifestyle changes. Unfortunately, these individuals are rare.

We hasten to add, however, that we've seen patients who've made lifestyle changes that did improve their general health and did reduce the severity of their symptoms. And without making those changes, patients with poor metabolic health will get less than satisfactory results from thyroid hormone. But, without appropriate thyroid hormone therapy added to the lifestyle changes, most patients will be unable to get well.

We recently wrote the chapter on fibromyalgia for the 3rd edition of *The Textbook of Natural Medicine*.[293] This authoritative textbook is edited by the eminent naturopathic physicians and educators Dr. Joseph Pizzorno and Dr. Michael Murray. To make the content of the chapter consistent with the current scientific literature on fibromyalgia, we spent months reviewing the published scientific studies.

During this research, we reviewed the studies on different types of treatments for fibromyalgia and chronic fatigue syndrome. What we found was that exercise, dietary improvements, and nutritional and herbal therapies enabled patients to improve somewhat—but in most cases, only slightly. Not a single study reported that any of these therapies enabled patients to fully recover from their symptoms.

Despite this evidence, Dr. Jacob Teitelbaum is currently advertising and reporting that patients can recover from fibromyalgia and chronic fatigue syndrom e merely with the use of nutritional and herbal supplements.[400][401] To support his claim that this approach enables patients to recover, he refers to his recently published double-blind, placebo-controlled study in which most patients recovered. It's important to note, however, as did Peter Warmingham,[402] that in the study, almost all of the patients used thyroid hormone—a therapy that's essential for most patients to recover from fibromyalgia and chronic fatigue syndrome. Teitelbaum's study, then, didn't show that patients with these diagnoses recovered with the use of nutritional and herbal therapies; instead, it confirmed our published studies showing that patients can recover only when they use nutritional therapy *and* thyroid hormone.

So, long clinical experience and the scientific literature show what we reported in the *The Textbook of Natural Medicine*.[293] Patients must make positive lifestyle changes to recover from fibromyalgia, but these lifestyle changes alone aren't enough. Most patients must also use the proper type of thyroid hormone in high enough doses. Never forget, however, that while the lifestyle changes alone aren't enough, they are *essential* if most patients are to recover their metabolic health.

SUMMARY

To achieve metabolic health, you must identify the symptoms you want to free yourself from. To improve your symptoms, you'll need to use therapies and lifestyle practices that correct or control the factors keeping your metabolism too slow. Identify the factors you believe are causing your hypometabolism and then write out your treatment program for correcting or controlling the factors.

Commit to follow through systematically with your regimen of metabolic rehab. This means monitoring the severity of your symptoms regularly, and adjusting your treatment regimen as needed so that you gradually eliminate your symptoms and achieve optimal metabolic health. If you're using thyroid hormone, when it increases your metabolic capacity, be sure to capitalize on the increase with lifestyle practices such as exercising to tolerance.

We want to emphasize an important point: Merely reading this book and making slapdash efforts to improve your health by using some of the information is likely to give you quite disappointing results. You're likely to achieve optimal metabolic health only if you use the entire system of metabolic rehab—monitoring your symptoms regularly and graphing your severity scores. With that in mind, let's now turn to *Chapter 3*. There, we'll explain how to measure the severity of your symptoms, and how to post the severity scores to line graphs.

Chapter 3

Numbers Count

IN THE LAST CHAPTER, WE wrote that you must identify the symptoms you want to free yourself from—the symptoms you suspect your slow metabolism is causing. After identifying them, you must estimate their intensity at intervals. How often you estimate the intensity of your symptoms will depend on your intention.

If you've never eaten a wholesome diet, taken nutritional supplements, or exercised to tolerance, you may want to first measure how much these practices alone reduce the severity of your symptoms. Monitoring the severity of your symptoms once or twice each week will be often enough.

If taking thyroid hormone is part of your rehab, you should measure the severity of your symptoms at intervals long enough to tell you the benefits of a particular dose. If you use desiccated thyroid or a synthetic T_4/T_3 product, monitoring every two weeks will be often enough. Two week intervals are enough because improvements in your symptoms after an increase of your dose can take up to two weeks.

If taking T_3 is part of your rehab, monitoring your symptoms once each week is appropriate. Improvements come much faster after an increase in a dose of T_3.

To estimate the severity of your symptoms, you'll need to use what we call a "severity scale" for each symptom. Below is a severity scale. Notice that it contains numbers ranging from 0 on the far left to 10 on the far right. Let's say this is your severity scale for fatigue. On each occasion that you estimate the intensity of your fatigue, you'll place a mark, such as a $\sqrt{}$, somewhere on the line. You'll mark 0 if you have no fatigue, 5 if it's moderately severe, and 10 if it's as severe as it can be. Or you can place a mark anywhere along the line that represents how severe your fatigue is.

We want to emphasize that you don't have to pick one of the numbers along the scale; instead, you can mark the scale anywhere you feel is accurate, including spaces between the numbers. For example, let's say you feel your fatigue over the past week has been about 7⅓, so you place a √ on the scale about ⅓ of the way between the 7 and 8.

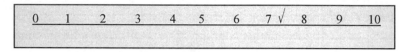

Fatigue

Don't worry about pinpoint accuracy. What's important is that you mark the spot that at the moment seems most accurate to you. Whether you're first estimating the intensity of the symptom, or whether you've done it many times, estimate the average intensity of the symptom over the past week, or past two weeks.

We've included a page in *Forms* that contains five severity scales. Copy the page and label the scales with your main symptoms. If you have more than five, use another copy of the page to label your other symptoms. Use as many scales as you want—one for each of the symptoms of slow metabolism from which you want to free yourself.

GRAPHING YOUR SYMPTOM SCORE

When you estimate the severity of a symptom, and you mark that symptom's severity scale, you then have a "score" for that symptom. Your next step is to post that score to a line graph. This is called "graphing." (We've included a line graph for you to copy and use. See *Forms*.)

In explaining how to think clearly and solve problems, writing and thinking expert Rudolf Flesch, Ph.D. advised the use of graphs:

> If the problem can be stated graphically, state it graphically. A graph often helps you understand something that looks unintel-

ligible in words or figures. Louis Bean, the only man who has been consistently right in predicting [political] election results, says he performs this magic trick with charts and graphs. If you are not up on this technique, pass the problem on to someone who is.[241,p.276]

We don't want you to pass the "problem" of graphing along to someone else. It's too important, and besides, we've learned that most doctors aren't going to do it anyway. We prefer that you learn to do your own graphing, and then share your graphs with your doctor. Some patients—Vicky Massey is the best example (see *Foreword*)—have found that their doctors became more cooperative when the patients shared their graphs with them.

We can't overemphasize the importance of graphing to your getting satisfactory results from your metabolic rehab. A little work is involved in getting scores for your symptoms and posting them to line graphs. Because of this, many people would prefer not to do it. But that's a mistake; failing to graph your scores can sabotage your efforts to get well.

I (GH-L) know this from personal experience. When we guide patients through metabolic rehab, we collect our patients' symptom severity scores, and we post them to line graphs. When I first began treating patients with metabolic rehab, I declined to do the "busy work" of graphing my patients' scores. Instead, I just looked at the changed scores on the monitoring forms I had patients fill out.

It was a mistake not to graph my patients' scores. At that time, I had just begun learning metabolic rehab from Dr. Lowe. When I was having trouble making decisions about my patients' treatment, I had to consult with him. He pointed out the source of my trouble—no graphs of my patients' scores. I promptly made the graphs, and doing so eliminated my trouble in making clinical judgments. The graphs enabled me to make quick and precise decisions, and I immediately felt a sense of control in guiding my patients in the right direction. There is no substitute for graphing, and we urge you to do it.

Our friend and colleague, the late Dr. John Gedye,[39] felt that a major problem with medical practice nowadays is doctors' failure to use data and graphs to guide their clinical decisions. He noted, though, that when it's really important, some doctors depend heavily on measures of how patients are doing—the equivalent of graphs. This is the reason for all the monitoring instruments around a patient who just came out of surgery, or a patient who is recovering from a heart attack. Making sure the patient recovers *critically* depends on measuring how she's doing, and some of the instruments provide graphs of the patient's changing status.

Dr. Alan Reichman, another of our colleagues and a family physician, once compared our monitoring and graphing to his management of patients with high blood pressure.[40] He said that a patient may not *look* like her blood pressure is high; measuring her blood pressure with an instrument (called a sphygmomanometer), however, shows that it is indeed high. Without the knowledge gained from measuring, Dr. Reichman wouldn't know to adjust his patient's treatment so that her blood pressure becomes normal. And without a record that shows the course of his patient's blood pressure over time, Dr. Reichman couldn't intelligently guide the patient in her treatment.

Consider this example: Jane's blood pressure was 144 over 98 until she stopped putting salt on her food. A week after she stopped the salt, her pressure went down to 135 over 95. The next week it dropped to 128 over 90. Since then, it's been 118 over 78. From this description, we know that Jane's blood pressure went down. But we don't have a clear picture of how it happened.

Now, compare your impression of the improvement in Jane's blood pressure with what you get from the line graph in Figure 1. The line with the ▲ symbol shows the changes in her systolic blood pressure during each of the six weeks. The line with the ◆ symbol shows the diastolic pressure during each week. The two lines are what we call "trend lines." Looking at the trend lines gives us a clear view of Jane's improvement over the six-week time frame.

The clear view that line graphs provide can have quite an impact on helping you to solve a health problem. We'll illustrate how in the example below.

A TYPICAL HYPOTHYROID PATIENT

Here we'll describe the use of scoring and graphing by a hypothetical patient as she goes through metabolic rehab. We'll call her Mary, although her story is a composite of several patients' experiences.

Mary is hypothyroid. Her main symptoms are depression, disturbed sleep, and widespread pain. One doctor told her that her depression was the cause of her other symptoms. But a year of treatment with several different antidepressants didn't improve any of her symptoms, including her depression. Another doctor diagnosed her pain as fibromyalgia, but six months of treatment with amitriptyline and cyclobenzaprine didn't help at all (see *Chapter 11*, section titled "Antidepressants as Sleep Aids").

Finally, Mary came under the care of a naturopathic doctor in her hometown in New Hampshire. At the same time, she consulted me (GH-L) long distance at our Boulder, Colorado Center for Metabolic Health. I agreed to work long distance with her and her naturopathic doctor. I diagnosed hypothyroidism, and her naturopathic doctor agreed to prescribe desiccated thyroid and to examine her at intervals. I taught Mary to make her own graphs to help guide her therapy. I also advised her to find a chiropractic doctor or therapist to evaluate her for physical sources of pain, such as trigger points or spinal subluxations.

Mary had tried for years to overcome her symptoms with lifestyle practices. She maintained a wholesome diet, took a wide array of nutritional supplements, and exercised regularly. Because she was already doing these metabolism-regulating practices, I expected her to have an uncomplicated recovery by using the desiccated thyroid.

Mary got her baseline symptom scores and posted them to her line graph before she began to take desiccated thyroid. Then she started taking 1 grain (60 mg) of desiccated thyroid at the beginning of the second week of her self-monitoring. Figure 2 shows what her graph looked like at the end of the first month.

The trend lines suggest that after her third week taking the thyroid hormone, all three of her major symptoms (depression, dis-

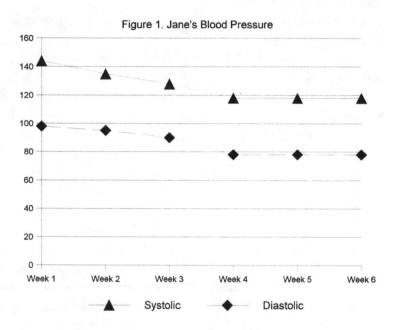

Figure 1. Jane's Blood Pressure

turbed sleep, and widespread pain) were improving. She was keeping a diary of her subjective feelings about her symptoms, and the diary reflected what the trend lines showed. She said she felt a little less depressed, was sleeping a little better, and that her pain wasn't as severe.

At the end of the fourth week, Mary increased her dose of desiccated thyroid to 2 grains (120 mg). She continued to assess her symptom severity with her three symptom scales, and she continued posting the scores to her graph. Her 2-grain (120-mg) dose apparently was effective for her.

Mary's graph suggests that by the end of eight weeks (see Figure 3), she had made substantial improvement. The trend line of her pain scores, however, suggests that the severity of her pain had reached a plateau. But a temporary leveling off of a trend line isn't unusual. When I asked Mary about physical treatment, she said she hadn't yet been able to find a doctor or therapist to evaluate her. She promised to diligently search for one.

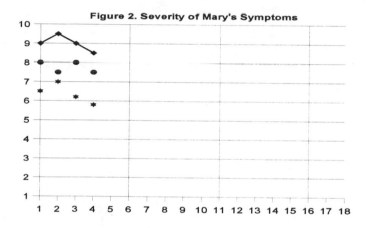

Figure 2. Severity of Mary's Symptoms

I recommended that she contact Richard Finn, Director of the Pittsburgh School of Pain Management in Pennsylvania to get a referral to a certified myofascial trigger point therapist (see *Resources*). Richard referred her to a therapist who practiced twenty miles from her. Fortunately, the therapist practiced in the same clinic as a chiropractic doctor—the therapist's wife. Unfortunately, both of them were on vacation, but Mary made an appointment for two weeks in the future.

At the end of the two weeks, but still *before* her appointment (look at weeks 9 and 10 in Figure 3), the trend lines show something we've often observed. We've seen it so often that we've described it in publications on fibromyalgia.[132][137] When a patient has a physical problem that's causing pain, and she doesn't get effective physical treatment to relieve the problem, her pain scores won't improve beyond a certain level—even though her metabolic treatment is improving her other symptoms. In addition, her other symptoms will improve only to a certain level; then the improve

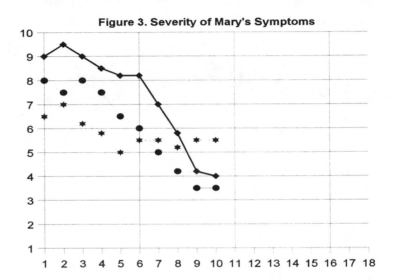

Figure 3. Severity of Mary's Symptoms

ment levels off and won't get any better. But as you'll see below, when the patient gets appropriate physical treatment, her pain and other symptoms continue to improve under the influence of the metabolic treatment.

At the end of the 10th week, the trigger point therapist and the chiropractic doctor evaluated Mary's muscles and spine. The therapist found multiple trigger points in the muscles of Mary's neck and upper back, and he began treating these. The doctor found subluxations in Mary's cervical and thoracic spinal areas and she adjusted them.

After the combined treatments, Mary felt immediate and profound relief from both pain and tension. She underwent the combined treatments three times a week for the next two weeks. The benefits are reflected by the trend lines in her graph over the next four weeks (weeks 11, 12, 13, and 14) shown in Figure 4.

At the end of the 15th week, Mary increased her dose of desiccated thyroid hormone to 2.5 grains (150 mg). She did this because

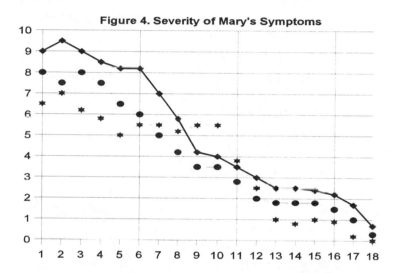

Figure 4. Severity of Mary's Symptoms

her symptom status, although dramatically improved, had leveled off again, and the extra ½ grain (30 mg) was calculated to be enough to totally relieve her symptoms. This indeed happened, and she was released from treatment after 18 weeks. It's now been two years, and Mary continues to maintain her full recovery.

More Than Graphing

Mary's line graph was instrumental in helping her fully recover. Had she not seen the leveling off of her trend line for pain, she might not have appreciated the importance of getting physical treatment. And without seeing her three trend lines level off after the 12th week, her substantial improvement may have caused her to mistakenly think she had improved as much as she could. She obviously had more improvement to come, and she got it with a slight increase in her thyroid hormone dose.

What we said in the previous paragraph bears repeating—that Mary's graph was instrumental in *"helping* her fully recover." This is what graphs are supposed to do: help. The trend lines in the graphs shouldn't alone dictate what treatment decisions the patient and her doctor make. The patient and her doctor should also calculate their subjective judgments into their treatment decisions.

Just as Mary's naturopathic doctor made progress notes on her status each time he saw her, Mary also made notes in her diary. And, she recorded the dates that she wrote the notes. It's important for all patients undergoing metabolic rehab to maintain diary notes. This is because it's too easy for a patient to forget exactly how she felt even a couple of days ago, a week ago, and especially further back in time. Usually, the patient's subjective judgment of how she's doing corresponds pretty closely to what her graphs show.

Unfortunately, the patient—like all of us—will occasionally have a bad day. On that day, she's likely to misjudge how much progress she's made since she began treatment. In fact, some patients who are nearly well will swear on bad days that they haven't improved a bit! Looking at the graphs and reviewing one's diary notes can effectively bring one's judgment closer to reality.

SUMMARY

In summary, here's the process you need to follow to guide yourself to recovery:

- Select the symptoms of slow metabolism you want to eliminate.
- Label a severity scale with the name of each symptom (see *Forms*).
- Decide how often you're to reassess your symptoms.
- Post your symptom scores to a line graph (see *Forms*).

- Decide what metabolic therapies and lifestyle practices you must include in your regimen of metabolic rehab. Read the chapters on the different therapies and lifestyle practices so that you understand them and can use them effectively.
- Commence your treatment program and reassess the severity of your symptoms at regular intervals.
- If the trend lines in your graph descend, indicating improvement, and your diary notes reflect the improvement indicated by your graph, continue with your current treatment regimen.
- If the trend lines don't indicate improvement, and this corresponds to your diary notes, troubleshoot your treatment regimen to figure out why you're not improving. Re-read any chapters about therapies and lifestyle practices that you may not fully understand or may not be using effectively.
- If you're stumped, see *Chapter 15*, Troubleshooting. If you decide you need help, we'll be happy to hear from you and help get you on the right track. In most cases, we can do this through long-distance consulting (see *Resources*).

■ For extensive information on monitoring metabolic status and using graphs to guide treatment, see Chapter 5.2, titled "Treatment Protocol," pages 937-979 in *The Metabolic Treatment of Fibromyalgia*.[1]

SECTION II
HOW TO OPTIMIZE
YOUR METABOLIC HEALTH

Chapter 4

Wholesome Diet

A WHOLESOME DIET IS ONE that sustains good health; it does so over the short and the long haul. We describe this diet below.

First, though, we'll look at what we call the "typical American diet." This diet does *not* sustain good health—over neither the short nor the long haul. Instead, the diet quickly disrupts normal physiology. And when one subsists on it for long, the diet promotes frank disease. The typical American diet is distinctly unwholesome, and if you're to achieve optimal metabolic health, you must renounce it and take up a wholesome diet.

TYPICAL AMERICAN DIET

Some officials, such as representatives of the fast food industry, argue that the typical American diet is health-encouraging. They're right in two respects: The diet promptly relieves hunger, and it provides some protein and calories.

The *least* nutritious foods can, of course, relieve our hunger, and they can keep us alive. But feeling free from hunger and merely being alive is a paltry definition of health. If this is a person's definition of health, she's likely to feel false security in subsisting off the typical American diet.

The diet does indeed provide some protein. And it provides people with calories. The problem is that it provides them with far too many calories. In addition, it also provides some forms of fatty acids that are likely to lead to cardiovascular disease and premature death from a heart attack or stroke.

Before one's early demise, however, the excess calories from the diet will be stored in the body as fat. Taste enhancers in many fast foods ensure that some people who eat these foods will eat them to excess, taking in far more calories than their bodies can deplete. As a result, many people who subsist off the diet have enough calories stored as fat to sustain them through a month, maybe two months, of starvation.

The excess calories the typical American diet provides come from the foods' high concentration of refined carbohydrates and bad fats. Refined carbohydrates consist of white flour and white table sugar.

Refined Carbohydrates

A high, regular intake of white sugar can cause irregular blood sugar levels. The blood sugar irregularities can cause a low energy level, poor mental function, and emotional instability.

Many patients who have unstable blood sugar from eating refined carbohydrates, and who are also taking thyroid hormone, have symptoms that resemble thyroid hormone overstimulation. By eliminating refined carbohydrates from their diet, the patients find that they remain free of the symptoms although taking the same or higher doses of thyroid hormone.

Long range, refined carbohydrates can lead to a wide array of other health problems. Cardiovascular disease is among them.

A diet high in refined carbohydrates is low in dietary fiber. Too little fiber intake can also cause a host of health problems (see section below titled "Fiber"). An occasional patient will try to get around these potential health problems by adding supplemental fiber to a diet heavy in refined carbohydrates. This is a self-sabotaging approach; adding fiber can avert problems from too little fiber, but it won't fend off the other problems that refined carbohydrates are likely to cause. As time progresses, and the patient continues to consume refined carbohydrates, these health problems will take a toll. Some, such as low blood sugar, will often cause unpleasant symptoms; others, such as cardiovascular disease, will insidiously progress, heightening the patient's risk for premature death.

Bad Fat

The typical American diet contains large amounts of "transfatty acids." These have the same types and numbers of atoms as naturally-occurring fatty acids, but they're structured more like saturated fats.[73] They can cause problems with fat metabolism that lead to obesity, heart attacks, and strokes. At least one fast food corporation—apparently fearing a class action lawsuit from customers—recently announced that it will lower the transfatty acid content of its foods.

Salt

In addition to the sugar and bad fat, the typical American diet also contains too much table salt, sodium-chloride. Excess sodium creates an imbalance of sodium and potassium in the body (see *Chapter 5*, section titled "Potassium"). This imbalance can contribute to poor metabolic health.

We often encounter a patient for whom massive salt intake is an obstacle to recovery. The patient's high salt intake (usually combined with poor physical fitness) has caused dangerously-high blood pressure. Often, the patient's doctor has prescribed a beta-blocker to lower her blood pressure into a safer range. Beta-blockers, however, are a sort of antidote to the effects of thyroid hormone on the body. While using the beta-blocker on a daily basis, the patient is, so to speak, immune to the benefits of thyroid hormone (see *Chapter 15*, section titled "Beta-Blocking Drugs"). If effective thyroid hormone therapy is crucial to her recovering metabolic health, she can't improve while she uses the beta blocker. The solution, of course, is for her to adopt a wholesome diet that includes a low intake of sodium in relation to potassium. She will then recover normal blood pressure and can stop using the beta-blocker.

Nutritional Deficiencies

The typical American diet also doesn't provide enough vitamins, minerals, trace elements, and other nutrients such as omega-3 fatty acids. Most people who subsist off this diet usually take no nutritional supplements and may have multiple nutritional deficiencies. They either presently have poor metabolic health, or they're destined to suffer from it.

To our amazement, an occasional new patient of ours doesn't realize how bad the typical American diet is. She surely wants to achieve metabolic health. But she assumes that it's fine to continue with her typical American diet as she starts metabolic rehab—not realizing that the diet contributes to poor metabolic health.

For some of these patients, the bad diet consists mainly of "convenience" or "fast foods." For others, the diet consists of over-feeding on red meat and greasy gravy. Most of these patients don't take nutritional supplements. Some of them do take a supplement but without much benefit, since it's one of the heavily-advertised brands of nutritional supplements. These generally contain only the RDAs of vitamins and minerals—enough perhaps to prevent frank deficiency diseases, but far too little to contribute to optimal health.

A wholesome diet provides enough proteins, carbohydrates, and good fats to meet the body's needs, but not so much of any one of these that health becomes impaired. The diet also includes a wide variety of foods. And it includes fresh fruits and vegetables and whole grains.

CAVEMAN DIET

Sixty million years ago, our animal ancestors lived in trees in areas now called Africa and Europe. They fed themselves on vege-tation, such as leaves, fruits, young shoots, and new bark. They also supplemented their diet with insects like the prehistoric kin of worms, termites, and ants.[64]

Some 30 million years ago, the climate changed and the forests began to thin. This forced some of the creatures to descend the trees to become land dwellers. When permanently on the ground, these creatures maintained their diet of *mostly* plant food. The diet consisted of roots, leaves, berries, grasses and the like, supplement-ed by small terrestrial animals. In regions with too little vegetation, the creatures included in their diet a wider range of animal foods. For example, they included "small, slow-moving animals, young birds before they are fledged in the nest, [and] infant and other easily secured animals."[243,pp.18-19]

The shift from a diet of mainly plant foods to one including more animal foods was a boon to humans; it contributed a lot to their immensely successful survival and spread over the earth.[244,pp.386-387] Most hunter-gatherers (humans not living in civilization) consume about 35% animal food and 65% plant food.[245]

The ice sheets of the fourth glaciation melted and receded some 15,000 years ago. At this time, the large cold-adapted mammals such as the mammoth gradually disappeared with the ice. This left humans without this previously important animal food source.

At the same time, the climatic changes due to the ending of the ice age enabled wild grasses to flourish in areas like southeast Asia and the Mideast. Humans found the seeds of these grasses, called "grains," edible. They settled among the grasses and began cultivating them for the grains, especially in river valleys with fertile soil. This abundant food source made it possible for large groups of people to live in close proximity to one another. In this way, roughly 12,000 years ago, agriculture began. And so, too, did the first civilization, Mesopotamia.[64]

This historical development was the beginning of humans' dependence on grains as a major source of food—a food that wasn't part of our evolution. Because heavy grain consumption wasn't part of human evolution, our bodies don't function as well on them as they do on vegetables, fruits, and lean animal meats. These foods make up the "caveman" diet—the diet we evolved consuming,[64] and the diet recent studies show is most likely to provide us with optimal health.

Some twenty-three years ago, I (JCL) conjectured that this caveman diet is necessary for optimal health.[60][64][65][79] The conjecture is supported by Dr. Barry Sears's recent articulation of the same idea in his book, *The Zone*.[246] In short, the idea is that we humans evolved with a diet consisting largely of fiber-rich vege-tables, fruits, nuts, and low-fat proteins as in lean meat. This diet is best for our health. In contrast, a high-grain diet is harmful to our health—especially when one also eats a lot of saturated fats. We strongly recommend the diet Dr. Sears describes in detail. But we staunchly disagree with his meager nutritional supplement regimen (for our recommendations, see *Chapter 5*).

Caveman Diet and Fibromyalgia

Recently, some people have argued that a variety of dietary changes or dietary supplements can relieve patients' fibromyalgia symptoms. It's true that a wholesome diet can improve patients' symptoms; the closer a patient's wholesome diet is to a caveman's, the more helpful it is. And as we wrote above, adopting a whole-some diet is essential to acquiring optimal metabolic health.

Except for the rare patient, however, dietary changes or supple-ments don't by themselves enable patients to recover. This is evi-dent from studies of different dietary changes and supplements as fibromyalgia treatments. The studies show that the therapies, when used alone, may improve patients' fibromyalgia symptoms but the improvement is limited.[317][318][319][320][321][322][323][324][325]

Unfortunately, some studies of dietary supplements for fibro-myalgia were conducted or paid for by the companies that sell the dietary supplement that was tested. Some of these studies are clear-ly nothing more than thinly-veiled marketing ploys. We've come to expect fraudulent science from many pharmaceutical companies. But it's been disheartening to learn that some nutritional and diet-ary supplement companies are willing to make fraudulent use of science to mislead potential customers about the therapeutic value of their products. *Caveat emptor!*

FAT: GOOD AND BAD

An important feature of the caveman-type diet is that it pro-vides a sufficient intake of "good fats" and a low intake of "bad fats."

Some fats are bad in that they're harmful to us in excess. When we ingest them in excess, they produce harmful substances in our bodies. An example is arachidonic acid.

Arachidonic acid is a polyunsaturated fatty acid and is important to health. Animals deprived of fats develop scaly skin, and infants can develop an eczema-type dermatitis. Ingesting arachidonic acid clears up these skin abnormalities. Ingesting linoleic acid, which the body can convert to arachidonic acid, also clears up the abnormalities.[261,p.82]

Animal fats contain small amounts of arachidonic acid. Consuming too much animal fat—and at the same time, too much arachidonic acid—can harm us. The harm comes in part from our cells converting the arachidonic acid to three classes of substances: prostaglandins and prostaglandin E2, leukotrienes, thromboxanes.

Space is too limited here for us to describe all the potentially harmful effects of these substances. However, some effects of one of the substances, prostaglandin E2, are highly relevant to patients with poor metabolic health. Stimuli that initiate inflammation cause cells to produce an otherwise absent enzyme that increases production of prostaglandins, especially prostaglandin E2. People with higher levels of prostaglandin E2 have more pain and inflammation, and they're more susceptible to breast, colon, and rectal cancer. Researchers recommend two ways to block production of the prostaglandin-generating enzyme and prostaglandin E2: Take an NSAID each day, and take omega-3 fatty acids.[264] Using these two blocking methods may prevent the diseases that prostaglandin E2 can produce. We do not recommend taking NSAIDs on a daily basis. It is preferable to decrease your intake of foods that contain arachidonic acid.

Foods Rich in Arachidonic Acid

Foods with a high arachidonic acid content are egg yolks, fatty meats, organ meats such as liver, and deli meat products. By reducing our intake of such foods rich in arachidonic acid, we also reduce our intake of saturated fats, as in red meat and whole-fat dairy products. Saturated fats raise one's insulin blood level. When someone's insulin level is chronically high, she can develop insulin resistance. Insulin resistance impairs energy metabolism and can lead to one feeling fatigued.

We can reduce our intake of arachidonic acid and saturated fats, of course, by eating more low-fat animal protein foods such as white meat poultry and fish. These, along with high-fiber fruits, vegetables, and nuts, make up the caveman diet (see section above titled "Caveman Diet").

Mediterranean Diet

Good (monounsaturated) fats don't raise the insulin level and don't contribute to insulin resistance. A diet of foods containing large amounts of good fats has been called the "Mediterranean diet." The diet reduces the risk of cardiovascular disease, partly by controlling blood insulin and sugar levels. Foods that contain good fats are olive oil, olives, avocados, macadamia nuts, walnuts, canola oil, almonds, almond butter, peanuts, and peanut butter. Tahini, a paste made of ground sesame seeds, is also rich in good fats.

Nuts

Nuts are rich in good fats and are an important part of a caveman-type diet. Eating more nuts makes it easier to reduce our intake of foods that contain arachidonic acid and saturated fats.

We have a precaution, though, concerning nuts. If you have herpes simplex and are prone to cold sores, eating lots of nuts can activate the virus. Nuts contain large amounts of the amino acid methionine. The virus selectively feeds on methionine and can become active if you take in enough of the amino acid.

If you have a tendency toward cold sores, and you want to eat nuts for their good fats, we advise taking 2000-to-4000 mg of the amino acid lysine in divided doses each day. When lysine is present in large enough amounts, the virus feeds on it instead of methionine. But lysine has no nutritional value for the virus; when it feeds on lysine rather than methionine, the virus becomes less active, reducing the tendency toward cold sores.

Arachidonic Acid:
A Good Fat in Small-Enough Amounts

We have a final note on arachidonic acid. To brand arachidonic acid as strictly bad for our health would be a mistake. If we don't ingest enough arachidonic acid, or substances that the body can convert to it, our bodies won't produce enough "prostaglandins." These are unsaturated fatty acids that induce smooth muscle contractions, help control inflammation and body temperature, and help regulate many other body functions. Prostaglandins are essential to having normal metabolism, and arachidonic acid is essential to having enough prostaglandins.[264]

Balance With Omega-3 Fatty Acids. Our ancient hunter-gatherer ancestors consumed animal foods from both the land and sea. Land animals provided more arachidonic acid (a long chain omega-6 fatty acid), and sea animals provided more omega-3 fatty acids. Evidence suggests that potential harmful effects from higher body levels of arachidonic acid are reduced when body levels of omega-3 fatty acids are also high.[262] This suggests that fanatically avoiding foods that have a higher arachidonic acid content may not be as important as making sure we consume enough foods rich in omega-3 fatty acids. Most people in industrialized societies take in too little omega-3 fatty acids. To prevent or hopefully correct the harmful health effects from this low intake, they can eat more foods that contain these good fats and take omega-3 fatty acid supplements (for our recommendations, see *Chapter 5*, Table II, "Fatty Acids").

Low Omega-3 Fatty Acids and Hypothyroidism. One harmful effect of low omega-3 fatty acid intake may be increased vulnerability to or severity of hypothyroidism. Japanese researchers found that among hypothyroid patients, those with lower levels of fatty acids in their blood had more severe hypothyroid symptoms. And conversely, patients with higher levels of fatty acids in their blood had less severe hypothyroid symptoms.[263]

Based on this finding, the Japanese researchers suspected that fatty acids may somehow enable the thyroid gland to function better despite being impaired. To test their idea, they gave rats a chemical that made them hypothyroid. The chemical damaged the thyroid gland follicles where thyroid hormones are produced. This reduced the rats' blood levels of thyroid hormone.

The researchers had some of the rats that were exposed to the chemical also ingest an omega-3 fatty acid derived from fish oil. In rats who ingested the fatty acid, the chemical was less damaging to thyroid gland follicles and the rats' thyroid hormone levels remained higher.

Low omega-3 fatty acid intake may also compound some effects of hypothyroidism. Hypothyroidism can impair brain function; the impairment may result in poor memory and concentration. Low omega-3 fatty acid intake can worsen poor memory and concentration in hypothyroid patients. Brain cells are dependent on glucose for their energy. Low omega-3 fatty acid intake appears to decrease molecules in brain cell membranes that transport glucose (sugar) into the cells. When rats had a low omega-3 fatty acid intake, glucose entry into their brain cells decreased by 30%.[265] Lowered glucose entering brain cells due to low omega-3 fatty acid intake can thus accentuate the already poor memory and concentration of hypothyroid patients.

Animal Meat and Good and Bad Fats. As we wrote above, humans began cultivating grains about 12,000 years ago, and the grains became their food staple. Before this agricultural revolution began, humans got most of their dietary fat from eating wild "ruminant" animals.

Ruminants are cloven-hoofed, cud-chewing mammals. Examples are bison, buffalo, deer, antelope, giraffe, and camel. In the wild, the main food source for ruminant animals is wild grasses and other plants they graze on. When humans began raising ruminants as food livestock, they kept the animals in pastures where they grazed. After the agricultural revolution, however, humans began to feed grains to their ruminant animals. Today, of course, most domestic cattle are fed almost exclusively grains. But grains as a food staple for the ruminants we eat, such as domestic cattle, appear to have led to health problems for us.

Researchers recently found that grain-fed cattle have a combination of body fatty acids that differs from that of wild animals. They also found that pasture-fed cattle have a combination of fatty acids similar to that of wild ruminants, including North American and African elk, mule deer, and antelope. The researchers proposed that the combination of fatty acids in grain-fed cattle may promote chronic diseases in humans who eat those cattle. But the fats in pasture-fed cattle, like those in wild ruminants, may protect us against those same human diseases.[260]

Accumulating evidence is teaching us a lesson about the animal foods we choose to eat: Our health is favored by food products from animals raised as closely as possible to the way livestock lived before the agricultural revolution began—freely roaming and grazing, and free from the antibiotics, estrogen, and growth hormone that hasten the maturity of the animals and fatten them in preparation for marketing.

PROTEIN

Ingesting enough protein is crucial to good health. The structure of the body is largely protein, and the enzymes that help keep our metabolism normal are mainly proteins.

Get plenty of protein, but not too much. On average, the body of a person who weighs 155 lbs expends about 30 grams of protein each day. The person must replace this amount to avoid a loss of protein from her body. Stress may increase the amount of protein the body expends. The extra protein expended due to stress may be small, but it's probably safe to take in an additional 10 grams each day to allow for the stress-induced increase. A good target amount of dietary protein for a person of 155 lbs is 40-to-45 grams each day.[70]

In Table 1, we've provided a list of some common foods and their respective protein content. By referring to the list, you can get some idea of how much protein you're getting from the foods you usually eat.

Keep in mind that the protein in some foods, such as eggs and meat, have a high "biologic value." This means the foods contain the full array of the twenty-two essential amino acids. The amino acids are "essential" in that we must get them from food because our bodies can't manufacture them.

Other foods, such as most vegetables and grains, contain only a portion of the twenty-two amino acids. The biologic value of these foods is therefore lower.

Having a rough knowledge of the biologic value of foods is important. If we're to meet our daily requirement for protein, and we eat mainly foods of low biologic value, we must eat more of them. If the foods we eat have a high biologic value, we can consume a lower amount and still meet our protein requirement. But just because foods derived from animals usually have a higher biologic value doesn't mean that you must eat animal foods. If you prefer not to, you have other options which we discuss below.

Animal or Vegetable Protein

Either animal or vegetable protein is okay. We base this belief on reports of some anthropologists of the diets of people in "preliterate societies." People in these societies have had little contact with modern, industrialized societies. The assumption is that the diet of these people is similar to that of our ancient ancestors before civilizations formed. In modern pre-literate societies where ample food is available, people consume about 70% plant foods and 30% animal foods.

Table 1. Protein content of some foods*

Food (Plant)	Amount	Approximate grams of protein
Almonds	10 nuts	1.9
Apples	3-in. diam	0.3
Bananas, medium	1 banana	1.3
Beans, lima	1 cup, boiled	12.9
Beans, red kidney	1 cup, boiled	14.4
Bread, white	1 slice	2.4
Bread, whole-wheat	1 slice	2.6
Beer	12 fl. oz.	1.1
Broccoli, boiled	1 cup	4.8
Carbonated sodas	12 fl. oz.	0.0
Carrots, raw	1 cup	1.2
Cauliflower	1 cup	2.7
Cherries, raw	1 cup	1.2
Chestnuts, fresh	10 nuts	2.1
Cucumbers, raw	1 cup	0.9
Eggs, chicken	1 egg, large	6.5
Figs, raw & whole	1 cup	1.2
Fudge, chocolate	1-oz	0.8
Grapes, Concord	1 cup, approx. 38 grapes	1.3
Grapefruit, raw	Half, 3½ in. diam.	0.5
Green olives	10 whole, small	0.4
Macaroni	1 cup	0.5
Macaroni & cheese	1 cup	16.8
Mushrooms	1 cup, raw	1.9
Oatmeal	1 cup, cooked	4.8
Okra	10 pods boiled	2.1
Oranges	Medium (2⅝ in)	2.1
Lentils	1 cup, cooked	15.6
Peaches	¾ lb	0.9
Pecans	10 large nuts	0.8
Peanut butter	1 tbsp	4.0
Peanuts	10 jumbo nuts	4.7
Tomatoes, raw, whole	4¾ oz	1.4
Wine, table	Glass, 3½ fl. oz.	0.1

Foods (Animal)		
Beef, lean & ground	¼ lb, broiled	31.0
Beef, rump roast	¼ lb, roasted	6.7
Cheese, cheddar	1 oz	7.1
Cheese, cottage	1 oz	3.9
Cheese, Swiss	1 oz	7.8
Chicken, light	¼ lb, roasted	35.8
Chicken, dark	¼ lb, roasted	31.7
Halibut	¼ lb, broiled	28.5
Herring, canned	¼ lb	22.5
Ice cream	1 cup	6.0
Lamb	¼ lb, lean	32.5
Liver, chicken	1 liver, simmered	1.1
Liver, calf	¼ lb, fried	33.4
Mackerel, Atlantic	¼ lb, broiled	24.7
Milk, cows	1 cup	8.5
Sardine	1 can	22.0
Oyster	3, 1 oz each	2.4
Ocean perch	¼ lb, fried	21.5

*Adams, C.F.: *Nutritive Value of American Foods: In Common Units.* Agricultural Handbook No. 456, Washington, D.C., U.S. Dept. of Agriculture, 1975.

Whether you get your protein mainly or solely from animal or vegetable sources, however, may be a philosophical choice to you. That's fine with us, as long as you get enough—but not too much—protein.

High Protein/High Fat Diets

We don't advocate a diet high in animal fat and protein. An example is the traditional American diet of large amounts of steak, pork chops, bacon, and butter and fatty gravy on potatoes. Such a diet can leave one's body chemistry too acidic. The high saturated fat content contributes strongly to cardiovascular disease and some cancers.

Part of the disease-generating potential of this type of high-fat diet is what it's deficient in: a wide variety of nutrients that vegetables, fruits, nuts, and seafood can provide. Traditionally in the U.S., people who eat high protein diets don't take in enough vegetables, fruits, and nuts. Because of this, they have dietary and nutritional deficiencies that contribute to cardiovascular disease and cancer.

One food constituent the high-fat diets are usually deficient in is indigestible fiber. Too little fiber can contribute to a wide array of illnesses and even premature death (see section below titled "Fiber"). The combination of saturated fats dawdling in a colon because of too little dietary fiber has resulted in a high rate of colon cancer and other intestinal diseases.

The Atkins Diet. A recent study showed that the Atkins diet contributes to cardiovascular health and weight loss. It was superior in these respects to the diet recommended by the American Heart Association. People on the Atkins diet markedly decrease their carbohydrate intake and liberally eat animal foods with high protein content. The high fat content of the foods decreases the people's appetite. As a result, they eat less. Despite this, they feel less hunger than they would from eating carbohydrate-loaded foods.

By comparison, foods high in refined carbohydrates can increase one's appetite. Foods such as pasta, bread, and some fruits and fruit juices can cause the blood sugar to surge. This can cause the insulin levels to peak, followed by a rapid drop in blood sugar. The blood sugar drop usually stimulates hunger, and the affected person tends to overeat carbohydrates. This pattern can lead to weight gain and increased risk for diabetes and heart disease.

The Atkins diet, however, practiced in the extreme, may suffer from the same deficiencies and health risks as the traditional American diet. The high-protein, high-fat diet may be immediately harmful to people with diabetes, heart disease, or kidney disease. Dr. Atkins openly cautions people about this, stating that the diet isn't for everyone.

Our concern is the long-range consequences for some people consuming almost exclusively a high-protein, high-fat diet of animal foods. Our advice is that if you're going to use the Atkins diet, be sure to take in enough fiber and plant foods in addition to high-protein, high-fat foods.

Of course, nuts and a variety of vegetables such as avocados contain high concentrations of good fats. Using these fats to suppress the appetite is preferable to using saturated fats in animal foods such as steak and lobster.

Protein Supplements

When many patients begin calculating how much protein they ingest each day, they find that they're getting too little. For some of these patients, using a protein supplement enables them to take in enough.

The protein supplement we presently use is the type we recommend—although, as always, we never endorse a particular brand. Many brands are available that meet our criteria for good quality (they contain all the essential amino acids). The brand we use contains enzymatically-processed rice protein from organic brown rice. And it has the important notice on its label, "GMO Free," signifying that it contains no genetically-modified organisms. The powder tastes good even when mixed with water. A heaping table-spoon contains 12 grams of vegetable protein.

CARBOHYRATES: REFINED AND COMPLEX

A wholesome diet contains ample amounts of complex carbo-hydrates; that is, carbohydrate foods that are as close to their nat-ural state as possible. And, it contains few refined carbohydrates. Complex carbohydrates can sustain good health, whereas refined carbohydrates can destroy it.

Refined Carbohydrates

In industrialized countries, refined carbohydrates (white sugar and flour) are a major contributor to many health problems. Hypo-metabolism is one of them.

Refined carbohydrates provide us with energy through their calories. But it's often said that the calories are "empty." This means that the carbohydrates provide at best paltry amounts of a few vitamins, minerals, and trace elements. And, for all practical purposes, they provide no fiber.

It's natural that most humans enjoy consuming large amounts of refined carbohydrates. According to some scientists, sugar (the basic unit of refined carbohydrates) has served a useful purpose in an interactive cycle between animals and plants. Enjoyment of the taste of sugar has provided an incentive for animals, including hu-mans, to eat certain plant foods. Seeds from these plants were then deposited in other locations from the feces of the animals. This enabled the strain of plants to flourish; it also eventually provided the animals with new plants to eat.

Sugar-containing plant foods also provided energy for cellular functions in humans and other animals. The sugars contain energy bonds that cells use in energy metabolism. In addition, plant foods contain fiber, and by eating the pleasant-tasting plant foods, hu-mans and other animals took in fiber that helped their intestinal tracts work efficiently (see section below titled "Fiber").

But then humans acquired advanced technological abilities. One of those abilities was to extract the sweet part of plant foods—the sugar—refine it, and provide it in concentrated form in beverages and foods. This is when the trouble with refined carbohydrates began. Between 1544 and 1689, sugar refineries were established in London and New York City. But the refining of carbohydrates on a large scale began in the late 1800s with the advent of advanced food-processing machinery.

During the 20th century, conventional medicine colluded with the food-processing industry to assure people that eating refined sugar had no harmful effects. I (JCL) recall, for example, a television exposé in the 1980s that illustrated this. In the segment, someone interviewed Frederick Stare, M.D., head of Harvard University's nutrition department.

During the interview, Dr. Stare assured viewers that eating refined sugar was fine for their health. He also said that the added sugar would make it more likely that children would eat nutritious foods they otherwise would avoid. The scene then changed to a child who had long eaten high-sugar foods undergoing radical dental surgery for massively rotten teeth. The scene then changed again, and the interviewer was standing outside the building that housed Harvard's nutrition department. He pointed to a plaque on a wall of the building. On the plaque were words of thanks from the food corporation that, at the time, put more sugar in children's foods than any other food company. The corporation had provided money to build the edifice occupied by Dr. Stare's nutrition department.

So, during the 20th century, some food companies used the authority of mainstream medicine to persuade people that eating refined carbohydrates regularly was not only safe, but actually fostered health. The companies also stimulated people, especially children, to desire their sugar-rich, fat-laden foods through the sophisticated and manipulative methods of Wall Street advertising experts. They further stoked desire by attention-holding cinematic methods that Hollywood movie producers had learned to effectively use over the last hundred years.

Food companies also used the talents of chemists to induce consumers to desire their products. The chemists concocted potpourris of taste-titillating chemicals that intensified the pleasure of eating the companies' foods. Some of the foods are so tasty that many people crave more even when they've already filled their bellies with them. Many consumers are enraptured by some of the engineered tastes, and they can hardly satiate themselves with the foods imbued with these tastes. Many people have consumed so much of these high-fat, high-sugar foods that obesity is epidemic in the United States. And some of the companies have now spread their food products and the accompanying obesity across the globe.

Despite the opinions of "authorities" such as Dr. Stare, people who regularly indulge themselves with the refined sugar and bad fats in fast foods are almost guaranteed to ruin their health. Normal metabolism is one of the main features of health many will lose. The refined sugar, for example, impairs metabolic health by overworking body systems not adapted to handle massive, concentrated sugar intake. We assure you of one thing: *Unless your intake of refined sugar is an extremely minor part of your diet, you won't achieve optimal metabolic health.*

As you proceed with metabolic rehab, be sure to watch out for the signs and symptoms of hypoglycemia. If you're diabetic, continue good management.

Complex Carbohydrates

Carbohydrate foods such as fruits, vegetables, and grains provide our bodies with energy. By doing so, they contribute to our health. When the carbohydrates are complex, they also provide us with vitamins, minerals, trace elements, and indigestible fiber. Having adequate amounts of each of these is essential to good health.

Whole Grains: Wholesome—But Harmful in Excess. Adopting a caveman diet doesn't mean you can't eat grains at all. Eating them in moderation is fine. The point is to make vegetables, fruits, and lean meat the staples of your diet.

To favor good health, however, the grains you eat in moderation, except for being cooked, should be close to their natural state. This means eating whole grains rather than refined and bleached grain products like white flour.

The milling of grains began hundreds of years ago. The purpose was to preserve the foods during prolonged storage. When weevils can reach whole grains stored in a hot, humid environment, they quickly infest them. Milling removes the most nutrient-rich parts of the grains and produces white rice or flour. This refining process protects the grains from weevils; they leave it for less prudent humans to consume and move onto foods with a high enough nutrient content to sustain health and life.

Many humans appear to lack the wisdom of the weevils, preferring refined grain products to whole grains. In some studies, people continued to eat milled grains in lieu of whole grains, even though they had full knowledge of the disease-inducing potential of their preference.

In regions where humans eat milled rice as their food staple, they fall victim to a vitamin deficiency disease called "beriberi." The deficient vitamin, "thiamine" or "vitamin B_1," is contained mostly in the outer layers of whole rice that are discarded during milling. People with beriberi have inflamed nerves, paralysis, general debility, and severe pain. And, they may die from the disease.

To prevent vitamin deficiency diseases such as beriberi, humans began in the 1940s to "enrich" white flour and bread with several vitamins and iron. Only a few nutrients were added back into the milled grain products. At the time, these were the nutrients known to prevent severe deficiency diseases in humans. As Professor Roger Williams noted in 1977, based on advances in nutritional knowledge since that earlier time, many other nutrients should also be added to milled grains. He noted that people's apathy had allowed food producers to ignore these advances in knowledge and decline to further enrich the foods.[57,p.94]

Since the time Professor Williams made that statement, a growing number of people have become interested in optimizing their health. These people are willing to pay for whole gains, and this has led to a bustling industry that provides more wholesome foods.

If you choose to include grains in your diet, and if you intend to achieve optimal metabolic health, you too must join the ranks of whole-grain enthusiasts, if you haven't already. Continuing to consume foods made mainly of milled, refined, bleached, and enriched white flour is simply incompatible with optimal metabolic health.

Even when the grains in your diet are whole, you still may not get enough vitamin B_1 if you also take thyroid hormone. You must use a supplement containing vitamin B_1 to ensure that you get enough. (See *Chapter 5*, section titled "Vitamin B_1, Thyroid Hormone, and Heart Health.")

Whole grains contain much more indigestible dietary fiber than do refined grains. This fiber is crucial to both intestinal and overall health. (See section below titled "Fiber.")

LOW CALORIE DIET

We don't advocate diets that severely restrict one's calorie intake. They are counterproductive in that they slow metabolism to survival level. The body, sensing the low calorie intake, shifts into a state that preserves calories by reducing energy expenditure. This state causes the person to remain fatter than she wants despite restricting her intake of calories.

We understand that people who often severely limit their calorie intake want to feel more attractive by reducing their body fat. But severely restricting calorie intake isn't the best way to accomplish the goal. Most patients can recover good metabolic health only by forgoing these excessively low calorie diets. And many rid themselves of excess body fat without restricting calories as they undergo metabolic rehab.

VEGETARIAN DIET

Most people who eat a vegetarian diet have higher metabolic rates. The carbohydrates, fats, and proteins in the diet don't cause the higher metabolic rates—two other factors do.

First, vegetarians have a higher intake of micro-nutrients: vitamins, minerals, and trace elements. Thus, their bodies have more of the substances needed for metabolic functions.

Second, they have more sympathetic nervous system activity. The sympathetic nervous system is a network of nerves that helps us adapt to stress. When this stress-adapting system is active, its nerve endings release a chemical (called "noradrenaline") that increases transmission of nerve impulses. Also, it speeds up the chemical reactions in cells. It does so by binding to beta-adrenergic receptors stationed in cell membranes. (For more on beta-adrenergic receptors, see *Chapter 15.*) When the receptors and noradrenaline bind, they set off a cascade of chemical reactions, and many processes inside the cells temporarily speed up. Vegetarians have higher blood levels of noradrenaline, and the higher levels keep their metabolism functioning at a faster rate. Their faster metabolism contributes to their fairly low percentage of body fat.

An especially important benefit of a vegetarian diet is that it provides dietary fiber. This fiber is essential for intestinal and overall health.

FIBER

A diet rich in dietary fiber can protect you from constipation and a variety of diseases. The diseases include diverticulosis, cancer of the colon, diabetes, obesity, and cardiovascular disease.[247] Moreover, getting enough fiber can ward off headaches, and it can possibly prevent or reduce the severity of autoimmune disease.

Headaches From Stretching of the Colon

I (GH-L) often have patients whose health problems result largely from how they eat. A typical case is a Canadian woman with whom I recently consulted by telephone. Her main complaints were chronic constipation and headaches. But she was also chronically fatigued and just felt bad most of the time. She also had trouble keeping off excess fat.

When I asked about her diet, she told me she ate with the aim of keeping her body fat low. For breakfast and dinner, she usually ate a "power bar"—essentially a high-protein candy bar. She ate what she considered a "normal" lunch, which consisted of tuna salad. She said she calculated that she took in 800 calories a day, with plenty of protein from the bars.

These types of "meals" are common among patients with symptoms doctors diagnose as fibromyalgia or chronic fatigue syndrome. Humans are designed to eat real food several times each day. Adequate protein intake is important, of course. But we must also get enough calories from complex carbohydrates and good fats. And we must get enough fiber from fruits, vegetables, and perhaps a modicum of whole grains.

Without the grains, many patients have the exact symptoms that the Canadian woman had: chronic constipation and headaches. We know that too little indigestible fiber in the diet causes constipation, and constipation can cause headaches. The famous intestinal specialist Walter C. Alvarez artificially created constipation in volunteer patients.[91,p.638] He accomplished this by stuffing their colons with gauze. A major complaint of the gauze-stuffed volunteers was headaches. When Alvarez removed the gauze from their colons, their headaches stopped.

As did Alvarez's volunteers, many patients experience headaches caused by overstuffed colons—not overstuffed with gauze, of course, but with dawdling or impacted feces. Most of these patients can easily relieve both their constipation and headaches. All they must do is get enough fiber and liquid from fruits and vegetables, and possibly some whole grains, into their intestinal tracts each day.

For some people, the fiber from fiber-rich foods isn't enough; they must also use supplemental fiber, such as inexpensive wheat or oat bran. The need to take large amounts of supplemental fiber to stay free from constipation raises the possibility that the patient has a thyroid hormone deficiency or resistance. This is because the main intestinal symptom of hypothyroidism and thyroid hormone resistance is constipation.

Autoimmune Disease and Proteins From the GI Tract

Mary Shomon recently interviewed us for her book, *Living Well With Autoimmune Disease*.[248, p.258] In the interview, we noted that dietary proteins can be absorbed from the colon into the blood. These absorbed proteins are foreign to the body; once in the blood, they become "antigens" against which antibodies form.[250][251]

Through "cross-reactivity," the antibodies may come to mistake normal body proteins as foreign. The normal body proteins that now become targets of the antibodies are those with a structure similar to that of the proteins absorbed from the intestine. When antibodies attack normal body proteins, we call the disorder "autoimmune disease." Proteins within the joints, the thyroid gland, the cortex of the adrenal glands, the intestinal lining, and other body tissues may become targets of cross-reacting antibodies.[65][70] Among patients with autoimmune disease, we most often work with the patient whose thyroid gland proteins are the target of the antibodies. The thyroid disease she's afflicted with is called "autoimmune thyroiditis."

The formation and dispatch of antibodies against antigens— including normal tissue proteins—will be especially strong in patients whose adrenal cortices are suppressed. Cortisol, secreted by the cortex of the adrenal glands, suppresses autoimmune reactions. But when the adrenal glands release too little cortisol, the virulence of antigen/antibody reactions is enhanced. Autoimmune attacks on normal body proteins will then proceed swiftly.

Adrenal cortical suppression is especially common in patients with hypothyroidism and thyroid hormone resistance. Thyroid hormone regulates the metabolism of the cortex of the adrenal glands. When a patient has too little thyroid hormone, or when the cells of her adrenal cortices are resistant to the thyroid hormone she does have, the cortices produce less than normal amounts of cortisol.

Adrenal function returns to normal in the hypothyroid or thyroid hormone resistant patient after she begins taking enough of the proper form of thyroid hormone. Her increased cortisol level may then slow down or halt autoimmune destruction of her thyroid gland.

Direct Effects of Inadequate Thyroid Hormone Regulation of the GI Tract. Patients who are hypothyroid or resistant to thyroid hormone have slowed motion of the GI tract. They also digest their food poorly because they secrete too little stomach acid and too few digestive enzymes. As a result, partially digested food passes into their colons. It dawdles there, along with cells that are sloughed off the inner lining of the tract, and microbes that are nurtured by the food residue. The food, cells, and microbes spend too much time in the sluggish GI tract. This provides time for proteins to pass into the blood from the tract, potentially contributing to autoimmune disease.

Many patients whose doctors give them a diagnosis of leaky gut syndrome fail to diagnose the hypothyroidism or thyroid hormone resistance that underlies it. When we see some of these patients, they've gone to tremendous effort and expense using dietary and nutritional methods to control the leaky gut. Proper thyroid hormone therapy promptly relieves the problem because it corrects the underlying cause. (For extensive information on the GI effects of too little thyroid hormone regulation, see Chapter 3.14, pages 681-687 in *The Metabolic Treatment of Fibromyalgia*.)

Throughly Digesting Proteins: The First Way to Stop or Prevent the Absorption of Dietary Proteins Into Your Blood. The first thing you can do to stop or prevent the absorption of proteins into your blood from your GI tract is to thoroughly digest the proteins in your food. In this section, we describe practices that increase the breakdown of proteins in your food. These practices will reduce the number of intact proteins that reach your colon.

Relax When You Eat. Being tense or anxious reduces the secretion of digestive juices and enzymes. It also slows the movement of food residue through the colon. The tense or anxious person may not fully digest the food she eats. The partially digested food that reaches her colon will dawdle there. As it does, microbes will work on it, putrefying proteins and fermenting sugars. Some of the undigested proteins will have time to enter her blood and activate her immune system.

You can prevent these potentially harmful processes from occurring in your colon by thoroughly digesting the food you eat. Keep in mind that digestion proceeds normally in most people *only* when they're relaxed while eating and for an hour or so afterward.

Some people aren't always able to relax completely when they eat. A sales person, for example, may have to discuss business with clients at lunch. Focusing on the business at hand rather than the food on the plate can make it impossible for him to relax. This is especially so if the sales person is tense about making the sale. Much of the person's swallowed lunch may go undigested.

If you often eat in such circumstances, and especially if you have indigestion and gas after doing so, talk with your doctor about prescribing a small dose of propranolol. Taking a small amount, about 20 mg, an hour or so before eating can be highly effective in blocking the nervous activity that can impede digestion.

Thoroughly Chew Food. To completely digest proteins, fats, and carbohydrates, chew your food thoroughly. Thorough chewing is important for three reasons.

First, the mouth and pancreas secrete enough food-dismantling enzymes only under certain conditions. These are when we:

1) relax before a meal
2) concentrate on the food we're about to eat
3) chew the food thoroughly, allowing enough
   time for saliva to mix with and moisten the food
4) savor the panorama of tastes from thoroughly
   chewing food and mixing it with saliva

Eating this way is the key that opens the door of good digestion. A person declines to use that key when she eats with her attention on the clock rather than on her food, gulps down her food, and ends the chore of eating as soon as she can to get back to whatever else is fully occupying her mind. Eating this way can give her indigestion; doing it habitually can impair her health.

The second reason to thoroughly chew our food is to disrupt the connective tissue encasement of proteins. Disrupting the encasement exposes the proteins to enzymes that will break them into amino acids. The amino acids can then absorb into your blood before reaching your colon.

The third reason to chew thoroughly is that saliva contains antibodies called immunoglobulin A (IgA). These antibodies protect us against some food-borne agents that are capable of causing intestinal or internal health problems. Chewing food thoroughly gives IgA time to do its intended job.

Protein-Digesting Enzymes and Betaine Hydrochloride. You may also want to take protein-digesting enzymes. These will increase the breakdown of dietary proteins into amino acids. Taking betaine hydrochloride will lower the pH of your stomach and small intestine, and this will activate the protein-digesting enzymes. Many over-the-counter digestive aid products contain both protein-digesting enzymes and betaine hydrochloride.

Ingesting Enough Fiber: The Second Way to Stop or Prevent the Absorption of Dietary Proteins Into Your Blood. The other thing you can do to reduce the amount of dietary proteins that enter your blood is to increase your fiber intake. Eating enough fiber ensures that food residue will move through your colon at a normal speed.

When food residue travels through the GI tract too slowly, intact proteins in the colon have more time to absorb into your blood. In addition, bacteria and fungi decompose some partially digested food matter that passes into the colon. Some molecules from this putrid substance may also enter your blood. (Putrefaction accounts in part for the obnoxious odor of some people's stool.)

Ingesting enough fiber shortens the transit time of proteins through the colon; the shortened time reduces the number of proteins that absorb into your blood. In the GI tract, water binds to the fiber, causing it to swell. The swollen fiber provides bulk that stretches the intestinal wall. The stretching activates nerve receptors in the wall that set off wavelike contractions of the colon. These contractions then move the food residue through the colon at a normal rate. (The contractions are akin to squeezing fingers sliding down an open toothpaste tube, moving the paste out the end.) The contractions usher the food residue along to evacuation, preventing the harm that tarrying proteins can cause.

Even when proteins are fully digested in the small intestine, some of their amino acids may still cause health problems if they fail to pass through one's colon quickly enough; they can dawdle there and get absorbed into the blood. Consider the toxic breakdown products of the amino acids arginine and ornithine. The three breakdown products are called polyamines. After they form, they can pass from one's colon into the blood. In selecting names for the three polyamines, researchers assisted us in feeling appropriate repugnance at the thought of them entering our blood: putrescine, cadaverine, and spermidine.

Patients with active psoriasis have high levels of these polyamines, and when levels decrease, the psoriasis improves.[253][254][255] Naturopathic physicians Dr. Michael Murray and Dr. Joseph Pizzorno write that some natural compounds can block the formation of the polyamines. Vitamin A and alkaloids of goldenseal (such as berberine) are examples. The goldenseal alkaloids inhibit an enzyme inside intestinal bacteria that converts arginine and ornithine into polyamines.[142,p.764]

Along with vitamin A and goldenseal, we can decrease the amount of polyamines that absorb into our blood in another way: eating enough fiber-containing foods or using supplemental fiber. Enough fiber in the GI tract will ensure that food residue and the polyamines move through the colon at a normal speed rather than lingering and being absorbed into the blood.

Supplementing With Bran. For most people, unprocessed vegetables, fruits, whole grains, and nuts can provide enough fiber to keep the transit time through the colon normal. Other people may have to use a fiber supplement.

If you need to use supplemental fiber, you can do so inexpensively by purchasing it as organic oat and wheat bran in health food stores. You can mix these together and ingest them in one of two ways. You can mix the bran with cereals, salads, baked goods, liquids, or with anything else that's agreeable to your taste. Or you can spoon or pour the bran directly into your mouth, soak it briefly with a liquid, swallow it, and wash it down with water or some other liquid. If you have a sensitivity to wheat products, only use the oat bran.

We hear a lot about the relative benefits of soluble versus insoluble supplemental fiber. At this time, however, researchers don't agree on what type of fiber is best for avoiding any particular disease. Nor do they agree on what the optimal daily dose is. One thing is clear, though: High fiber intake (more than 25-to-30 grams per day) from a variety of food sources such as fruits, vegetables, legumes, cereals, and possibly bran, protects us against many diseases.[247]

An Advantage of Getting Fiber From Food: Avoiding Adrenaline-Induced Symptoms. When humans ingest white sugar, it rushes into their bloodstream. Its rapid entry steeply raises the blood sugar level, provoking a large release of insulin into the blood. The insulin binds to insulin receptors in cell membranes to rapidly shunt the sugar from the blood into the cells. The large amount of insulin may rush so much sugar into cells that the blood sugar level plummets. If so, the adrenal glands will respond to the low blood sugar level by releasing adrenaline. The purpose of the adrenaline is to raise the blood sugar level, which it does. But a heavy load of adrenaline can also induce disturbing symptoms: nervousness, tremors, rapid heart rate, muscle tension, sweating, and anxiety.

(*NOTE:* Many patients who eat sugary foods throughout the day regularly experience adrenaline-induced symptoms. Taking thyroid hormone can accentuate their symptoms, and the patients often mistake their worsened symptoms as overstimulation from the thyroid hormone. The proper solution to their worsened symptoms isn't to settle for a lower dose of thyroid hormone. Of course, they must reduce their dose until they get their blood sugar under control. And that's the proper solution. After their blood sugar becomes normal and stable, most find their optimal thyroid hormone dose. That dose for many patients is much higher than the amount that previously worsened their adrenaline-induced symptoms.)

The adrenaline release set off by low blood sugar will also temporarily affect the GI tract. It will reduce the secretion of hydrochloric acid and digestive enzymes, and it will slow the movement of food residue through the intestinal tract. The slowed movement through the GI tract can cause two problems: bacteria in the colon will have time to putrefy food residue, and proteins have time to pass into the blood.

In contrast to refined sugar and white flour, starches and sugars ingested as part of unprocessed fruits, vegetables, nuts, and grains are released slowly into the circulation. The starches and sugars release slowly because they're intertwined in the complex structure of the fiber-containing foods.[252]

To completely disrupt the fiber complexes of the plant foods and release the sugars they contain takes time. As enzymes gradually disassemble a food, its complex carbohydrates are released, and enzymes break them down into simpler compounds and eventually to sugar. The sugar absorbs into the blood *gradually* as it's released from the food step by step. As the sugar gradually absorbs into the blood, the pancreas secretes only small amounts of insulin. The adrenal glands aren't provoked into secreting adrenaline, and the person doesn't experience adrenaline-induced symptoms.[65]

Fiber and Thyroid Hormone Work Together to Keep Cholesterol Normal. For patients concerned about high cholesterol, taking in enough of both fiber and thyroid hormone is important. Thyroid hormone is one of the most potent cholesterol-lowering agents. Many people who take cholesterol-lowering drugs today probably have untreated or under-treated hypothyroidism or thyroid hormone resistance.

Some people, however, have cholesterol levels too high despite their use of enough thyroid hormone. Taking in too little fiber may be the cause of their high cholesterol.

As we explained above, when someone ingests enough fiber, food residue moves through her GI tract at a normal rate. The residue takes with it a salt derived from bile acid called lithocholate. But when she doesn't take in enough fiber and food residue moves too slowly through the GI tract, lithocholate has time to absorb from the colon into the blood. The blood transports the lithocholate to the liver. There, the salt slows the rate at which the liver converts cholesterol to bile acids. The slowed conversion causes the cholesterol blood level to rise. For the person's cholesterol level to decrease into the normal range, she'll have to increase her fiber intake.

How to Tell When You're Getting Enough Fiber. You need a practical way to know when you're getting enough fiber. The most useful gauges are your bowel movements and your stools.

If your stools are hard, or if you must strain to pass them, you're constipated. You should increase your fiber intake to soften your stools.

If your stools are loose or watery, and you pass them more than a couple of times each day, you may be taking too much fiber. If this is the case, you should cut back your fiber intake until your stools are closer to ideal.

By ideal stools, we mean that they're large, well-formed, low in odor, and soft enough to pass without straining. The ideal frequency and timing are in the morning or after a meal, once or twice a day. If this describes you, then you're consuming the right amount of fiber.[249]

HIGH-NUTRIENT CONVENIENCE FOODS AS SUPPLEMENTS TO A WHOLESOME DIET

Protein bars are essentially convenience foods, but they aren't as potentially harmful as fast foods laden with bad fats, salt, and sugar. Still, protein bars shouldn't be a substitute for wholesome meals. These convenience foods don't provide all the essential nutrients, and health problems can develop if we use them as a substitute for a wholesome diet (see section above titled "Headaches from Stretching of the Colon").

These high-nutrient convenience foods are best used as a supplement to, rather than a substitute for, a wholesome diet. For example, I (GII-L) eat one every hour or two when I'm on long hikes into the mountains or on long bike rides. At these times, the nutrients in the bars provide me with extra fuel that sustains me in my physical work.

ORGANIC FOODS

Make as much as possible of the food you eat organic. *Many* environmental toxins—toxins that we can't totally avoid—constantly assault our bodies (see *Chapter 12*). Because of this, it makes sense to eliminate the intake of the toxins whenever we can. We do so by eating organic foods.

Some people complain that organic foods are too expensive.

They *are* generally more expensive, and the higher cost may strain some people's budgets. But the savings from not buying organic foods may be only temporary. Over time, diseases caused by the toxins in conventional foods may be far more costly, chronic diseases that make life miserable or cancer that can end life prematurely.

Even if you live a long time eating conventionally grown or raised foods, the quality of your life may be low. Consider, for example, that some toxins impede metabolism; they do so especially by interfering with the thyroid system. If you suffer from symptoms of hypometabolism, man-made toxins taken in through conventional foods may be one of the causes (see section named "Dioxins and PCBs" in *Chapter 12*).

LIQUIDS

We need more than three quarts or liters of liquid per day for the best health.[5,p.39] On average, people should drink about eight 8-oz glasses of liquid each day. We strongly recommend water as the main liquid you drink.

Getting Enough Water Each Day

A convenient way to make sure you get enough water is to fill and drink a 1 liter bottle three times each day. The 3 liters are roughly equal to the eight 8 oz glasses of water most people need. Using a water bottle in this way will enable you to easily keep track of how much you've drunk.

A good habit to develop is to drink a glass of water each hour. Drinking this much water will keep your urine dilute. Excreting dilute urine is easier on the kidneys than excreting concentrated urine.[5,p.39]

Drinking this much water may be inconvenient for patients whose hypothyroidism or thyroid hormone resistance isn't yet effectively treated. Some of these patients excrete a small volume of urine many times each day. They may tend to drink less to reduce the number of times they have to urinate. But since concentrated urine is more burdensome to the kidneys, it's prudent for them to drink more despite the inconvenience. When patients reach an effective dose of thyroid hormone, their urine volume increases and they have to urinate less often. (For extensive coverage of urinary urgency and frequency, see *The Metabolic Treatment of Fibromyalgia*, pages 745-766.)

How much water you should drink each day, of course, will depend on several factors. One is how large you are. Smaller people may need less than the eight 8 oz glasses of water; larger people may need more. If you live in a humid area, you may need a little less water. But if you live in a dry region, such as where we live in Colorado, you may need to drink as much as four rather than three liters each day.

If you exercise vigorously and lose body water through sweat, you may need to drink even more water. I (GH-L), for example, take yoga classes where the room temperature is kept at 105°F (40.5°C). The room temperature and activity induce profuse sweating. Because of this, I carry a bottle of water with me, and during the class, replenish the water my body loses.

Water, Eating, and Fat Retention. Candice Pert, Ph.D. noted that some people eat to relieve thirst that they don't recognize. The food doesn't relieve their thirst, so they keep on eating. Over time, this practice makes some people fat.[224] By drinking more and reducing their intake of calories from food each day, they can reduce their excess body fat.

For some reason, an occasional person finds drinking water objectionable. The person may eat excessively, unwittingly driven by her body's need for liquid. Those who have this problem can overcome it by making water palatable for them to drink. They can do so by adding a flavoring substance to filtered water. We recommend a natural substance such as lemon juice, and we *strongly* discourage the use of sugar or artificial sweeteners.

Why No One Should Drink Tap Water

Community water systems use chlorine as a disinfectant in water intended for human use. No one who wants to achieve or maintain good health should be drinking tap water except on rare occasions when filtered water isn't available.

Most restaurants, of course, make tea and coffee from water straight from the tap. If you eat in a restaurant, chances are you'll ingest tap water, along with its chlorine, while doing so. Otherwise, though, make every effort to avoiding consuming tap water.

The Environmental Working Group reported that in 1996, the drinking water of 4.3 million US citizens contained "excessive" amounts of pesticides. The amounts exceeded new federal standards of acceptable risk. People in farm regions, especially the Midwestern corn belt, "are being served a cocktail of farm chemicals in their tap water." The Group reported, however, that some cities are trying to improve the quality of their water.[27]

Despite the cleanup efforts, we strongly recommend that you *not* drink tap water in *any* city! In 1993, researchers analyzed studies to learn whether chlorination by-products in drinking water are associated with cancer. They found a positive association between humans consuming chlorinated drinking water and their developing bladder and rectal cancer.[28]

A 1997 study found that women who drink more heavily chlorinated water have more cancers.[29] The researchers found a clear, positive relationship between the level of chloroform (a chlorination by-product in water) and the incidence of all cancers in women in Iowa. Women who drank chlorinated city water had a 72% increase in colon cancer.

Of special concern to hypometabolic patients is chlorine's potential for harming the thyroid gland. We cover this in the section titled "Chlorine and the Thyroid Gland" in *Chapter 12.*

Clean, Filtered Water

Water is the "old-fashioned health drink,"[274] but nowadays, for optimal health, we must drink only filtered, or treated, water. Over the last ten years, steadily more supermarkets in the U.S. have come to provide machines in which customers can refill water bottles. Most of the machines treat the water with several methods. If you subscribe to a water delivery service, make sure the water you purchase is treated in these same ways. Preferably, your drinking water will be treated with several of seven common treatment methods.

Water Treatment Methods. The most basic form of water treatment is sediment filtration. In the process, filters remove dirt, rust, algae, and other particles from the water.

Activated carbon treatment is another basic form. In the process, water runs through activated carbon, removing odor-causing chemicals and much of the chlorine. This improves the taste, color, and odor of the water.

The water in some bottled brands may also be injected with ozone. This disinfects the water.

High quality water is subjected to these treatments, but the addition of other treatments can raise the quality of the water even further. One method is deionization, a process of ion exchange.

Another method is reverse osmosis. Reverse osmosis is the most effective system for removing potentially harmful materials from water. In reverse osmosis, the water is forced through an ultra thin semipermeable membrane. This filters out dissolved solids such as lead, mercury, salts, and pesticides. Reverse osmosis filtering can also remove many pathogens due to the size of the microscopic pores in the semipermeable membrane.

Another method is exposing water to ultraviolet light. The exposure kills any microbes in the water.

Distillation involves boiling water and condensing and collecting the steam. Distillation is used with deionization and reverse osmosis to remove most of the dissolved minerals in the water, producing what is called purified water. We don't recommend that distilled water be your major source of liquid. Water can be an important source of health-sustaining minerals, but distilled water contains precious little of them.

Soft Water

Health problems are especially likely with soft water—water without minerals such as calcium and magnesium. Soap lathers more easily with soft water, but people may pay a high health price for the convenience if they depend on soft drinking water. Soft drinking water may dissolve nickel from pipes and containers. Nickel leached in this way may accumulate heavily in the water.[275] Drinking the nickel-laden water may dangerously increase one's body level. Potential harmful effects include skin allergies, lung fibrosis, kidney and cardiovascular poisoning, and cancer.[276]

Spring Water

We prefer not to drink spring water except when we rarely don't have access to water treated by filtration, activated carbon filtering, and reverse osmosis. Spring water comes from underground sources and flows naturally to the surface of the earth.[274] The likelihood that the water contains contaminants is high, and we prefer to avoid them.

Soft Drinks

Drink few soft drinks, or even better, none at all. While occasionally drinking a soft drink isn't likely to harm you, soft drinks definitely shouldn't be your main source of liquids. Unless they are diet soft drinks, they contain a large amount of refined sugar. However, we don't recommend that you drink diet soft drinks either (see section below titled "Aspartame").

Soft drinks also contain phosphoric acid to make the drinks bubble. In the small intestine, the phosphorus from phosphoric acid binds to calcium. The binding forms calcium-phosphate. The small intestine can't absorb calcium-phosphate into the blood. As a result, the person who consumes a lot of soft drinks through the day and with meals may develop a calcium deficiency. The deficiency can contribute to osteoporosis. It can also cause nerves and muscles to be excessively excitable. The excitability can cause symptoms such as restlessness, anxiety, and muscle tension.[200][201]

Aspartame. Some people have switched to soft drinks that contain artificial sweeteners, especially aspartame. Aspartame is 180 times sweeter than sugar. The FDA has allowed its use in dry foods since 1981, and in carbonated drinks since 1983. It's also used in multivitamins, fruit juices, stick-type confections, breath mints, and iced tea.[338] We've also seen it in the list of ingredients on ice cream, candy, and cookie packages in the supermarket.

Recently, a panel of researchers reviewed the evidence for the safety or health risks of using aspartame. The panel represented the NutraSweet Company of Mt Prospect, Illinois. NutraSweet is the brand name under which aspartame is marketed. Although we doubt that we have to tell you what the panel's official conclusion was, it decided that the sweetener is entirely safe.[337] The company, of course, has a gargantuan financial interest in consumers thinking aspartame is safe. Because of this, no one should be surprised that a panel of researchers on the company's payroll concluded that consuming the sweetener carries no health risks.

Since the FDA approved the use of aspartame in carbonated beverages, the agency has received increasing numbers of reports concerning adverse reactions. These include complaints of neurologic, gastrointestinal, and allergic reactions.[338]

One researcher has warned that substances such as aspartame can destroy brain cells. He wrote that aspartame and glutamate can be called "excitotoxins." This means that the chemicals both arouse and damage the brain. Some excitotoxins from food reach some regions of the brain and silently destroy cells. He noted that some people are more sensitive to excitotoxins than others, and these people are at particular risk. He summarized, ". . . data supports the conclusion that excitotoxins, as used in foods today, may produce blood elevations high enough to cause damage to the nervous system of young children, damage which is not detectable at

the time of occurrence but which may give rise to subtle disturbances in neuroendocrine function in adolescence and/or adulthood."[339]

(*NOTE:* Another researcher reported that 25% of people who
eat foods containing MSG have adverse reactions to it.[340] MSG
contains glutamate, a flavor enhancer that's also an excitotoxin.
Common adverse reactions are headache, weakness, muscle tight-
ness, numbness or tingling, and flushing.[341] One study showed that
when fibromyalgia patients stopped consuming glutamate and aspartame, their symptoms markedly improved.[320])

Consuming soft drinks containing sugar or aspartame is likely
to compromise your health. Filtered water is a far healthier way
to quench thirst. If you want a flavored drink, add a little lemon or
lime juice to your water. If you don't at first, you'll soon come to
like the taste of naturally flavored water, and soft drinks will lose
their taste appeal.

Coffee

The question of whether or not people should drink coffee or
use caffeine from other sources is important enough that we devote
a separate chapter to it—*Chapter 14.*

SOY

Soy products contain "isoflavones." These are plant compounds that have estrogen-like effects in the body. They are also
called "isoflavonoids," "flavonoids," "lignans," or "phytoestro-
gens." Soy, however, isn't the only food that contains isoflavones;
tea, fruits, and vegetables also contain them.

Women may want to consume a sufficient amount of isoflavones to help regulate their estrogen levels. Using isoflavones
is especially important for women who want to minimize or stop
their use of estrogens foreign to the human body, such as those in
Premarin. (See *Chapter 9*, section titled "Isoflavones.")

Isoflavones in excess, however, may cause hypothyroidism.

Those who consume a lot of soy products are at risk of taking in excess isoflavones. Those whose health may be more adversely affected are those who already have borderline hypothyroidism.

How much soy is too much? Perhaps no one is better prepared to answer this question than Mary Shomon. Few people have provided more thyroid patients with more information about the potential dangers of heavy soy intake. We asked Mary her opinion of the dietary use of soy:[10]

"You've extensively explored and written about the issue of soy products impairing thyroid gland function. Do you have any advice for people about the healthy use of soy—use of it that doesn't impair the thyroid gland?" Mary answered:

> My primary concern with soy products is for people who are already hypothyroid due to autoimmune thyroid disease, or those who are from a family with a history of autoimmune thyroid disease. In those people, over-consumption of soy products (here, I'm most worried about soy supplements, isoflavone pills, and so-called "menopause" aids like Revival or Promensil) may worsen their thyroid problem, or trigger a problem in someone not yet diagnosed. I also caution those who are having trouble regulating their TSH levels to look at the quantity of soy.
>
> That said, I think for those without autoimmune problems, and those who can eat soy while remaining regulated and doing well on their thyroid medications, it's not a problem. And even those with autoimmune thyroid disease can benefit from some soy in the diet . . . I eat soy burgers, soy patties, and some tofu and miso periodically. I'm just not going to take soy powders or pills.[10]

We agree with Mary's view, and also the conclusions of some published reports. Some researchers have noted that the estrogen-like and antioxidant effects of isoflavones can help protect people from diseases such as heart disease and cancer. They also noted that these potential health benefits have led to a dramatic increase in people's consumption of soy supplements.[336]

These same researchers, however, caution that soy isoflavones ingested in excess are potentially toxic. High doses of isoflavones can induce mutations and oxidation reactions that generate free radicals. Isoflavones may also inhibit enzymes involved in hormone metabolism. They concluded: "Thus, in high doses, the adverse effects of flavonoids may outweigh their beneficial ones, and caution should be exercised in ingesting them at levels above that which would be obtained from a typical vegetarian diet. The unborn fetus may be especially at risk, since flavonoids readily cross the placenta."[336]

Excess consumption can also cause metabolic problems. In one study, about 50% of participating people developed metabolic problems when they consumed 30 grams of soybeans (which contain isoflavones) each day for three months. The people in the study had no history of goiter or elevated thyroid antibodies. Despite this, half of them developed symptoms of hypometabolism: malaise, constipation, and sleepiness. One month after they stopped eating soybeans, their symptoms of slow metabolism disappeared.[164]

Recently, researchers wrote of a 45-year-old woman whose use of a soy supplement reduced her absorption of T_4. She had thyroid cancer, so surgeons removed most of her thyroid gland and treated her with radioactive iodine. Still, it was necessary to suppress her TSH level so that the remainder of her thyroid gland wouldn't develop tumors. She had to take a very large amount of T_4 to accomplish this. She had been taking a "soy cocktail" protein supplement right after taking her daily T_4 dose. When she began taking her T_4 hours from the time she took the soy cocktail, she was able to suppress her TSH level with a much lower dose of T_4. The researcher concluded that the soy product had been reducing her absorption of some of her daily dose of T_4.[335]

The soy cocktail the patient was ingesting after taking her daily dose of T_4 was a complex food. It may have contained calcium, iron, or any of a variety of other food constituents that can reduce the amount of thyroid hormone that absorbs into the blood from the small intestine. As a rule, patients absorb the maximum amount of thyroid hormone when they take it on an empty stomach.

Soy does contain isoflavones, antioxidants, and high-quality protein; all of these can contribute to good metabolic health. If you want to use soy, however, temper your use of it.

Don't use large amounts of soy each day, and don't make it your only source of protein. If you use soy isoflavone capsules or tablets, the same advice applies. As with other foods, be sure to read the packaging of the product; note the content of isoflavones, and adjust your intake so that it's not excessive.

We have one last recommendation about soy. A lot—perhaps most—of the available soy products contain soy that has been genetically modified. On principle, we choose not to eat foods artificially mutated to better serve the financial interests of corporations. If you feel the same, make sure the packaging of any soy product you purchase contains a particular statement: that the product contains no genetically modified organisms or GMOs. (See *Chapter 12*, section titled "Protecting Yourself Despite Official Assurances.")

■ For more on soy products, isoflavones, and hypothyroidism, read "Soy Formulas and Soy Foods—A Thyroid Danger," pages 269-271 in Mary Shomon's book, *Living Well With Hypothyroidism* (New York, Avon Books, 2000).[11]

FAT AND WEIGHT LOSS
AND THYROID HORMONE DOSE

Many patients, though not all, who've had a low energy level for years because of hypothyroidism or thyroid hormone resistance are fatter and weigh more than they prefer. When they begin taking the proper form and dose of thyroid hormone, some of them lose the fat and weight without any particular effort.

Other patients, even though they're now taking enough thyroid hormone, retain the excess body fat and weight they've accumulated. Usually, there are two factors involved that promote the build-up and retention of excess body fat in these patients: a diet that adds body fat and a sedentary lifestyle.

Sometimes these patients have an unrealistic expectation. They assume the thyroid hormone they now take will deplete the excess fat and reduce their weight with no other effort on their part—without them adopting a good diet and exercising to tolerance.

With this unrealistic expectation, the patients make mistakes that could dreadfully harm them. They fail to adopt a wholesome diet, decline to take nutritional supplements, and refuse to exercise to tolerance. Along with these, they increase their thyroid hormone dose higher and higher with the aim of getting the hormone alone to deplete their excess fat. As a result, these patients may harm themselves with excessive doses of thyroid hormone.

The patient's poor diet and sedentary lifestyle may have rendered her heart more susceptible to damage from overstimulation of any kind, including that from high doses of thyroid hormone. The outcome can be disastrous if she increases her dose to a high level without protecting her heart with a wholesome diet, nutritional supplements, and exercise to tolerance. We urge patients under the care of other doctors *not* to take this approach. In our own clinical practice, we refuse to cooperate in the thyroid hormone treatment of patients who decline to include in their lifestyle a heart-protective diet, nutritional supplementation, and exercise to tolerance.

If you don't lose excess body fat after reaching a health-sustaining dose of thyroid hormone, it's extremely important for you to educate yourself about two things: how people get and retain excess fat through lifestyle, and how to get rid of the fat in a healthy way. The most helpful resources we could find for this information are two books by biochemist (and stand-up comedian extraordinaire) Covert Bailey: *Fit or Fat* and *The Ultimate Fit or Fat*. We also recommend three books by Oprah Winfrey's personal trainer, Bob Green: *Make the Connection*, *Keep the Connection*, and *Get With the Program.*

If you want to count calories and be aware of nutritional information for the food you eat, we recommend two sources. One is Allan Borushek's book, *The Doctor's Pocket Calorie, Fat & Carbohydrate Counter.* The other is the website: <www.CalorieKing.com>. This website provides a free online diet diary.

Wholesome Diet in a Nutshell

- The typical American diet is too high in bad fats and sugar to promote health.

- The diet natural to humans and that best promotes health is what has been called a "caveman diet." It consists of vegetables, fruits, nuts, lean animal foods, and a small amount of whole grains. You should eat most vegetables, fruits, nuts, and grains as close to their natural state as possible.

- Make as many of your foods as possible organic; organic foods are more expensive than conventional foods in the short run, but less so in the long run.

- A normal transit time of food through your GI tract is crucial to health. Provide yourself with this by eating enough fiber-rich foods and taking an organic fiber supplement. And if you're hypothyroid or resistant to thyroid hormone, work with your doctor to arrive at an effective dose of thyroid hormone that will normalize transit time through your GI tract.

- Take in the equivalent of eight 8-oz glasses of liquid each day. Don't drink carbonated soft drinks or tap water. Treated water is necessary nowadays for good health.

- Soy products are a good source of plant estrogen-like compounds, antioxidants, and protein. Ingesting soy products in excess, however, can impair the thyroid gland and cause other health problems. Keep your consumption of soy products low, and make sure the product's packaging contains a statement such as "GMO Free."

Chapter 5

Nutritional Supplements:
Vitamins, Minerals, Trace Elements,
and Other Substances

IN 1978 AND 1979, I (JCL) taught clinical nutrition in the Clinical Science Division of the Texas Chiropractic College. I obtained this teaching position partly because of several papers on nutrition I'd written for publications.[77][78][79][200] A published paper that especially helped was one I completed during my internship at the Los Angeles Chiropractic College. The paper, titled "The Nutritional Treatment of Arthritic Diseases," won the Annual Scientific Paper Award of the *Journal of the American Chiropractic Association*. I was delighted with the award and with the forthcoming publication of the paper in the journal.[77] But as a student living at poverty level, I was delighted with the $500 prize that came with the award (a considerable amount in 1977). And, of course, I was happy when this honor helped me get a position teaching clinical nutrition. The year I taught clinical nutrition, I wrote 14 papers on the subject that were published in journals and trade papers.[59][60][61][62][63][64][65][66][67][68][69][70][71][72] After I quit the teaching position, I used clinical nutrition in my private practice.

I mention my background in nutrition for one reason. From what I learned through it—by writing, teaching, and practicing—I finally reached a conclusion that I expressed in a 1982 desk manual for doctors on nutritional therapy: "The dosages I recommend here are *practical target amounts* rather than scientific quantifications. Our base of scientific information in nutrition is not sufficient to specify exact dosages that are scientifically defensible. Therefore, *practical targets* are my present aim. Treatment cannot be determined on the basis of statistics; rather, it remains uniquely individual and empirical. Your clinical judgment, based on scrutiny of your patients, is the ultimate determinant of the dosages you specify."[7,p.4] I again published the same statement in 1989[6] and 2000.[1,p.968]

While writing this book, we've carefully considered whether this conclusion is still true. We agree that it is, and that it warrants emphasis. So, here in a nutshell are our recommendations to you about nutrient dosages:

• Take all the nutrients we now know benefit humans. At minimum, take those we list in Table 2.

• Initially, aim for *practical target amounts*, such as those Dr. Earl Mindell recommends.[74][75] You'll find that different authorities recommend different doses. The discrepancy between their recommendations isn't too important. Start with the amounts recommended by an authority your trust. Then adjust the doses so that you feel they are fulfilling your individual needs.

• Except for the fat-soluble vitamins D, E, A, and K, there's virtually no risk of overdosing with vitamins. For most patients, it's best to err on the side of wastefully high doses than mistakenly low ones.[1,p.968] As eminent nutritional scientist Dr. Roger Williams wrote: "Widely different levels of vitamins A, C, and E are required by different individuals, and since in reasonable amounts they are all harmless, I tend to take generous amounts."[57]

• If you feel you need help in designing your nutritional supplement program, find someone qualified to advise you. In college, chiropractic students take more hours in nutrition than do medical students. Some chiropractic physicians also become board certified in clinical nutrition. Your chiropractic physician may be your best source of information on nutrition. Of all types of physicians, however, naturopathic physicians who are graduates of accredited naturopathic medical schools by far have the most education in nutrition. CNCs (Certified Nutritional Counselors) are also well qualified to advise you. We have a precaution, however, regarding nutritional counselors. In our experience, too many registered or licensed dieticians are patently unscientific in their beliefs, and they're prejudiced against the use of nutritional supplements. Among dieticians, of course, there are admirable exceptions. But if you consult one, find out right away whether the person believes we don't need nutritional supplements. If this is the advice the dietician gives you, following this advice is almost guaranteed to sabotage your efforts to achieve metabolic health.(For more detailed information on this problem with some dieticians, see the section below titled "Optimal Vitamin and Mineral Intake." Also, see the following page on our website: <www.drlowe.com/news/bushletr.htm>)

In the sections below, we have some comments on nutrients we consider especially important to your achieving metabolic health.

VITAMINS

Vitamins are minute substances in natural foods. The word "vitamin" comes from the Latin term that means "vital for life." Vitamins are essential if life is to continue, and an optimal amount is crucial for metabolic health. When people ingest too few vitamins, metabolism slows, and the people may develop deficiency diseases.

Taking nutritional supplements is imperative if you're to achieve metabolic health. For most patients, however, taking vitamins isn't enough to acquire and sustain metabolic health. At minimum, they must also make other practices a regular part of their lives—eating a wholesome diet, exercising to tolerance, and avoiding metabolism-impeding drugs. Many people must also use the proper form and dose of thyroid hormone.

Vitamins and Enzymes

Enzymes are proteins, most of which have a mineral or vitamin attached to them. The minerals and vitamins are called coenzymes. Vitamin C is the only vitamin that doesn't serve as a coenzyme. When we increase our intake of vitamins that serve as coenzymes, we increase the amount of active enzymes in our bodies.[5] An increase in active enzymes may be one reason some people's symptoms of slow metabolism go away after they begin using nutritional supplements.

Taking in more vitamins and minerals that act as coenzymes may speed up your metabolism. The opposite is also true—if you don't take in enough vitamins and minerals that act as coenzymes, the number of active enzymes in your body will decrease, and your metabolism will then slow down. Your metabolism may slow so much that you begin having symptoms that resemble those of hypothyroidism. Your regimen of self-treatment *must* include the use of vitamin and mineral supplements.

Vitamins and the Use of Thyroid Hormone

When we take thyroid hormone, the hormone drives our metabolism at a faster rate. In fact, thyroid hormone is the single most potent metabolic stimulant. For thyroid hormone to speed up our metabolism in a healthful way, we must also have an increase in active enzymes. Thyroid hormone increases the production and activity of a host of enzymes. As we said in the section above, taking nutritional supplements can also increase the number of active enzymes. By these effects on enzymes, thyroid hormone and nutritional supplements work hand-in-hand to optimize metabolism. The mutually enhancing metabolic effects of B complex vitamins and thyroid hormone make optimal amounts of these agents especially important to metabolic health.

B Complex Vitamins

Some B complex vitamins are critically important to normal metabolism. Taking in too little of them can slow metabolism. If metabolism slows enough, symptoms develop. An example is slowed metabolism and related depression suffered by many people deficient in vitamins B_1, B_{12}, and folic acid. People with even low-normal folic acid levels tend to have low body temperature and feel cold. They may tire easily, sleep poorly, and feel discouraged and depressed.[9] The deficiency of the vitamin also causes poor memory and concentration.

Vitamin B_1, Thyroid Hormone, and Heart Health. Vitamin B_1 is essential to normal metabolism. In addition, it augments the metabolic effects of thyroid hormone. Taking thyroid hormone without also taking vitamin B_1 as a supplement may be hazardous. For one thing, a deficiency of vitamin B_1 increases the irritability of trigger points and referred pain.[9,p.120] This is especially bad for fibromyalgia patients since they already have chronic, widespread pain. When a vitamin B_1 deficiency causes pain referral by trigger points, the patients have even more pain.

There is an even worse risk for patients who take thyroid hormone without also taking vitamin B_1. Speeding up metabolism with thyroid hormone in a person not taking nutritional supplements is likely to create vitamin deficiencies. As thyroid hormone speeds up metabolism in the person not taking vitamin B_1, a heart disorder may develop. The disorder is a "beriberi-type heart syndrome." The syndrome may lead to heart failure.[8][9] For this reason, it is imperative that patients taking thyroid hormone also take vitamin B_1 as part of their nutritional regimen.

ANTIOXIDANTS

We're bombarded by damaging chemicals in the air we breathe, the food we eat, and the water we drink. Antioxidants help us prevent adverse effects to our health from these toxins. Antioxidants act as scavengers for the free radicals created by the reactions of these toxins with normal body chemicals. Free radicals can cause cancers and make us look old before our time. The main nutritional antioxidants are vitamins C and E, beta carotene, and selenium.

Selenium, a mineral, is a potent antioxidant. It is essential for the production of an antioxidant enzyme, "glutathione peroxidase," found in all body cells. Increased production of this enzyme helps prevent some cancers and strokes. As with many minerals and vitamins, processing and cooking foods destroys selenium, decreasing its content in foods.

VITAMIN C

Vitamin C supplements are essential to our health. We simply cannot get enough in our food to maintain good health and resistance to disease. To achieve and maintain optimal health, we need high daily doses of vitamin C.

On November 5, 1997, I published an article in my (GH-L) newsletter for patients regarding how much vitamin C I believe we should take, and how often we should take it.[4] The sections below on vitamin C are based on the article.

How Much and How Often

In 1970, Professor Linus Pauling's book *Vitamin C and the Common Cold*[26] was published. That year, the book was chosen for the Phi Beta Kappa Award as the year's best book on science. Those who were familiar with Professor Pauling weren't surprised. Few scientists in history have received equal acknowledgments for extraordinary contributions to science and medicine. Pauling, a chemist, was the only person in this century to receive two unshared Nobel Prizes. One was for chemistry which he received for unraveling the mystery of the structure of proteins. The other was the Nobel Peace Prize. He is acknowledged as one of the most important scientists in history, on a par with Darwin, Newton, and Einstein. In fact, he was considered the Albert Einstein of chemistry, and before Einstein died, he acknowledged Pauling's genius.

Despite his unique standing in the world of science, the political wing of the medical profession protested Pauling's views. Their claim was that vitamin C is good for nothing but preventing the deficiency disease scurvy. As Pauling pointed out, there was ample scientific evidence to show that there are scores of health benefits from regularly taking the vitamin in large amounts. In the years since, scientific studies have vindicated Pauling's views. It's now established that vitamin C potently protects our health in many ways. Taking it in large amounts is critical for preventing a host of diseases. These include the common cold, the flu, some mental illnesses, learning disabilities, metabolic diseases, cardiovascular disease, viral and bacterial infections, and cancer. In addition, its use hastens the healing of injuries, recovery from surgery, and spinal disc disease. And those who take vitamin C have a longer and healthier life span on average than those who don't.

How Much Vitamin C Should We Take? We should take more vitamin C than any other vitamin, and more than is provided by the usual amounts of fruit and vegetables in our diet. Most animals produce vitamin C in their bodies. Humans and a few other animals don't produce the vitamin internally and must obtain it through food or in nutritional supplements. How much you should take depends on your objective. Many people, including doctors, mistakenly believe that health is ensured by taking only the "recommended daily allowance" (RDA). For adults, the RDA is 60 mg per day. The RDA is the amount that in the average person will prevent the deficiency disease scurvy, plus 50% more. However, the Food and Nutrition Board (that calculates the RDAs for nutrients) makes something clear in their official publication: The RDA is not the amount that provides optimal health; it's only the amount on average needed to ward off deficiency disease, plus a little more. Optimal health is provided only with considerably greater amounts than the RDA.

Professor Pauling calculated how much vitamin C humans probably must take for optimal health. His calculations are based on the amounts of vitamin C other animals produce in their bodies. The assumption is that the same rate of production is necessary for humans. Pauling's conclusion was that the optimum daily intake is between 2300-to-10,000 mg per day. During stress, the requirement climbs to 8500-to-20,000 mg per day.

Can We Get Enough Vitamin C in a "Good" Diet? Probably not. The U.S. Department of Health, Education, and Welfare conducted a large study to learn the average vitamin intake. A third of the people studied got less than the RDA of 60 mg of vitamin C per day. Only 30% took in more than 100 mg, and only 17% took in more than 150 mg. What a federal agency considers a "good" diet, including vegetables and orange or tomato juice, may provide only 100 mg per day. Cooking at high temperatures destroys about 50% of the vitamin C content of food, especially if copper or some other metals are present. Pauling advised, "The loss of the vitamin can be kept to a minimum by cooking for a short time, with a minimum amount of water and with the water not discarded, because it has extracted some of the vitamin from the food." Still, it's not likely that you can get enough vitamin C from your diet. Taking it as a nutritional supplement is the most practical way to get enough for optimal health.

A Precaution When Increasing Your Vitamin C Intake. We want to emphasize that vitamin C—even in very large doses—is *not* harmful. In the latter part of the 20th century, some physicians who were medical editors published warnings that large doses of vitamin C can cause kidney stones. Their warnings were unwarranted. The physicians had come to their false conclusion from an ignorance of chemistry. Pauling graciously and eloquently explained their errors in a book addressed to the public.[5,pp.308-309,349-351] He had to explain in such a book because medical editors had a habit of refusing to print Pauling's explanations of physicians' errors in medical journals. The editors' censoring of Pauling deprived practicing doctors of the benefit of accurate information, perpetuating a false belief about vitamin C. Some twenty years after Pauling corrected the physicians' warning, I (JCL) was still encountering practicing physicians who innocently believed that vitamin C causes kidney stones. In my early twenties, before I began taking vitamin C, I was hospitalized because of a kidney stone. I haven't had another stone despite having taken between 5000 and 20,000 mg almost every day for the past 30 years.

Clearly, large doses of vitamin C are harmless. Despite this, if you haven't taken the vitamin as a supplement before, or if you've only taken small doses, be cautious while increasing your daily dose. If you suddenly increase your dose by a large amount, you may experience some GI symptoms. The most common symptom is loose stools, but some people experience flatulence. These symptoms last only for a few days after you increase your daily dose. But you can avoid them entirely by increasing your dose gradually. What works for most people is to increase the dose by roughly 250 mg every three days until they reach their target dose.

How Often Should We Take Vitamin C? It's best to take vitamin C several times each day. The reason for this becomes clear when we consider what happens to the vitamin after we ingest it. After entering the small intestine, some is absorbed into the body, and the rest is eliminated in the stool. The portion that passes all the way through the intestines isn't wasted; it protects us from GI diseases such as rectal polyps. This is important because polyps can develop into malignant cancer.

Most of a dose of vitamin C is absorbed through the mucous membrane of the small intestine into the blood. After entering the blood, most of the vitamin enters internal organs. Some, however, is excreted in the urine. That "lost" in the urine isn't wasted; it protects us from diseases such as urinary infections and bladder cancer.

The larger the amount of vitamin C we take at one time, the less is absorbed into the blood, and the more is eliminated in the stool. If we take up to 250 mg at one time, about 80% is absorbed into the blood. But if we take 2000 mg at one time, only 50% is absorbed. As we noted, though, we benefit from good quantities of vitamin C traveling through the intestines.

Still, we should strive to get a large supply of vitamin C to our internal organs. We can accomplish this by taking smaller amounts several times each day rather than larger amounts less often. Professor Pauling advised that under non-stressful conditions, people take 1000 mg every three hours or so. Certainly, it's wise to take your daily allotment of the vitamin in no fewer than three divided doses. If it is utterly impossible for you to do so, you should make your absolute minimum intake two widely separated half-doses each day.

TRACE ELEMENTS

Unlike essential minerals such as calcium and magnesium, we need only minuscule amounts of trace elements. Foods may not contain enough of the elements due to being grown in the depleted soils of industrialized farms. Processing of foods can also destroy trace elements. Some water filtering systems also remove trace elements. Examples of trace elements are boron, copper, chromium, iodine, manganese, molybdenum, selenium, and zinc.

MINERALS

Calcium

Calcium is an essential mineral. It's important to bone density, and adequate amounts are necessary for normal nerve and muscle function.[200][201] Several forms of calcium are available in supplements. Calcium citrate is considered one of the best because it is most readily absorbed into the blood. Other forms are calcium carbonate and calcium phosphate. Another is hydroxyapatite which is derived from bovine (cow) bone. In *Earl Mindell's Supplement Bible*,[74] Dr. Mindell recommends hydroxyapatite as a superior source of calcium. It is the exact form of calcium that normal bone tissue contains. An advantage of hydroxyapatite is that along with calcium, it contains collagen and other essential minerals and trace elements found in bone. If you don't consume animal products, of course, you should choose another type of calcium supplement.

Most of us need 1000-to-1500 mg of calcium each day. Young

people with growing bones and postmenopausal women need more than other people. Some calcium is obtained through our diet. But in discussing dietary intake of calcium with my (GH-L) patients, I've found that some actually don't get much in their diets. During a recent telephone consultation, a woman told me she eats lots of yogurt as a source of calcium. When I asked how often she eats yogurt, she thoughtfully replied: "Well, maybe twice a week. But you know what? I just realized that I may go weeks without eating any." Generally, this woman has a very good diet of organic foods. But clearly, her diet doesn't provide enough calcium. It's worth noting that she doesn't eat enough green vegetables to take in enough calcium in her diet. Taking a calcium supplement is important even for those who eat mostly organic foods.

As important as calcium intake is to bone health, other factors are also important. Exercise to tolerance is crucial, and sex hormone supplements may be needed (see *Chapter 9*). Books with excellent information on preventing and treating osteoporosis are *What Your Doctor May* Not *Tell You About Menopause* by Dr. John R. Lee,[13] *Natural Woman, Natural Menopause* by Dr. Marcus Laux,[202] and *Preventing and Reversing Osteoporosis* by Dr. Alan Gaby.[14]

Magnesium

Magnesium is another essential mineral. It's crucial for the activity of many enzymes, the transmission of nerve impulses, nerve regulation of heart function, bone health, regulation of blood sugar, and contraction and relaxation of muscle. The mineral also helps prevent atherosclerosis and high blood pressure.

A severe deficiency of magnesium can cause symptoms similar to those of a calcium deficiency. Prominent among the symptoms is heightened irritability of the nervous system and chronic, excess muscle tension.[200][201] Excess muscle tension from a magnesium deficiency can compound excess muscle tension from hypothyroidism or thyroid hormone resistance.

Most people should take about half as much magnesium as calcium. If you take from 1000-to-1500 mg of calcium each day, you should also take from 500-to-750 mg of magnesium. Too much magnesium in a single dose may cause diarrhea.

Potassium

The body uses potassium to keep nerve and muscle function normal. When people take diuretics, they lose more potassium in their urine. The same happens when people drink extremely large amounts of liquids, have heavy diarrhea, vomiting, or undergo colon irrigations.

A potassium deficiency can severely impair nerve and muscle function. By impairing the nerves and muscles in the intestines, for example, a potassium deficiency can cause "ileus." This is a condition in which stools fail to pass through the colon. If non-passage of stool is severe enough, the bowel becomes obstructed. The patient's abdomen distends, and the patient may have colicky pain, fever, and dehydration.

Potassium depletion can also cause mild-to-severe muscle weakness. When severe enough, the weakness can progress to paralysis. Before becoming a chiropractic physician, I (GH-L) was a registered respiratory therapist. Once, while on staff in an intensive care unit, I treated a gentleman who had been using diuretics to lose weight. He collapsed at work and was unable to communicate or breathe for himself. Paramedics resuscitated him in an ambulance until he arrived at the hospital. We placed him on a ventilator while lab tests were performed. The tests showed he had almost no potassium in his blood. He rapidly improved once treatment restored his potassium level to normal. Diuretic abuse, resulting in potassium depletion, nearly cost him his life.

Potassium depletion can also cause severe heart problems and abnormal electrocardiograms. When fresh out of chiropractic college, I (JCL) briefly practiced in a holistic clinic. Many patients at the clinic received series of colon irrigations. All of the patients should have been taking a potassium supplement. Doing so is important because series of irrigations can critically lower the amount of the mineral in the body. Another physician at the clinic failed to have his patients take supplemental potassium. A near-fatal experience of one of his patients illustrates the gravity of the physician's negligence. The patient, a famous actor in his late 60s, had a heart attack induced by potassium depletion after several irrigations.[59] Fortunately, he survived, and his physician learned a valuable lesson about the risk of potassium depletion.

If chronic fatigue is a feature of your poor metabolic health, you may fail to recognize muscle weakness that develops from a diuretic-induced low potassium level. If you're using diuretics by medical necessity, insist that your doctor check at intervals to make sure your blood potassium level is in a safe range.

Drs. Michael Murray and Joseph Pizzorno are eminent naturopathic physicians. They've explained well the need for most people to increase their potassium intake and decrease their salt (sodium choride) intake.[142,pp.58-60] They wrote that the average person's high sodium and low potassium intake make it tough for the kidneys to keep the body's water volume balanced. High sodium intake causes high blood pressure and water retention. Low potassium intake can predispose people to the type of nerve and muscle malfunctions we described in the paragraphs above.

Drs. Murray and Pizzorno explain how people taking in too much sodium and too little potassium can avoid or correct health problems. They do so by increasing their intake of high-potassium foods and avoiding high-sodium foods. Most processed, convenience, and fast foods have a high sodium content and should be avoided. The doctors advise reading labels to keep your total daily salt intake below 1800 mg.

The doctors also note that most people in the United States have a diet with a potassium-to-sodium ratio of less than 1:2. This means they consume less than half as much potassium as sodium. Yet researchers state that to maintain health, people must have a dietary potassium-to-sodium ratio of more than 5:1. This means that they should ingest at least five times more potassium than sodium. Drs. Murray and Pizzorno write that this ratio is five times higher than the average person's potassium intake. They also point out that an optimal ratio of potassium-to-sodium may be 100:1. As Table 1 shows, most fruits and vegetables have a potassium-to-sodium ratio of at least 50:1.

Table 1. Potassium-to-sodium content of some foods (mg per serving)*

Food	Portion Size	Potassium	Sodium
Fruits			
Apple	1, 3-in diam.	182	2
Banana	1, medium	440	1
Fig	1 fig	97	1
Grapefruit juice	1 cup	454	2
Orange juice	1 cup	496	2
Vegetables			
Mushroom	1 cup	290	11
Bean, lima	1 cup	717	2
Carrot	1, 7½ in long, 2⅞ oz	246	34
Corn (boiled)	1 cup	272	trace
Cucumber	1 small	272	10
Grains			
Amaranth	¼ lb	466	none
Barley	1 cup	320	6
Oatmeal	1 cup	528	146
Wheat, rolled	1 cup, dry form	323	2
Wheat, shredded	1 cup	174	2

*Nutritive Value of American Foods. Agriculture Handbook No. 456. Washington, D.C., United States Department of Agriculture, 1975.

Sodium

Many patients with a diagnosis of fibromyalgia, chronic fatigue syndrome, or ME have low blood pressure because they take in too little salt (sodium chloride). Some of the patients keep their salt intake low to avoid high blood pressure. They avoid salt-laden foods and abstain from putting table salt on foods. Some have been too extreme in the effort, and as a result, their body's sodium level is too low.

An adverse effect of too little salt intake is low blood pressure. Some patients' blood pressure is always too low, whether they are standing, sitting, or lying. Others' blood pressure is high enough until they get up abruptly from lying, sitting, or squatting. Then they feel faint and may even pass out.

For the patient to raise her blood pressure, she must add enough salt to her diet. She can do this by sprinkling table salt on some foods, but *she definitely should not take in more salt by adding processed foods to her diet.* While adding table salt to some foods, she should still maintain a diet of foods with a high potassium content (see Table 1). To achieve optimal health, the ratio of sodium-to-potassium in one's diet must be proper. For information on the proper ratio, see the section above titled "Potassium."

NUTRIENTS AND OTHER AGENTS TO TAKE FOR TISSUE DAMAGE

In our chapter on exercise to tolerance (*Chapter 10*), we discuss tissue damage from overuse during exercise and work. Patients who are hypothyroid or thyroid hormone resistant may not have enough growth hormone and somatomedin C, hormones that are essential to effective tissue repair. Taking the proper form and dose of thyroid hormone should relieve deficiencies of growth hormone and somatomedin C. Then you'll have enough of the hormones to heal damaged tissues completely and at a normal rate. Your tissue will heal best, however, when you have enough protein in your diet, take supplemental MSM, glucosamine sulfate, megadoses of vitamin C, and bromelain. These agents interact in complex ways to counter tissue damage and aid tissue repair.

MSM

MSM is a sulfur compound named "methyl-sulfonyl-methane." Cells use MSM to produce enzymes, antibodies, and glutathione (an important antioxidant). Cells also use MSM to make compounds important to healing injured tissues. The compounds include collagen (which gives tensile strength to connective tissues), cartilage, hair, nails, skin, and amino acids needed to produce proteins.[74,p.104]

Food sources of MSM are fresh vegetables, fresh fruits, meat, seafood, eggs, poultry, and non-pasteurized milk. Heat and food processing reduce the amounts of MSM in foods, making it hard to get enough from food. MSM is harmless even in large doses. Most patients take between 250 and 1500 mg of MSM per day. When Dr. Stanley Jacob, a pioneer in MSM research, had patients use up to 5000 mg per day, no adverse effects occurred.

Glucosamine Sulfate

Glucosamine sulfate is made up of the sugar glucose and an amine. It promotes the incorporation of sulfur into cartilage.[142,p.698] Glucosamine sulfate is a natural component of cartilage, and it stimulates the production of connective tissues. Its main effect is to stimulate the production of water-binding molecules (glycosaminoglycans) in connective tissues.[144] These molecules are important constituents of all connective tissues.[1,p.427]

Glucosamine sulfate can reduce pain, stiffness, and tenderness when cartilage is damaged in the degenerative process called osteoarthritis.[74,p.104] The compound can also reverse some damage of joint cartilage and halt the progression of osteoarthritis.[74,p.58] Taking glucosamine sulfate with MSM enhances these therapeutic effects.

In one arthritis study, glucosamine sulfate worked better than piroxicam (Feldene). Patients taking glucosamine sulfate had fewer adverse effects than even those taking placebos[24]—meaning, of course, that the compound was virtually without adverse effects. The two most common adverse effects of glucosamine sulfate are nausea and heartburn. These sometimes occur when a patient takes her dose on an empty stomach. But even these effects are rare, and you can avoid them by taking the compound with food.[74,p.59]

Bromelain

All injured tissues are inflamed. To counteract the inflammation, we recommend that you take the anti-inflammatory agent bromelain. Bromelain is a group of sulfur-containing enzymes obtained from the pineapple plant.[142,p.798] The enzymes digest proteins. In a study of professional boxers, the use of bromelain reduced trauma-induced bruising, inflammation, swelling, and pain.[145] Bromelain can help patients with poor metabolic health recover more quickly from inflammation sustained in injuries when they exercise beyond their tolerance.

Doses of MSM, Glucosamine, Vitamin C, and Bromelain

When tissue injuries are acute, we generally recommend that adult patients take large amounts of MSM—between 3000 and 5000 mg twice per day. We recommend 1500 mg of glucosamine sulfate each day. You should take this amount in three doses of 500 mg. We also recommend megadoses of vitamin C *to bowel tolerance* (see section above titled "A Precaution When Increasing Your Vitamin C Intake"). Taking a combination of vitamin C and bioflavonoids may increase your absorption of MSM. We recommend that you take 250-to-750 mg of bromelain three times per day *between* meals. When you take bromelain with a meal, much of it is expended by digesting proteins in the food. More will enter your blood stream and reach inflamed tissues when you take it on an empty stomach.

OPTIMAL VITAMIN AND MINERAL INTAKE

We insist that our patients take nutritional supplements. We also insist that they dispense with the "one-a-day" mentality and use optimal doses of nutritional supplements. You must do so, too, if you're to achieve metabolic health.

We want to emphasize that you should strive for *optimal* nutritional intake. Linus Pauling defined optimal nutritional intake. It is the amounts of nutrients that enable chemical reactions in the body to proceed at a rate that leads to the best of health.[5,p.340]

Understanding the Difference Between Optimal Nutritional Intake and the Recommended Daily Allowances (RDAs)

The RDAs are the minimum amounts of vitamins needed, on average, to ward off deficiency diseases, plus 50% more. Many clinicians believe that the RDAs are all the nutrients humans need for health. This is patently false. Bear in mind: The RDAs tell us *nothing* about what nutrient intake may provide optimal health; they only estimate what intake may prevent severe deficiency diseases. What you need for metabolic health is *optimal* intake.

We don't have enough scientific information on individual nutrient requirements to give scientifically justifiable recommendations for nutrient doses.[6,p.4][7] Because of this, the best anyone can recommend in the way of nutrient doses is *practical target amounts*.

Most old guard AMA-type doctors and dieticians tell patients they don't need any vitamin and mineral supplements except for calcium. Some obliquely dismiss their importance with comments like, "Well, at least they won't hurt you."

Taking the unscientific advice of these doctors and dieticians is one of the worst things you can do for your health. Throughout the 20th century, their advice has been responsible for a great deal of disease and premature death. A vital part of your metabolic health regimen is to disregard their poor advice. We recommend that you read my (JCL) 1999 letter to then Texas Governor George W. Bush. I urged him to veto a bill that would have restricted paid nutritional counseling only to licensed or registered dieticians. The URL to the letter is: <www.drlowe.com/news/bushletr.htm> Since the advice of most dieticians is based on false beliefs about the need for nutritional supplements, putting them in control of nutritional counseling would have had disastrous results for Texas citizens. Fortunately, the vociferous protests against passage of the bill influenced Governor Bush to veto it.

We want to emphasize that we aren't condemning all dieticians. As my letter to Governor Bush explains, many dieticians are scientifically-oriented and provide patients with accurate and valuable information about nutritional supplements. Unfortunately, though, most don't. You must protect yourself from the harm their false beliefs are likely to cause you.

We've listed in Table 2 the minimum amounts of nutritional supplements we recommend everyone take. At the very least, your nutritional supplement regimen should include B complex vitamins, antioxidants, minerals, and trace elements.

"TOO MANY PILLS TO SWALLOW"

Some patients complain about having to swallow too many tablets and capsules. If swallowing pills bothers you, we have several recommendations. First, take your supplements with food. Second, space out your supplements through the day, taking a portion of your daily allotment with different meals. Third, purchase nutritional supplements as liquids, wafers, or powders.

I (GH-L) am among those who prefer not to swallow lots of tablets and capsules. I use Bronson's "All Insurance Vitamin Powder." (Although the product is called "Vitamin Powder," it also contains minerals, trace elements, amino acids, and other nutrient substances.) This powder, and others like it, are easier to consume than pills; we can mix it in water, juice, or rice or soy milk. An added benefit of the powder is that it doesn't contain the fillers or binders that are in tablets. For people with sensitivities to fillers and binders, using a powder product will eliminate the potential for allergic reactions to them.

You may have to work to devise a strategy that enables you to regularly take in enough nutritional supplements. Whatever you do, however, you *must* ingest them. I (GH-L) made a rule for myself that I cannot have my morning coffee until I take my nutritional

Table 2. Minimum supplemental nutrients we recommend for everyone, including those working to optimize their metabolic health. Take these each day.

B Complex Vitamins. Synergists in the cellular actions of thyroid hormone. Taking thyroid hormone increases the amounts of some B vitamins that cells use. Everyone taking thyroid hormone should take a B complex vitamin supplement. In quality B complex vitamin products, B vitamins other than B_1 are in roughly appropriate proportions. Making sure the product you use contains at least 50mg per tablet or capsule may ensure that the product contains enough of the other B vitamins.

Bronson product #6: Super B Take with food. One tablet two times each day.

Individual nutrients • B_1 (thiamine mononitrate) (50mg) • B_2 (riboflavin) (50mg) • B_6 (pyridoxine hydrochloride) (50mg) • Biotin (400mcg) • B_{12} (cyanocobalamin) (100mcg) • Folic Acid (400mcg) • Pantothenic acid (calcium D-pantothenate) (100mg) • Niacinamide (300mg)

Carotenoids. Antioxidant nutrients. Occur naturally in plant foods.

Bronson product #351: Carotenoid Complex • A mixture of carotenes as they occur in nature. They provide a variety of antioxidant protective nutrients for various parts of the body. (See alternate below.)* Only 9% of people consume enough vegetable & fruits to obtain sufficient antioxidants to protect health. These people may benefit from using a complex of carotenoids, understandably more expensive than beta carotene. Two capsules once each day.

*Alternate to product #351: #127 Natural Beta Carotene (derived from specially grown and harvested algae) • Equivalent to activity of 25,000 IU of vitamin A. Use beta carotene instead of a complex of caretenoids only if you consume a wide variety of vegetables & fruits. Two capsules once each day.

Vitamin E. Occurs naturally in oils (wheat germ, cotton-seed, palm, rice), whole grain cereals, & lettuce. Also occurs naturally in animal tissue, such as liver, pancreas, heart, muscle, uterus, testes, & blood. Has a wide range of protective effects on the body. Take with food containing fat or oil.

Bronson product #71: Natural Vitamin E Complex Two-to-four capsules once each day.

Individual nutrients: • Vitamin E (80% d-alpha tocopherol and 20% of other naturally-occurring tocopherols: d-beta d-delta, and d-gamma) (400 IU)

Minerals. As important to health as vitamins. Take with food.

Bronson product #12: Mineral Insurance Formula One tablet two times each day.

Individual nutrients: • Molybdenum (amino acid chelate) (33.3mcg) • Calcium (calcium phosphate) (108mg) • Phosphorus (calcium phosphate) (83mg) • Zinc (gluconate) (5mg) • Iron (ferrous fumarate) (5mg) • Magnesium (oxide) (66.7mg) • Iodine (kelp) (50mcg) • Copper (gluconate) (0.67mg) • Manganese (gluconate) (1.67mg) • Chromium (amino acid chelate) (66.7mcg) • Selenium (sodium selenate) (6.7mcg)

Calcium, Magnesium & Vitamin D. For adults, we recommend roughly 1500mg of calcium and 750mg of magnesium per day. Take with food.

Bronson product #16: Calcium Complex & Magnesium (Elemental calcium: 375mg) Two tablets two times each day. (See alternate below)**

Individual nutrients: • Elemental calcium derived from oyster shell (providing 225mg calcium) • Magnesium (oxide) (187mg) • Calcium citrate (providing 25mg calcium) • Eggshell (providing 125mg calcium)**

****Alternate to product #16: #111 Calcium, Magnesium, & Vitamin D*** Two tablets two times each day.

Individual nutrients: • Elemental calcium (derived from calcium carbonate) (250mg)

 • Magnesium (80% from magnesium oxide & 20% from magnesium carbonate) (125mg) • Vitamin D (cholecalciferol) (100 IU)

Vitamin C. Use one of two options below, either tablets or crystals. Adjust dose to bowel tolerance.

Bronson product #47: Vitamin C (ascorbic acid) Take one-to-six 1000mg tablets, three times each day.

Bronson product #84: Vitamin C as Calcium Ascorbate Crystals (See alternate below[†]) Mix with juice or other liquid, or sprinkle on food. One scoopful (scoop provided with order), or ¼ teaspoon, provides approximately 1000mg: One-to-six scoops (¼ teaspoon) three times each day.

Individual nutrients: • Vitamin C (approx. 1000mg) • Calcium (approx. 115mg)

[†]***Alternate to product #84: NutriBiotic's Calcium Ascorbate Cyrstalline Powder*** 100% pure buffered vitamin C, pharmaceutical grade. Sold in some health food stores. (NutriBiotic, Lakeport, CA 95453)

Individual nutrients: • Vitamin C (approx. 1000mg) • Calcium (approx. 115mg)

Fatty Acids. Take with food containing fat or oil. We recommend organic flax seed oil for its omega-3 fatty acids. Many people are deficient in omega-3. There are several brands of organic flax seed oil, and we have used Sundown brand with good results. You can use capoules in the liquid oil. A daily dose of 1000mg is recommended. Omega-6 deficiency isn't as common, but we list evening primrose oil because its omega-6 benefits some patients.

Organic flax seed oil. Take 1000mg daily.

Bronson product #427: Evening Primrose Oil 100% pure cold pressed evening primrose oil. Two capsules with food each day.

Individual nutrients: • gamma linolenic acid (45mg) • linoleic acid (300mg) • oleic acid (55mg)

If you have trouble swallowing pills, use a product such as #353. The product should provide amounts of nutrients as close as possible to those we recommend in this table.

Bronson product #353: All Insurance Vitamin Powder Contains vitamins, minerals, & amino acids. You will need to take several supplements in addition to the powder. These include 1000mg vitamin C, omega-3 fatty acids, 400mg calcium, and a Super B tablet. Two scoops of powder two times each day.

supplements. Use whatever management techniques you need to ensure that you form a habit of taking your supplements. You have no other option, if you're to attain a high level of metabolic health.

Multi-Vitamin-Mineral Supplements

One way to reduce the number of nutritional tablets or capsules you ingest each day is to take a multi-vitamin-mineral supplement. Most such products contain vitamins, antioxidants, and minerals.

Many good brands are on the market to choose from. Whenever you choose a brand, make sure the company that markets it emphasizes quality control. Some good companies are Bronson Pharmaceuticals, Twin Labs, Wilner Chemists, Rexall, Metagenics, Nutriwest, and Anabolic.

Check the contents of the products you choose to take against our list in Table 2. Make sure the products provide the specific nutrients we recommend in roughly the same amounts.

Be aware that the amounts of some nutrients in multi-vitamin-mineral supplements aren't high enough. Nutrients that your multi-vitamin-mineral product will probably contain too little of are vitamin C, calcium, magnesium, and vitamin E. If you take a multi-vitamin-mineral supplement, you'll most likely also need to take additional amounts of these nutrients—especially vitamin C.

In general, we advise patients to take 1500 mg of calcium and 750 mg of magnesium each day. We recommend between 800 and 1600 IUs of natural vitamin E complex each day. We believe that patients should take *at least* 2000 mg of vitamin C each day in divided doses. Taking 500 mg four times each day is preferable. If for some reason that's impossible, we advise patients to take 1000 mg twice each day. See Table 2 for the minimum amounts of other nutrients we recommend everyone take.

"I CAN'T AFFORD ALL THE SUPPLEMENTS LISTED IN THE TABLE"

We appreciate that some people can't afford all or most of the supplements in our list. If this is true for you, we recommend that you purchase a product such as Bronson's "All Insurance Vitamin Powder" (product number 353), which I (GH-L) discussed in the above section. The powder contains a wide array of vitamins, minerals, trace elements, amino acids, and other nutrients. Two scoops of the powder twice a day provide enough of the nutrients to help get your metabolic rehab underway. When you can, though, get the additional supplements we recommend. To keep costs under control, you can take lower amounts than we recommend so that you have to repurchase less often. By taking the full array of supplements, even in less than preferable amounts, you're more likely to have optimal nutrition.

Of course, brands by different companies are available. If you use other brands, we suggest that you make sure the nutrients the products contain are roughly proportional to those in Bronson's.

■ For more information on the role of nutrition in metabolic function, see *The Metabolic Treatment of Fibromyalgia*,[1] pages 967-969 and 1031-1035.

A PRECAUTION ALL PATIENTS SHOULD HEED

All patients who want to achieve metabolic health should observe a particular precaution—don't expect nutritional supplements and herbs to substitute for a wholesome diet. Nutritional supplements and herbs serve you best when you use them to augment the health benefits of a wholesome diet.

Researchers at the American Institute of Cancer Research (AICR) recently took a poll to find out who was taking nutritional supplements and why.[41] In their report on the results, the researchers wrote that to prevent cancer, the older Americans polled preferred to take vitamin supplements rather than adopt a healthy diet. Melanie Polk, a nurse who works with AICR wrote: "The telephone survey of 1,000 adults found that just 13% of Americans aged 18-to-35 take supplements to lower their risk of cancer. But 24% of those aged 55-to-64 did. And 54% of those above the age of 65 took vitamins with the specific aim of lowering cancer risk."

She also noted, "People tend to look for a quick fix." Our clinical and personal experiences support her assertion.

The wording of many reports from organizations such as AICR belie a prejudice against the use of nutritional supplements, and we feel this is true of the wording of this particular report. However, the results of the poll echo an observation of ours: Many patients take nutritional supplements and herbs intending to sustain their health, hoping and praying that this will make up for their disease-inducing diet of fatty, high-sodium, sugar-laden, pollutant-loaded foods, with little or no organic whole grains, vegetables, and fruits. They hope that vitamins, minerals, and herbs will compensate for their daily ingestion of large amounts of red meat, potatoes and fatty gravy, and quasi-foods such as pastries, candies, soft drinks and other beverages full of refined sugar.

Let us make one thing perfectly clear: You'll most likely get some benefits from taking the supplements and herbs alone, but this approach won't stem the tide of deteriorating health. By taking this approach, it's highly unlikely that you'll achieve optimal metabolism and recover your health.

Incidentally, it's worth emphasizing another precaution once again: Your diet should consist largely of *organic* grains, fruits, and vegetables, along with some organic meats. The AICR report noted that grains, fruits, and vegetables help prevent cancer. It's interesting that they failed to mention that grains, fruits, and vegetables containing pesticides and other man-made chemical pollutants subject people to cancer risk. As much as you possibly can, *eat organic foods*. (See *Chapter 4*, "Organic Foods.")

Chapter 6

Herbs

MANY OF OUR HYPOMETABOLIC PATIENTS use herbs to help them recover and sustain their health. Most patients don't have to use herbal agents permanently. They use them early in their metabolic rehab to control bothersome symptoms. After their health has improved enough, they only occasionally need the help of the herbs.

DOSAGES OF HERBS

Humans are biochemically individual. That is, our needs for assorted nutrients vary considerably among people. Also, we respond in highly individual ways to nutritional supplements, synthetic drugs, and herbs. Because of your unique biochemical makeup, you may not respond to a particular dose of an herb as most others do. The dosage may be too low to meet your needs, or it may be too high and cause adverse effects. Accordingly, your effective dosage may be higher or lower than that of someone else.

The doses of herbs we recommend in this chapter are standard, and are for available preparations of the herbs in capsules or tablets. They are reasonable starting doses for the average person. You may choose, however, to use a liquid form of an herb, such as a tincture. If so, either use the dose recommended on the label, consult your health care practitioners about the proper dose, or consult an authoritative book on herbal medicines.

ST. JOHN'S WORT

Many hypothyroid and thyroid hormone resistant patients are depressed. To provide relief from the depression, we often recommend that the patients use St. John's wort. After going through metabolic rehab, most patients are no longer depressed. They can—and should—then stop using the herb without concern that the depression will return. Until then, however, their use of St. John's wort can be lifesaving. In addition to relieving mild-to-moderate depression, St. John's wort can be mildly sedating and lessen anxiety.

St. John's wort acts in several ways in the body. One is by inhibiting serotonin reuptake in the brain. This makes more serotonin available to transmit nerve impulses from one nerve to the next.

Another way St. John's wort acts is by inhibiting an enzyme (monoamine oxidase, or MAO). This enzyme breaks down nerve transmitters, such as serotonin and norepinephrine, in the brain. When St. John's wort inhibits the enzyme, more of these substances are available to transmit nerve impulses.

Different pharmaceutical antidepressants have the same actions in the brain as St. John's wort. Because of this, taking a pharmaceutical antidepressant at the same time you're taking St. John's wort might cause a compound effect. In some instances, a compound effect may be beneficial. In others, the effect may be harmful. We recommend that you have the guidance of a practitioner with experience in the use of St. John's wort and other antidepressants. If you are already using a pharmaceutical antidepressant prescribed by your doctor, be sure not to begin using St. John's wort without first discussing with him the prudence of also using the herb.[102]

You may want to switch from a pharmaceutical antidepressant to St. John's wort to see if it is more effective for you. Or you may want to switch to take advantage of better tolerance of St. John's wort or its lower incidence of adverse effects.[167][168] If so, talk with your prescribing doctor first. If you switch from the pharmaceutical drug to St. John's wort, do so gradually. We describe how you should do this in the section below titled, "Caution in Your Use of Herbs."

Dose. A reasonable starting dose of St. John's wort for most people is 300 mg (with 0.3% hypericin content), three times per day. Some patients improve more when they use 5-HTP (5-hydroxytryptophan) with St. John's wort.

Studies have shown that with some patients, 5-HTP is as effective as Prozac, Paxil, or Zoloft. They also show that it's better tolerated and causes fewer adverse effects. In addition, it is less expensive than pharmaceutical antidepressants.[169][170][171][172] The starting dose of 5-HTP is 100 mg, three times each day.

KAVA-KAVA

Kava-kava (*Piper methysticum*) is an herb used to calm anxiety, restlessness, and stress and to relieve insomnia. Some authors mention that kava improves depression,[142,p.397] and some preparations of St. John's wort (an antidepressant herb) contain kava. Other authors caution that patients with endogenous depression shouldn't use kava because it may increase the risk of suicide.[17,p.1043] Kava is also used in some preparations that ease menopausal symptoms including hot flashes.

Studies indicate that for some patients, kava is as effective as benzodiazepines (see *Glossary*). At the same time, kava doesn't have the adverse effects of benzodiazepines, such as addiction and hindrance of memory and attention.[173]

When we first see some patients with a diagnosis of fibromyalgia, they are extremely anxious from their experiences since becoming ill. The main cause of most of these patients' symptoms is too little thyroid hormone regulation of their tissues. This affects them at the molecular level, and is invisible to family and doctors. Because the cause isn't visible, as a tumor or lacerations would be, some family members and doctors have questioned the patients' honesty about how bad they feel. Family members or doctors may have accused them of malingering. And some doctors may have blamed their symptoms on emotional illness and referred them to a psychiatrist. Some patients are angry at this absurd suggestion; others come to question their own sanity. Such experiences have left some of these patients full of self-doubt and fearful of their future. This fear compounds the dread that their symptoms are caused by some yet undetected lethal disease. We explain to these patients what the probable cause of their symptoms is, and we reassure them that most patients recover with proper care. Often, we recommend kava to help them relax until they soon learn, through experience with metabolic rehab, that we're telling them the truth about the cause of their illness.

Kava can exaggerate the effects of sleeping pills or tranquilizers. Because of this, if you're using such medications, don't begin using kava without expert guidance. In general, it is best to use kava instead of, but not with, these other drugs.

Dose. The potency of kava products is based on their concentration of kavalactones. An effective dose for the average person is 45-to-70 mg of kavalactones, three times per day.[142,p.259]

VALERIAN ROOT

Valerian (*Valeriana officinalis*) is an herb used to produce relaxation, sedation, and sleep. Studies have shown that valerian improves sleep quality without the problems associated with benzodiazepines such as Xanax.[142,p.608] Valerian can also help with muscle spasms that may be due to mechanical stress overload. Without expert guidance, patients shouldn't use valerian when taking prescription medications such as sleeping pills or tranquilizers.

Dose. We advise that patients select a standardized preparation. Those using a dry powdered extract should begin with 150-to-300 mg (containing 0.8% valerenic acid). Those using a tincture should begin with 1-to-1.5 teaspoons (4-to-6 mL). Those using dried valerian root or tea should begin with 2-to-3 grams.[142,p.608] Valerian is safe and non-habit forming, but since it causes sleepiness, patients shouldn't use it during the day.

GINKGO

Humans benefit in several ways from the use of extract of ginkgo *(Ginkgo biloba)* leaves. Most of the benefits result from ginkgo relieving deficient blood flow to the brain (cerebral vascular insufficiency).[174] Ginkgo improves brain circulation by decreasing the stickiness of blood platelets. This increases the delivery of oxygen and glucose to brain cells.

The improved circulation from the use of ginkgo reduces or relieves several symptoms: short-term memory loss, impaired mental performance, deficient vigilance, depression, headache, vertigo, and ringing in the ears.[142,p.608] Ginkgo may also improve or relieve impotency when decreased blood circulation is the source of the problem.[175]

The thyroid hormone deficiency or resistance that underlies most patients' fibromyalgia and chronic fatigue syndrome severely reduces blood flow through the brain. (See *The Metabolic Treatment of Fibromyalgia*, pages 394 & 401-407.[1]) Increasing the blood flow to normal requires the use of the proper form and dose of thyroid hormone. Until a patient finds the dose of thyroid hormone that is effective for her, ginkgo can help reduce symptoms of decreased blood flow, such as poor memory and concentration.

Dose. Standardized preparations of 24% ginkgo flavonglycosides are available. The starting dose should be between 40 and 80 mg, three times per day.[142,p.608][155,p.189]

GINSENG

People in Asia have used the herb ginseng for centuries. They've used it to increase stamina and resistance to the effects of physical and emotional stress. Modern studies have verified that ginseng indeed confers these benefits.[176][177][180]

Ginseng is an "adaptogen"—that is, a general tonic. It increases resistance to stresses by normalizing actions of hormones, especially those of the adrenal glands, and other body chemicals.[142,p.186] Chinese ginseng (see below) also reduces or relieves anxiety. Its anti-anxiety effects compare favorably to those of benzodiazepines.[179] The stress-reducing and anti-anxiety effects of ginseng can be especially helpful to patients intolerant of stress and anxious due to hypothyroidism or thyroid hormone resistance. Ginseng is also a phytoestrogen and can be helpful to menopausal women.

We recommend that patients take care to obtain high-quality products from reputable companies. As with other herbs, some products on the market don't contain the amounts of active ingredients their labels claim.

The two forms of ginseng practitioners usually recommend are Siberian ginseng and Chinese (Panax or Korean) ginseng. Both forms effectively reduce the impact of stress.[178] Chinese ginseng is more potent than Siberian ginseng.[155,p.107]

Dose. The usual dose of Chinese ginseng (at 7% ginsenoside) is 200 mg, one to three times per day. The typical dose of Siberian ginseng (standardized to more than 1% *eleutheroside E*) is 100 mg, three times each day. If you begin to feel jittery when using ginseng, try a different form, or reduce your use of other stimulants such as caffeine.

ECHINACEA AND ASTRAGALUS

Dr. Broda Barnes (with his coauthor Lawrence Galton) was the first physician we know of to publicize how hypothyroidism lowers the resistance of many people to infections.[185] The most thorough explanation of impaired immunity from hypothyroidism and thyroid hormone resistance ever published is in Chapter 3.13 of *The Metabolic Treatment of Fibromyalgia*.[1,pp.635-679]

Many patients have impaired immunity due to thyroid hormone deficiency or resistance. We advise these patients to use two herbs on a limited basis until the proper form and dose of thyroid hormone returns their immunity to normal. These herbs, echinacea and astragalus, increase the competence of several components of the immune system. To boost patients' immune function, we also have them use vitamin A and mega-doses of vitamin C. We have most patients use 50,000 units of vitamin A for as long as two weeks. We have them take the highest doses of vitamin C their bowels tolerate well for up to four weeks (see *Chapter 5*, section titled "Vitamin C").

Echinacea. Echinacea is an herb used to boost the immune system. Numerous components of the plant have nonspecific stimulating effects on the immune system. Echinacea increases the white blood cell activity, which helps fight infection. Macrophages (which Dr. Julian Whitaker calls the "Pac-Man" cells of the immune system[155,p.119]) are especially responsive to echinacea. These cells ingest and destroy bacteria, cellular debris, and other matter that might impair our health. When stimulated by echinacea, machrophages produce agents that increase immune competence, such as tumor necrosis factor, interferon, and interleukins. The herb has antiviral activity, and it stops the spread of bacteria by blocking the action of a bacterial enzyme (hyaluronidase) that breaks down connective tissue barriers.[142,p.160] Echinacea also increases body temperature enough to activate the immune system and thereby destroy bacteria. Echinacea has been effective in the treatment of colds; flu; and respiratory, urinary tract, and vaginal infections.[181][182]

Dose of Echinacea. The typical dose of tinctures of echinacea is ½-to-1 teaspoon (2-to-4 mL, or 30-to-60 drops), three times a day. We prefer tinctures since they are more readily absorbed from the GI tract. The usual dose of dried echinacea root is 0.5-to-1 gram three times per day. The usual dose of dry powdered extract (standardized to 3.5% echinacoside) ranges from 100-to-300 mg three times each day. To avoid toxicity, we advise patients to limit their use of echinacea to no longer than eight weeks at a time.

Astragalus. Astragalus, like echinacea, is an immune booster. In Chinese medicine, practitioners have prescribed *Astragalus membranaceus* as an antiviral agent. It increases the white blood cell count, the production of interferon, and the activity of natural killer cells. It also activates monocytes and macrophages, and has been found to reduce the incidence of the common cold.[183][184]

Dose of Astragalus. The usual dose of dried root of astragalus is 1-to-2 grams, three times per day. The dose of astragalus tincture is ½-to-1 teaspoon (2-to-4 mL), three times each day. And the dose of the herb as dry powdered extract (standardized to 0.5% 4-hydroxy-3-methoxy isoflavone) is 100-to-150 mg, three times per day.[142,p.161]

CAUTION IN YOUR USE OF HERBS

Patients should be cautious in their use of herbs. Herbs can have potent effects on the body, and they can interact with different medications. You can learn about interactions from various publications and through the Internet.

Dr. Jesse Coats is a registered pharmacist and chiropractic physician. He recently explained some precautions in the use of herbs.[80,p.9] His explanation was directed toward chiropractic physicians who prescribe herbal medicines for their patients.

Dr. Coats noted that humans have always searched for and used plants as medicines. This search for natural medicines in the outdoors led to the production of man-made medicines behind the doors of pharmaceutical laboratories. Today, health care practitioners are returning in droves to the use of natural medicines in the form of herbs.

Dr. Coats pointed out that herbs are drugs. As such, some have the potential to cause adverse effects. Some herbs may themselves cause adverse effects, or they may do so by interacting with other herbs or man-made medicines. "Very often," he wrote, "the pharmacology or mechanism of action of the natural drug and a prescription drug is identical. This means that the two should not be given concomitantly at therapeutic doses, for this would be the equivalent of an overdose of either when given alone."

Dr. Coats gave chiropractic physicians advice that patients should also heed: "When the prudent physician decides to prescribe a natural product for a patient, this obligates him to take a careful history. The information gathered in this segment of the physician-patient interview will be valuable in determining allergies to medications, failure of the patient to respond to certain medications, and will provide the physician with a starting point for the drug selection process." When you're considering the use of an herb, you too should consider such issues as allergies to different over-the-counter and prescription drugs. When you learn how the herbal medicine you're considering works, if other drugs that work in the same way have caused an allergy, you should exercise caution in a trial use of the herb.

We recommend that you learn as much as you can about the herb you're considering using. You can gather a great deal of information through the use of Medline on the Internet. (In the *Resources* section at the back of this book, see Websites: PubMed.) We also recommend that you read about the herb you're thinking of using in the *Herbal PDR*.[17] Be especially alert to possible interactions of the herb with other herbs, over-the-counter medicines, and prescription drugs.

Dr. Coats also noted that a patient may decide to change from a pharmaceutical medicine to an herbal medicine because herbs have fewer potential adverse effects and are less expensive. He advised that when doing so, the patient make this changeover carefully and gradually. The patient should slowly reduce the dose of the pharmaceutical drug while she begins the herbal medicine, slowly increasing its dose. "This," he explained, "will allow no interruption in treatment and provide a smooth transition to the new medication, with the fewest possible side effects."

Dr. Coats had a final precaution for those switching from a pharmaceutical to an equivalent herbal medicine: "Keep in mind that this natural medication is just as potent, has virtually the same side effect profile, and will interact with the same drugs, foods, and nutrients that the prescription medication does." We agree with Dr. Coats' precautions.

For another point about the use of herbs, please read the section titled "A Precaution All Patients Should Heed" at the end of *Chapter 5.*

Chapter 7

Safely Getting Well
with Thyroid Hormone

ONE OF THE WORST DISASTERS in the history of medicine is the endocrinology specialty's modern guidelines for diagnosing and treating patients whose bodies are under-regulated by thyroid hormone. These guidelines and the beliefs they're based on have caused a worldwide public health crisis. It involves the chronic illness of scores of millions of people and the premature deaths of incalculable numbers more. Each year, billions of dollars are spent for drugs intended to control patients' chronic symptoms; the drugs are largely ineffective and often induce adverse effects in the patients. Researchers who fail to recognize that the cause of the patients' symptoms is under-regulation by thyroid hormone do studies looking for other causes. Since they are blinded to the real culprit, their fruitless efforts squander billions of research dollars.

We learned of this public health disaster through our study of fibromyalgia patients. Our research taught us the main underlying cause of most of the patients' fibromyalgia symptoms: under-regulation of their bodies by thyroid hormone. After learning this, we developed metabolic rehab, a treatment method that helps patients recover normal metabolism. The treatment involves the use of thyroid hormone, but in ways that differ from the method the endocrinology specialty has imposed on most doctors and patients.

Most patients who undergo conventional thyroid hormone therapy remain ill. In stark contrast, some 85% of patients who undergo metabolic rehab fully and lastingly recover. In this chapter, we explain how patients use thyroid hormone in metabolic rehab.

MOST HYPOTHYROID PATIENTS DISSATISFIED
WITH T₄-REPLACEMENT THERAPY

T_4-replacement therapy is defined as the treatment of hypothyroid patients with the thyroid hormone T_4, adjusting their doses according to their TSH levels.[85][89][101][212] Some advocates of T_4-replacement therapy argue that most patients are satisfied with the treatment. Among those expressing this view is endocrinologist Anthony Toft. In 1999, he wrote of the use of T_4 alone, "It should not be forgotten that the majority of patients taking a dose of thyroxine that satisfies the recommendations of the American Thyroid Association have no complaints about their medication."[391]

Not surprisingly, Toft provides no scientific evidence to back up his claim. The reason is that no scientific evidence supports his view. On the contrary, substantial evidence shows that enormous numbers of hypothyroid patients are disappointed with their T_4-replacement therapy.

We receive thousands of requests for information through our website question-and-answer service at <www.drlowe.com>. One of the most common questions we receive comes from hypothyroid patients being treated with T_4-replacement therapy. Why, they ask, do I still suffer terribly from hypothyroid symptoms? Our answer is that T_4-replacement is the least effective approach to thyroid hormone therapy.[210][211] Over the past fifteen years, we have carefully evaluated the relative effectiveness of different types of thyroid hormone. Our evaluations have led us to a firm conclusion about T_4-replacement: It enables some patients to recover from their hypothyroid symptoms. For most, however, it provides modest improvement at best. Many patients don't benefit from it at all no matter how high they raise their dose of T_4.

Toft's opinion is contradicted by the popularity of websites that provide information on alternative approaches to thyroid hormone therapy. During 2002-2003, we've had an average of 22,000 visitors to <www.drlowe.com>[396] each month, most of whom are hypothyroid patients dissatisfied with the kind of thyroid hormone therapy Toft advocates. Other popular websites are Mary Shomon's thyroid information site[394] and Thyroid-UK.[395] Totaled, hundreds of thousands of dissatisfied patients visit these sites and others, looking for information with which they can recover the health they've lost through T_4-replacement therapy.

Studies also contradict Toft's opinion. The Thyroid Foundation of America conducted a survey of patients whose thyroid glands had been removed. The majority were dissatisfied with their treatment.[11,p.153]

Also, in 2003, thyroid patient advocate Mary Shomon conducted a survey of more than 850 patients. Over half were dissatisfied with their thyroid hormone therapy. Results of the survey showed that many thyroid patients still suffer from symptoms even though they're being treated with thyroid hormone. Table 1 gives the percentages of current symptoms reported by the thyroid patients who responded to Mary's survey.[389]

Table 1. Percentage of 860 hypothyroid patients with various symptoms despite treatment	
Symptom	Percentage still suffering from
• Fatigue	92%
• Inability to lose weight despite diet/exercise	65%
• Feel sluggish & lethargic	62%
• Trouble concentrating	60%
• No sex drive	58%
• Pains, aches, stiffness	51%
• Depression	45%
• Hair loss	43%
• Eyes dry & light sensitive	38%
• Strange feeling in neck or throat	38%

Interestingly, Dr. Toft has waffled in his viewpoint. At the 21st Joint Meeting of the British Endocrine Societies, April 2002, he made a concession that many thought they would never hear from him.[390] He cited studies showing that restoring normal levels of thyroid hormone in the cells of hypothyroid rats is possible only when they're treated with a combination of T_3 and T_4.[30][58] He then noted a study in which the use of both T_3 and T_4 by human patients was superior to that of T_4 alone. The patients' cognitive function was better when they used both hormones.[392]

"It would appear," he then stated, "that the treatment of hypothyroidism is about to come full circle." By this, Toft meant that the use of T_3 and T_4 in combination—as was used throughout most of the 20th century—is the superior therapy.

Then, on August 14, 2002, he contradicted his recent public statements. On that date, he wrote a letter replying to thyroid patient advocate Linda Thipthorp in Cornwall, UK. "I would reiterate," he wrote, "that the overwhelming majority of patients feel perfectly well taking Thyroxine [sic] alone in a dose that restores serum TSH to normal."[393] The absurdity of this view is obvious from the percentages in Table 1.

Rather than being satisfied with T_4-replacement, as Toft claims, thousands of hypothyroid patients are highly dissatisfied with their continuing hypothyroid symptoms. Many are outraged at endocrinologists' arrogant dismissal of their continuing symptoms as features of mysterious "new diseases" such as fibromyalgia, chronic fatigue syndrome, or myalgic encephalomyelitis (ME). And some patients, although relieved when they promptly recover their health with the thyroid hormone therapy we describe in this chapter, are furious that conventional therapy kept them sick for so long.

TWO MAJOR SOURCES OF
UNDER-REGULATION BY THYROID HORMONE

Under-regulation by thyroid hormone results from one or both of two disorders: hypothyroidism and partial cellular resistance to thyroid hormone.

Hypothyroidism

Hypothyroidism is abnormally low production of thyroid hormone by the thyroid gland. The hypothyroid patient, then, has too little thyroid hormone to properly regulate the metabolism of her cells. As a result, the metabolism of her cells is abnormally slow. If severe enough, she'll have symptoms of hypometabolism.

A patient may be hypothyroid because her thyroid gland is diseased. The most common disease of the gland that causes hypothyroidism is autoimmune thyroiditis. In this disease, antibodies attack and destroy the follicles of the gland. Thyroid hormone is manufactured in the follicles, and when they are destroyed, the gland isn't capable of producing enough thyroid hormone.

A patient may also be hypothyroid because something is wrong with either the hypothalamus or the pituitary gland in her brain. Each of these structures produces a hormone that helps regulate the thyroid gland. The hypothalamus produces TRH, and the pituitary produces TSH (see the *Glossary* for an explanation of these hormones). Too little TRH or TSH can reduce the thyroid gland's production of thyroid hormone, leaving the patient hypometabolic.

Cellular Resistance to Thyroid Hormone

A patient's body may be under-regulated by thyroid hormone because her cells are partly resistant to the hormone. Patients who are hypometablic due to resistance to thyroid hormone are classified as having "partial peripheral cellular resistance to thyroid hormone." These patients have "normal" laboratory thyroid hormone levels. In other words, they have normal amounts of thyroid hormone in their blood, but these normal amounts are not enough to overcome the resistance in their cells.

Some patients' thyroid hormone resistance is caused by mutations of the thyroid hormone receptor. Many other causes have been proposed, as I (JCL) detailed in *The Metabolic Treatment of Fibromyalgia* (pages 322-329).[1] The causes are debatable, but what isn't debatable is that among patients with a diagnosis of fibromyalgia, the disorder is common.[161][162] Our clinical experience has also shown that the disorder is far from rare among other hypometabolic patients.

Deciding Whether a Patient is Hypothyroid or Resistant to Thyroid Hormone

Deciding whether a patient is hypothyroid or possibly thyroid hormone resistant is important. The decision should determine what type of thyroid hormone the patient begins treatment with.

Deciding if a Patient is Hypothyroid. When we evaluate a patient, we first consider whether she has symptoms typical of hypothyroidism. If she does, but also has a wholesome diet, takes nutritional supplements, exercises, and doesn't take metabolism-impairing drugs, we consider that she may have hypothyroidism or thyroid hormone resistance.

To learn if she is hypothyroid, we order a particular profile of laboratory thyroid tests for new patients. The profile includes tests for TSH, total T_4, T_3-uptake, and free-T_4 (thyroxine) index.

Until recently, if a patient's thyroid profile didn't indicate hypothyroidism, we could order a TRH stimulation test. Results of this test helped us to decide if a patient had hypothyroidism due to a problem with her hypothalamus or pituitary gland. If so, we diagnosed her disorder as "central hypothyroidism." Two of our studies indicated that among fibromyalgia patients, 44% had TRH stimulation test results consistent with central hypothyroidism.[2][3] Most of these patients recovered when treated for hypothyroidism, even though their standard thyroid test profiles hadn't indicated hypothyroidism. At this time, however, the TRH stimulation test isn't available.

An alternate profile contains tests for TSH and free T_4. We prefer the other profile, however, because it permits us to identify problems with the proteins in the blood that carry thyroid hormone. Your doctor may use either profile. However, if he orders only a TSH, we recommend that you protest and insist upon the other component(s) of one of the profiles.

We also order tests of thyroglobulin and thyroid peroxidase (microsomal) antibodies. Some patients with chronic muscle pain and other symptoms of hypometabolism have elevated antibodies, but their other lab thyroid test results are within the reference ranges. Most of these patients respond well to a thyroid hormone product that contains both T_3 and T_4.

If the patient has a high TSH, low measures for T_3 or T_4, or high antithyroid antibodies, it's safe to tentatively conclude that she is hypothyroid. Technically, the decision that the patient is hypothyroid is always tentative unless the patient has a medical history that suggests that her thyroid gland is damaged in some way. The history might include surgical removal of part of her thyroid gland (thyroidectomy), previous drug therapy to destroy part of her thyroid gland, or high levels of antithyroid antibodies that might have damaged her gland. But even if she doesn't have such a history, she may still have abnormal thyroid test results and symptoms of hypothyroidism. If so, a trial of therapy using a product that contains both T_3 and T_4 is warranted. (For an explanation of why our patients don't use T_4 alone, see section below titled "Use of T_4 is the Least Effective Approach to Thyroid Hormone Therapy.")

When a patient's thyroid hormone levels are normal, but her TSH is high, the assumption is that her thyroid gland is undergoing failure. Even if she doesn't have hypothyroid symptoms, some doctors would start her on thyroid hormone therapy. The purpose of the therapy is to prevent her from developing hypothyroid symptoms. The diagnosis her doctor gives her is "subclinical hypothyroidism." In general, we agree with this preemptive therapeutic approach.

It's common for a patient with hypothyroid-like symptoms to have borderline thyroid test results.[205] If the patient doesn't have another condition that plausibly explains her symptoms, it's reasonable for her to begin a trial of thyroid hormone therapy.

The question naturally arises: What is a borderline thyroid test result? The answer shows that the diagnosis of hypothyroidism isn't scientifically precise, but is in fact arbitrary.

When I (JCL) began working with hypothyroid patients in the mid-1980s, the endocrinology specialty argued that a TSH level of around 6.0 was the upper end of normal. According to them, it was proper to diagnosis hypothyroidism only if the TSH was higher than that number. So at that time, if a patient of mine had a TSH of 5.7, I would have considered it borderline for the diagnosis of primary hypothyroidism.

Recently, the American Association of Clinical Endocrinologists[16] (AACE) and the National Academy of Clinical Biochemistry[342] decided that the range of TSH values indicating normal thyroid function is narrower than they formerly believed. The AACE has decided that 0.3-to-3.0 is the new reference range. According to this new range, if a patient's TSH level is above the upper limit, the doctor should diagnose hypothyroidism. As a result, when a patient's TSH is perhaps 2.8 or so, I (GH-L) might consider it borderline. Today, both of us would consider a TSH of 5.7 clearly high, not borderline.

We want to emphasize that decisions based on the results of lab thyroid test results are fallible.[1,pp.794-798,824-826][404][405] The tests aren't especially reliable: test results on one day may be markedly different from those on the next day or the following week.[404] And, as we just noted, those who continue to attempt to establish reference ranges (what used to be called "ranges of normal") periodically change the ranges. What conventional medicine considers a "normal" test result today, it may consider abnormal tomorrow.

Despite their faults, lab thyroid tests are a useful tool for classifying patients. And classifying patients provides some basis for choosing the type of thyroid hormone they begin treatment with.

When hypothyroid patients use T_4-containing products such as desiccated thyroid, they can expect the therapeutic effects from a newly increased dose from one-to-two weeks later. It's reasonable, then, for them to wait about two weeks before reevaluating the intensity of their symptoms (see *Chapter 3*).

Deciding if a Patient is Resistant to Thyroid Hormone. Resistance to thyroid hormone is a relatively new but well-researched field.[1,pp.295-338] Researchers first documented a family whose cells are partly resistant to thyroid hormone in 1967.[221] In 1990, other researchers found one cause of the resistance: a mutation in a gene on chromosome 3.[220] More than a hundred mutations have now been found in this gene in different patients who are resistant to thyroid hormone.

Mutations in the gene, however, aren't always the cause of thyroid hormone resistance. Some of our patients who clearly had resistance and fully recovered by using T_3 (within the context of metabolic rehab) were free from mutations in the gene.[1,p.277] Resistance may result from several possible mechanisms (for a full description, see Chapter 2.6, *The Metabolic Treatment of Fibromyalgia*, pages 303-313, 319-321, 323-329[1]). Regardless of the cause of a patient's resistance, our current statistics suggest that 34% of our patients with a diagnosis of fibromyalgia have resistance.[161]

Unfortunately, we can't determine when we first evaluate a patient whether she has thyroid hormone resistance. We can only suspect that she might. If she has a diagnosis of fibromyalgia, chronic fatigue syndrome, or ME, this means that she has symptoms typical of hypothyroidism or thyroid hormone resistance.

The symptoms, of course, are also typical of other possible conditions. The most common ones are multiple nutritional deficiencies, cortisol deficiency, low physical fitness, or the use of metabolism-slowing drugs. Any of those may cause symptoms remarkably similar to those of thyroid hormone deficiency or resistance.

Commonly, when a patient consults us, she's already gone to great lengths to recover her health; she's adopted a wholesome diet, taken nutritional supplements, exercised to tolerance, and abstained from the use of metabolism-impairing drugs. With this patient, our first aim is to learn whether she has a thyroid hormone deficiency. Often her history and thyroid test results don't suggest a deficiency. In these cases, we next look for lab test results that suggest some other disorder that could account for her symptoms of hypometabolism. If we find none, we then suspect that her symptoms are caused by thyroid hormone resistance.

We wrote above that TRH stimulation tests aren't available right now. Without this test, we can't rule out central hypothyroidism. The only way to determine its likely presence is through a trial of T_4/T_3 therapy. If this treatment doesn't relieve the patient's symptoms, it's possible that she may have thyroid hormone resistance. A trial of T_3 therapy is then warranted.

During the trial, the patient carefully progresses through metabolic rehab using plain T_3. The method of adjusting her dose of T_3, and the safety monitoring she undergoes, are based on our experiences with hundreds of resistance patients and our scientific studies of those patients.[36][38][92][93][94][135][137][188][189][292][403]

We want to emphasize that our patients use plain T_3—*not sustained-release or timed-release T_3*. They take their full dose of T_3 on an empty stomach (one hour before a meal, or three hours after) once each day (see Figure 1).

When thyroid hormone resistance patients use T_3, therapeutic effects from a newly increased dose may occur within several days to a week. It's reasonable for these patients to reevaluate the intensity of their symptoms a week after they increase their T_3 dose (see *Chapter 3*).

We can't give a specific starting dose for patients in general. It varies for different patients, depending on their health status, severity of their symptoms, and other factors. Many patients, however, start with what the clinician calculates to be a full replacement dose—one that provides all the thyroid hormone a normal thyroid gland would produce to regulate metabolism. The patient's doctor should help her calculate an appropriate starting dose.

From the starting dose, the patient gradually increases the thyroid hormone at intervals that may vary from several days to a week or two. She increases her dose based on her doctor's calculations; the amount of each increase is most often small. Gradually, through these increases, she reaches what we call her "therapeutic window"—the dose at which she has no symptoms of overstimulation, and her hypothyroid-like symptoms improve or disappear altogether. In most cases, her therapeutic window involves doses of T_3 that would overstimulate people whose cells respond normally to thyroid hormone.

Let us say emphatically, however, that this doesn't mean that all patients who think they are resistant should take high doses of T_3! Treatment with thyroid hormone must *always* be individualized. Bear in mind that many patients who have failed to benefit from T_4 alone or combined T_3 and T_4, recover from their symptoms on *fairly low doses* of T_3. Patients and the doctors treating them with T_3 shouldn't forget this. High enough doses of T_3 can be harmful to anyone, and it's crucial that patients not subject themselves to overstimulation from excessive doses.

Used responsibly, however, T_3 has no adverse effects.[12] In fact, it's far safer than any of the drugs doctors commonly prescribe to control the symptoms from untreated or under-treated hypothyroidism.

If a patient reaches her therapeutic window, and she meets the following four criteria, we conclude that she has partial cellular resistance to thyroid hormone:

- Before beginning to use T_3, her lab thyroid test results suggested that she didn't have hypothyroidism.

- Her hypothyroid-like symptoms are improved or relieved by her use of a dose of T_3 that would overstimulate most other people.

- After markedly improving or recovering from her symptoms with the use of T_3, her free T_3 blood level is high.

- *She has no evidence of tissue overstimulation*: she has no symptoms of overstimulation, and repeatedly, her results are normal on EKGs, serum and urine lab tests, and bone densitometry.

We want to emphasize that patients undergoing treatment for possible thyroid hormone resistance must be under the care of a doctor. Not just any doctor, however. The doctor must be educated about thyroid hormone resistance and experienced in guiding patients through proper treatment for the disorder.

We believe it's important to emphasize this for several reasons. First, patients can now obtain different thyroid hormone products, including plain T_3, without a prescription over the Internet. We feel this is a boon to patients. It means they can buy T_3 for a *far* lower price than buying it in most pharmacies in the United States. Also, being able to buy T_3 without a prescription essentially removes the shackles of T_4-replacement therapy that conventional endocrinology has strapped on patients the world over who need thyroid hormone therapy.

But this new freedom to obtain T_3 without a prescription imposes a responsibility on all those who take advantage of the freedom. To maintain it, patients must not give the fascist factions within conventional medicine justification for enlisting the help of legislators and regulatory agencies to take away the freedom. It matters not that conventional medicine, through T_4-replacement therapy, has now ruined the lives of scores of millions of people, and brought the lives of others to a premature end. It would only take a patient or two being harmed by self-administered T_3, and conventional medicine would quickly move to deprive all patients of this freedom.

What we're saying here is that safety must be the foremost concern—not only for doctors who treat patients with T_3, but for the patients themselves. So, if you suspect that you have thyroid hormone resistance, enlist the guidance of a collaborative doctor educated about the condition and experienced in its treatment.

■ For the most extensive document ever written on thyroid hormone resistance, please see *The Metabolic Treatment of Fibromyalgia*, Chapter 2.6, pages 295-338.[1]

**Educational Information on
Thyroid Hormone Therapy**

The information we provide in this section on thyroid hormone therapy is strictly for educational purposes. We believe it's important to help educate patients about what safe and effective thyroid hormone therapy is and isn't.

It's important that patients be well-educated about thyroid hormone therapy. This is so because, in general, doctors don't know how to safely and effectively treat patients with the hormone. If most patients are to get safe and effective treatment, they must be well-informed about what is proper thyroid hormone therapy.

With accurate knowledge, for example, a patient can judge the competence of the doctor whose care she's presently under. If necessary, she should try to educate him. Or, if he isn't open to learning, she can dismiss him and find another doctor she judges to be competent to help her. This is the exemplary assertive approach of Vicky Massey, LMP, who wrote the *Foreword* to this book.

OPTIMAL IMPROVEMENT WITH THYROID HORMONE THERAPY

To get optimal improvement with thyroid hormone, the patient should follow two rules. First, she should *not* permit her doctor to adjust her dosage according to lab thyroid test results. TSH and thyroid hormone levels have nothing whatever to do with making correct decisions about safe and effective doses of thyroid hormone.[045][106] Using the results of thyroid tests to adjust a patient's dose is likely to sabotage the patient's effort to recover from her symptoms of hypothyroidism or thyroid hormone resistance.

Second, the patient should enlist her doctor's assistance in adjusting the hormone dose according to changes in her symptoms due to the last dosage increase. The patient should monitor for changes in her symptoms using the method we describe below and in *Chapter 3*. The patient's doctor can help her by monitoring how she's responding in other ways (see section below titled "Tissue Responses to Thyroid Hormone that Your Therapist or Doctor Can Monitor").

Other Responses to Treatment
the Patient Can Evaluate

Three useful measures of patients' tissue responses to thyroid hormone are the pulse rate, blood pressure, and basal temperature. It's useful to take these measures at least a couple of times each week and record them. Reviewing the list of measures can be a helpful gauge of treatment progress. Graphing the measures is even more useful.

Pulse Rate and Blood Pressure. Many patients with poor metabolic health have low blood pressure and a slow pulse rate. This is especially true of those with a diagnosis of fibromyalgia or chronic fatigue syndrome.

If a patient has low blood pressure and a slow pulse rate, effective thyroid hormone therapy will most likely increase both. Some patients, however, must make lifestyle changes to further increase their blood pressure. For example, a patient who has avoided table salt for health reasons may have to begin ingesting some to help raise her blood pressure.

Unfortunately, your doctor's office probably isn't the best place for your blood pressure or pulse rate to be measured. A rise in blood pressure in a doctor's office is so common that it's called "white coat hypertension." Patients' pulse rates are also usually higher in their doctors' offices.

For the patient to get her true resting blood pressure and pulse rate, she'll most likely have to purchase a device that measures both. These devices are widely available in drug stores and athletic stores. They can be useful not only for taking one's blood pressure and pulse rate, but to help distinguish thyroid hormone overstimulation from other causes of increased blood pressure and pulse rate.

To get a true measure of resting blood pressure and pulse rate, sit in a quiet and comfortable room. With your eyes closed, think of something pleasant for a minute or two. Then, when you feel deeply relaxed, take your blood pressure and pulse rate. If possible, have someone else take the measures while you remain relaxed with your eyes closed.

Basal Body Temperature. The basal temperature is the body temperature at rest. Body heat depends on the amount of foodstuff the body oxidizes or burns. Thyroid hormone is the main agent that regulates the rate at which foodstuff is burned. In patients with hypothyroidism and thyroid hormone resistance, the rate is too low. As a result, most have a body temperature lower than normal.

During World War II, Dr. Broda Barnes and Dr. Joseph Ehrlich studied the basal body temperatures of a thousand soldiers. Over the next thirty years, Dr. Barnes studied the temperatures of many thousands of other patients. He established that the normal armpit temperature is between 97.8° and 98.2° Fahrenheit. Most patients with hyperthyroidism or infections had armpit temperatures above 98.2°, and most hypothyroid patients had temperatures below 97.8°. As thyroid hormone normalized the metabolic health of hypothyroid patients, their basal body temperatures increased into the range of 97.8°-to-98.2°.[185,pp.42-47]

Men can take their basal body temperature on any day. Women, on the other hand, have temperature variations during their menstrual years. The typical woman's temperature is lowest at the time of ovulation, and it's highest just before the start of her menstrual flow. Dr. Barnes recommended that the woman take her basal temperature on the second and third days of the period after her flow starts.

Figure 1. How our patients take thyroid hormone

Our patients take their thyroid hormone in a single daily dose when their stomach is empty. This means that they take their thyroid hormone—no matter what form of thyroid hormone they take—at least one hour before meals or taking nutritional supplements, or three hours after.

The patient should shake down a thermometer before she goes to bed and place it on a night stand. When she wakes in the morning, she should place the thermometer deep into her armpit and leave it there for ten minutes by the clock, while remaining still the entire 10 minutes.

Dr. Barnes noted that young children may have trouble lying still for ten minutes. It may be best to take their rectal temperature for two minutes. The normal range is 98.8°-to-99.2° Fahrenheit.[185,p.48]

As with the blood pressure and pulse rate, the patient should record her temperature readings and the dates she took them. The readings are most useful when posted to a line graph. (For extensive information on body temperature as a tissue response to thyroid hormone, see *The Metabolic Treatment of Fibromyalgia*, Chapter 4.3, pages 842-849.[1])

Body Temperature May Not Change. Effective thyroid hormone therapy doesn't always increase some patients' low body temperatures, and not all patients with hypothyroidism or thyroid hormone resistance have low body temperatures. For these types of patients, the basal body temperature isn't a good gauge for monitoring change with thyroid hormone therapy.

Dr. Barnes warned, "The basal temperature is not a perfect test for thyroid function. There are conditions other than hypothyroidism that may produce a low reading—for example, starvation, pituitary gland deficiency, or adrenal gland deficiency. But starvation is certainly not difficult to rule out—and some thyroid is frequently indicated, anyhow, for the other conditions."[185,p.46]

Tissue Responses to Thyroid Hormone
That Your Therapist or Doctor Can Monitor

Health care practitioners can help the patient monitor for tissue changes in response to thyroid hormone therapy. Most useful are changes in the puffiness of skin and muscle and the speed of the Achilles reflex.

Puffiness of Skin and Connective Tissue in Muscles. When a patient is going through metabolic rehab, a practitioner who examines and physically treats her at intervals can look for changes in her skin and muscles. A massage therapist, certified myofascial trigger point therapist, naprapath, or chiropractic physician who works on the patient's muscles can be especially helpful.

Some patients whose hypometabolism is caused by hypothyroidism or thyroid hormone resistance have puffy skin and puffy swelling of the connective tissue around muscles. We've observed this for many years in hypometabolic patients, especially those with a diagnosis of fibromyalgia. Substantial evidence shows that the puffiness results from too little thyroid hormone regulation of connective tissue cells.[1,pp.425-446] Starlanyl and Jeffrey reported the swellings in fibromyalgia patients,[18][22] and in a study of one patient, they found that treatment with T_3 relieved the swellings.[18]

An attentive therapist or doctor who treated you before and after you began to use thyroid hormone may find that your puffiness has disappeared. Its disappearance is a valuable sign that your current dose of thyroid hormone is benefitting you, at least in this one respect. If they haven't already, other benefits are likely to soon follow.

Achilles Reflex Speed. The relaxation phase of the Achilles reflex is abnormal in about 80% of patients who are hypothyroid or resistant to thyroid hormone. Accordingly, it's abnormal in roughly the same percentage of patients with a diagnosis of fibromyalgia.[1,pp.879-880]

The Achilles reflex is abnormal in that the relaxation phase is slower than the contraction phase. When the doctor hits a patient's Achilles tendon at the back of the ankle, the calf muscles contract at a normal rate, and the foot dips down. Normally, the foot comes back up at the same speed at which it dipped. But for most patients with too little thyroid hormone regulation, the calf muscles relax too slowly. This causes the foot to come back at a slower speed. The speed is so much slower that it's obvious to most anyone watching.

An occasional hypometabolic patient has a variation of the slow relaxation phase. After the doctor taps the tendon, her foot dips quickly. But the foot stalls briefly, or may jerk slightly, before beginning a slow or normal relaxation phase.

As patients increase their doses of thyroid hormone into the effective range, the relaxation phase of the Achilles reflex becomes more rapid. Eventually it equals the speed of the contraction phase. And any jerks or pauses before or during the relaxation phase cease. (Overstimulation with thyroid hormone speeds both the contraction and relaxation phases of the reflex.)

Before beginning to use thyroid hormone, the patient should ask a doctor or therapist to test her Achilles reflex. If the relaxation phase is slow at this baseline measurement, changes in the speed of the relaxation phase can serve as a measure of the patient's tissue response to thyroid hormone. (For extensive information on the Achilles reflex as a tissue response to thyroid hormone, see *The Metabolic Treatment of Fibromyalgia*, Chapter 4.3, pages 850-852.[1])

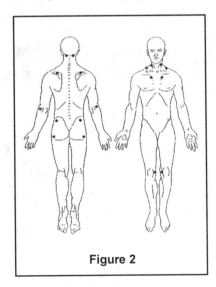

Figure 2

Algometer Exam of Tender Points. If your diagnosis is fibromyalgia, measuring the sensitivity of your tender points can be useful. We examine 18 tender points represented by dots on the body drawing (see Figure 2).

Using a finger or thumb to gauge how sensitive the points are isn't reliable. A doctor or therapist, however, can use a pressure gauge called an "algometer" to measure the sensitivity of the tender points. After measuring how much pressure is needed to set off the perception of pain at each tender point, the doctor or therapist should calculate the average amount of pressure that initiated pain at the 18 points. It's most useful to create a line graph for the average tender point sensitivity. Changes in the sensitivity during metabolic rehab are a useful gauge of a patient's tissue responses to thyroid hormone.

Responsiveness of Trigger Points to Treatment. The muscles of many hypometabolic patients contract too easily. This can cause trigger points in the muscles to refer pain too readily. Commonly, these patients must be treated physically far more often to keep their trigger points from referring pain.

When the patients undergo metabolic rehab including the use of thyroid hormone, their trigger points respond better to physical treatment. Relief that may have lasted only days may now last for weeks. A practitioner who has treated the patient both before and during her metabolic rehab may note her improved response to physical treatment.

REALISTIC PERSPECTIVE ON THE
SAFE USE OF THYROID HORMONE

The potential harm from the use of thyroid hormone has been *grossly* exaggerated by the endocrinology specialty. Despite this, patients and their doctors should exercise caution to avoid thyroid hormone overstimulation. They can best do so by ignoring the endocrinology speciality's exaggerations, and seeing the potential for harm with proper perspective.

Needless Worry Over Potential Harmful
Effects of Thyroid Hormone

The three main potential harmful effects from the misuse of thyroid hormone are bone thinning, heart problems, and acute adrenal crises.

Osteoporosis. Through the 1980s and 1990s, doctors forced millions of patients' to keep their thyroid hormone doses too low in order to avoid causing osteoporosis. In the early 1990s, studies began appearing in journals showing that TSH-suppressive doses of thyroid hormone *don't* cause excessive bone thinning, and certainly don't cause osteoporosis or an increased rate of fractures.

For years, I've (JCL) talked with bone density radiologists about the potential for bone thinning from the use of thyroid hormone. Some have chuckled over the absurdity of the endocrinologists' belief that TSH-suppressive doses of thyroid hormone cause significant bone thinning, osteoporosis, or an increase in fractures.

Bone density tests of our own patients have shown that those taking higher-end thyroid hormone doses usually have higher bone density. The main cause of their higher bone density is that their thyroid hormone doses are high enough to enable them to exercise vigorously enough to thicken their bones. And, of course, their wholesome diets and nutritional supplements also contribute.

It appears that the conventional endocrinologists' scientifically false belief that TSH-suppressive doses of thyroid hormone cause osteoporosis has actually contributed to bone thinning among patients. Those restricted to T_4-replacement therapy usually are too weak and fatigued to exercise vigorously. Their low physical activity level has undoubtedly caused progressive thinning of their bones, as well as deterioration of their health in general.

Table 2. Nutrient complex that favors bone thickening

- Vitamin D
- Calcium (from hydroxyapatite)
- Phosphorus (from hydroxyapatite)
- Magnesium (from magnesium oxide)
- Zinc (as amino acid chelate)
- Copper (as amino acid chelate)
- Manganese (as amino acid chelate)
- Boron (as amino acid chelate)

If a patient already has osteoporosis when she begins using thyroid hormone, caution is prudent. If she hasn't recently had a bone density study, she should ask her doctor to order one. She should ask him to order follow-up studies at intervals, perhaps every six months. She may have to teach the doctor that, despite the opinion of conventional endocrinologists, we *absolutely cannot* accurately infer from a TSH level the effect of a dose of thyroid hormone on bone density. If the doctor wants to know the effect, he should measure it directly by ordering a bone density study.

When the patient's dose of thyroid hormone is high enough to enable her to exercise, she should do "bone-jerking" types of exercises to tolerance each day. She should also make sure she gets enough nutrient complex and protein each day to help thicken her bones. The complex we take includes the nutrients listed in Table 2.

Heart Problems. "You're going to have a heart attack and die!" is the warning many doctors give their patients when they ask to be treated with desiccated thyroid—and especially if they ask for T_3. (If you haven't read the *Foreword* to this book by Vicky Massey, LMP, you may find interesting her experience with a doctor who bellowed this warning at her.) Where these doctors get this idea is a mystery, but they certainly don't get it from the scientific literature.

The belief of these doctors that patients using desiccated thyroid or T_3 run a high risk of heart attacks is clearly ignorance. Still, though, it's prudent for each patient to take reasonable precautions when using thyroid hormone. We recommend that each patient at least get a baseline EKG before starting to use thyroid hormone. If the patient's doctor has any doubts about the health of her heart, a consultation with a cardiologist is wise. We've referred many patients for cardiac consults before they began taking thyroid hormone. Rarely, a cardiologist has recommended that the patient only cautiously increase her thyroid hormone dose. Never has a cardiologist reported to us that a patient should not use thyroid hormone.

Most patients with heart disease can safely use thyroid hormone. In fact, using the hormone is likely to improve the patients' heart disease. These patients, however, should use thyroid hormone cautiously. And they—just like every other person who takes thyroid hormone—should have a wholesome diet, take a full array of nutritional supplements, and get regular aerobic exercise to tolerance.

Figure 3. Atrial fibrillation

The atria are the two small upper chambers of the heart. They receive blood from the veins and in turn force it into the large chambers of the heart called the "ventricles." Fibrillation is uncontrolled twitching or quivering of muscle fibrils. Normally, the muscles of the atria contract rhythmically. In atrial fibrillation, however, the atrial muscles twitch rapidly and irregularly. The irregular twitching of the atria bombards the ventricles, potentially causing them, too, to contract irregularly.

If a patient has compromised heart function, her initial dosage should be low enough to avoid aggravating the heart condition. If her doctor finds that she tolerates the dose well, he should guide her through small dosage increases until she reaches her optimal dose. He must monitor her each step of the way using all appropriate procedures to ensure her safety.

Recently, endocrinologists have warned that TSH-suppressive doses of thyroid hormone increase the risk of atrial fibrillation by 33%. A number of studies showed that a certain set of people who had low TSH levels had a higher incidence of atrial fibrillation (see Figure 3).

But don't conclude from this finding that if you take a dose of thyroid hormone that suppresses your TSH level, you'll have atrial fibrillation. What endocrinologists—the main doctors who warn of this risk—don't bother to tell you is that these studies were done on elderly, sedentary individuals. In fact, in some of the studies, the patients were bedridden in nursing homes. In none of the studies did the researchers control for a heart-protective diet, nutritional supplements, or cardiovascular exercise to tolerance. The patients appear to have been in such poor health that they may have developed atrial fibrillation if they drank too much coffee each day. It's ludicrous and outrageously wrong to conclude that the results of these studies apply to healthier people using TSH-suppressive doses of thyroid hormone.

We require all patients under our care to adopt a wholesome

diet, take nutritional supplements, and exercise to tolerance. These practices are what we call (as in the previous paragraph) "heart-protective," meaning that they encourage healthier hearts that are resistant to disease and other problems such as atrial fibrillation. Because we require our patients to engage in heart-protective life-style practices, we haven't had a single patient under our care ever have a heart problem from the use of thyroid hormone—despite the fact that many of them take enough of the hormone to suppress their TSH levels.

Acute Adrenal Crisis. The risk of an acute adrenal crisis—collapse of the patient from too little cortisol—is a risk from the use of thyroid hormone that many endocrinologists unrealistically exaggerate. The fact is that the published medical literature contains only a few reports of acute adrenal crisis. These reports were of patients in extraordinary circumstances.[120][121][122][123]

It is simply irrational to conclude from these few exceptional reports that most patients using thyroid hormone should be concerned about having an acute adrenal crisis. We've worked with many patients who developed symptoms of adrenal insufficiency after they began using thyroid hormone. Not a single one of these patients, however, has experienced acute adrenal crisis.

Relieving Thyroid Hormone Overstimulation

Occasionally a patient inadvertently increases her thyroid hormone dose too high. The symptoms of overstimulation she experiences are usually rapid heart rate and tremors. We've listed other symptoms of overstimulation in the form titled "Are You Over-stimulated?" (See *Forms*.)

Tremors can be detected more easily if the patient will sit with the balls of her feet on the floor, and raise both heels up. If her ankles quiver, this suggests thyroid hormone overstimulation. If the Achilles reflex speed is extremely rapid in both phases, this too indicates overstimulation.

Before concluding that thyroid hormone is causing these results, however, it's important to rule out other possible causes. The patient should make sure she hasn't taken stimulants such as ephedra, antihistamines, decongestants, or too much caffeine. Emotional upset or acute stress can also cause symptoms that resemble those of thyroid hormone overstimulation.

The patient truly overstimulated by thyroid hormone should decrease her daily dose. If the patient's thyroid hormone product is T_3, reducing her next scheduled dose can stop the stimulation within 24-to-48 hours. If her thyroid hormone product contains T_4, the overstimulation might not stop for a week or so despite her reduced dose. In this case, she should ask her doctor about using a small dose of propranolol several times each day until the overstimulation stops. In general, results are best when the doctor prescribes 20 mg plain (not sustained-release) propranolol tablets. Propranolol is highly effective at relieving symptoms such as tremors. Many public speakers, trial lawyers, and musicians and other entertainers use propranolol before their performances to prevent symptoms of anxiety or nervousness from interfering with the performances.

For most people, 20-to-40 mg of plain propranolol stops the symptoms of overstimulation within 30-to-45 minutes. Usually, the symptoms don't reappear until several hours have passed. Some patients get relief from the symptoms for 6-to-8 hours.

The 20-to-40 mg dose of propranolol is harmless for most patients except those with asthma. *In general, patients with asthma should not take propranolol or any other beta-blocker.*

In general, it's not necessary to completely stop taking thyroid hormone just because mild overstimulation has occurred. Suddenly stopping the hormone altogether may produce rebound hypometabolism. The rebound symptoms of hypometabolism can be more unpleasant than the overstimulation. Reducing a patient's dose by an amount calculated by her doctor will relieve the overstimulation.

IMPORTANT POINTS TO BEAR IN MIND

A Low TSH Level Does *Not*
Mean the Patient is Hyperthyroid

An unfortunate convention in orthodox endocrinology is to define "hyperthyroidism" as a suppressed TSH level. Distinct thyroid hormone excess (as in Graves' disease) does suppress the TSH level. If the hormone excess is severe enough, it will harm the affected patient.

But to describe a patient taking a TSH-suppressive dose of thyroid hormone as "hyperthyroid" is to imply that the patient will suffer effects similar to those of untreated Graves' patients. Certainly, if the TSH-suppressive dose of thyroid hormone is too large, it will harm the patient. But many patients' TSH-suppressive doses merely induce normal metabolism in them and have no harmful effects. Depriving these patients of TSH-suppressive doses of thyroid hormone, however, *is* likely to harm them; they'll have chronic symptoms of hypothyroidism and may develop advanced cardiovascular disease.

To define hyperthyroidism by a suppressed TSH level is, therefore, misleading. It fails to distinguish between the blood levels of thyroid hormone and TSH, and the effect of thyroid hormone on the metabolism of body tissues. A suppressed TSH and hyperthyroidism are *not* one and the same.

Use of T_4 Is the Least Effective
Approach to Thyroid Hormone Therapy

Our patients today don't use T_4 (thyroxine) alone. As we were developing metabolic rehab, many of our hypothyroid patients used T_4 alone. Some of them fully recovered, some improved but didn't fully recover no matter how high their dose, and many didn't benefit at all no matter how much they used.

Most every one of our hypothyroid patients who had a poor response to T_4 alone fully recovered when they switched to a product containing both T_3 and T_4, or T_3 alone. Because of our patients' comparatively poor responses to T_4 alone, and their excellent responses to combined T_3 and T_4 or T_3 alone, we decided that it was inhumane to restrict them to the use of T_4 alone. Using our method of treatment, it took months for us to learn that a particular patient wasn't responding well to T_4 alone. We couldn't justify the wait, just to learn eventually that the patient had to switch to a generally more effective product.

If your doctor insists on treating you with T_4 alone, your protest will be a reasonable one. If he won't cooperate, you'll be smart to find another doctor who will.

Potential Harm From Too
Low a Dose of Thyroid Hormone

For some patients, taking a low dose of thyroid hormone is worse than taking none at all. This is especially true if the patient is taking low-dose T_4.

Low doses of T_4 may actually slow metabolism further. This can happen when the T_4 the patient is taking lowers her pituitary gland's secretion of TSH. The lowered TSH in turn reduces her thyroid gland's secretion of T_3 and T_4. If her T_4 dose is too low to compensate for the thyroid gland's reduced release of T_3 and T_4, her metabolism will slow further. To her surprise, her symptoms of hypothyroidism will worsen after she begins the use of the low dose of T_4.

For a more detailed explanation of the harmful effects of low dose T_4, see <www.drlowe.com/QandA/askdrlowe/t4therapy.htm>.

Chapter 8

Cortisol, Pregnenolone, and DHEA

ATOP EACH KIDNEY IS A small hormone-releasing structure called an "adrenal gland." The outer layers of each adrenal gland are called the "cortex." The cortex produces and releases a hormone that's critical for normal metabolism; the hormone is named "cortisol."

The adrenal glands release cortisol throughout the day and night. They release the largest amount shortly after we get up from sleeping. This release causes a peak in the blood levels of cortisol, but the glands release less as the day goes on. They release the smallest amount while we sleep.

Cortisol helps regulate carbohydrate metabolism and other body functions all the time. But during times of stress, the adrenal glands release more cortisol, and the extra cortisol helps us adapt. For this reason, cortisol is called a "stress hormone."

Some symptoms caused by a cortisol deficiency resemble those of a thyroid hormone deficiency: a low metabolic rate,[105,p.578] fatigue, and widespread pain,[104,pp.42-43] chronic low blood pressure, and acute low blood pressure upon standing up rapidly (orthostatic hypotension). (See Chapter 3.2 in *The Metabolic Treatment of Fibromyalgia*, pages 385-423.)

In Addison's disease, the patient has a severe deficiency of cortisol due to disease of the outer layers of the adrenal glands. If the patient doesn't take supplemental cortisol, her metabolic rate decreases 25%-to-30% below normal.[105,p.578]

Fatigue during a cortisol deficiency can progress to severe malaise, and the patient usually has widespread aches and pains. The patient's symptoms are similar to those of the flu: general weakness, mental unrest, lethargy, and discomfort. When the patient takes a high-enough dose of cortisol, her symptoms quickly improve or completely cease.

Some people's adrenal glands produce enough cortisol to meet their needs when they aren't stressed. But when they are stressed, their adrenal glands aren't able to produce the extra cortisol their bodies need to adapt to the stress. We don't say that these people have a *deficiency* of cortisol; rather, we say that they have "decreased adrenal reserve." This means that their adrenal cortices (plural for adrenal cortex) don't have enough cortisol in reserve to help the people adapt to stress. Instead, their adrenal cortices are able to produce and release enough cortisol to meet their metabolic needs only when they aren't stressed. Decreased adrenal reserve commonly contributes to poor metabolic health.

SOME CAUSES OF DECREASED ADRENAL RESERVE

The patient with Addison's disease has a severe deficiency of cortisol caused by disease of the adrenal cortices. The patient may not have enough cortisol to meet her metabolic needs even under relaxed conditions. Stress, which increases the need for cortisol, can disastrously affect the patient. In the past, the main cause of Addison's was tuberculosis of the adrenal cortices. Exposure to toxic substances and autoimmune disease can also damage the cortices and cause Addison's.

The adrenal cortices may be damaged less severely than in Addison's. The damage doesn't leave the patient with a severe cortisol deficiency. Instead, she may have decreased adrenal reserve.

Decreased reserve may also result from decreased stimulation by ACTH from the pituitary gland.[84] This is the mechanism of "postpartum" (after childbirth) low adrenal reserve. Some women, after delivering a baby, develop a "postpartum mood disorder." The disorder occurs because function of the hypothalamus-pituitary-adrenal axis is impaired (see "HPA axis" in the *Glossary*). The decreased function makes the women more vulnerable to depression. When tested, the women's hypothalamic-pituitary-adrenal axis behaves as it does in women who have clinical depression; that is, function of the axis is impaired. It's important to consider, however, that the function of the thyroid gland may also decrease after delivery of a baby. A resulting thyroid hormone deficiency may itself cause the women to be depressed.[118] We believe it's important to test patients with postpartum depression for both adrenal and thyroid function.

Researchers at the University of Alexandria, Egypt, found altered function of the adrenal cortices in women using Norplant implants. (Norplant is a long-term contraceptive implant that contains progestigens.) The women's cortisol levels at 9 am were low, although within the normal range. Cortisol levels at 6 pm, however, were normal. The researchers gave the women ACTH stimulation tests (see section below titled "ACTH Stimulation Test"). In this test, clinicians injected women with the hormone ACTH. This is the hormone that the pituitary gland releases in response to stress. The hormone travels through the blood to the adrenal cortices. There, it stimulates them to release cortisol. The women's adrenal cortices responded sluggishly. The amount of cortisol they released was on the lower end of normal. The researchers reported that these women's low-normal release of cortisol might cause problems during acute or prolonged stress, as during surgery or shock.[119] It's important to consider these results in relation to women who have barely enough adrenal reserve. Norplant implants in them may decrease their cortisol secretion enough to cause symptoms such as fatigue and widespread pain.

Decreased Adrenal Reserve From Hypothyroidism or Thyroid Hormone Resistance

Virtually every tissue in the body must have adequate thyroid hormone regulation to perform its function efficiently. This is true of the adrenal cortices. In some patients, a deficiency of thyroid hormone causes low function of the adrenal cortices. In other patients, the cells of the adrenal cortices are partially resistant to thyroid hormone. In both cases, the adrenal cortices produce an abnormally low amount of cortisol.

The hypothyroid or thyroid hormone resistant patient usually doesn't have cortisol deficiency symptoms. The reason is that the patient's liver is also under-stimulated by thyroid hormone. As a result, the liver clears cortisol from the blood at a slow rate. Because of this, although the patient's adrenal cortices are producing cortisol at a less-than-normal rate, the amount of cortisol in the body remains normal. Despite the normal amount of cortisol on an hour-by-hour basis, the patient's adrenal cortices may not be able to produce enough additional cortisol to meet increased needs during stress.

When a patient begins taking thyroid hormone, her liver begins clearing cortisol from her body at a faster (more normal) rate. If, at the same time, her adrenal cortices aren't producing enough cortisol to keep normal amounts in the body, she may develop a cortisol deficiency. Some doctors have patients take cortisol by mouth to avert this possibility. Whether we should do this routinely, however, is debatable. Some doctors, such as the famed Dr. Barry Peatfield in England, begin many patients' metabolic treatment with cortisol. He then adds natural thyroid. Dr. Peatfield does this to allow time for the thyroid hormone to begin stimulating the adrenal cortices enough for them to produce normal amounts of cortisol. After a time, he gradually reduces the doses of patients' cortisol until they have stopped using it.

Our approach is to order lab tests for adrenal function if we suspect adrenal insufficiency or decreased adrenal reserve. If we don't suspect one of these conditions, the patient begins using thyroid hormone without supplemental cortisol. Our patients increase their thyroid hormone doses gradually, and we carefully watch for any evidence of adrenal insufficiency or decreased reserve. If the patient develops symptoms such as muscle weakness or increased fatigue, we then do lab testing for adrenal function. If the lab results suggest that the patient might benefit from the use of cortisol, the patient goes on an appropriate trial dose.

Unfortunately, we don't have enough evidence from studies to know whether Dr. Peatfield's approach or ours is usually the better. Both approaches, however, are safe and effective with most patients. Your doctor may prefer one approach to the other, and either may be fine for you.

ACUTE ADRENAL CRISIS

Many conventional endocrinologists discourage patients from using any dose of thyroid hormone other than one so low that it's ineffective. A reason they give is that higher doses of thyroid hormone may cause an "acute adrenal crisis." Such crises are *extremely* rare. Conventional endocrinologists' exaggerated concern over them has undoubtedly done far more harm than good. (See *Chapter 7*, Thyroid Hormone, section titled "Acute Adrenal Crisis.")

It is true that a patient with Addison's disease or impaired pituitary secretion of ACTH must take great care in finding an effective and safe dose of thyroid hormone. There are a few reports of acute adrenal crisis in patients using thyroid hormone.[120][121] Other authors have written describing precautions regarding thyroid hormone and adrenal crises.[122][123][124][125][126] In most reported cases, however, adrenal crises occurred in only one circumstance: when a single stressful event suddenly rendered the body's adaptive mechanisms unable to compensate for a long-standing pituitary or adrenal disorder.[122]

Despite many of our thyroid hormone resistant patients using extremely high doses of thyroid hormone when it was proper for them to do so, none have had an adrenal crisis. We have had many patients who, after beginning to use thyroid hormone, had mild symptoms suggesting the need for a cortisol supplement. The most common symptoms were muscle weakness and fatigue.

Your doctor and you should consider the possibility of adrenal insufficiency or decreased adrenal reserve before you begin taking thyroid hormone. Your doctor should look for evidence of adrenal insufficiency before starting you on thyroid hormone, and he should watch for any budding signs of it while increasing your dose.

We also caution, however, that you not be frightened by the

unrealistic expectations of conventional endocrinologists. In general, these practitioners lack proper perspective on this issue, and they seem prejudiced against the use of anything other than extremely small and ineffective doses of thyroid hormone. Tragically, for each patient who has suffered an adrenal crisis from using thyroid hormone, millions of others have suffered chronic illness and premature death because their thyroid hormone doses were too low.

TESTING ADRENAL CORTEX FUNCTION

We use several tests to evaluate the function of a patient's adrenal cortices. Most often, we use the ACTH stimulation test and the daily variations in salivary cortisol levels.

ACTH Stimulation Test

A test that can show whether you have decreased adrenal reserve is the ACTH stimulation test.[117] In this test, a blood sample is taken to measure your baseline cortisol level. Next, you are injected with the hormone called "ACTH." This is the pituitary hormone that stimulates the cortex of your adrenal glands to release cortisol (see "HPA axis" in the *Glossary*). Then, at sixty minutes, another blood sample is taken so that the level of cortisol can be measured again. This second measure tells us how your adrenal cortex has responded to the injected ACTH. (If Cortrosyn, a chemical similar to ACTH, is used for the injection, a cortisol level is usually drawn at thirty minutes. But despite the substance injected, many labs draw thirty, sixty, and ninety minute cortisol levels.)

The difference between the first and second cortisol levels is calculated. We consider your adrenal response normal if your cortisol level at least doubles after the ACTH (or Cortrosyn) injection. If your second level isn't double the first, this is evidence that you have low adrenal reserve.

A low baseline cortisol level is clinically important, even if the patient's second level is double the first. Let us say that the patient's baseline level is 5 mcg/100 mL. If this value doubles after the ACTH or Cortrosyn injection, the cortisol level will have risen to 10 mcg/100mL. This change barely brings the patient's cortisol to a low-normal level. When the patient's cortisol rises to this level during stress, she may not have enough to adapt to the stress.

Daily Variations in Salivary Cortisol Levels

Most people have peak cortisol levels at about 8:00 am. The level then gradually declines during the day, with the lowest level around midnight.

Of course, people whose sleep/wake cycles are unusual don't have this "normal" pattern of cortisol levels according to the clock. If you're awake at night and sleep during the day, you'll have peak cortisol levels shortly after you've awakened, and the levels will gradually decline through your time awake. Your lowest levels will occur while you're in deep sleep.

For example, a recent study showed that during deep sleep, the HPA axis (see *Glossary*) is inhibited. The inhibition reduces the production and release of cortisol. As a result, blood levels are low. Sleep deprivation, however, caused an increase in cortisol levels.[127] This suggests that cortisol secretion is dependant upon deep sleep times rather than clock times. So, people who normally have a different time structure to their sleep/wake cycles also have, by the clock, different times when their cortisol levels are high and low. Because of this, the times of the 24-hour cycle medical labs use for the "normal" reference range (see *Glossary*) should be adjusted based on an individual's sleep/wake cycle.

PHYSIOLOGIC DOSES OF CORTISOL

Dr. William Jefferies is the father of treatment with physiologic doses of cortisol. In 1996, he emphasized a most unfortunate fact—medical writers have failed to distinguish between "pharmacologic" and "physiologic" doses of cortisone and cortisol.

Pharmacologic doses are large. They raise the blood levels of cortisone or cortisol above what labs consider normal. And they often harm patients. They can cause cataracts, stomach ulcers, breakdown of connective tissues, and loss of bone mass. As I (JCL) wrote in 1989, pharmacologic doses can have several harmful effects, especially when taken for prolonged times:[109]

> The doses exaggerate normal actions of the hormones and lead to the clinical picture of 'Cushing's syndrome' (a disease in which the adrenal cortex secretes excess cortisol): fat tends to redistribute from the extremities to the trunk and face, leaving the face rounded and puffy; there may be an increased growth of fine hair over the thighs, trunk, and face; acne may appear or worsen; insomnia and increased appetite develop; proteins are continually broken down and their amino acids converted to glucose; this increases the need for insulin; over a period of time this leads to weight gain, fat deposition, muscle wasting, and thinning of the skin with striae; the patient comes to bruise easily, becomes hyperglycemic, and after a time may develop osteoporosis and diabetes. The patient may become psychotic and develop posterior subcapsular cataracts. Increased intraocular pressure is common and glaucoma may be induced. Benign intracranial hypertension may also develop. Even when used for less than a week, the drugs occasionally induce behavioral changes and acute peptic ulcers.[110,p.349]

In addition, pharmacologic doses can disrupt the body's connective tissues. In fact, connective tissue researchers have used large amounts of these hormones to study the breakdown of connective tissues.[111] I (JCL) have observed patients who had used pharmacologic doses for prolonged times and whose connective tissues were so disrupted that they couldn't provide adequate support for the patients' spines.

Prednisone is a cortisol derivative that's stronger than cortisol. In one study, it worsened the status of fibromyalgia patients.[112] This finding was important because it confirmed previous research showing that fibromyalgia is not an inflammatory disorder. These studies should lay to rest the ill-conceived belief of Andrew Weil, M.D.[113] and Jeffery Bland, Ph.D.[114] that fibromyalgia is an inflammatory condition.

In stark contrast to pharmacologic doses of cortisol, physiologic doses are safe.[104,p.18] This makes sense in that physiologic doses are equal to the amounts the adrenal cortices normally release; these doses don't raise the blood levels above what's considered normal. As Dr. Jefferies wrote, "That cortisone and cortisol are normal hormones of the adrenal cortex implies that in physiologic dosages they must be safe." He noted that clinical experience has shown that patients with adrenal insufficiency can take physiologic doses of cortisol indefinitely with no adverse effects. In fact, he wrote that the patients "enjoy perfectly normal health."[104,p.11] Moreover, his experimental studies showed that physiologic doses of cortisone or cortisol produced no blood, urine, or metabolic effects typical of cortisol excess.[104,p.16][116] Patients and their doctors should, of course, observe reasonable precautions (see "Precautions" below).

HOW TO TAKE CORTISOL TO CORRECT
DECREASED ADRENAL RESERVE

Dr. Jefferies advised that most patients with decreased adrenal reserve take 5 mg of cortisol four times each day. He wrote that patients should take a dose before each meal (assuming they eat three per day) and before going to bed. He advised patients to take their bedtime dose with either milk or an antacid.

Jefferies wrote that this schedule makes it easy for patients to remember to take their doses of cortisol. Also, taking the doses with food avoids the acid indigestion cortisol may cause. (Cortisol can cause indigestion by stimulating the release of gastric acid and the enzyme pepsin.[104,pp.14-15])

Jefferies advice that patients take cortisol four times each day is based upon one of his research findings. He found that a single dose of cortisol kept the blood cortisol level and metabolic effects normal for only eight hours.[115] Taking cortisol at these intervals during the day and night is important for getting the desired metabolic benefits from use of the hormone. The therapeutic effects of cortisol taken on this schedule may not occur until 10-to-14 days after the patient starts treatment.[104,p.17]

Another way to use cortisol, which we prefer, is to mimic the adrenal glands' normal daily pattern of release of the hormone. (Typically, the glands release the largest amounts in the first few hours after waking. They release diminishing amounts through the day.) With this method of cortisol use, most patients take the largest dose about 8:00 am. They take a smaller dose around noon; and they take an even smaller one, their third and last for the day, around 4:00 pm. Taking the last dose at 4:00 pm avoids the insomnia some patients experience when they take cortisol in the evening.

PRECAUTIONS

If you use cortisol, your doctor and you should note several precautions.

How to Take Cortisol

If patients take cortisol on an empty stomach, they may experience acid indigestion. To avoid this, they should take the hormone with food or an antacid.

Allergic Reactions

Some patients are allergic to the filler in cortisol tablets.[104,p.11] They should be careful not to confuse an allergic reaction to the filler with a reaction to cortisol.

Proper Medication

Dr. William Jefferies[104,p.18][106][107][108] gave a precaution that bears repeating here. He recommended cortisol or cortisone for the treatment of decreased adrenal reserve. Some doctors confuse these hormones with drugs derived from them that are more potent. The more potent drugs include prednisone, prednisolone, methyl prednisolone, triamcinolone, and dexamethasone. The effects of the derivatives also last longer than those of cortisol and cortisone.[104,p.17]

Dr. Jefferies pointed out that taking 5 mg of cortisone or cortisol four times each day is a physiologic—and therefore safe—dose.

But the derivatives are at least four times more potent. Taking 5 mg of one of these derivatives four times each day may cause the adverse effects we listed above (see section titled "Physiologic Doses of Cortisol"). If your doctor decides that you need to use cortisone or cortisol therapy, make sure he doesn't inadvertently prescribe one of the more potent derivatives.

Potassium Supplements

Patients with decreased adrenal reserve may have both low cortisol and low "aldosterone" levels. Aldosterone is a hormone that stimulates the kidneys to keep sodium in the body. It also stimulates the kidneys to release potassium into the urine. When a person has a deficiency of aldosterone, her body will excrete more sodium and retain more potassium. When severe enough, this can cause low blood pressure.

The person with too little aldosterone may have a potassium level that's too high.[117] Because of this, if you think you have decreased adrenal reserve, you should ask your doctor to check your potassium level before you begin taking a potassium supplement. Some people add potassium to the nutritional supplements they take each day just to make sure they get enough. But for the person with decreased adrenal reserve, this may be harmful. It's best to first make sure your potassium level isn't too high. We order a potassium level as part of a screen panel of blood tests on each new patient. If the potassium level is high, this is a signal that we should test the patient for decreased adrenal reserve.[117] (See "ACTH Stimulation Test" above.)

LICORICE AND CORTISOL

Licorice is the dried underground stem (rhizome) and root of Glycyrrhiza glabra. People have used licorice as a mild laxative and expectorant. They've also used it to soothe irritated membranes, and, because it's sweet, to disguise the taste of unpalatable remedies.

The active component of licorice is "glycyrrhizic acid." This acid inhibits an enzyme in the adrenal cortex, and inhibition of the enzyme leads to salt retention. This effect mimics the action of the adrenal hormone aldosterone which influences the kidneys to keep salt in the body (see section above titled "Potassium Supplements").

The enzyme (that licorice inhibits) in the adrenal cortex normally changes cortisol into cortisone.[146] Cortisol markedly affects carbohydrate metabolism, but cortisone is inactive in the body until changed back into cortisol. When licorice inhibits the enzyme that converts cortisol to cortisone, less cortisol is changed to cortisone. This increases the amount of cortisol in the body. Salt retention occurs because the receptors that normally bind to aldosterone to keep salt in the body also bind to cortisol. When the receptors bind to cortisol, the salt-retaining effect is the same as when they bind to aldosterone. When the body is working correctly, the enzyme keeps cortisol levels low enough to prevent excess salt retention.[148]

One researcher has expressed concern, however, about children eating too much licorice as candy. If children eat too much over a long-enough time, they'll retain so much salt that it's toxic.[147] By increasing cortisol levels until they are too high, then, licorice can be a "hormone disruptor" with the potential for harm. On the other hand, in people whose adrenal glands produce too little cortisol, licorice can be a useful medication. Naturopathic physicians and other alternative doctors have long used licorice to treat patients with adrenal insufficiency.

In 1996, Dr. Jacob Teitelbaum wrote: "I do not recommend treating with licorice because everybody reacts differently to it, and ascertaining just how much it has increased the adrenal-hormone level is difficult. Although I prefer natural products to pharmaceuticals, in this case I am most comfortable with standardized hormones."[23,pp.31-32] We agree with Dr. Teitelbaum in regard to licorice products that aren't standardized. Fortunately, today we have standardized licorice products, and with these, we can better control the effects of licorice on patients' cortisol levels.

If you use licorice, be sure to let your doctor know. If he recommends that you take physiologic doses of cortisol, he should have the benefit of knowing you're also using another agent that increases cortisol levels.

PREGNENOLONE

Pregnenolone is first in the series of hormones made from cholesterol in the adrenal cortex. This means that cells of the adrenal cortex can then transform pregnenolone into all the other hormones. So, pregnenolone can be called the mother of the other hormones of the adrenal cortex. (See Figure 1 for the sequence of steps involved in production of the different hormones, first from cholesterol, and thereafter from pregnenolone.)

Brain cells also produce pregnenolone from cholesterol, and the pregnenolone alters brain function. Pregnenolone and DHEA alter GABA receptors in the brain.[372] GABA receptors mainly bind to a nerve-transmitting chemical in the brain called GABA, and the binding sets off excitatory responses. By altering the receptors, pregnenolone and DHEA alter nerve function and mental experience.

Research shows that pregnenolone and DHEA in the brain modify electrical brain wave patterns in a manner that suggests they are memory enhancers.[373] The brain contains a structure called the hippocampus. Normal function of the structure is critical to good memory. When the pregnenolone level was low in the hippocampus of aged rats, they performed poorly on memory tests. When researchers injected pregnenolone into the hippocampus of the rats, their memory temporarily improved. This research suggests that pregnenolone may help stave off age-related changes in the hippocampus that otherwise would impair memory.[397]

Pregnenolone has been found to improve sleep quality and to decrease intermittent waking during the night.[294] The improved sleep may have resulted from reduced anxiety. This is suggested by the finding that patients with generalized anxiety[315] and generalized social phobia[316] had lower blood levels of pregnenolone. Taking pregnenolone as a supplement may reduce anxiety, and the lower anxiety may allow sleep to improve.

In the 1940s, researchers tested the effects of pregnenolone on factory workers and airline pilots. They found that the hormone improved concentration, increased learning, elevated mood, and improved job performance.[74,p.261]

Rheumatoid arthritis improves when patients use pregnenolone. The hormone reduces swelling, stiffness, and pain. Improvement usually occurs in about two weeks.[74,p.122]

Pregnenolone induces alterations in brain cells that may enable the brain to make adaptive changes in response to experiences. The ability to make adaptive changes is called neuroplasticity.[371]

Supplemental Pregnenolone

We strongly recommend lab testing for levels of pregnenolone and other steroid hormones of the adrenal cortices before supplementing with pregnenolone. As we wrote above, cells of the adrenal cortex can convert pregnenolone to all the other hormones of the cortex. In different people, pregnenolone may increase the production of any one or more of the other hormones.

Since we can't predict which adrenal hormones supplemental pregnenolone will increase in any individual patient, we must experiment in each case. Some people feel comfortable simply taking pregnenolone, feeling the effects, and altering their dose based on their feelings. But feelings can be misleading; this is true because they are affected by any number of mental, biochemical, biomechanical, and environmental factors each moment of the day. Because of this, we use the results of lab tests to make sure we aren't throwing the levels of any hormone out of range, and we also use the monitoring method we describe in *Chapter 3*. The monitoring enables us to determine more accurately what the effects of different doses are.

If testing shows that one of the other hormones, say testosterone, is high, we don't recommend the use of pregnenolone—not without close and repeated monitoring of the testosterone level to see if it increases further. It's extremely important not to cause an excess of testosterone or any other adrenal hormone by supple-

**Figure 1. Sequence of steps involved in production
of hormones of the adrenal cortex**

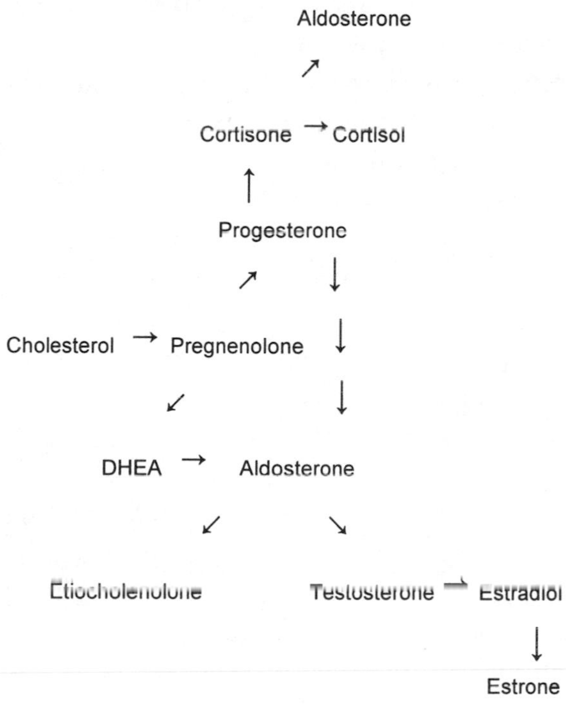

Aldosterone

↗

Cortisone → Cortisol

↑

Progesterone

↗ ↓

Cholesterol → Pregnenolone ↓

↙ ↓

DHEA → Aldosterone

↙ ↘

Etiocholenolone Testosterone → Estradiol

↓

Estrone

menting with pregnenolone.

Consider another case. Let's say the patient's progesterone level is low, but her cortisol, DHEA, estrogen, and testosterone levels are normal. The patient may increase her progesterone level to normal by taking pregnenolone. Our preference, however, is to have

183

the patient supplement with the specific hormone that is low, in this case progesterone. But if you use pregnenolone to raise your progesterone level, we again strongly recommend lab tests to see what result you get.

Pregnenolone, of course, has benefits other than correcting a low production of other adrenal hormones. As we noted above, pregnenolone exerts effects in the brain. It may improve memory, reduce anxiety, improve sleep, and enable the brain to make more adaptive changes. If achieving these effects is your aim in using pregnenolone, you may want to use the hormone even if you don't have a deficiency of other adrenal hormones. If so, we suggest you begin with a small dose, perhaps 10 mg, and gradually work up to 50 mg, and then possibly to 100 mg. Again, we strongly recommend that you monitor your adrenal hormone levels with lab tests.

Pregnenolone itself has no known adverse effects. Doses as high as 200 mg haven't produced adverse effects.[398,p.569] Because of this, if you need higher-end doses to benefit from its use, we wouldn't expect them to be harmful. However, if scrutiny of your responses to the hormone suggests that you're getting some adverse effect, you should lower your dose of pregnenolone and possibly consult a clinician experienced in its use.

When taking pregnenolone, it's important to also take a wide array of nutritional supplements. The nutrients, acting synergistically with thyroid hormone and many enzymes, can help optimize your production of adrenal hormones. The most important nutrients for optimizing the functioning of the adrenal cortex are pantothenic acid, vitamin C, and vitamin B_6.

Patients who are hypothyroid or resistant to thyroid hormone usually achieve optimal function of their adrenal cortices only after beginning the use of an effective dose of a thyroid hormone product. For hypothyroid patients, products containing both T_4 and T_3 will be most effective. For those who are resistant to thyroid hormone, plain T_3 will work best. (See *Chapter 2* and *Chapter 7*.)

DHEA

DHEA (dehydroepiandrosterone) is another hormone produced by the adrenal cortex. DHEA-S, sulfated DHEA, is the same hormone containing sulfur. DHEA and DHEA-S are the most abundant steroid hormones (see *Glossary*) in the blood.

DHEA levels are high in the fetus and decrease after birth. Before puberty, levels increase, and during young adulthood, they reach their peak. Eventually, perhaps by age 30, levels begin to decline. By age 70, levels in men have decreased to only 10%-to-20% of the peak levels during young adulthood.[149]

At menopause, women's ovaries cease producing estrogen and progesterone, lowering their blood and tissue levels of these hormones. Levels of estrogen drop even further because the women's levels of DHEA (a source of estrogen) have also markedly dropped. Between the highest DHEA levels in young adulthood and the decline at menopause, DHEA levels have decreased by about 60%. As a result, less estrogen is produced from the DHEA in most women's adrenal cortices and other tissues. Tissues other than the adrenals change the DHEA and DHEA-S, which reach them through the blood, into male sex hormones (androgens) and estrogen. So, when the adrenal cortices produce and release less DHEA into the blood, less estrogen is produced in other tissues.[152] Postmenopausal women thus have decreased estrogen for two reasons: their ovaries have ceased making it, and their adrenal cortices produce less DHEA.

Benefits of DHEA

Low levels of DHEA and DHEA-S in the body harm humans in many ways. Low levels may contribute to diabetes, obesity, high cholesterol, heart disease, arthritis, impaired immune function, and other diseases typical of older people.[154] Declining levels later in life may contribute to senility, formerly considered an unavoidable effect of brain aging.[154] Taking supplemental DHEA can prevent, improve, or reverse such diseases.

Increased levels of tissue androgens from supplemental DHEA may protect the postmenopausal woman from breast and uterine cancer. Increased levels may also stimulate bone formation and decrease insulin resistance.[152]

In rats, DHEA-S enhances memory. As yet, studies haven't shown that the hormone improves the memory or attention of humans.[150] Nevertheless, the level of DHEA in the brain is higher than in other body parts, and the hormone has positive effects on the central nervous system. In some studies, DHEA-S improved people's global sense of well-being. When elderly people used the hormone, their mood improved and depression lifted.[150]

Dr. Julian Whitaker wrote, "DHEA seems to rejuvenate the systems required for optimal functioning of the human body. It helps protect the body from the malfunctions associated with age. The exciting part of the action of DHEA is that it may reverse many of the aspects of aging previously thought to be irreversible."[155,p.98] I (JCL) share Dr. Whitaker's enthusiasm for the potential benefits of DHEA, having experienced some personally. Among other benefits, I (like Dr. Earl Mindell[74,p.46]) have had increased energy and stamina; I find it far easier to maintain a rigorous schedule and endure physical and psychological stresses.

DHEA and Androgens. DHEA is chiefly converted into male sex hormones (androgens).[151] This is true in both men and women, and both benefit from the androgen production. For men, this may eliminate any need for Viagra. For women, it may provide protection from some cancers. For example, two androgens (testosterone and dihydrotestosterone) formed in breast tissue from DHEA prevent some breast cancers in rats.[152]

More to the point of this book, increased androgen production from DHEA can positively influence metabolism. Low levels of androgens decrease muscle mass and strength in both men and women. Conversely, raising androgen levels increases muscle mass and strength. Larger muscle mass increases the basal metabolic rate.[153] (For extensive details on the relation of metabolism to muscle mass, see *The Metabolic Treatment of Fibromyalgia*, Chapter 5.5 "Complementary Methods: Increasing Metabolic Capacity and Decreasing Metabolic Demand," pages 1029-1030.[1])

Men generally have a larger muscle mass than women. The greater mass results from their higher androgen levels and provides men with a higher metabolic rate. The higher rate may partly explain their lower susceptibility to fibromyalgia or chronic fatigue syndrome.[1,p.516] In one study, women with chronic fatigue syndrome had low DHEA-S levels,[156] and women with fibromyalgia had low androgen levels. The lower the patients' androgen levels, the more severe their fibromyalgia symptoms.[157] Such findings in women may partly explain their greater susceptibility to fibromyalgia and chronic fatigue syndrome. In women with low DHEA levels, taking DHEA may increase their androgen levels. With higher androgen levels, exercise will increase their muscle mass enough to give them a higher metabolic rate.

Low androgen levels decrease the body's protein production. Lower protein production decreases the thickness of the body's connective tissues. The person is then more vulnerable to injuries. Higher androgen levels have the opposite effect—increased protein production, thicker connective tissues, and a lower injury rate. Women's lower androgen levels and thinner connective tissues make them more prone to injuries. Taking DHEA may increase a woman's androgen levels, enable exercise to thicken her connective tissues, and enhance her resistance to injury.

Note: Thyroid Hormone, Growth Hormone, and Injuries. Thyroid hormone is one of the most powerful regulators of growth hormone secretion. (For a detailed review of this topic, see *The Metabolic Treatment of Fibromyalgia*, Chapter 3.12 "Growth Hormone and Somatomedin C," pages 619-633.[1]) Both hypothyroidism and thyroid hormone resistance can lower levels of growth hormone. They can also cause low levels of "somatomedin C"— the hormone that responds to growth hormone by stimulating protein production in tissues.

If a woman's thyroid hormone deficiency and/or resistance has caused low levels of growth hormone and somatomedin C, she'll also have low protein production in her tissues. As we've stated, low protein production in her connective tissues will make her more vulnerable to injuries. To reduce her vulnerability, she must raise her levels of growth hormone and somatomedin C. The proper way to do this is to use the form and dosage of thyroid hormone that's proper for her. Lately, however, it has become popular for patients to take human growth hormone or amino acids that stimulate growth hormone release. When a patient is hypothyroid and/or resistant to thyroid hormone, this latter approach is a poor second to using the proper form and dose of thyroid hormone. Taking human growth hormone can make patients feel somewhat better, but not without a price. Among fibromyalgia patients treated with growth hormone, 24% had fluid retention, 60% had joint pain, and 28% developed carpal tunnel syndrome.[166] In stark contrast, there are no adverse effects from using the proper form and dose of thyroid hormone—only benefits.

As we've said elsewhere in this book, resistance to injury is important to people in the initial stages of improving their metabolic health. They must be able to exercise without injury because exercise is *crucial* to recovering from poor metabolic health.

DHEA Dosage

Not everyone needs to take DHEA. Most people below age 40 have enough. From about age 40 on, the percentage of people with low levels increases. We recommend lab testing before anyone begins the use of DHEA.

Dose recommendations vary widely among doctors; some advise as little as 12.5 mg, others advise as much as 100 mg. We agree in general with Dr. Earl Mindell's recommendation of one 25 mg tablet daily for women, and one 50 mg tablet for men.[74,p.48] We ask our patients to use the lowest effective dose. You may have to work with your doctor to find your optimal dose, based on lab tests and clinical results.

The most common symptoms in our patients who take excessive doses of DHEA have been those of metabolic overstimulation. Most feel restless, unable to relax, irritable, and uncomfortable. Rarely, women who have taken more than 90 mg per day have had a mild adverse effect: masculinization with increased facial hair and a lower voice.[155,p.98] These effects subside when a patient lowers her dose.

When men take DHEA and their testosterone levels rise, they may form too much of the highly potent byproduct of testosterone called "dihydrotestosterone." Prolonged exposure to this hormone can cause the prostate to enlarge. The enlargement may cause the man to have to urinate too often, to have trouble getting the flow of urine going, and trouble emptying his bladder. He may also feel a vague but attention-holding discomfort in his lower pelvis.

To avoid prostate enlargement, we advise men taking DHEA to also take three herbs, pygeum (*Pygeum africanum*), saw palmetto (*Serenoa repens*), and stinging nettle (*Urtica dioica*). Pygeum and saw palmetto block the enzyme (5-alpha reductase) that converts testosterone to dihydrotestosterone. Saw palmetto also blocks androgen receptors within the prostate, and pygeum has anti-inflammatory effects in the structure.[158][159][160] Stinging nettle relieves the symptoms of prostate enlargement without eliminating the enlargement itself. It does so by increasing urine volume, maximizing urine flow, and reducing residual urine in the bladder.[117,pp.1197-1198]

We recommend as starting doses the following amounts three times each day with meals: 100 mg pygeum extract, 320 mg saw palmetto extract, and 900 mg stinging nettle leaf. Men may have to alter their doses of the different herbs according to individual needs. We encourage men to enlist the participation of a reputable herbalist or of a doctor knowledgeable about herbal medicine. Please contact the Herb Research Foundation for more information (see *Resources*).

Chapter 9

Female Sex Hormone Balance

WHEN A PATIENT HAS IMPROVED, but the improvement isn't optimal, it's possible that a sex hormone imbalance is an obstacle to further improvement. One reason we're prepared to consider such imbalances is that some of the symptoms of sex hormone imbalance closely resemble those of hypothyroidism and thyroid hormone resistance.

The similarities can be striking. For example, a progesterone deficiency can cause fatigue, weight gain, irritability, depression, memory and concentration problems, headaches, irregular and painful menstrual cycles, fluid retention, loss of sex drive, and cold hands and feet. These symptoms, of course, are also characteristic of hypothyroidism and thyroid hormone resistance. Some symptoms of estrogen and testosterone deficiencies also resemble those of hypothyroidism and thyroid hormone resistance.

During the female's fertile years, a high percentage of sex hormone imbalances and female problems are caused by hypothyroidism or thyroid hormone resistance. Effective metabolic therapy that includes a high-enough dose of the proper form of thyroid hormone can correct the sex hormone imbalances and female problems.

During perimenopause and menopause, diminishing levels of estrogen and progesterone can cause symptoms that complicate those of hypothyroidism or thyroid hormone resistance. To reduce these perimenopausal and menopausal symptoms, most woman will have to use both a high-enough dose of the proper form of thyroid hormone, and natural therapies that reduce the effects of lower sex hormone levels. (See section below titled "Sex Hormone Problems Due to Under-regulation by Thyroid Hormone.")

SEX HORMONE PROBLEMS DUE TO
UNDER-REGULATION BY THYROID HORMONE

Before menopause, women who are hypothyroid or resistant to thyroid hormone are likely to have a range of female problems: abnormality of the menstrual cycle including irregular periods, absence of menstrual periods, painful menstruation, frequent or profuse bleeding; PMS; infertility; first-trimester spontaneous abortion, stillbirth, miscarriage, and premature birth.[1,pp.525-533]

Men who are hypothyroid or resistant to thyroid hormone may also have problems related to sex hormones. Many have low testosterone levels, low libido, and impotence.[1,pp.558-559] They may have an increased ratio of estrogen to testosterone, and this may lead to insulin resistance. The resistance may render the men more susceptible to energy-deficient muscle contractures and painful myofascial trigger points.[1,p.560]

During perimenopause or menopause, women who are hypothyroid or resistant to thyroid hormone are likely to develop fibromyalgia symptoms or see their symptoms get worse. Under-regulation of a woman's hypothalamus, pituitary, and ovaries by thyroid hormone is likely to cause far worse perimenopausal and menopausal symptoms.[1,pp.510-511]

For a detailed and comprehensive description of sex hormone-related health problems in hypothyroidism and thyroid hormone resistance, see Chapter 3.6, pages 509-571, in *The Metabolic Treatment of Fibromyalgia*.[1]

REDUCED ESTROGEN AND PROGESTERONE AND
MENOPAUSAL SYMPTOMS: NATURAL PROCESS
OR HEALTH PROBLEM?

For some women, symptoms and signs of perimenopause and menopause are merely bothersome. For other women, they create or worsen other health problems and degenerative diseases.

Hot flashes aren't inherently dangerous, and some women simply regard them as a nuisance. Other women view them with disgust and are embarrassed when they have to mop perspiration from their brows in public.

But hot flashes can be hazardous to a woman's health. This can occur when hot flashes and night sweats wake her at night and make it hard for her to get back to sleep. If the woman isn't able to get enough slow-wave sleep because of recurrent hot flashes, she can develop symptoms that can lead to a diagnosis of fibromyalgia.[288]

Her disturbed sleep can complicate her perimenopausal or menopausal symptoms. As a result she may suffer steadily worsening depression, fatigue, irritability, and poor memory and concentration. For the woman with worsening symptoms facing fluid imbalance, unstable blood sugar, and osteoporosis, restoring hormone balance to some degree seems a worthy goal. In fact, the severity of the symptoms and fear of other diseases undoubtedly accounts for many women submitting to conventional hormone replacement therapy (HRT) and, in many cases, suffering its potentially dreadful consequences.

I (GH-L) have watched several patients who refused to check estrogen and progesterone levels unnecessarily suffer from menopausal symptoms. I appreciate the women's desire to let natural processes occur. But I also see the sense in restoring balance enough to offset adverse health effects from reduced levels of female sex hormones.

Fortunately, gentle and natural alternatives are widely available. We hope those who choose to undergo treatment for perimenopausal and menopausal symptoms use these alternatives rather than conventional HRT.

TESTING FOR HORMONE IMBALANCES

Many conventional doctors don't order lab tests to measure women's progesterone and estrogen levels. Instead, if a woman of perimenopausal age complains of hot flashes or fatigue, the doctors reflexly prescribe a conjugated estrogen such as Premarin. Sometimes they also prescribe a progestin—a synthetic chemical resembling progesterone but different in that it has severely adverse effects on most women.

Most alternative doctors order blood tests to measure progesterone and estrogen levels. We prefer the option of testing hormone levels to see if there is an obvious deficiency or excess. The only problem with blood or serum tests is that they measure the amount of the hormone attached to carrier proteins. This hormone may or may not actually be able to release from the carrier protein and be of use to the body. (Only a tiny percentage of hormones circulating in the body are actually used.)

While blood tests have been the most common method of testing, in the past few years more and more labs are offering saliva testing. The benefit of saliva testing is that the amount of free hormone circulating in the body can be measured. This is more useful information than knowing how much of the hormone is attached to carrier proteins in the blood. Also, if you are using transdermal progesterone, the blood tests won't measure its level at all since this free hormone isn't attached to carrier proteins.

Urine testing for metabolites of progesterone can also be performed, and some doctors think this style of measurement is even more valuable than saliva testing. We aren't discounting the validity of this, but we're most familiar with saliva testing and have seen very good results with this simple, convenient type of test.

Regardless of the style of testing, be sure to note where you are in your menstrual cycle when the samples are collected, and also note what kind of hormone supplements you may be using. Patients often bring lab results from other doctors' offices that show no indication of when during the patient's menstrual cycle the tests were performed. Also, if the lab testing is inconclusive, it's safe to try natural progesterone to see if your symptoms can be alleviated. We are all too familiar with the phenomenon of normal lab tests excluding people from treatment they desperately need.

TREATMENT OF SEX HORMONE IMBALANCES

For decades, conventional medicine promoted the use of sex hormone "replacement therapy." The horrors of this approach are now too evident to deny. Because of this, steadily more women are using natural alternatives to the conventional approach.

Conventional Hormone Replacement Therapy

Until 2002, conventional doctors treated most women who had menopausal symptoms with progestins and conjugated horse estrogens. This approach to female sex hormone imbalance, called hormone replacement therapy (HRT), has recently received widespread attention. In one published study, postmenopausal women who used HRT over a 5-year period had an increased incidence of breast cancer, stroke, and pulmonary embolism.[218] Another study showed that HRT reduced the risk of bone fracture and colorectal cancer, but these benefits were outweighed by an increased risk for cardiovascular disease and breast cancer.[214][216] The increased risk for heart disease, stroke, and cancer are so extreme that the FDA recently ordered companies to put safety warnings on labels for estrogen.[217]

Women who use artificially altered progesterone, called progestins, are likely to suffer especially severe consequences. Provera is a progestin, and Prempro contains progestins. Rather than marketing natural progesterone, drug manufacturers synthesize progestins from natural progesterone so that they can patent them as "medicines" and make higher profits. Natural progesterone cannot be patented, and therefore is not a lucrative venture for drug manufacturers to pursue. Progestins are much stronger than natural progesterone, and have a much more potent effect in the body. They are also more slowly processed by the liver and therefore stay longer in the body. They have more time to produce their strong effects, and this increases their potential for causing side effects. Impaired glucose metabolism is only one possible side effect from progestins.

If a woman has an estrogen deficiency, she can reduce or eliminate the symptoms with the use of one or more natural agents. The most common way until 2002, however, was for her to use Premarin or similar synthetic products. Premarin is a conjugated estrogen synthesized from the urine of pregnant horses. Many of the estrogen molecules synthesized from pregnant horse urine are not identical to human estrogens. Because of this, women often have adverse effects from them. Conjugated estrogens have a more potent effect on our bodies than natural estrogens. (On another level of concern, the synthetic estrogen industry destroys mares when they are no longer producing estrogens in an economical manner. The foals produced by many of the mares are fortunate if they are adopted. The unlucky ones are destroyed.)

The progestins and conjugated estrogens used in oral contraceptives or for HRT can cause serious health problems. Progestins, even those in low-dose oral contraceptives, can impair glucose metabolism.[81][82] The effect is similar to an episode of hypoglycemia (low blood sugar),[86] and can cause energy-deficient muscle contractures. These become new or reactivated myofascial trigger points that can refer pain. It's difficult to eliminate trigger points as long as cells are affected by the progestins. And on a more lethal level, conjugated estrogens can also increase the risk of blood clots, heart attacks, strokes, and breast and endometrial cancers.

Inadequate Thyroid Hormone Regulation:
A Cause of Sex Hormone Imbalances

Under-regulation by thyroid hormone of the glands that produce sex hormones is a common cause of sex hormone imbalances. For this reason, with our patients, we first consider whether hypothyroidism or thyroid hormone resistance is causing the sex hormone imbalance. For some patients, using a high-enough dose of the proper form of thyroid hormone relieves symptoms characteristic of sex hormone imbalances. Other patients must also use natural therapies to effectively control or fully relieve the symptoms.

Natural Alternatives to HRT

Research hasn't yet clearly specified the exact mechanism of the hot flashes and other symptoms that most women in menopause experience. Despite this, some medical writers argue that the best available treatment for hot flashes is the use of estrogen and/or progesterone. They estimate that using them reduces hot flashes by 80%-to-90%.[209][213] Fortunately, most women don't have to resort to conjugated horse estrogen or progestins to reduce their hot flashes. Women can now use natural progesterone and estrogen-like chemicals in herbs and foods such as soy. A recent study confirmed that isoflavones from soy effectively reduce hot flashes. A soy product high in isoflavones reduced the hot flashes of 76% of patients.[208]

Natural Progesterone. Natural progesterone cream is safe, and easily obtained over the counter in health food stores. The cream absorbs through the skin into fatty tissue beneath the skin. From there, the cream's chemicals gradually enter the blood stream.

Drs. John R. Lee and Jesse Hanley recommend brand name products that independent labs have tested for strength.[13][197,p.257] Their list may not be all-inclusive, but it is a good guideline. Products without enough progesterone are ineffective, and those with too much can cause symptoms of excessive progesterone. The effective dose of natural progesterone for most women is from 15-to-30 mg per day.

Dosing guidelines differ in the product literature. Most sources I've (GH-L) consulted advise women to use ¼ to ½ teaspoon of progesterone cream once or twice each day. It's best to rub the cream on thin skin, such as that of your upper chest, upper arms, neck, and face. Even the soles of the feet are good sites of absorption, unless they are rough and calloused. The palms of your hands are good sites as well. If you always apply the cream to the same body site, the amount absorbed will decrease. Because of this, it's best to use several body sites to apply the cream, rotating from one site to another.

If you're still having menstrual cycles, you should begin using the progesterone twelve days after the start of your last period. In general, you should continue using it for fourteen days. But if you start another period before the end of the 14-day time frame, you should discontinue it then. Women who are postmenopausal (meaning you haven't had a menstrual cycle in one year) can use progesterone three weeks per month and take one week off. Symptom relief is the goal, so you'll most likely need to experiment to find your optimal dose. Even if you overshoot a little when adjusting your dose, you're not likely to experience adverse effects.

In that most women today are busy and have cycles that may be irregular, it's difficult to precisely remember a dosing schedule. Because of this, it's important to keep a written record. Use a calendar to note when to use progesterone during your cycle and when to discontinue it.

For detailed instruction on using natural progesterone cream to help with particular female problems, please refer to the book, *What Your Doctor May* Not *Tell You About Premenopause*[197,p.257] by Drs. Lee and Hanley. They give specific guidelines for women who have had hysterectomies, and for women with problems such as endometriosis, uterine fibroids, and fibrocystic breast disease.

Natural Sources of Estrogen. Women have several options in natural substances to reduce or eliminate symptoms of estrogen deficiency. If you use transdermal progesterone, some of it may be converted to estrogen in your body. If using the progesterone doesn't eliminate your estrogen-deficiency symptoms, you may have to use one or more of several sources of estrogen-like chemicals. Estrogen receptors are responsive to a wide array of chemicals, so you can use the receptors' responsiveness to your advantage.

Soy Isoflavones. The isoflavones in soy products have estrogen-like effects in the body. Ingesting enough of them may relieve your estrogen-deficiency symptoms. When postmenopausal women used 100 mg of soy isoflavones for four months, their menopausal symptoms diminished. Hot flashes decreased in 76% of the women, palpitations in 77%, sleep disturbance in 69%, and nervousness in 56%. The women's total cholesterol and low-density lipoprotein (LDL) also decreased significantly.[208] It's important, however, not to take in too much soy (see *Chapter 4*, section titled "Soy").

Gamma Oryzanol. Another safe and effective natural agent that can reduce the number and severity of hot flashes is gamma oryzanol. So that patients can use it as a supplement, it is isolated from rice bran oil.[190]

During perimenopause or menopause, the anterior pituitary gland increases production of leutinizing hormone (LH) and follicle stimulation hormone (FSH). Some medical writers believe that the overproduction of LH causes the troubling symptoms.[190] Gamma oryzanol decreases LH production,[186] thereby decreasing hot flashes and other menopausal symptoms. It also promotes endorphin release by the hypothalamus, which improves mood. Up to 85% of women had a reduction of symptoms with the use of gamma oryzanol.[100]

Taking 150 mg twice each day can reduce hot flashes, depression, sweating, and memory and concentration problems. This same daily dose of gamma oryzanol also decreases cholesterol and triglycerides. It does this by converting cholesterol to bile acids, and then increasing excretion of the bile acids. Gamma oryzanol can also help decrease the absorption of cholesterol into the bloodstream. Importantly, gamma oryzanol has no known adverse effects.[190]

Herbs. Compounds in several herbs appear to bind to estrogen receptors, especially in the hypothalamus in the brain. Some researchers believe that symptoms such as hot flashes are initiated in the hypothalamus. This happens, they argue, during perimenopause and menopause when estrogen production is low and too few of the estrogen receptors in the hypothalamus are occupied. The compounds in certain herbs may alleviate the estrogen deficiency symptoms by binding to the estrogen receptors.

Herbs such as black cohosh, red clover, dong quai, tribulus, and chaste tree berry exert these estrogen-like effects. A combination of 50 mg black cohosh, 100 mg dong quai, and 60 mg soy isoflavones significantly reduces the incidence of migraine headaches associated with menopause.[204] In another study, 500 to 750 mg of tribulus per day improved menopausal symptoms for 98% of women.[207,p.41] In the UK, chaste tree berry has long been used to reduce intense PMS symptoms during the perimenopausal time.[206]

One herbalist, Kerry Bone, states that herbal treatments for menopausal symptoms are intended to ease adaptation to lower levels of female sex hormones. Women shouldn't use them indefinitely, but can benefit from doing so for six to eighteen months.[207,p.42]

Ginseng is an "adaptogen," which means it helps us adapt better to stress. The herb increases energy production and stamina. In one study, 193 postmenopausal women with symptoms used a standardized ginseng extract. Their menopausal symptoms improved slightly, but they had significant improvement in depression, well-being, health, and quality of life. Testing suggested that the improvements from the patients' use of ginseng didn't result from a hormone-replacement-like effect.[98] The benefits probably derived from the herb's adaptogen effects.

Ginseng also helps normalize the balance of some hormones. Postmenopausal women with symptoms including fatigue, insomnia, and depression took 6 grams of Korean red ginseng for thirty days. After doing so, their scores on psychological tests improved. The researchers wrote that the therapeutic effects of the ginseng were related to its decreasing the women's ratio of cortisol to DHEA.[99]

Bioidentical Estrogen. Some women get little relief from menopausal symptoms when they use transdermal progesterone, soy isoflavones, herbs, or gamma oryzanol. For these women, bioidentical forms of estrogen, which are available by prescription, may work better. Bioidentical means that their molecules are the same as those of human estrogen. It's important, though, to use the smallest effective dose of these estrogens, and balance it with natural progesterone. Compounding pharmacies often formulate bioidentical estrogens.

Vitamin E. To control mild symptoms that don't interfere with sleep or daily function, some doctors recommend that women use 800 IU of vitamin E.[209] Remember, though, that nutrients work synergistically in the body. Because of this, it's important not to take only select vitamins and minerals but to take the full array of nutritional supplements (see *Chapter 5*).

Diet and Exercise. A wholesome diet and exercise to tolerance can reduce symptoms of perimenopause and menopause. In countries where most women regularly do physical labor and eat a wholesome diet, any menopausal symptoms they have are usually milder than those of women in highly industrialized countries. In Europe and North America, the high intake of refined carbohydrates and red meat by many women, added to their sedentary lifestyles, appears to worsen menopausal symptoms.[13]

The wholesome diet (see *Chapter 4*) and exercise to tolerance (see *Chapter 10*) that are essential parts of metabolic rehab can reduce menopausal symptoms to a level consistent with those of the more active and well-fed women of some other areas of the world. We agree with Dr. John Lee and Dr. Jesse Hanley[13][197,p.257] that natural sex hormones work best when women also stick to a wholesome diet, take nutritional supplements, and exercise to tolerance.

An excellent source book for foods that contain natural estrogen-like chemicals is *The Natural Estrogen Diet* by Dr. Lana Liew.[97] She gives many recipes in the book that can make it palatable and easy to take in enough of these foods to reduce menopausal symptoms.

Chapter 10

Exercise to Tolerance

TO ACHIEVE OPTIMAL METABOLIC HEALTH, you *must* exercise to tolerance. By "tolerance" we mean that you should exercise as intensely as you can *without worsening your symptoms*. If you are hypothyroid or resistant to thyroid hormone, exercising beyond your tolerance is likely to worsen your symptoms of slow metabolism. Metabolic rehab increases exercise tolerance. As your rehab progresses, you should eventually be able to exercise vigorously without your former symptoms recurring. In the meantime, you must exercise enough to start improving your metabolic health without making your symptoms more severe. In this chapter, we explain how you can do this. (For detailed coverage of exercise to tolerance, see Chapters 3.4 and 5.2 of *The Metabolic Treatment of Fibromyalgia.*[1])

BENEFITS OF EXERCISE TO TOLERANCE

The benefits of exercise are too extensive for us to cover in this book. Here, we describe only the benefits we believe are especially important to those with poor metabolic health: relaxation, reduced pain, decreased anxiety and depression, improved mental abilities, and easier menstrual periods and menopause.

Relaxation and Reduced Pain

Patients who fail to exercise pay a dear price for doing so. Lack of sufficient exercise impairs their health and well-being in many ways. The harmful effects are usually worse for those of middle and old age. But for patients who have fibromyalgia and chronic fatigue syndrome, the effects of too little exercise can especially worsen their symptoms.

In the early 1980s, I (JCL) reported in two journal articles the research evidence that exercise improves mental and emotional well-being. The evidence also showed that not exercising—or not

exercising enough—contributes to mental and emotional disturbance.[44][47] One source of the disturbance is the higher muscle
tension of those who don't exercise enough. Sufficient exercise
reduces muscle tension, and the reduction soothes emotions and
mollifies the mind.

Some people will be happy to learn that they don't have to run
or jog to reduce their muscle tension. In one study, researchers
found that walking relaxed people more than taking a tranquilizer (meprobamate) popular at the time. When people in the study
walked and increased their heart rate to 100 beats per minute,
instruments showed that their muscles relaxed. Immediately after
the exercise, their muscle activity was 20% lower than before the
exercise. At 30 minutes, their muscles were 23% more relaxed.
And at an hour, 20% more. The tranquilizer didn't relax the people's muscles at all.[42] Other researchers also found that exercise
tranquilizes people.[43][44][45][46]

The muscle-relaxing effects of exercise can be especially important for fibromyalgia patients. Consider a finding researchers
recently reported: the tenderness of fibromyalgia patients' tender
points was correlated with how much muscle tension they felt
when going to sleep. The more muscle tension they felt, the more
sensitive their tender points were.[49] If fibromyalgia patients exercise enough, and this reduces their muscle tension, their tender
points may be less tender.

Unfortunately, exercise alone doesn't relieve most fibromyalgia patients' widespread aches and pains. Fibromyalgia patients'
pain is *chronic*. Studies tell us that relaxation may reduce *acute*
pain;[50] they don't show that relaxation reduces *chronic* pain.[51][52]
But exercise may relax a fibromyalgia patient and reduce some
acute pain that compounds her chronic pain. If so, she's likely to
welcome the relief, albeit incomplete.

Humans have a mechanism within the spinal cord and brain
stem that normally protects them from excessive pain. Nerve fibers
continually deliver barrages of nerve impulses to the spinal cord

from other body tissues such as our muscles, tendons, and joints. If these impulses were to freely enter the spinal cord and reach the brain, we would experience widespread and intense pain. But, other nerves in the spinal cord release chemicals close to these incoming nerves. These chemicals (norepinephrine and serotonin) stimulate still other nerves—very small ones—to release another set of chemicals called "endorphins." Endorphins are powerful, opium-like chemicals. When released, they reduce the entry of incoming impulses into the spinal cord from other tissues. The reduced entry has a pain-killing effect.

Evidence suggests that the chronic, widespread pain fibromyalgia patients experience results in part from a less-than-normal release of norepinephrine (and possibly serotonin) where outside nerve impulses enter the spinal cord. Too little thyroid hormone regulation of nerves in the brain stem is probably the cause of most fibromyalgia patients' pain. This is likely because too little thyroid hormone regulation can reduce production of norepinephrine and serotonin. Reduced production of these chemicals would reduce the release of endorphins, and reduced endorphins would permit the entry of too many nerve impulses into the spinal cord.

Regular exercise increases the release of endorphins in the spinal cord, making humans more resistant to pain. When athletes, for example, exercise vigorously enough, they can endure severe injuries without pain while endorphin levels remain high. On the other hand, a lack of exercise reduces endorphin release. The reduced release accounts largely for the aches, pains, and general discomforts of sedentary people.

Many hypothyroid and thyroid hormone resistant patients have too little thyroid hormone regulation of the brain stem. As a result, they may have reduced norepinephrine and serotonin, which can lead to reduced endorphins and chronic, widespread pain. Many of the patients don't exercise because of their low energy levels. The combination of no exercise and reduced norepinephrine in the spinal cord causes pain that is resistant to pain-killing drugs. To begin reducing their pain, these patients *must* exercise to tolerance—even though their tolerance may be extremely low.

Fibromyalgia patients also have excessive amounts of another chemical in their spinal cords—substance P. This chemical encourages the entry into the spinal cord of nerve impulses from other tissues. The increased entry heightens patients' perception of pain. Again, too little thyroid hormone regulation of certain brain and spinal cord nerves causes extremely high production and release of substance P. (See *The Metabolic Treatment of Fibromyalgia*, Chapter 3.15, pages 689-694.)

In summary, too little thyroid hormone regulation of the spinal cord, brain stem, and brain cells is the cause of many patients' chronic, widespread pain. For patients' to free themselves from pain, they must use the proper form and dose of thyroid hormone. Our studies show that this form of treatment effectively relieves fibromyalgia patients' pain[92][93][94][135][138][187][188][189]—but only when they use thyroid hormone as part of a comprehensive program to improve their metabolism. An *indispensable* component of that regimen is exercise to tolerance.

Exercise and Anxiety

Many people with poor metabolic health are more anxious than others. Consider fibromyalgia and chronic fatigue syndrome patients. They're often subjected to conditions that promote anxiety. When a patient asks her conventional doctor, "What's causing my pain?" she doesn't get a satisfactory answer—only a prescription for a pain-killer. Typically, the drug doesn't help, and the patient is left fretting over the source of her pain. When she complains of anxiety to her doctor, he prescribes another drug to control that symptom. The anti-anxiety drug may sedate her and worsen her fatigue, adding to her woes worry over whether she can drag herself through the days.

Moreover, many fibromyalgia and chronic fatigue syndrome patients have financial distress. Medical expenses may have depleted their money reserves. Not being able to work and produce more money usually escalates their anxiety.

The abnormalities underlying fibromyalgia and chronic fatigue symptoms are biochemical and molecular—abnormalities invisible to others. Many patients anxiously endure doubts from family, friends, and doctors who see no obvious cause of the patients' symptoms. (For a detailed description of the factors that contribute to psychological disturbance among fibromyalgia patients, see pages 121-123 in *The Metabolic Treatment of Fibromyalgia*.[1])

When patients are anxious, their muscles tense;[2,p.248][53][54][55] they contract more tightly and for longer times. The contractions expend more energy than normal, even when the patients are resting.[56][259] The energy loss may profoundly weaken the patient with poor metabolic health, as her energy is already in short supply.

Exercise to tolerance can reduce the patient's anxiety and help increase her energy reserves. She may have to start, though, with the smallest baby steps. Reassurance from a clinician who understands the nature of her illness can reduce her anxiety and enable her to recover at least a modicum of energy to exercise. But she may have to wait a few weeks until an improved diet, nutritional supplements, the wise use of caffeine, and thyroid hormone increase her energy reserves. But she shouldn't wait for this: even squeezing a rubber ball or raising her arms out from her sides a few times each day will get the anti-anxiety process of exercise to tolerance under way.

Exercise and Depression

Exercise physiologist Dr. Herbert deVries wrote, "The wisdom of the ages that suggested that vigorous exercise makes you feel good is now supported by laboratory evidence."[194,p.249] Exercise increases people's feelings of well-being.[47][48] Researchers found that even brief exercise reduced depression,[43] and ten weeks of jogging markedly improved patients' depressive disorders.[191] Studies revealed a positive relationship between middle-aged men's fitness levels and their emotional stability.[192] And daily exercise improved both the physical and psychiatric status of institutionalized elderly mental patients.[193]

Exercise and Mental Abilities

Studies have shown that patients with hypothyroidism, fibromyalgia, and chronic fatigue syndrome have reduced blood flow through the brain. The reduced blood flow can impair mental abilities. (For a detailed description of the mechanisms, see *The Metabolic Treatment of Fibromyalgia*, pages 394 & 401-407.[1]) When hypothyroidism or thyroid hormone resistance is the cause of reduced blood flow to the brain, the proper form and dose of thyroid hormone is needed to completely correct the problem. But patients can also use exercise to increase the flow of blood to their brains.

Highly credible testimony on this issue comes from no other than one of the most important biochemists of the 20th century, Roger J. Williams, Ph.D. Between 1941 and 1963, more vitamins were developed by his laboratory than any other in the world. Dr. Williams discovered the B vitamin pantothenic acid; he also concentrated and christened the B vitamin folic acid.[57]

Dr. Williams didn't use nutritional therapy until he was in his seventies. When he began, his health improved remarkably, especially his mental functions. In middle age, however, he'd found that exercise was essential for his ingenious brain to work properly. In 1977, when he was 83 years old, he wrote of this middle-age experience:

> I had previously written a book on biochemistry, and the publishers were asking for a revision. I started to work, but immediately became stalled. It was difficult to write anything, and nothing I wrote seemed worthwhile. Quite unlike my normal self, I gave up. A couple of weeks later I began to realize what my difficulty had been; the weather had been rainy. I had failed for several weeks to get adequate exercise. Soon, however, the weather cleared, and I played golf several times. On returning to the writing job, I had no trouble whatever. Evidently my brain wouldn't work properly without exercise. (I now know, of course, that exercise helps to convey good nutrition to the brain.)[57,pp.126-127]

About the time he retired, Dr. Williams added nutrition to his health regimen. This gave him what he called a "rejuvenation." He wrote that he exercised regularly and judiciously:

> This, in my experience, is *absolutely essential*. I could not have written *Nutrition Against Disease* or its sequels *The Physician's Handbook of Nutritional Science*, and *The Wonderful World Within You*—if I had not walked from two to four miles every day. Such exercise, as I have noted, helps in transporting good nutrition to the brain, where it is conspicuously needed.[57,p.131]

We urge you to read two books by Dr. Williams, *Nutrition Against Disease*[195] and *The Wonderful World Within You*[57] (see *Resources*). He wrote these important books in his 80s. His ability to continue high-level mental function so late in life was a benefit of his exercise and nutritional supplements. He wrote:

> The most noteworthy sign of rejuvenation has been the retention of the ability and—more importantly, the strong inclination—to do constructive mental work. I believe, in fact, that my mental ability is superior to what it was ten years ago.[57,p.129]

Easier Menstrual Periods and Menopause

Dr. John Lee recently wrote, "Menstrual cramps and PMS are soothed by a good workout."[197,p.308] Many women who exercise agree with Dr. Lee's assertion, which preliminary studies support.

Teenage girls who rated their health as poor had a higher incidence of menstrual pain. They had low levels of physical fitness and reported that they preferred not to be physically active in the mornings.[196] Studies have shown that exercise decreases the prevalence of abnormal menstrual periods and the severity of menstrual symptoms.[203]

Two common and potent causes of abnormal menstrual periods are hypothyroidism and thyroid hormone resistance. Some of our female patients, before consulting us, had hysterectomies to stop profuse menstrual bleeding. Their medical records and a careful history show that the bleeding was caused by untreated or under-treated hypothyroidism. They later consulted us for other hypo-thyroid symptoms that had accompanied the profuse bleeding, and treatment with the proper form and dose of thyroid hormone re-lieved these symptoms. Most likely, their profuse bleeding would also have stopped with proper treatment; tragically, though, it's too late for proper treatment to save them from the hysterectomies. (For extensive coverage of this topic, see *The Metabolic Treatment of Fibromyalgia*, pages 525-532.)

Too little physical activity can worsen abnormal menstrual periods caused by thyroid hormone deficiency or resistance. Maxi-mum improvement comes when women exercise to tolerance and use thyroid hormone properly.

HOW TO EXERCISE

With patients working to improve their metabolic health, we emphasize four points about exercise:

1) Exercise at an intensity that doesn't worsen your symptoms.
2) Take baby steps first and *gradually* condition your body.
3) When there's a choice, walk instead of riding, and run instead of walking.
4) Do exercises you *will* do.

Exercise Intensity That Doesn't Worsen Your Symptoms

When we say patients should "exercise to tolerance," we mean they should exercise, but not so intensely that they worsen their symptoms of slow metabolism.

Many fibromyalgia and chronic fatigue syndrome patients complain that exercise aggravates their symptoms. The truth is that their symptoms worsen when they exercise *beyond their toler-ance*—that is, to an intensity that makes their symptoms worse.

We know of two reasons that vigorous exercise worsens symptoms of slow metabolism. One is that patients simply overdo it—they strain muscles, connective tissues, and other body structures. The other reason is that most hypometabolic people have too little thyroid hormone regulation of their genes. This results in an excess on their cell membranes of proteins called "alpha-adrenergic receptors."

Normally, when we exercise vigorously, our sympathetic nerves release the stress hormone, "noradrenaline." And our adrenal glands release both noradrenaline and another stress hormone, "adrenaline." When these hormones bind to proteins called "beta-adrenergic receptors," metabolism speeds up. This makes energy available that enables us to adapt to the stress of vigorous exercise.

In hypothyroid and thyroid hormone resistant patients, however, adrenaline and noradrenaline released during exercise bind to an excess of alpha-adrenergic receptors. Binding of the hormones to these receptors causes metabolism to slow down. The metabolic slowdown may cause an energy crisis. When the crisis reaches a critical level, the patient's symptoms worsen. Her aggravated symptoms may persist for days or even weeks.

Baby Steps First and Gradual Conditioning

Many people think that tiny bits of exercise can't possibly have any benefit. It may seem ridiculous to them to do tiny bits. This is especially true when, in the past, they did high-impact aerobics or ran marathons.

Fibromyalgia and chronic fatigue syndrome patients have reduced blood flow through their brains. Studies show that the most minor muscle contraction dilates blood vessels in parts of the brain, increasing the flow of blood. So, even a low-stress resistance exercise like squeezing a ball may increase blood flow through patients' brains.

A recent study showed that doing common housework contributes to conditioning. We caution you, though, not to restrict yourself *only* to housework, considering that enough. What we're saying is this: If housework is all you can do at the start, then do that. But if you're going to achieve metabolic health, you *must* steadily increase your level of exertion as time goes on. Only by exerting yourself steadily more can you gradually condition yourself and raise your fitness level. So, if all you can do is lightly squeeze a rubber ball, do it. If all you can do is walk to the end of your driveway and back, do that. And if all you can do is raise your arms from your sides up to shoulder level, then do that. Do whatever you can, and as the days pass, do it more often and more vigorously—always, though, at an intensity level that doesn't aggravate your symptoms.

A useful way to begin with baby steps is exercising in water. Some patients with extremely low physical fitness find it easiest to begin with "aquatic" exercises. Some have physical limitations that restrict them to this form of exercise. But most gradually progress to more stressful forms, such as riding a bicycle, running, or working out with weights. (For more on exercising in water, read the section below titled "Warm Water Exercises.")

Need for Exercise to Tolerance. Many patients with poor metabolic health are hardly able to exercise before beginning to use thyroid hormone therapy and nutritional supplements. After beginning, they find they are able to exercise more vigorously. Of course, to detect an increased ability to exercise, the patient must be doing some amount of baseline activity to start with. As thyroid hormone and nutritional supplements increase her energy and stamina, she can compare increases in her physical abilities to the baseline. (We urge you to use visual analog scales and graphs to objectively assess changes in your physical abilities. See *Chapter 3.*)

If you are hardly able to exercise, keep an important point in mind: By baseline activity, we don't mean activity so intense that it worsens your symptoms. The intensity of baseline activities should be below the level that aggravates your symptoms. As your ability to exercise more intensely gradually increases, you must take advantage of the increase. The way to do that is to gradually increase the intensity of your exercise, and exercise more often. Throughout this process, always be careful not to overdo.

Once you've recovered your metabolic health, you should be able to exercise as often and as intensely as anyone else. When now-and-then you overdo it, you shouldn't relapse into severe symptoms of slow metabolism. Instead, you should suffer nothing more than brief post-exercise soreness—soreness that the healthiest individuals experience when they exceed their limits.

Avoid Overdoing It. When your pain wanes and you have more energy, be careful not to overdo it exercising. Many patients come into my (GH-L) office complaining of sore muscles. When I ask them what caused the soreness, they excitedly report, "I felt so good I cleaned out the garage and three closets, and shampooed the carpets—all in one day!"

Most patients who make themselves sore this way don't mind. They say their soreness from overwork has a positive meaning, as opposed to the chronic, agonizing aches and pains they've suffered from for so long. But some patients become so sore that they have to temporarily suspend their regimen of exercise to tolerance. The time off from the regimen delays their full recovery.

It's best to avoid overuse injuries by pacing yourself. This is especially important if you're hypothyroid or resistant to thyroid hormone. Thyroid hormone powerfully regulates the production and release of both growth hormone and somatomedin C. Growth hormone stimulates the release of somatomedin C, and somatomedin C stimulates damage-repairing protein production in tissues. If you have low levels of growth hormone and somatomedin C, tissues you've damaged from overuse will repair slowly and perhaps incompletely.

In many people, too little thyroid hormone regulation decreases growth hormone and somatomedin C release. Low levels of these hormones in fibromyalgia patients are most likely caused by hypothyroidism or thyroid hormone resistance. (See Chapter 3.12 in *The Metabolic Treatment of Fibromyalgia.*[1])

After you begin taking the proper form and dose of thyroid hormone, your levels of growth hormone and somatomedin C should become normal. Then you'll heal damaged tissues completely and at a normal rate. This is especially true if you get enough protein in your diet, take supplemental glucosamine sulfate, MSM, megadoses of vitamin C, and bromelain. For explanations of these agents and recommended doses, see *Chapter 5*, the section titled "Nutrients and Other Agents to Take for Tissue Damage." (For more information on thyroid hormone, growth hormone, and somatomedin C, see *Chapter 8*, section titled "Note: Thyroid Hormone, Growth Hormone, and Injuries.")

Don't Ride When You Can Walk; Don't Walk When You Can Run

People can enhance their physical conditioning by taking opportunities to stress their bodies throughout the day. (This is *good* stress!) This advice comes from social worker, Alissa Nelson, a former exercise instructor. Taking such opportunities is part of her personal commitment to lifelong physical fitness.

Alissa's fitness-sustaining policy is exemplified by her practice of taking the stairs rather than the elevator. Through this practice, she's able to go about her daily duties in downtown Houston, Texas, and at the same time, reinforce the conditioning of her cardiovascular system and thigh and leg muscles. She also runs and works out at a gym, but even if she didn't, her policy of choosing fitness-sustaining options (like using the stairs instead of the elevator) throughout her day would enable her to maintain some conditioning. This policy gives her momentum in the direction of fitness and health; it can stave off the physical and mental deterioration that accrues from always taking the easiest routes during the day.

We share Alissa's fitness policy. Today, stores that sell similar types of products are often grouped together in shopping communities. Some of these communities, like the computer store community where we often shop, are sprawled over areas as large as city blocks. When we're at this shopping community, we leave our car parked in front of the first store we go to. We walk the rest of the way, often to the most distant store next, walking back to the car when we're done. We're confident this practice contributes to our cardiovascular and metabolic health.

At times, of course, social propriety decrees that we not take the fitness-sustaining option. When walking to lunch and talking with your boss, the best decision might not be to break into a run and leave him or her behind. When escorting a slow-moving grandparent to an office on the tenth floor of a high-rise, decorum dictates that you not insist on taking the stairs rather than the elevator. And, of course, the relaxation from leisurely strolls can contribute to good metabolic health as well. With this allowance, though, and within the boundaries of good taste, never ride when you can walk, never saunter when you can scoot, and never walk when you can run.

Do Exercise You *Will* Do

When deciding what exercises to do, pick those you like doing. If you like particular exercises, you're more likely to do them regularly enough to benefit from them. If you force yourself to do exercises someone else prefers but you don't, you're likely to find them objectionable, and you're not as likely to continue them.

If no exercises in particular appeal to you, recall when you were 10 years old, and think of how you spent your free time. Children are in constant motion and except for doing their homework and chores, they do what they enjoy. Did you ride a bike? Play basketball? Swim? Skate? Thinking about activities you enjoyed then might spark your interest in exercises you can do now that you'd enjoy and that would help you build good metabolic health.

You may have to find an exercise partner other than your spouse, sibling, or best friend—someone else who shares your preference for certain exercises. Or you may have to exercise alone. Regardless, you'll fare best by doing exercises you'll continue doing regularly because you prefer or even enjoy them.

TYPES OF EXERCISE

Each day, patients working to improve their metabolic health should do toning, aerobic, and stretching exercises. They should also use horizontal rest several times each day as a form of exercise. Those with extremely poor physical fitness may make the fastest progress by starting their exercise program in warm water.

Warm Water Exercises

Gravity exerts a more powerful pull on our bodies than we customarily recognize. Consider how the former U.S.S.R.'s Cosmonaut Valeri Ryumin described his landing on earth:

> As we descended farther, the pressure on our bodies mounted. The engine of the soft landing started up, and we hit the ground and turned to one side. The hatch opened and we saw the sky and human faces peeking in. I had lost coordination. My body, arms, and legs were terribly heavy. Dear Earth, how heavy you are, sitting on my shoulders.[128,p.124]

When we do exercises like running, the pull of gravity stresses body structures such as the hips and knee joints. For most people, exercising to tolerance doesn't damage the body. For others, however, exercising under the full force of gravity becomes painful and can cause joint and other tissue damage.

Water enables these other people to exercise without the full pull of gravity on their bodies. The buoyancy of the water softens the pulling force of gravity. Warm water exercises are especially gentle and relaxing. Exercising in water can tone muscles, make joints and connective tissues more flexible, and provide aerobic fitness. To find a water exercise program, phone your local fitness centers, especially those associated with hospitals.

(For a precaution when exercising in swimming pools, see the section named "Chlorine and Bath, Hot Tub, and Swimming Pool Water" in *Chapter 12*.)

Horizontal Rest

Some readers may find it odd that we consider lying down and resting an exercise. They may think of exercise as a way to improve health through mental or physical *exertion*. But improving our health through intentionally *not* exerting ourselves is also exercise—a form in which too few people engage in the United States. Like exercising in water, horizontal rest reduces the stress gravity imposes on our bodies. By reducing gravitational stress, horizontal rest reduces demands made on our metabolism. The reduced demands can contribute to achieving optimal metabolic health.

Getting horizontal and remaining that way, even for a short time, can have dramatic, positive effects. When we're upright, the weight of our bodies compresses our ankle, knee, hip, and spinal joints. Also, ligaments stretch and muscles contract to resist the pull of gravity. Nerve endings in joints, ligaments, and muscles activate, sending volleys of nerve impulses into the spinal cord and brain. Through nerve circuits, the impulses excite parts of the brain that keep us aroused, alert, and thinking at an accelerated pace.[198][199]

When we get horizontal, relax, and rest, much of this brain activity subsides. The subsiding, even for a few minutes, can leave us feeling better. It can also increase how much work we get done in a day. Some companies now recognize the benefits of rest; they encourage workers to refresh themselves by lying down and taking a nap one or more times throughout the work day.

A visit to the clinic of your chiropractic doctor or massage therapist can benefit you in too many ways for us to list here. A benefit relevant here, however, is the relief from gravitational stress on your body and mind as you lie on the doctor's or therapist's treatment table. The chiropractor's or therapist's treatment room is the only place where some people get horizontal rest during the day. The stress-relief, relaxation, and increased energy aren't the only benefits you're likely to get from the visit, but these alone can make the visit worthwhile.

Toning Exercises (Resistance Training)

Toning exercises are essential to optimizing your metabolic health. Increasing your muscle mass increases your metabolic rate. Conversely, losing muscle mass slows your metabolic rate. The typical patient with severely poor metabolic health doesn't have the energy or drive to work her muscles. As a result, her muscles lose mass. As the loss of mass slows her metabolic rate, her metabolic health declines further. If she is to recover her health, she must recover her lost muscle mass.

The definition of resistance training is contracting muscles against resistance. Some examples of resistance training are lifting weights, stretching rubber tubing or bands, and contracting muscles against the resistance of swimming pool water.

Fortunately, most of our patients require only guidance and encouragement to begin using toning exercises. Most must start with small steps, as we've described above. But as proper diet, nutritional supplements, and hormone balancing increase their energy levels, the patients are soon able to steadily increase the intensity of their toning exercises. You may have to start with the smallest of possible baby steps. No matter where you start, however, you *must* start and persist. Only by obtaining enough muscle mass through toning exercises will you eventually achieve metabolic health.

Posture and Toning Exercises. Many patients with poor metabolic health have too little strength to maintain good posture. By chronically slumping, the muscles needed to maintain good posture gradually weaken. Then, muscle weakness and low energy work in concert to keep the patient in a slumped posture.

Slumped posture is common among hypothyroid and thyroid hormone resistant patients with a diagnosis of fibromyalgia. They have a "flexed" posture. The typical patient's head juts forward, her upper back is humped, her shoulders drop forward, and her low back is swayed. Renowned chiropractic physician and rehabilitation expert Dr. Craig Leibenson recently explained the harmful effects: "Conditions such as headache, jaw pain, neck pain, shoulder pain, numbness or tingling in the arms or hands, or shoulder blade pain can all arise without any injury, yet be due to cumulative factors associated with the repetitive strain of poor posture."[165]

When the slumped posture of fibromyalgia patients was improved with training, tender points of 94% of patients became less tender.[163] Improved tenderness is only one possible benefit from improving slumped posture. Improved posture also reduces muscle tension. The reduced tension relieves an energy drain that can worsen poor metabolic health. The reduced tension also decreases brain-bombarding nerve impulses from tight muscles, strained joints, and stressed tendons and ligaments. Adopting good posture, as Dr. Leibenson explained, can improve or eliminate a host of ailments caused by slumped posture.[165]

Some people's posture is slumped because they inherited abnormal spinal structure. Some, for example, inherited "scoliosis," a sideways curvature of the spine. Others inherited a short leg, which also causes sideways curvatures of the spine. Still others inherited severely swayed low back or humped upper back. These people can't completely correct these abnormalities. They fare best when they are under regular care of practitioners who specialize in treating patients with these disorders. Such practitioners include chiropractors, naprapaths, physiatrists, myofascial trigger point therapists, massage therapists, physical therapists, occupational therapists, and in some countries, osteopaths.

Other people have slumped posture simply because of their neglect to practice "good" posture. Many of them can improve their posture by awareness of the need to do so, and then with conscious practice.

As we mentioned at the beginning of this section, still other people have slumped posture because of slow metabolism. They are simply too fatigued to resist the relentless pull of gravity when they are sitting or standing. The fatigue that promotes slumped posture may result from one or more causes: unwholesome diet, nutritional deficiencies, poor physical fitness, adrenal insufficiency, and hypothyroidism or thyroid hormone resistance.

Our studies and others show that about 90% of patients with a diagnosis of fibromyalgia have hypothyroidism and/or thyroid hormone resistance.[161][162] Many of these patients have too little strength to hold themselves erect. After patients begin metabolic rehab (including the proper form and dosage of thyroid hormone), most are soon able to hold an erect posture.

For many patients, correcting all the causes of slow metabolism, fatigue, and weakness isn't enough to regain an erect posture. Some will require professional guidance in rehabilitating their posture muscles and realigning their spines. Many patients, however, can retrain themselves to have good posture. Three exercises Dr. Craig Leibenson recently described will help them do so. The exercises are for improving or correcting slumped posture.[165] They are simple and require no equipment other than a mirror and a stool or chair.

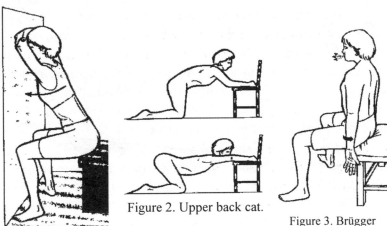

Figure 2. Upper back cat.

Figure 1. Wall lean.

Figure 3. Brügger relief position.

© Reprinted from *The Journal of Bodywork and Movement Therapies*, vol.5, no.2., Craig Leibenson, D.C., "Self-treatment of the slump posture," pages 99-100, 2001, by permission of the publisher Churchill Livingston.

Figure 1. Wall lean. Starting position, five steps:
  1. sit on the edge of a chair with your feet turned slightly out
  2. fold your arms, prop them against the wall, and lean forward
  3. make sure the chair is far enough away from the wall so that as you lean, your mid-back can fall toward the wall
  4. keep your chin slightly tucked in
  5. avoid shrugging your shoulders

When you're in the proper position, breathe in deeply. Notice that your mid-back rounds slightly. Next, let the breath go while you let your breast bone collapse toward the wall. Finally, when you're almost out of breath, actively exhale or cough to bring your chest even closer to the wall.

Figure 2. Upper back cat. Starting position, four steps:
  1. kneel on a carpeted floor facing a chair
  2. place your forearms on the seat of the chair
  3. move your knees away from the chair until your hips are directly above your knees
  4. bend your elbows slightly without pushing your arms into the chair

Begin the upper back cat exercise by rounding your back up. After a moment, let your back fall towards the floor. As you do, allow your head and neck to follow the movement and extend back slightly. You should feel the movement in your mid-back, especially when you let your back fall towards the floor.

Figure 3. Brügger relief position. Starting position, four steps:
  1. sit at the edge of a chair
  2. place your feet on the floor further apart than your hips

3. turn your feet out slightly

4. tuck your chin in slightly

To perform the exercise, first breathe deeply into your abdomen. Then exhale actively while you make two movements: Turn your palms out with your fingers extended and raise your breastbone slightly. Dr. Leibenson recommends two to three repetitions of the Brügger relief position at each exercise session. He also advises patients to do the exercise every 20-to-30 minutes when they're sitting for prolonged times.

Keep in mind that what you want to accomplish with these exercises is to strengthen postural muscles so that it's easier for you to stand and sit corrrectly. To accomplish this, you must do the exercises several times each day. Doing the exercises occasionally or even once each day won't help much. You will know when you're doing these exercises often enough: You'll find it easier and even enjoyable to stand or sit up straight.

It's important, of course, that before you begin doing the exercises, you make sure they won't worsen any health problem you have. If you're not certain, be sure to talk with your health care practitioner before deciding to do them.

Right now, you may have low energy and weak muscles from conditions such as untreated hypothyroidism or nutritional deficiencies. If so, you may have to correct these before you get the best results from postural exercises. Despite this, you shouldn't wait for thyroid hormone or nutritional treatment to give you enough energy and strength to maintain good posture. You may not be able to do a lot of repetitions, but you should start the exercises anyway—taking care to exercise *to tolerance*. You will probably see some benefit from the exercises shortly after you start using them. When your metabolism begins to increase with metabolic rehab, however, you're likely to find that the exercises become much easier and the results much more satisfying.

(For extensive coverage of posture in relation to metabolism, see *The Metabolic Treatment of Fibromyalgia*, pages 607-618.)

Aerobics

The word "aerobics" scares some patients because the term to them means *extreme* exertion. They find this objectionable because they know or fear that the exertion will worsen their symptoms for days or maybe weeks.

"Aerobic" refers to the fact that your body uses oxygen during an activity. Aerobic exercise improves the blood's delivery of oxygen to tissues, and it improves the use of oxygen by cells. By doing so, aerobic exercise has a wide variety of health benefits. This form of exercise is crucial to our cardiovascular and metabolic health. It helps our bodies burn fats such as cholesterol and triglycerides. It also helps prevent breast cancer,[95] and it lessens anxiety and depression. By increasing blood flow to the brain, aerobic exercise can improve memory and concentration and enhance our general sense of well-being.

For aerobic exercise to be beneficial, you must exert yourself enough to increase your heart rate above your usual resting rate by a certain percentage, depending on your age. This is called your "target heart rate." (See Covert Bailey's book, *Fit or Fat*, or most any other book on exercise.) To be able to push yourself to achieve this rate, you'll need to gradually increase your aerobic fitness. If you're just beginning to use aerobic exercise, pace yourself; always being careful to exercise to your own tolerance.

Walking. Walking is a superb way to start moving more and to increase your aerobic and metabolic conditioning. Since walking is a weight-bearing activity, it can also increase the density of some bones. But the benefits of walking aren't limited to conditioning and bone-building. Walking can be a good way to watch the seasons change, meet neighbors, or socialize with friends. On the other hand, when you're overwrought by responsibilities and interactions with others, walking can be quality time alone.

You can walk as leisurely or as briskly as your tolerance allows, gradually increasing your walking time and distance. As we mentioned earlier, you can get small but valuable amounts of conditioning by taking opportunities to walk even a little more. You can, for example, park further from the door of the grocery store or take the stairs instead of the elevator.

All you need for walking is a good pair of shoes and a safe place to walk. People who don't feel safe in their neighborhoods can go to shopping malls to walk. When we're traveling and can't find walking trails, we often walk briskly around inside a large grocery or department store. At home, we routinely ride bicycles fairly long distances when walking doesn't meet our need for aerobic exercise. But when conditions of traveling have forced us to be sedentary for several days, a brisk walk—even inside a store—relaxes, refreshes, and energizes us.

Running. Compared to walking, running provides more cardiovascular conditioning, more metabolic capacity, and higher gain in bone density. You don't have to run great distances or lengths of time to obtain health benefits. Researchers found, for example, that only 60 seconds of running activated "osteoblasts," the cells that thicken bone.

Bicycling. Bicycling is an excellent aerobic exercise. It tones the muscles of the legs, thighs, hips, and buttocks. It provides cardiovascular and metabolic conditioning that equals that of walking and running. An advantage of bicycling is that it imposes less stress on hips, knees, and ankles than does walking or running. A drawback is that weight-bearing during bicycling is less than in walking or running. Because of this, bicycling has less potential for increasing bone density.

You can travel faster and further on a bicycle than by walking or running. (Our preference in aerobic exercise is probably obvious by now!) If you have time, you can pack a picnic and a book and make an afternoon of it. If you choose to ride a bicycle, you should wear a helmet and abide by the safety rules of the road. We know bicyclists who've paid a dear price for not doing so. Some people leave their cars at home and ride their bicycles to work or school or to run errands—a choice on their part that contributes not only to their health but also to the quality of our environment.

Stretching

Whenever our cat, Geno, wakes up—and this happens many times during the day and night—the first thing he does is stretch. Humans don't have the lithe anatomy that makes cats so limber; our anatomy is more rigid. But we could be far more limber and relaxed by mimicking the stretching schedule of cats.

Muscles naturally shorten as we sleep or rest. This is called "nocturnal" shortening. Most patients with thyroid hormone deficiency or resistance already have shortened muscles from a muscle energy deficiency. Additional nocturnal shortening causes these patients to be extremely stiff when they wake up, and some patients loosen up only after several hours. This stiffness is common among patients beginning metabolic rehab. The proper form and dose of thyroid hormone will eventually relieve their morning stiffness. (See *The Metabolic Treatment of Fibromyalgia*, pages 735-743.) But until that happens, we encourage patients to use hot showers or baths. Then while their bodies are still warm, they can gently stretch until their muscles are comfortably loose.

Stretching is important for several reasons. First, it can take pressure off body structures caused by tight muscles and ligaments. The pressure-relief can reduce or stop aches and pains. This can be especially useful after sleeping. Some people wake up and take pain-killers to reduce body discomforts. Often, stretching can accomplish the same thing but more completely, and it helps us avoid taking pain-killers like NSAIDS. The painkillers can cause stomach and intestinal bleeding and kidney damage, and the death rate from these effects is enormous. Whenever you relieve aches and pains by stretching, you also relieve the desire to take pain-killing drugs.

Be sure to stretch gently before, during, and after other exercises. When you've been immobile for a time, as when you've been sitting watching television, your muscles may be "cold" from inactivity. At these times, it's especially important to stretch gently before beginning other exercises. This will help you avoid tearing tissues. If your muscles tighten during an exercise, take time out to gently stretch them. When you resume the exercise, you'll be able to perform better and you'll be less prone to injury. You can also avoid muscle soreness by taking time to stretch after an exercise.

Yoga. Yoga is perhaps the oldest form of "exercise to tolerance," and is the traditional mainstay of the discipline of systematic stretching. For the most part, other stretching programs are offshoots of yoga.

The systematic stretching of your body that yoga encourages can benefit you in many ways. It can keep you flexible, free from muscle tension, mentally calm, and more in touch with your body. By reducing the tension of your muscles and connective tissues, the practice of yoga can also improve the circulation of blood and lymph through your skin and internal organs.

The mental benefits of yoga can be remarkable. Absence of the discomfort of excess muscle and connective tissue tension is remarkable enough. But concentrating on your body while you execute the yoga positions can calm you and produce a state of mind that's hard to describe because of its less-than-tangible nature.

For those striving for optimal metabolic health, the practice of yoga can decrease metabolic demand. The decreased demand comes partly from relaxing your muscles. When tense, muscles expend an enormous amount of energy that metabolic activity must constantly replenish. Relaxing your muscles reduces the amount of energy they require.

Caution

If you take an exercise class, don't feel intimidated by other students or the instructor. Tell your instructor you're going to pace yourself for your individual fitness level and you may not keep up with the class at first. You should pace yourself even if you start with a beginner class. If an instructor tries to bully you into keeping up with the class, find a class with a different instructor. We congratulate you for starting an exercise program of any kind—you should feel very good about yourself for doing so!

Chapter 11

A Good Night's—or Day's—Sleep

FAR MORE TIMES THAN WE can count, we've heard hypometabolic patients plead, "I'd give anything for a good night's sleep!" They go on: "I don't sleep well at all, and I'm still tired when I get up. I'm tired all day long, and I even fall asleep through the day."

These patients have insomnia, an inability to get enough sleep to feel rested and restored. Insomnia can involve trouble falling asleep, staying asleep, or waking too early.

Insomnia is also called sleeplessness and unrestful or non-restorative sleep. No matter what term we use, however, patients with insomnia don't get enough sleep—or enough good quality sleep—to feel rested.

Insomnia is a problem for about a third of the population in industrialized countries. The problem is so widespread and troublesome that many hospitals now have sleep clinics. In the clinics, sleep-study (polysomnographic) technologists use high-tech methods to find the causes of patients' insomnia.

HARM FROM TOO LITTLE RESTFUL SLEEP

During sleep, our bodies heal from physical traumas and our psyches heal from emotional ones. Heart and respiratory rates slow down, and blood pressure decreases. With deep sleep that's prolonged enough, we awaken energized and ready to meet the day. The benefits of enough sleep are so substantial that some businesses now allow their employees to take short naps during the day. The companies allow this—in fact, encourage it—because the naps increase employees' productivity.

The aftereffects of too little deep sleep can, of course, be unpleasant and troubling. We may wake up fatigued, achy, headachy, cranky, and stiff. And during the day, we may be forgetful and have a hard time concentrating on any task at hand.

Psychologist Joan Borysenko cited some harmful effects of insomnia. She wrote, "The indirect costs in terms of decreased ability to function and to solve problems, as well as absenteeism, make insomnia an economic issue as well as a pressing personal problem." She also wrote that some 200,000 sleepy drivers in the U.S. have car wrecks each year, and it was excessive sleepiness that led to the nuclear meltdown at Three Mile Island. "Most of us," she went on, "have experienced the personal kind of meltdown that poor sleep causes. It lessens appreciation for life, interferes with relationships, and is linked to poor health."[215,p.48]

The day after we sleep poorly can be quite unpleasant. In 1967, researchers reported what people experienced after electric shocks disrupted their deeper stages of sleep. The people "became physically uncomfortable, withdrawn, less aggressive, and manifested concern over vague physical complaints and changes in bodily feelings."[238]

In other studies in the mid-1970s, students had similar unpleasant effects from too little deep sleep. Canadian psychiatrist Harvey Moldofsky disrupted the sleep of healthy college students with 20-second bursts of sound. The day after their disrupted sleep, the students complained of several symptoms that could have led to a diagnosis of fibromyalgia: unpleasant mood, tender points in their tendons and muscles, and widespread aches and pains.[239][240]

The students in Moldofsky's studies experienced fibromyalgia-like symptoms only *temporarily*; their symptoms disappeared after they got a good night's sleep—one in which they stayed long enough in the deepest phase of slow-wave sleep called "delta" sleep.[239] Unlike the students, patients to whom we give a diagnosis of fibromyalgia or chronic fatigue syndrome have these symptoms *chronically*. When they don't sleep well, which is often for some, their symptoms worsen.

The unrestful sleep of fibromyalgia patients has led some doctors to conclude that a sleep disorder is the main cause of the patients' symptoms. Recently, Dr. Jacob Teitelbaum came to this conclusion, stating that fibromyalgia is basically a sleep disorder.[287,p.7] He implies by this statement, of course, that disturbed sleep is the cause of fibromyalgia. But this is not true, as we recently explained in the sleep-study technologists' journal.[288] The idea that disturbed sleep is the main cause of fibromyalgia was originally proposed in the mid-1970s by the psychiatrist we mentioned above, Dr. Harvey Moldofsky. But studies debunked the theory, and even Dr. Moldofsky abandoned the idea long ago.

In the section below, we explain how insomnia—although not the cause of fibromyalgia—is a feature of the condition for many patients. And it can worsen the symptoms. Keep in mind that what's true of fibromyalgia regarding unrestful sleep is possibly also true of chronic fatigue syndrome. It's true too for many other patients with hypothyroidism and resistance to thyroid hormone.

INSOMNIA: A FEATURE OF POOR METABOLIC HEALTH THAT CAN WORSEN ITS SYMPTOMS

To understand why many hypometabolic patients have insomnia, we need to know a little about brain wave patterns during sleep. Sleep-study technologists record a patient's electrical brain waves with an instrument called an EEG. The EEG records the waves through electrodes pasted to the sleeping person's head.

Faster Brain Wave Intrusion Into
Slower Waves During Sleep

Sleep that leaves hypometabolic patients feeling unrested often involves an abnormality of brain waves. What recordings reveal is that faster waves (alpha waves) appear too often during the slower waves (delta waves) that occur during deep sleep.

Researchers say that the faster waves "intrude" into the slower ones. The intrusion is extremely important because it shortens the time we spend in slower delta wave sleep. We must get enough delta wave sleep to wake up rested and restored. If brain waves speed up too often to the frequency of alpha waves, we won't wake feeling fully rested and restored.

Metabolic Status

Not getting enough slower wave sleep certainly leaves some people feeling unrested and fatigued. Also, as we said above, the day after experiencing sleep deficient of enough slow waves, some people have fibromyalgia-like symptoms. In studies, people deprived of slow-wave sleep experienced vague physical discomfort, social withdrawal, unpleasant mood, tender points, and widespread aches and pains.[238][239][240] And as we said before, the symptoms of people who already have fibromyalgia become much worse. But, faster wave intrusion into slower waves during sleep isn't the whole story.

Remarkably, people who are athletic and physically fit, and as a result, have high metabolic efficiency, are resistant to the unpleasant effects of too little slow-wave sleep.[240] One of the researchers who found this, Moldofsky again, wrote that the fibromyalgia-like symptoms people developed when deprived of slow-wave sleep didn't result solely from the deprivation; low physical fitness might also have contributed.[240,p.43]

In one of Moldofsky's studies, none of the people studied exercised regularly; they led sedentary lives as students. When deprived of slow-wave sleep, they developed fibromyalgia-like symptoms.

In his previous study,[239,p.349] however, Moldofsky used three people who were "quite physically fit." Two of them ran 3-to-7 miles each day, and they continued to exercise this way during the study. When deprived of slow-wave sleep, these people didn't develop fibromyalgia-like symptoms. Their tender point body sites became even less tender than at the beginning of the study.

Moldofsky noted that in other studies, too little slow-wave sleep didn't cause the people in the studies to develop fibromyalgia-like symptoms. The reason was probably their high physical fitness level: They were "young naval recruits who presumably would be quite physically fit and unlike our sedentary nonathletic university students."[240,p.43]

Moldofsky pointed out that as far back as the 12th century, Maimonides had remarked that sedentary people easily developed fibromyalgia-like symptoms[240,p.43] (although Maimonides, of course, didn't use the term fibromyalgia). Maimonides wrote, "If one leads a sedentary life and does not take exercise, neglects the calls of nature, or is constipated—even if he eats wholesome food and takes care of himself in accordance with medical rules—he will, throughout his life, be subject to aches and pains and his strength will fail him."[314]

Sedentary people today are no different from those who had low physical fitness in Maimonides' day. Ancient and modern sedentary people alike have lower metabolic rates. Because of this, sedentary people have always been more susceptible to developing fibromyalgia-like symptoms—especially when deprived of slow-wave sleep. But physically fit people are more resistant to doing so, even when deprived of slow-wave sleep.

Physical fitness, then, protects us from the troubling effects of too little slow-wave sleep. For good physical fitness to be protective, however, our metabolism must not be impaired by some other factor. Too little thyroid hormone regulation is a powerful factor that does impair metabolism. And in doing so, it can leave even physically fit people susceptible to the unpleasant effects of insomnia.

Sleep Brain Waves of Hypothyroid and Fibromyalgia Patients: The Same

The brain wave patterns of hypothyroid patients[305] show that they are virtually the same as those of fibromyalgia patients.[139][140] [279] And just as many fibromyalgia patients don't sleep well, many hypothyroid patients don't sleep well either.[312][313] In some patients in both groups, faster brain waves disrupt the slower waves during sleep. The result is that patients don't get enough slow-wave sleep to restore them to a fully rested state.

Thyroid Hormone Therapy. When hypothyroid patients with abnormal brain wave patterns during sleep undergo treatment with thyroid hormone, their brain wave patterns become normal.[305] When fibromyalgia patients underwent metabolic rehab including the use of T_3, they recovered from their sleep disturbance.[92][93] [94][188][189] Their normal sleep, after they started to use thyroid hormone, may have resulted in part because their brain wave patterns during sleep became normal, allowing them to get enough slow-wave sleep.

Why Hypometabolic Patients Have Disruption of Sleep

Why would hypometabolic patients have fast-wave intrusion into slow waves during sleep? To understand this, it's helpful to consider that a variety of stimuli can cause the brain wave abnormality.

This wave speed-up can occur in response to electric shock or loud buzzers in sleep clinics.[238][239][240] But, faster wave intrusion into slower waves during sleep is rare among people with chronic insomnia.[308] The intrusion is far more common among patients with pain—in whom the intrusion *can* cause insomnia.

Pain easily disrupts the slower sleep waves with faster ones.[307][310] When researchers induced deep pain in fibromyalgia patients, faster waves intruded into the slower waves.[309] The more severe the fibromyalgia patients' pain, the worse the quality of their sleep,[309][310] presumably because of more severe fast-wave intrusion into the slow waves.

Why, then, does the fibromyalgia patient experience enough pain to disrupt her sleep? Because the typical patient has too little thyroid hormone regulation of the cells of her spinal cord. This causes an increase of a chemical called substance P in the spinal cord.[343][344]

Substance P amplifies sensory impulses that enter the spinal cord from the muscles, joints, and other tissues of the body. And substance P intensifies the transmission of the nerve impulses to the brain stem and brain. As the impulses pass through the brain stem, they whip into motion a network of nerves called the "reticular activating system."[198][199] This network of nerves in turn stirs up the rest of the brain, arousing the person so much that she either can't go to sleep, can't stay asleep long enough, or wakes up too early—in other words, it gives her insomnia.

Increased muscle tension is common in hypothyroid and fibromyalgia patients.[311] So are trigger points in their muscles.[9] Both tense muscles and trigger points send a type of nerve impulse into the spinal cord, brain stem, and brain that's especially unpleasant.[198][199] These nerve impulses produce excess arousal and a generalized state of discomfort. (The impulses serve to mobilize the person to do something to rid herself of the unpleasant stimulus.[103])

We know from many years of clinical experience that relieving patients' muscle tension and inactivating their trigger points can produce extreme sedation. Some patients even go to sleep on the treatment table during their therapy. Patients commonly report that on the night after the physical treatment, they sleep better than they have in years.

Insomnia, then, is *not* the main cause of fibromyalgia patients' symptoms. But it is a problem for many patients with a diagnosis of hypothyroidism, thyroid hormone resistance, fibromyalgia, or chronic fatigue syndrome. Insomnia can worsen the patients' symptoms, and because of that, they should try to improve the quality of their sleep. Below we explain how they can do exactly that.

■ For in-depth coverage of sleep disturbance in hypothyroidism, thyroid hormone resistance, and fibromyalgia, see Chapter 3.18 in *The Metabolic Treatment of Fibromyalgia*, pages 713-730.

HOW TO GET A GOOD NIGHT'S—OR DAY'S—SLEEP

For people with poor metabolic health, what's most important for getting enough good sleep is to acquire normal metabolism.[288] This is true regardless of whether their diagnosis is hypothyroidism, thyroid hormone resistance, fibromyalgia, chronic fatigue syndrome, or one of the other so-called "new diseases" that have sluggish metabolism as their cause.

Until a patient can acquire normal metabolism, however, she may be able to improve her sleep by using a combination of sleep aids. Many factors, of course, can cause insomnia, and even after her metabolism is normal, she may have to occasionally or continually use the sleep aids that work for her. Table 1 includes different aids to try.

Developing Good Sleep Hygiene

Poor sleep hygiene is the practice of sleep habits that cause insomnia and can impair health.[300] Especially disrupting to sleep, for example, is shifting one's work and sleep schedule—from day to night, or the other way around. So is flying across geographical meridians, inducing jet-lag.[299] A low daily level of physical activity can interfere with sleep; without enough activity, we may not be fatigued enough to go to sleep or stay asleep. And using our bed for activities that keep us awake, such as watching television programs, can keep us too alert to fall asleep.

Good sleep hygiene is the practice of sleep habits that foster restful sleep. These habits help our mind-body clock adjust so that we get into a rhythm of being asleep and awake about the same time each 24-hour cycle.[289] Several good sleep hygiene practices can help us acquire a sleep/wake rhythm that enables us to sleep more restfully.

Good sleep hygiene includes exercising to tolerance each day to make us fatigued and sleepy at bedtime. Also, we should try to sleep at roughly the same time in the 24-hour cycle, whether it's during the day or night. It's helpful, too, to sleep in the same room

TABLE 1. LIST OF METHODS TO AID RESTORATIVE SLEEP

Improve sleep hygiene
- Sleep at the same time each night
- Eat nutritious meals and take nutritional supplements

Exercise
- Engage in enough low intensity aerobic, stretching, and muscle-toning exercise each day to contribute to nighttime fatigue
- Avoid vigorous exercise before bedtime

Reduce chemical sleep disruptors
- Avoid caffeine, theobromine, theophylline, and ephedrine for at least 8 hours before bedtime
- Stop smoking cigarettes
- Don't drink alcohol to excess

Reduce psychological sleep disruptors
- Reduce psychological distress or anxiety
- Consider muscle relaxation training, meditation, or listening to relaxation tapes or CDs
- Consider counseling or psychotherapy

Reduce sleep-disturbing physical stimuli
- Get effective treatment for muscle tension, trigger points, and other physical problems
- Learn stretching and self-massage to relax muscles
- Use hot baths and moist heat packs before bed
- Undergo massage therapy, spinal manipulation, and acupuncture regularly
- Use good neck support, such as a buckwheat pillow
- Abstain from eating large meals within 3 hours of bedtime

Reduce sleep-disrupting noises
- Avoid sleeping with someone who snores loudly or sleeps restlessly
- Close windows or use sound-proofing materials to shut out neighborhood noises
- Use earplugs or a white noise generator
- Don't leave the television on while sleeping

Use non-addicting oral agents such as
- L-Tryptophan
- Valerian and passiflora
- Diphenhydramine
- Melatonin
- Small amount of high carbohydrate food before bed

Treat sleep apnea
- Have a sleep study done at a sleep clinic
- Get proper treatment with a CPAP unit or dental appliance if indicated

and bed.

Of course, some activities in bed encourage sleep, and we can consider these good sleep hygiene practices. One such activity for many people is lying in bed and reading. Reading helps them get their minds off sleep-disturbing matters; at the same time, lying down decreases nerve bombardment of the brain from muscles and joints. This enables people to drop off to sleep (see section below titled "Lying Down: Shutting Off the Nerve Bombardment of Your Brain").

A practice that helps many people develop regular sleep times is for them to expose themselves to bright light during their waking hours.[245] During their sleep time, they should make the room dark. This practice can help realign our sleep/wake rhythm so that our sleep shifts to the times we prefer.[300]

For other people, though, trying to sleep in a dark room can *result* in insomnia. A totally dark room causes some people to be anxious; they're usually more comfortable with some light in the room. Their anxiety in a dark room may disrupt their sleep more than light in the room would. They must do what works best for them. But they're more likely to cultivate a good sleep/wake rhythm if they use lighting that's soft, and preferably dim and red. Research subjects were exposed to bright blue or green light for up to five hours. During subsequent sleep, their core temperatures didn't decrease normally, and their melatonin levels didn't rise normally. Exposure to dim or red light didn't have these effects.[346] This finding implies that exposure to dim red light at night, as when one gets out of bed to urinate, isn't as disrupting to sleep as exposure to bright light of other colors.

Avoiding Environmental Sleep-Disrupters

Some people are naturally light sleepers and the least noise can awaken them. If this is true of you, you should make arrangements to prevent sources of noise from awakening you. It may be enough for you to use earplugs that block out high decibel sounds.

But you may also have to take other steps to protect yourself from noise. You may have to sleep in a room away from someone who snores loudly or moves about too much during sleep. If a dog in the neighborhood barks early in the morning and wakes you, you may have to sleep in a room as far away from the dog as you can get. Remove a telephone if it's in the room where you sleep, and if you have a pager, leave it in another room.

If your bedroom is situated so that traffic wakes you, sleep in another room away from traffic sounds. If you can hear the traffic in any bedroom in your dwelling, you may have to change your sleep time so that you're awake and rested before the traffic starts.

Identifying and Treating
Sleep-Disrupting Medical Problems

Problems such as sleep apnea, restless leg syndrome, and periodic limb movement often disrupt sleep. If you suspect you have one of these problems, getting a sleep study done at a sleep clinic is most important.[300] Sleep apnea is usually effectively managed by a CPAP machine, which administers continuous positive airway pressure while the person sleeps. Some drugs, such as the anti-epileptic drug gabapentin, improve restless leg syndrome.[347] And periodic limb movements may be controlled with dopamine drugs.[306]

In considering a sleep study, you might want to start by visiting the website for the National Association of Polysomnographic Technologists: <www.aptweb.org> These are the specialists who conduct sleep studies.

Adopting a Wholesome Diet

A wholesome diet, as we describe in *Chapter 4*, is one that promotes good health; it can also contribute to our getting restful sleep. In one study, poor dietary habits was the lifestyle factor most responsible for people failing to get enough sleep. The people didn't eat often enough, ate at irregular times, snacked on unwholesome foods, seasoned their food too much, and ate too few vegetables.[298] Such study findings make it clear that a wholesome diet is important to good sleep.

Our clinical experience has taught us that patients can improve their sleep through several dietary practices. These practices contribute in different ways to better sleep.

Avoiding Indigestion. To be wholesome, our diet must consist of foods that don't cause indigestion. Which foods cause indigestion is to some degree an individual matter, and you must learn which foods give you trouble and avoid them before bed. You may still choose to continue eating foods that give you indigestion. For some people, the joy from ingesting some offending foods is worth the subsequent indigestion. But if you're intent on improving your sleep, you should abstain from eating these foods within several hours of your bedtime.

You may improve your digestion by following good principles of wholesome eating. In *Chapter 4*, we describe these principles (section titled "Throughly Digesting Proteins: The First Way to Stop or Prevent the Absorption of Dietary Proteins into Your Blood"). They include: relaxing when you eat, focusing on your food, and chewing thoroughly before swallowing. You may also want to take digestive enzymes. (For more on digestive enzymes, see "Protein-Digesting Enzymes and Betaine Hydrochloride" in *Chapter 4*.)

You can also avoid indigestion by not overeating. Overeating can interfere with sleep in several ways. It can cause an uncomfortable sensation of excess fullness in the upper abdomen. It can also cause bloating from the gas that forms from undigested food that has passed into your colon. And if you have gastric reflux, overeating can cause severe upper abdominal and chest pain.

The opposite of eating too much can also disturb sleep. Hunger can interfere with sleep just as much as overeating.

Abstaining From Sugary Foods. Eating sugary foods close to bedtime may cause your blood sugar level to drop a couple of hours later while you're asleep. This can awaken you.

Oddly, some of our patients who have these blood sugar drops during sleep don't realize the cause of their awakenings. They became aware of it only after following a suggestion we give them: keep a high-protein/good-fat food (such as cashew nuts) close at hand while they sleep; if they wake up, promptly eat some of this food. When this enables them to go back to sleep, they realize the role that low blood sugar has played in awakening them.

Of course, we strongly recommend that these patients give up eating sugary foods before bedtime. And except in extreme moderation, they should also give them up at other times during the day.

Low Intake of Foods High in Arachidonic Acid. We encourage patients to reduce their intake of foods that contain the omega-6 fatty acid, arachidonic acid. Our bodies convert arachidonic acid into two chemicals (prostaglandin E2 and leukotrienes B4) that foster inflammation and chronic pain.[291][292]

The heightened pain perception from these chemicals can interfere with sleep. The chemicals may also worsen the chronic pain of hypometabolic patients who have a diagnosis of fibromyalgia.[293] Several commonly-consumed foods are high in arachidonic acid (see *Chapter 4*, section titled "Foods Rich in Arachidonic Acid"). We recommend that people with insomnia eat only small amounts of these foods and only on occasion.

Eating a Complex Carbohydrate Food Before Bed. Eating a small amount of a high carbohydrate food before bed may aid your sleep. This is because carbohydrate foods can increase the level of serotonin in the brain, and the increased serotonin level may improve sleep.[268] Increased serotonin may also reduce anxiety that otherwise might interfere with sleep.

Nutritional Supplements

A number of nutritional supplements can contribute to better quality sleep. These include B complex vitamins, calcium and magnesium, tryptophan, and 5-hydroxytryptophan.

B Complex Vitamins. B vitamin deficiencies can cause nerve and muscle irritability, and the irritability can interfere with sleep. People with even slightly low folic acid levels, for example, may sleep poorly.[9] The sleep of the affected person may be disturbed by restlessness, or by pain from trigger points that form in muscles. Nerve impulses from the trigger points can excessively arouse all areas of the brain, as we described in the above section titled "Why Hypometabolic Patients Have Disruption of Sleep." The brain arousal can cause insomnia and reduce the quality of sleep.[198][199]

Calcium and Magnesium. Calcium and magnesium deficiencies can also cause irritability and excessive activity of nerves and muscles.[200][201] As with B vitamin deficiencies, these mineral deficiencies can make it tough to get restful sleep.

To prevent nutritional deficiencies from interfering with your sleep—as well as slowing your metabolism—you should take a wide array of nutritional supplements. See Table 2 in *Chapter 5* for the supplements and doses we recommend.

Tryptophan and 5-Hydroxytryptophan. Tryptophan is an effective sleep aid, especially for those who have a tryptophan deficiency.[76] A few years ago in the U.S., contaminated tryptophan caused a disease in some users. The FDA used the incident as a pretext to deprive the public of supplemental tryptophan. Presumably, the reason for this action was that U.S. citizens' increasing use of tryptophan threatened the financial profits of pharmaceutical companies that market drugs for sleep.

U.S. citizens who want to use tryptophan now have two choices: they must obtain it illegally, or from foods with a high content, such as turkey. They can also take 5-hydroxytryptophan, the chemical that cells convert to serotonin. It's available over the counter. The dosage range of 5-hydroxytryptophan that patients have found useful for various conditions is 100-to-600 mg.[267,p.296] In one study, 100 mg before bed increased the depth and duration of sleep.[273]

Herbal Sleep Aids

Valerian is the most potent herbal sleep aid; it promotes relaxation, sedation, and sleep. Many herbal sleep-aid products contain valerian. A dosage of 300-to-400 mg taken 30 minutes before bed may make it easier to go to sleep and to sleep more deeply. To read our recommendations for the use of this herb, see the section titled "Valerian Root" in *Chapter 6.*

Other herbs that are mildly sedating are chamomile, hops, passion flower, lemon balm, scullcap, catnip, and the volatile or essential oil of lavender.[267,p.106] Many herbal preparations containing several or all of these herbal sleep-aids are available in health food stores and pharmacies.

If anxiety interferes with your sleep, kava-kava may reduce the anxiety enough to improve your sleep. The herb also reduces restlessness and stress. Please refer to the section titled "Kava-Kava" in *Chapter 6.*

If you're taking prescription drugs such as sleeping pills or tranquilizers, be cautious in using herbal sleep aids at the same time. The herbs may exaggerate the effects of the prescription sleep drugs. If you're thinking of using herbs with a drug, it's best to consult a clinician who is expert in the use of both herbs and drugs for sleep.

Hormones

At least three hormones can potentially aid sleep: thyroid hormone, melatonin, and pregnenolone.

Thyroid Hormone. In this book, we focus mainly on the safe and effective use of thyroid hormone. We wrote above that some untreated hypothyroid patients have unrestful sleep; the slow or delta brain waves during deep sleep too often speed up to the faster alpha waves, and this leaves the patients feeling unrested. Effective thyroid hormone therapy can correct the brain wave speed-up and enable the patients to wake up feeling rested.[305]

Correction of the brain wave/sleep problem may be the means by which thyroid hormone therapy improved the sleep of fibromyalgia patients in our studies.[92][93][94][188][189] Prudent use of the proper form and dose of thyroid hormone will be the most important aid to sleep many patients can use.

Taking Too Much Thyroid Hormone. Taking too much thyroid hormone for her needs can keep a patient from falling asleep easily enough. It can also keep her from sleeping long and deeply enough.

Unfortunately, some doctors are too ready to blame insomnia on patients' use of thyroid hormone. These doctors blame the hormone even when patients are taking so little of it that it couldn't interfere with their sleep.

A patient can, of course, take too much thyroid hormone for her so that it disrupts her sleep. When this happens, the patient must reduce her dose to resume sleeping well.

For various reasons, a patient may take slightly too much thyroid hormone on occasion. If the product she's taking is T_3, and on the next day she reduces the dose, it's likely to disrupt her sleep only for one or perhaps two more nights.

If the product is T_4 or desiccated thyroid, her sleep may be disturbed for more than a week after she reduces her dose. In that case, her doctor can prescribe propranolol for her to take thirty minutes to an hour before bed. For most patients, 20-to-40 mg of propranolol stops overstimulation from thyroid hormone. Some patients must take another dose of propranolol after several hours sleep. If a patient has asthma, however, she definitely shouldn't take propranolol; it can worse asthma symptoms, particularly bronchoconstriction, and it should be avoided.

If you think your insomnia is caused by too much thyroid hormone, use the overstimulation form in the *Forms* section. I (GH-L) designed the form to help patients decide whether or not they are overstimulated. It can help your doctor and you more accurately decide whether your dose is too high. Chances are, if your dose is high enough to disturb your sleep, you're also having some other symptoms of thyroid hormone overstimulation. The form can show this, and we recommend that you use it.

Melatonin. Melatonin is a hormone secreted by the pineal gland in the brain; this gland regulates body rhythms. As we age, our production of melatonin declines, and reduced amounts in our bodies can make it more difficult to sleep.

Taking supplemental melatonin can improve sleep in both young[271] and elderly people.[272] The dose of melatonin that works for most people is 1-to-3 mg, 1½-to-2 hours before bed.[267,p.106]

Pregnenolone. Pregnenolone improved sleep in healthy men ages 20-to-30. The quality of their sleep improved and they had less intermittent waking during the night.[294]

The hormone may have improved the men's sleep by reducing anxiety. Patients with generalized anxiety[315] and generalized social phobia[316] had lower blood pregnenolone levels. It's possible that taking pregnenolone will reduce some people's anxiety, and by doing so, improve their sleep. (For our recommendations on the use of pregnenolone, see *Chapter 8*, section titled "Pregnenolone.")

Female Sex Hormones. When a woman is experiencing perimenopause or menopause, she is often awakened by hot flushes and throws off her bedcovers to cool off. As her perspiration evaporates from her skin, she cools down. If in the meantime, she's gone back to sleep, she may wake up again because she's too cold.

Balancing sex hormones during these phases of the woman's life often helps her to sleep better. See *Chapter 9.*

Cortisol. Low function of the outer layers (cortices) of the adrenal glands can cause the blood level of cortisol to be too low. A low cortisol level causes some people to be more sensitive to noises. If the person is a light sleeper already, her heightened sensitivity to noise from the low cortisol can cause insomnia. If this is a possibility for you, you should consult a doctor experienced in treating cortisol deficiency, often called adrenal hypofunction. See *Chapter 8.*

Cigarettes

Some of the chemicals in cigarette smoke tend to disrupt sleep, and insomnia is more common among smokers than nonsmokers.[270] Of course, the health benefits of giving up cigarette smoking extend far beyond improved sleep.

Relaxation and Stress Reduction

You can most likely improve your sleep by using relaxation techniques. I (GH-L) strongly advise patients to read *The Relaxation Response*[295] by Dr. Herbert Benson and use the techniques he describes in the book. I've taught many patients to use these techniques, and most people can learn them by reading about them and practicing them. Many people have initially felt frustrated by the fact that the first few times they begin to practice this, or any other meditative technique, they do not easily fall into a relaxed state. It takes regular practice, just like any other new skill.

Meditation is another useful way to relax. And relaxing is only one of the benefits to be gained from meditating. We strongly encourage patients to begin practicing meditation techniques.

When you're ready to go to sleep, rather than counting sheep, focus on relaxing your body. Feel your head, neck, back, arms, abdomen, pelvis, thighs, legs, and feet against the bed. Note any areas of tension and let them go. It's likely that when you take note, you'll find that your head isn't completely at rest on the pillow—instead, muscles are holding it up at least slightly. Let your head go completely and feel what it's like to fully rest it on your pillow. Feel the bed support your body.

Also focus on your face. Most likely, you'll find some areas where the muscles are tense. (Don't intentionally tighten a muscle even more when you find one that's tense. Some people advise this, but we do not.) Purposefully let the tension go, and feel the difference when it's suddenly gone. That feeling is relaxation.

Hot Baths. Lininger and coauthors recommend a 15-to-20-minute hot Epsom salts bath before bed. They wrote that the magnesium sulfate in Epsom salts acts as a muscle relaxant.[267,p.105] Hot water itself is a potent sedative. (It was used to tranquilize agitated psychiatric patients before the advent of powerful chemical tranquilizers.) And, drinking a cup of chamomile tea can enhance the sedation from the hot bath.

Lying down in the hot bath will also help you relax. Lying horizontally reduces the bombardment of your brain by nerve impulses from your spine, joints, muscles, and tendons. (See section titled "Flexed Posture" in Chapter 3.11 in *The Metabolic Treatment of Fibromyalgia*.[1,pp.612-615]) See the section below titled "Lying Down: Shutting Off the Nerve Bombardment of Your Brain."

Emotional and Psychological Issues. When you have emotionally charged issues to deal with, say with your spouse or a child, take care of them as early in the day as possible. Dealing with such issues too close to bedtime can intensely disrupt sleep.

If you use methods such as those above but still don't feel you're relaxing enough, you might consider a course of psychotherapy or counseling. Psychotherapy and counseling may help you resolve or deal better with personal matters you're disturbed about. By choosing this option, you can help reduce the stress, discontent, or inner turmoil that's interfering with your sleep.[269]

Some people have insomnia from the fear that they won't be able to go to sleep.[299] With professional help, they may be able to overcome the fear. The importance of getting professional help for poor sleep related to psychological or emotional causes can't be overemphasized. Insomnia is most common among people who are divorced, separated, widowed, unemployed, or have a very low income.[299] The adverse effects of too little restful sleep can make it tougher for these people to cope with the psychological effects of their life circumstances.

The suggestion that psychotherapy or counseling may help you is not an implication that you're mentally or emotionally ill. These services are certainly valuable when any of us have an emotional crisis. But perhaps for most people nowadays, psychological services aren't solely a way to deal with crises. Taking advantage of them has become a way to personal growth, and also allows us to tweak practical aspects of our lives—like improving our sleep.

Exercise to Tolerance

Life in Western civilization and competition in the workplace leave many people stressed, anxious, and depressed. And as we said at the outset, about 30% have trouble sleeping.

Exercise is a highly effective antidote to the sleep-disturbing effects of modern society. Not only does exercise counter the effects of stress, it has other health benefits, too. To be effective in helping you relax, your exercise should meet several criteria: It should be noncompetitive, of moderate intensity, and done in pleasant surroundings.[303] (See *Chapter 10* for more on exercise to tolerance.) Your exercise should be an activity that you enjoy—if it's not, you probably won't do it consistently.

Lying Down: Shutting Off the
Nerve Bombardment of Your Brain

Eminent medical physiologist Author Guyton wrote that when we're standing, we're resisting gravity. To effectively resist it and not crumple to the ground, some of our muscles must stay contracted and others must contract over-and-over again. The muscles, working in synchrony with our tendons and ligaments, act like guy wires to keep us erect.

Similar muscle contractions occur when we sit without a backrest, especially if we lean slightly forward, as over a computer keyboard. Back muscles work vigorously to hold us in this upright posture. When we're upright, we're usually using our hands, arms, and legs to carry out the activities of living.

The muscle contractions cause nerve impulses to bombard our spinal cord and brain. The nerve impulses come up through the brain stem. There, some of the impulses pass to a structure called the reticular activating system. As its name implies, when stimulated, it activates the rest of the brain. The activating effect can make it impossible to go to sleep. (This commonly occurs in patients with myofascial trigger points.[198][199] Until their trigger points are effectively treated, they may fail to get restorative sleep. From their poor sleep, they may develop fibromyalgia-like symptoms.[296])

From the brain stem, the nerve impulses reach a structure called the thalamus. The thalamus sorts and transmits the impulses to all parts of the brain. One part is the cerebral cortex. This is the place where we experience awareness and formulate thoughts. Another part is the limbic system that sits lower in the brain. This area gives rise to emotion and motivation.

Heavy and prolonged bombardment of these parts of the brain by nerve impulses can be harmful. Aside from disrupting our sleep, the bombardment can cause highly unpleasant thoughts and feelings.[198][199] When we lie down long enough, however, the impulses reaching the brain settle down. If they settle down enough, the brain stem activating system, the cortex, and the limbic system all calm down. This partly explains why most people gradually become sleepy when they lie in bed for a time, as when they read for a while. The effects on our thoughts and feelings can be soothing and pleasant.

Merely lying down for a time can serve as a sleep aid. In this practice, you simply lie for a while and wait for sleep to come. Some people have trouble lying down long enough for nerve signals to subside unless they have something to distract them from thoughts that reverberate in their minds. For some, reading works. For others, listening to the radio, mellow music, or environmental sounds (such as waves on a beach) works just as well.

We recommend that you adopt the practice of lying down one or two times throughout the day. When you lie down, mentally scan your body looking for tense muscles. When you find them— and you definitely will—relax them. This will increase your chances of fully benefitting from lying down.

You may find that lying in bed for a while doesn't relax you enough to sleep. And you may find that consciously relaxing your muscles doesn't help much either. If so, you may be able to relax more by undergoing physical treatment.

Clinicians Who Provide Physical Treatment

Sleep can still be elusive for people whose muscle tension is so intense that lying a prolonged time doesn't shut off nerve bombardment of their brain. For these people, physical treatment can remarkably improve their ability to relax and sleep. Some of the most enthusiastic reports we've heard from patients about improved sleep have come after we treated them for trigger points and vertebral subluxations.

In one study, fibromyalgia patients reported that chiropractic physicians and massage therapists best provided them with palliative relief.[139] These clinicians provide patients with relief partly by correcting spinal problems or reducing muscle tension that can interfere with sleep. But other clinicians such as certified myofascial trigger point therapists, physical therapists, occupational therapists, naprapaths, and naturopathic physicians can also provide helpful physical treatment.

Ask your clinician to help you find whatever physical problem is keeping you from relaxing enough. If the clinician treats you effectively for the problem, you should relax more when lying down even after the first treatment.

Caffeine and Sleep

Using caffeine prudently can actually be a sleep aid. For example, caffeine can improve mental function so that we're able to work more efficiently and accomplish more during our work days. The satisfaction from having a highly productive day or from completing an important project, aided by the wise use of caffeine, may relax us enough at bedtime to get high quality sleep. But to get such a positive effect from the use of caffeine, we emphasize that you must use it wisely.

In her recent book, *Inner Peace for Busy People*, Joan Borysenko, Ph.D. wrote , "As a society, we are out of rhythm. We were meant to go to sleep when it's dark and to awaken with the dawn.

Yet," she continued, "even with the advent of the electric light, most of us have managed to get our rest."[215,p.49]

But some individuals who'd otherwise get their rest, don't because they use caffeine improperly. "Energy tends to cycle down in the afternoon after lunch," Dr. Borysenko wrote. "Rather than taking a refreshing nap, most of us are more likely to reach for a cup of coffee. Ignoring the body's signals that it's time for rest, we just keep on keeping on. The result is that natural, cyclic patterns of wakefulness and drowsiness get flattened out. As a scientist, my guess, which is properly called a hypothesis, is that disorder in these subtle daytime rhythms contributes to sleep disturbances at night."[215,p.49]

Most people don't have adverse reactions to the *proper* use of caffeine, and we teach most of our patients to use caffeine properly—that is, to augment their metabolic health (see *Chapter 14*). We have a few rules for the proper use of caffeine: First, use enough of it but not too much. Second, don't use it so close to bedtime that it interferes with your sleep. Third, if you don't tolerate it well, please don't use it at all.

It's a good idea not to consume caffeine for eight hours or so before you intend to go to sleep. Researchers tell us that on average, our bodies eliminate about 50% of caffeine in five hours. Avoiding caffeine for an extra three hours or so will eliminate more from your body; this will decrease the chance that it will interfere with your sleep.

Keep in mind that coffee isn't the only source of caffeine. Black and green teas, chocolate, cocoa, soft drinks, and many over-the-counter medicines contain caffeine. Chocolate also contains two other caffeine-like stimulating chemicals, theobromine and theophylline. These, too, can disturb sleep. For several hours before bed, you should also avoid ephedrine or pseudoephedrine. These are ingredients in some over-the-counter asthma and cold medicines.

For some people—probably rare ones—the stimulating effects

of caffeine may last up to 20 hours.[266] These individuals' sleep at night may be disturbed even by caffeine ingested in the morning.[267]

We advise patients to use just enough caffeine soon after waking up so that it *gently* bolsters their mental sharpness, sense of well-being, and drive. But we caution them to use it sparingly enough so as not to dim their awareness of the drowsiness that signals the need for a nap. As Dr. Borysenko wrote: "Listen to your body. When you're tired, take a nap or try a short meditation, which can be equally restorative. Hang some sort of *Do Not Disturb* sign on your door. *Genius at Work* might do nicely. And it's the truth. Getting in tune with your body's natural rhythms will make you more creative, productive, and peaceful. Napping awakens the genius within."[215,pp.49-50]

Two Constructive Ways of Using Caffeine. Some people use caffeine to extend the time they're alert. I (GH-L) use it this way. I have a fairly regular sleep pattern: I go to sleep late in the evening and I wake up early in the morning. When I'm tired in the early evening, I don't want to go to sleep then. Doing so might disrupt my sleep/wake pattern.

So, in the early evening, when my energy is low, and I still have a significant amount of work to do, I drink organic coffee to give me a lift. The lift is enough for me to do mental work up until the late evening when I get tired and go to sleep. I'm not overly sensitive to caffeine and it doesn't disturb my sleep pattern.

I (JCL), on the other hand, have a fairly irregular sleep pattern. Sometimes I sleep during the night and work during the day. At other times, I sleep during the day and work through the night. I especially do this when I'm working on a long or difficult writing project. For my writing and research, I have to have a sharp mental edge.

Sleeping deeply and long enough gives me that edge during my work hours. Ingesting caffeine when I get up sharpens my mental edge even more. I sometimes drink organic coffee, but more often,

I take caffeine pills. The pills allow me to take a carefully measured amount of caffeine—usually 100 mg, sometimes 150 mg. This makes my mental processes far more efficient. When I get tired, I don't take caffeine. Doing so would keep me awake, but my dull mental edge would persist. Only sleep sharpens it again, so I go to sleep.

Drugs as Sleep Aids

Getting restful sleep in natural ways is an excellent goal. But at times, nothing natural does the job. At those times, people can get some decent sleep by using a drug *wisely*. This is better than not getting sleep at all.

In using some drugs to get better sleep, people make a trade-off with potential side effects. But when they are struggling with sleep that's not restful, we think it's acceptable to use whatever means they must to break the cycle of poor sleep. Ideally, of course, metabolic rehab will improve sleep enough to eliminate the need to use drugs as sleep aids.

Diphenhydramine. For many people, diphenhydramine is an effective sleep aid. Diphenhydramine is the active ingredient in Benadryl and over-the-counter sleep aids such as Nytol. It's non-addicting and has a short half-life, so you won't wake up feeling groggy if you use a dose that's effective, but not excessive, for you. People's sensitivity to diphenhydramine differs, so experiment to find if the drug works for you and how much you need. First, try 25 mg. If that dose doesn't work for you, increase it to 50 mg. If you wake up in the middle of the night, take another dose that's effective for you.

Hypnotics. Hypnotics such as Ambien or Zolpidem work well for inducing sleep. They are especially useful for sporadic and brief insomnia, as when unusual circumstances make it hard for you to go to sleep. (See "Special Circumstances" below.) The half-life of Ambien is short. Because of this, the drug usually doesn't leave people feeling drowsy. Also, drug dependence is less a problem than with benezodiazepines such as Xanax. Because of their longer half-life, drugs such as Xanax are more likely to produce grogginess after waking.[301][304]

Hypnotic drugs help initiate and maintain sleep, and they reduce daytime tiredness. But they don't provide restorative sleep or reduce pain. Except for thyroid hormone,[305] no available drug improves the sleep disrupting intrusion of faster brain waves into slower ones during sleep.[289]

For more information on Ambien and Zolpidem, see *The Metabolic Treatment of Fibromyalgia*, Chapter 5.1, page 911, section titled "Ambien (Zolpidem)."

Beta-Blockers. Propranolol and other beta-blockers may help patients sleep better when anxiety disrupts their sleep. Using propranolol on an as-needed basis is harmless for most people. When used properly, it's so harmless that we can't figure why it's on the prescription list in the U.S.

However, taking large amounts of propranolol, especially at intervals throughout the day, carries a risk. It may produce symptoms remarkably similar to those of hypothyroidism and fibromyalgia.[297]

Antidepressants as Sleep Aids. For some patients, taking an antidepressant is necessary to alleviate depression. We always recommend, however, that patients first try other therapies that have powerful antidepressant effects, such as exercise, nutritional supplements, and thyroid hormone.

We don't think it's wise for any patients to use tricylic antidepressants as sleep aids, but especially if the patients have a diagnosis of fibromyalgia.[1] The potential for adverse effects from these drugs make them a poor choice compared to other sleep aids. If hypothyroidism or thyroid hormone resistance is the cause of a patient's poor sleep, it seems irresponsible to use antidepressants to merely improve the patient's sleep when there are better choices of medications.

A high-profile rheumatology fibromyalgia researcher named I.

Jon Russell promotes the use of amitriptyline to improve fibromy-algia patients' sleep.[282] And Dr. Moldofsky, whom we mentioned before, appears to agree. He wrote that in improving sleep, tricyclic drugs, such as amitriptyline and cyclobenzaprine, may provide fibromyalgia patients long-term benefit.[289] Their viewpoint would seem to be supported by an analysis of nine studies of antidepressants as fibromyalgia treatments. The analysis suggested that improved sleep quality was the main benefit fibromyalgia patients got from using the drugs.

The improvement from using tricyclic drugs, however, was minimal.[277] In one study, the drug didn't improve the abnormal brain wave pattern that 36% of fibromyalgia patients had. The drug improved patients' sleep quality by only 25%.[279] Other researchers reported that neither amitriptyline nor Prozac enabled fibromyalgia patients to wake up feeling rested.[280] And in another study, amitriptyline as the only treatment actually worsened patients' fibromyalgia symptoms.[278]

Dr. Russell also recommends the use of cyclobenzaprine (Flexeril) as a sleep aid for fibromyalgia patients. In one study, though, more patients quit using the drug because of adverse effects than benefitted from its use: only 12% of patients using the drug had slight and brief improvement, but 13% quit taking it because of noxious effects.[283][284] This track record for the drug leaves one wondering why Dr. Russell would continue advising patients to use the drug.

Potential Harm From Use of Antidepressants. Patients would do well to consider some of the potential harmful effects from antidepressants. Some of the adverse effects are merely annoying to some patients. For example, amitriptyline can cause dry mouth, digestive symptoms, vertigo, and "neuro-psychic symptoms."[281] Far worse, however, is the potential of antidepressants to increase the risk of death. They can do so by adverse effects on the heart, and by increasing the incidence of some cancers.

Antidepressants can alter heart rate and blood pressure,[330] and they can induce or worsen abnormal electrical rhythms of the heart (arrhythmias).[329][333] Tricyclic antidepressants can cause low blood pressure, especially in patients with ischemic heart disease.[332] They also make it more likely that a patient will die after a heart attack.[331] The use of Prozac and amitriptyline have been associated with death.[334] Because of these potential adverse effects, it's important for doctors to monitor the blood pressure, heart rate, and EKG of patients taking antidepressants—especially elderly patients and those who have cardiac disorders.[330] Fibromyalgia patients are generally deconditioned, and this makes many of them highly vulnerable to harmful cardiac effects from antidepressants.

Studies have revealed an association between the use of amitriptyline and liver cancer in humans.[327] In a recent study of some 40,000 patients, researchers found more lymphoma among patients who took tricyclic antidepressants.[326] In lymphoma, tumors that are usually malignant appear in tissues such as lymph nodes and the spleen. The tumors may invade the blood and develop into leukemia. Prozac (fluoxetine) and amitriptyline have been linked to a benign skin disorder resembling malignant lymphoma in which lymph cells infiltrate the skin.[328]

Amitriptyline and other antidepressants increase the risk of some female cancers.[285][286] The use of amitriptyline, nortriptyline, desipramine, and phenelzine is associated with an increased risk of breast cancer.[327]

Alcohol and Sleep

If you don't have a problem with alcohol, experiment with it (if you're inclined to) to see if it helps you go to sleep. Some anti-alcohol fanatics will be horrified at this suggestion, just the way anti-caffeine fanatics are horrified at our advice about prudent caffeine use. The best argument they have against this advice is along this line: "Everybody knows that alcohol worsens sleep problems, so anybody with a sleep problem should get off alcohol altogether!"

We're not the sort of people to leap on bandwagons and joyfully sing a certain tune just because others loudly and persistently proclaim its truth. Instead, when we hear someone chanting a belief, we check the available evidence before reaching our own conclusions about its truth or falsehood.

So, we checked the available evidence on alcohol use. Some researchers found no relationship between people not getting enough sleep and their alcohol drinking habits.[298] Other researchers found that alcohol-dependent people had disturbed sleep, psychiatric disorders, and social problems. These effects improved, however, when the people abstained from alcohol or controlled or minimized their drinking.[302]

Based on the evidence we found, we disagree that *all* people with sleep problems should definitely avoid alcohol altogether. We believe that most people, if they choose, can use alcohol temperately as a sleep aid without harm to themselves.

So, if you don't have a problem with alcohol, try a small amount of beer or wine before bed if you'd like. You may find that it relaxes you and enables you to go to sleep easier. Some people find that although alcohol helps them go to sleep, it makes them wake up after a while. If that happens to you, you might best avoid alcohol before bed. But if you have restful sleep and you don't wake up after a while, you may want to use alcohol as one of your sleep aids—at least when you otherwise aren't able to fall asleep.

As we advise in Table 1, don't drink to excess since this can disrupt sleep. If you're a chronic alcoholic, we recommend that you join a Rational Recovery group (see *Resources*) in your city. If a Rational Recovery group isn't available in your city, consider joining Alcoholics Anonymous. And, some people need residential treatment to help them break the pattern of harmful alcohol consumption.

Liquid Interference With Sleep. One problem with drinking alcohol to help us get to sleep is that it's a liquid, and a while after you drink it, your bladder will distend. When it does, nerve signals from your bladder will reach your brain and arouse you from sleep. Getting out of bed to urinate may then leave you too awake to fall asleep again. Anyone who wants to get up to urinate as seldom as possible during sleep hours should take in as little liquid as possible.

Drinking beer to help you get to sleep can be especially problematic, since beer is a diuretic. One way around this problem is to drink an alcoholic beverage that has a higher alcohol content. Wine, for example, has a higher alcohol content per volume of liquid. A smaller amount may help you get to sleep. If so, the lower liquid intake will cause your bladder to distend less.

Distilled liquors such as scotch, whiskey, and vodka are much stronger. In using these as sleep aids, the same amount of alcohol content can be taken in with a much lower volume of liquid.

Some patients with a diagnosis of fibromyalgia have what we call "urinary frequency." Some of them urinate ten or more times each day, although they release only a small amount of urine each time. They have two powerful sleep disrupters that keep them unrested: pain and the need to urinate often. As I (JCL) documented in detail in *The Metabolic Treatment of Fibromyalgia*, urinary frequency can be caused by too little thyroid hormone regulation of the bladder and some brain stem centers.[1,pp.745-766] Effective thyroid hormone therapy is the solution to this problem. Until a patient with urinary frequency undergoes thyroid hormone therapy, using alcohol as a sleep-aid is probably not a good idea.

Special Circumstances

Many people aren't able to sleep restfully on trips out of town when they sleep in unfamiliar rooms and on unfamiliar beds. On these occasions, drugs such as Ambien or other sleep aids can help them get enough sleep. On the other hand, you may find that, like me (GH-L), you sleep better on trips out of town. Trips take me away from endless concerns in town, such as my clinical practice, that often make it a challenge to get enough restful sleep.

Occasionally in my (JCL) clinical practice, I was consulted by a mother whose baby woke her up several times through the night. The mother was able to get back to sleep—if at all!—only after walking the baby for a length of time that left her fully awake. Usually, the mother and I were able to enlist her husband's help. He took the night shift for a time, allowing her to sleep in another room where the baby's crying wouldn't wake her up. This allowed her to get enough deep, restful sleep for several nights, restoring her energy and clarity of mind.

We have enough ways to aid sleep so that most people can improve their sleep without the use of prescription sleep aids. We encourage you to try different combinations until you find what works best for you.

Chapter 12

Avoiding Chemical Contaminants

WE HUMANS ARE SURROUNDED BY and saturated with chemical contaminants. As part of our industrialized world, people in laboratories have created a plethora of chemicals and oozed them into our lives from every direction.

Since the late 1940s, petrochemicals have provided us with a colossal array of comforts and conveniences. Pesticides, by killing plant, fungal, and animal pests, have made life more pleasant and convenient, and they have reduced the cost of plant foods and the incidence of some diseases. Insecticides have decreased disease transmission by mites, mosquitoes, fleas, and flies. At the same time, petrochemical residues have increasingly polluted our food, water, and air—causing major health problems.

DDT is the first pesticide/insecticide to come to our minds. It does so because of our childhood memories: Growing up in different parts of the United States, we often ran joyously with playmates in the streets through clouds of DDT sprayed from trucks to kill mosquitoes. The chemical served that purpose, making life more tolerable and decreasing the transmission of disease. But it also sickened many humans and other animals, killed some, and damaged ecosystems.

The government restricted the use of DDT in the United States in 1972. The restrictions were prompted by evidence linking DDT to human cancer risk.[242,p.201] However, people in developing countries in Latin America, Africa, and Asia still use large amounts of DDT.[242,p.136] It's plausible that through various routes from those countries, the chemical can still reach and contaminate those of us in countries that have outlawed the chemical's use.

Artificial fertilizers, preservatives, and food additives increase our food supply and keep it fresh longer. We now know, though, that some of those most commonly used also cause allergic reactions, nerve and brain damage, and cancer.

Our automobiles give us freedom and mobility. They also defile the air we breathe. To provide hydrocarbon fuels, people created refineries in oil and gas producing regions across the world. The petrochemical pollutants in the air in the surrounding communities damage lungs, brains, and other parts of the human body, and shorten life through cancer. Still other health problems come from chlorine in our drinking water, and vapors emitted from carpets and sofa covers sprayed with "protective" man-made chemicals that resist soil and stains.

A major cost of chemical contaminants is damage to the thyroid system. Dioxins, PCBs, chlorine, organo-phosphates, and other man-made chemicals disrupt various parts of the thyroid system.

Radioactive fallout from aboveground nuclear weapons testing causes cancer of the thyroid gland. All 48 contiguous states in the United States have had some degree of radioactive contamination; and of course, the heaviest concentrations were nearest to test sites. The U.S. government has recently, and quietly, offered financial restitution to victims of thyroid cancer who lived near test sites.

Diagnostic x-rays have also undoubtedly induced considerable thyroid gland disease. Indeed, recent evidence shows that the smallest amount of x-ray exposure can induce gene mutations. The radiological industry has effectively suppressed public awareness of this; we know of at least one prominent whistle-blowing x-ray researcher who was silenced by a premature end to his career.

The problem of impaired metabolism due to a disrupted thyroid system is pervasive, especially in industrialized countries. We can protect ourselves from radiation exposure in general by supporting organizations and legislators who encourage only limited and safe uses of radiation by governments and industries. And we can protect our thyroid glands from x-ray damage by avoiding x-rays except when they are truly indispensable to our health.

Protecting ourselves from chemicals that can cause hypothyroidism or thyroid hormone resistance requires almost constant vigilance. It can also increase one's cost of living and be inconvenient. Nonetheless, avoiding or minimizing exposure to the chemicals is just as important as avoiding radiation. Below, we describe the chemicals that are most important to avoid as much as possible.

FOOD CONSTITUENTS

In *Solved: The Riddle of Illness*, our friends Dr. Steven Langer and medical writer James Scheer make excellent points about thyroid hormone-lowering constituents of some foods.[227,pp.36-37] A food constituent that reduces the thyroid gland's output of thyroid hormones is "progoitrin." The body converts this substance to goitrin, which blocks thyroid gland function. Foods that contain progroitrin are cabbage, cauliflower, kale, kohlrabi, mustard greens, rutabaga, and turnips. Cabbage and turnips also contain cyanide, a substance that can block thyroid gland production of thyroid hormones.

As Langer and Scheer note, eating these plant foods isn't likely to cause hypothyroidism except under a special condition: when a person lives in an area with too little iodine in food and water and he eats large amounts of progoitrin-containing foods.

An observation of Langer and Scheer is wise to note. They point out that researchers have never studied the effects on the thyroid gland of thousands of substances that food processors add to foods. This fact is good reason to avoid, or minimize in the extreme, one's consumption of processed foods.[227,p.37]

COMMONLY PRESCRIBED DRUGS

Many commonly prescribed drugs can cause or contribute to poor metabolic health by lowering thyroid hormone levels. Some drugs lower thyroid hormone levels by interfering with iodine metabolism in the thyroid gland. The interference reduces the amount of thyroid hormone that the gland releases into the blood. Other drugs lower thyroid hormone levels by interfering with the metabolism and excretion of the hormone after the thyroid gland releases it into the blood.

For a list of drugs that potentially interfere with thyroid hormone metabolism, see Table 1. For a more detailed account of interfering drugs, we recommend the chapter titled "What's Sabotaging Your Thyroid" in Dr. Steven Langer and James Scheer's 3rd edition of *Solved: The Riddle of Illness*.[227,pp.33-38] (See *Resources*.)

**Table 1. Chemicals that, in various ways,
lower thyroid hormone levels***

- estrogen in birth-control pills & HRT
- salicylates (such as asprin)
- barbiturates
- sulfa drugs
- iodide
- antidiabetic agents
- lithium
- nitrothyrosines
- prednisone and its analogs
- oral radiopague substances for gallbladder x-ray visualization
- amiodarone
- phenobarbital
- rifampin
- thiocyanate
- thionamides (propylthiouracil, methimazole, carbimazole)
- carbamazepine
- phenytoin
- ClO_4^-
- TcO_4^-

---

*After: Green, W.L.: Extrinsic and intrinsic variables. In *Werner and Ingbar's The Thyroid: A Fundamental and Clinical Text*, 6th edition. Edited by L.E. Braverman and R.D. Utiger, New York, J.B. Lippincott Co., 1991, pp.322-335, and Langer, S.E. and Scheer, J.F.: *Solved: The Riddle of Illness*, 3rd edition. Lincolnwood, Keats Publishing, 2000, p.35.

We include salicylates such as aspirin in Table 1 because they may reduce the amount of T_4 and T_3 that reaches the brain. Salicylates block the binding of T_4 and T_3 to the proteins that transport them in the blood.[234,p.337] The potential problem comes from salicylates displacing T_4 and T_3 from a blood protein called "transthyretin."[235][236][237] This protein normally transports T_4 and T_3 into the brain. If enough of the hormones are displaced from the protein, it's possible that too little will reach the brain. This could cause hypothyroid-like brain effects. The potential hypothyroid-like effects include low blood flow through the brain and slow metabolism of brain cells. The effects on the person could be anxiety, depression, low motor drive, and sluggishness.[225] (See "Chapter 3.2 Blood Pressure and Circulation," pages 385-423, and "Chapter 3.10 Depression, Anxiety, and Cognitive Dysfunction," pages 587-606, in *The Metabolic Treatment of Fibromyalgia*.) Other effects could be an increase of pain-heightening substance P, and a decrease of pain-inhibiting norepinephrine. These two changes could cause chronic, widespread pain and tenderness that doctors diagnose as "fibromyalgia." (See "Chapter 3.15 Pain," pages 689-694 in *The Metabolic Treatment of Fibromyalgia*.)

DIOXINS AND PCBS

When I (JCL) was writing the chapter on hypothyroidism for *The Metabolic Treatment of Fibromyalgia*, I reviewed the published studies on dioxins, PCBs, and similar chemicals and how they disrupt the human thyroid system.[1,pp.226-231] These chemicals are man-made pollutants, and they contaminate our air, water, and soil, and thus our food chain. The chemicals are so widely spread throughout our world that virtually every human is polluted with them, and accumulated body levels often exceed amounts considered to be a risk to health.[256]

Some people are exposed to dioxins by cotton and pulp sanitary products such as tampons and diapers.[257] Our major source of exposure, however, is a wide variety of foods such as meat, fish, and dairy products. Toddlers take in dioxins from the soil, but their exposure to the chemicals begins with breast-feeding. Cows take the chemicals in by eating grass, especially while grazing in the vicinity of incinerators. In turn, humans take them in by consuming the cows' meat and dairy products. Milk is further contaminated from the pulp used to make milk cartons. People who live along coastlines and eat fish caught in the coastal waters usually have higher levels of dioxins in their bodies. The risk of exposure is especially great through low-priced foods from developing countries that aspire to join markets in more developed countries.[258]

Dioxins and PCBs wreak havoc on the thyroid system. The scientific documentation for this is overwhelming. Because of this, I was perplexed and then appalled when I noticed that *Werner's The Thyroid*, considered the "bible" of thyroidology (the study of the thyroid system and its diseases), devotes only one of 1365 pages to the subject. Since *Werner's* is one of the main books conventional doctors use to learn thyroidology, it's little wonder that they ignore the issue of pollutants that disrupt patients' thyroid systems. The importance of this subject is obvious. Because of this, I thoroughly covered the subject in *The Metabolic Treatment of Fibromyalgia*.

Here we'll briefly touch on how these chemicals disrupt the thyroid system and contribute to symptoms of slow metabolism. Learning how these chemicals interfere with normal thyroid function may motivate you to avoid and lower your body's levels of the pollutants.

How Dioxins and PCBs Disrupt the Thyroid System

Dioxins and PCBs disrupt the thyroid system in at least three ways. First, dioxins and PCBs interfere with the thyroid gland's production of thyroid hormone, and they reduce the gland's release of thyroid hormone into the blood. The lower production and release of thyroid hormone can cause a low level in the blood. The lower blood level of thyroid hormone can raise the blood level of TSH. A chronically high TSH level may induce thyroid gland tumors, and the tumors may lead to surgical removal of the patient's thyroid gland.

Second, PCBs and other chemicals increase the activity of a liver cell enzyme that hastens the excretion of thyroid hormone into the bile. As a result, the level of thyroid hormone in the blood decreases. And again, the lower blood thyroid hormone level will increase the TSH level in the blood.

Third, PCBs displace thyroid hormone from its binding sites on a protein called "transthyretin." This blood protein transports thyroid hormone to the brain. As more PCB molecules bump thyroid hormone off transthyretin, more PCBs enter the brain. At the same time, as more PCBs enter the brain bound to the protein, less thyroid hormone gets in.

In these three ways, dioxins and PCBs may potently contribute to slow metabolism and symptoms of hypometabolism. Moreover, they're toxic to the liver, immune system, and reproductive system, and they can cause cancer. Obviously, reducing your intake of the pollutants may go a long way toward optimizing your metabolism and improving your health. Aside from improving or preserving your health, reducing the levels of dioxins and PCBs in your body is important for another reason: Doing so can prevent you from risking a potential horrific outcome at the hands of mainstream doctors.

Dioxins, PCBs, and Problems With Medical Specialists

If doctors remove a patient's thyroid gland because of dioxin- and PCB-induced tumors, the aftermath can be worse than the surgery itself. After the surgery, the patient will be hypothyroid. This is the point at which her worst troubles will begin. The reason is that the patient's mainstream doctor is almost certain to under-treat her with thyroid hormone. He's likely to prescribe T_4 alone, which is not effective for most patients even in high doses. And he'll keep her dose so low that she'll continue to suffer from hypothyroid symptoms.

The under-treated patient will then have chronic hypothyroid symptoms. If the patient's doctor is a conventional endocrinologist, he's likely to believe his thyroid hormone therapy infallible. Hence, he'll believe the patient's hypothyroid-like symptoms *must* be caused by some other disease. If the patient's main symptom is pain, the endocrinologist is likely to refer her to a rheumatologist. This specialist will diagnose "fibromyalgia" and prescribe a variety of drugs that worsen and complicate the patient's symptoms. If her main symptom is fatigue, the endocrinologist is likely to refer her to an infectious disease specialist. This specialist will diagnose "chronic fatigue syndrome" and similarly prescribe trouble-making drugs.

Fish and Omega-3 Fatty Acids

It's difficult to avoid ingesting dioxins and PCBs. And, hence, it may also be hard to elude the sequence of events with mainstream doctors we described in the section above. One reason it's difficult to avoid ingesting dioxins and PCBs is that they bind to fat molecules in foods. As a result, the pollutants are highly concentrated in fatty foods such as whole milk and salmon and other fatty fish.

Health enthusiasts know well that eating fish has health benefits. A benefit of eating fish from the ocean is that they are a major source of omega-3 fatty acids. Fish oil contains the fatty acids because the fish eat plant matter that contains them. Omega-3-fatty acids are essential to healthy cell membranes, and consuming omega-3-fatty acids may help guard against heart disease, neurological diseases, and cancer.

Nowadays, however, many health-conscious people avoid fish from the ocean. They do so because the fat in the fish is heavily laden with dioxins, PCBs, and other pollutants. (Another pollutant is mercury, which can block the conversion of T_4 to T_3.) Many people instead eat farm-raised fish. Unfortunately, most farm-raised fish are fed corn. Corn doesn't contain omega-3 fatty acids, so fish raised on corn aren't a good source of the fatty acids.

To get enough omega-3-fatty acids, you can take them as a supplement in capsules containing fish oils. But the oils from ocean fish also contain dioxins and PCBs. By consuming concentrated fish oil in capsules, you also take in large amounts of dioxins, PCBs, and other pollutants. Some companies market fish oils from which pollutants are presumably removed. If you choose to get your omega-3 fatty acids from ingesting fish oil, you should be sure that the company that produces the product has effectively removed the pollutants. We recommend that you ask the company to provide you with documentation of the effectiveness of its pollutant-removing process.

We recommend that you get omega-3-fatty acids by taking organic flax seed oil. By taking organic flax seed oil capsules, you'll get enough omega-3-fatty acids, and you'll reduce your intake of pollutants that promote disease. Among the pollutants you may avoid are dioxins and PCBs. Hopefully, by avoiding the intake of the pollutants, over time, the levels in your body will decrease. If the pollutants were disrupting your thyroid system, reduced body levels may eventually free your thyroid system from disruption. In addition, reducing the levels of dioxins and PCBs in your body will help you optimize your metabolism and your health in general. And, you may be able to avoid the life-threatening diseases the pollutants can cause.

The U.S. government banned the use of dioxins and PCBs in the 1970s. An assumption has been that over time, the amounts of these pollutants in lakes and oceans have decreased. The hope was that eventually we could eat fatty fish again without risks to our health. But some evidence suggests that pollution continues in some areas. Researchers recently reported, for example, that PCBs are still entering Lake Michigan.[25]

CHLORINE AND THE THYROID GLAND

Studies suggest that exposure to chlorine may lower the levels of T_4 in the blood. Researchers had African Green monkeys ingest chlorine dioxide in drinking water for 30-to-60 days. The chlorine inhibited the metabolism of the monkeys' thyroid glands. After four weeks of exposure to the chlorine, the T_4 levels in their blood decreased. The more chlorine the monkeys ingested, the lower their T_4 levels were.[33]

In another study, monkeys' T_4 levels decreased after they ingested chlorine dioxide for four weeks. After eight weeks of ingesting the chlorine, their T_4 levels increased again. In the same study, rats' T_4 levels decreased after they ingested the chlorine for eight weeks. The more chlorine they took in, the further their T_4 levels dropped. Unlike the monkeys' levels, the rats' T_4 levels didn't rise again as they continued ingesting chlorine.[34] In still another study, T_4 levels decreased in pups fed chlorine dioxide, and their development was delayed.[32]

Other researchers had human volunteers ingest chlorine dioxide in drinking water. The humans' T_4 blood levels, however, didn't decrease as the monkeys' levels had. But another form of chlorine (sodium chlorite) caused abnormalities that can produce symptoms of impaired metabolism. First, the chlorine decreased the humans' red blood cell and hemoglobin levels. (Hemoglobin is the oxygen-carrying pigment of red blood cells. It gives the cells their red color, and it carries oxygen to tissues.) The chlorine also increased levels of the liver enzyme SGPT, which suggested damage to the liver cells. Moreover, the chlorine caused the harmful substance "methemoglobin" to form in the humans' blood. Methemoglobin forms in arteries after poisoning with various substances such as nitrates. It forms when oxygen tightly binds to ferric iron in the hemoglobin molecule. The tight binding of oxygen to the iron transforms the hemoglobin to methemoglobin. Oxygen doesn't release from methemoglobin. So, unlike hemoglobin, methemoglobin is worthless for providing us with usable oxygen.[33] These effects of the chlorine (lower red blood cell levels and production of methemoglobin) reduce delivery of oxygen to cells. The reduced oxygen delivery is likely to cause symptoms such as fatigue and weakness.

Some people may take comfort in a finding of the above study: that only one form of chlorine—chlorine dioxide—suppressed T_4 levels, and only in monkeys. They may hope that chlorine dioxide is only a minor ingredient of their drinking water and not likely to harm humans. This comfort-taking, however, is risky. When a human takes chlorine into his intestinal tract, a host of other chlorine-containing compounds form from it. These "chloro-organics," as we call them, pass into his blood. He may be among the humans who are highly sensitive to various chloro-organics.[135] If so, they'll disrupt some body processes and cause disease. Among the harmful effects may be abnormally slow metabolism.

These studies don't show that all forms of chlorine interfere with the thyroid system. Nor do they show that ingesting small amounts of chlorine suppresses blood thyroid hormone levels. We cannot draw firm conclusions from the studies about the potential for chlorine to impair the thyroid system of humans. But the studies are enough to raise concern. Those who already have hypothyroidism, or those whose thyroid status is borderline, will probably be served well by avoiding chlorine intake. Some researchers reported that a diet high in iodide prevented chlorinated drinking water from lowering animals' T_4 levels.[35] We don't find this especially consoling. For even if a high iodide intake prevents one's T_4 level from decreasing, chlorine may damage one's health in other ways that make low T_4 levels of lesser concern.

Surely available studies are cause for precaution by those who value their metabolic health. Humans fall into a "bell curve" of sensitivity to pollutants, including chlorine. People on one end of the curve won't be harmed by exposure to large amounts. Most other people will be harmed by large amounts, but they're less vulnerable to smaller amounts. But individuals on the other end of the curve will be harmed by even small amounts of chlorine. If you prize good metabolic health, we recommend that you err on the side of safety: Ingest only the smallest amounts of chlorine that can slip into you without your notice.

Chlorine and Bath, Hot Tub, and Swimming Pool Water

Another liquid source of chlorine and other pollutants is exposure to tap water when bathing and when using hot tubs or swimming pools. People usually don't intentionally ingest this water. It's possible, though, to take in pollutants from water through the mucous membranes of the eyes and mouth. It's also possible to swallow swimming pool water. Intentional or not, taking tap water into the body is the consumption of polluted water.

A study of swimming pool water in Miami, Florida found substantial amounts of three potential disease-causing chemicals.[31] We encourage hypometabolic patients who have extremely low physical fitness to begin exercising in water (see *Chapter 10*, "Baby Steps First and Gradual Conditioning" and "Warm Water Exercises"). While doing water exercise, however, the patient should carefully avoid ingesting the water.

CIGARETTE SMOKING

Judging from available studies, some chemicals in cigarette smoke are highly likely to contribute to poor metabolic health. One way they do so is to interfere with the smoker's thyroid system.

Investigators report that smoking is associated with an increased risk of developing overt thyroid disease. The evidence suggests that the more people smoke, the more at risk they are for thyroid disease, especially autoimmune thyroid disease.[229]

Researchers at Emory University found that people who smoked more heavily had higher levels of thyroid gland toxins.[230] Smokers also had higher total T_4 levels. The higher T_4 levels, however, don't mean that the smokers had more thyroid hormone stimulation of their tissues. T_4 levels were higher because the smokers had higher levels of the proteins that bind and transport T_4 through the blood. The T_4 was bound to the proteins and not available for stimulating tissues.

Swedish scientists studied the effects of smoking on two groups of hypothyroid women.[232] Compared to women who didn't smoke, smoking women had worse hypothyroidism. Their TSH levels were higher, their total cholesterol and LDL cholesterol were higher, and their ankle-reflex time was slower. The more women smoked, the worse the metabolic effects of their hypo-thyroidism were.

Some studies show that smoking provides some protection from thyroid cancer.[228] But this potential benefit isn't worth the risk of smoking causing hypothyroidism.

Thiocyanate From Cigarettes

Japanese researchers studied female Hashimoto's thyroiditis patients who smoked.[231] They compared the incidence of hypo-thyroidism in smoking and non-smoking women. Among non-smoking Hashimoto's patients, 35% were hypothyroid. Among smoking patients, 76% were hypothyroid. This means that hypo-thyroidism was more than twice as common among smokers.

Interestingly, 62% of Hashimoto's patients in the Japanese study who had formerly smoked were hypothyroid. This high per-centage suggests that stopping smoking doesn't usually reverse hypothyroidism. Other researchers have reported that smoking has long-term anti-thyroid effects, and these seem to be irreversible.[233]

Smoking introduces into the body a chemical called "thiocy-anate" that's toxic to the thyroid gland. In the Japanese patients, levels of the toxin were highest in hypothyroid women who cur-rently smoked. The researchers wrote that thiocynate is a cause of the hypothyroidism in women with Hashimoto's.

Smoking and Graves' Disease

Researchers in the United Kingdom studied patients who had been treated for Graves' disease with thyroid gland-destroying drugs. They found that cigarette smoking increased the likelihood that male Graves' patients would have recurrences of the disease. The researchers concluded that among male patients, smoking is an important risk factor in both the Graves' disease process and treat-ment outcome.[226]

Graves' patients who are smokers have a higher incidence of eye diseases (called "ophthalmopathy"). The more heavily patients smoked, the more severe their eye diseases.[233]

PROTECTING YOURSELF
DESPITE OFFICIAL ASSURANCES

U.S. Secretary of State Colin Powell recently urged audiences in South Africa to accept and consume genetically modified crops from the U.S. Genetically altered crops contain a gene from another organism. The gene alteration makes plants resistant to some herbicides or enables the plants to produce their own toxin to kill pests. Critics argue that researchers have done too few studies to know whether gene alteration is harmful to the environment and public health. To the credit of the South African audiences, they were—to put it mildly—less than enthusiastic and rejected Powell's proposal.

Powell had assured the audiences that genetically-altered crops are harmless to humans. After all, he noted, researchers looked for harmful effects for five years and found none. This brief time should assure no one that these crops are harmless. The harmful effects of some man-made chemicals (and gene-altered corn is partly a man-made chemical) don't show up for as long as a generation.

Consider, for example, the drug diethylstilbestrol or DES. Initially, doctors prescribed DES to prevent miscarriages, but the chemical failed to accomplish this. Doctors also prescribed DES to suppress milk production after childbirth, and to relieve hot flashes and other symptoms of menopause. They also prescribed it to treat acne, prostate cancer, and gonorrhea, and to arrest growth in teenage girls who were becoming unstylishly tall. In 1957, Grant Chemical Company extolled the use of DES for "all pregnancies." The company pridefully advertised that DES produced "bigger and stronger babies." In her book, *Our Stolen Future* (see *Resources*), Theo Colborn wrote, ". . . doctors not only prescribed DES to prevent miscarriages, they began to recommend it for untroubled pregnancies as if it were a vitamin that could improve on nature."[242,p.48]

Beginning in the mid-1960s, some young women developed a rare cancer of the vagina. Researchers eventually found that the cancer was caused by DES taken by their mothers in the first trimester of pregnancy. Colborn refers to the "invisible damage caused by DES."[242,p.56] The damage didn't show up for 15-to-22 years after the chemical exposure. Surgically removing the uterus and vagina saved most of the young women's lives, but not all. Obviously, establishing the safety or potential harm of some man-made chemicals can take far longer than five years.

Assurances from politicians such as Powell are akin to those of public relations spokespersons from corporations that market chemical contaminants. The assurances are essentially appeals to lend ourselves as research subjects for the sake of economic benefit. Far in the future, economists and other analysts will compute whether the economic benefits (such as profits from the sale of gene-altered crops) are worth any harm done to the unwary research subjects. We personally decline to participate, and we advise our patients to do the same.

We humans swim every day in a sea of chemical contaminants. Many of the contaminants are highly toxic. In view of this, we're amazed that more humans don't succumb to their harmful effects. To increase our chances of being among those who don't succumb, we can take two protective steps: Avoid as many of the chemicals as possible,[61] and bolster our resistance to disease through the methods we describe throughout this book. These steps can contribute greatly to both recovering and sustaining metabolic health.

■ For a detailed description of how man-made chemicals disrupt the human thyroid system, see Chapter 2.4 in *The Metabolic Treatment of Fibromyalgia*.[1] Read the section titled "Environmental Contaminants" on pages 226-231.

Chapter 13

Physical Treatments

NOW AND THEN, A RECOVERED patient says something to us we've often heard many other patients say: "Before I got well with metabolic rehab," she says, "I barely had the stamina for a quick run to the grocery store and back. I never would've gotten *anything* done if it hadn't been for chiropractic and massage treatments. Lucky for me, I got both in the same clinic. The treatments didn't make me *well*, understand. But I felt *much* better for a few hours after my chiropractor and my massage therapist worked on me. During those hours, I had enough energy to get things done, so I got in the habit of running all my errands then. Those treatments helped me get through until I finally got well."

As with this patient, physical treatments—when well done—enable many patients with poor metabolic health to cope better with their illness. The treatments help by decreasing demands made on the patients' metabolism. This can help the patients, despite their low metabolic reserves, to fulfill their daily responsibilities and to feel better as they do.

Mainstream chiropractic care and massage therapy are especially effective at reducing metabolic demand. Partly because of this, chiropractic physicians and massage therapists are the clinicians most preferred by fibromyalgia patients.[19][70][139] Chiropractic doctors and massage therapists provide the range of physical treatments we describe in this chapter. Other clinicians also provide the treatments (see our comments under each form of treatment). Whichever type of clinician you consult, you're likely to fully recover good metabolic health only if your therapeutic regimen includes physical treatment.[137]

The typical patient in poor metabolic health doesn't benefit as much as other people from physical treatments. The treatments improve some of her symptoms, especially pain. But as long as her metabolism is abnormally slow, physical treatments provide

275

her with more moderate and short-lived improvement than other patients experience. As her metabolic health improves, however, she'll get more profound and lasting results from the treatments. Her response to physical treatment, then, can serve as a useful barometer of her level of metabolic health; the healthier she is, the more she'll benefit from physical treatment.

MYOFASCIAL THERAPY

"Myofascial" is a hybrid word: "myo" means muscle, and "fascial" refers to the connective tissues (fascia) that encase and support muscle. When you see raw chicken or beef, muscle is the red or pink substance; fascia is the white, often shiny substance that covers and adheres to muscle. When we treat patients' "muscles" in our clinic, we're actually treating both muscle and its ensheathing fascia as a single, functional unit. Because of this, we use the term "myofascial therapy."

Most clinicians view myofascial therapy as a variety of physical treatments doctors and therapists can use to correct abnormalities of myofascial tissues. The treatments include stripping massage; brief compression of "trigger points" (see next paragraph), often called "ischemic compression" or "Nimmo technique"; fascial release; dry needling of trigger points; stretching; ultrasound; and injection of local pain-killing solutions. Clinicians use such treatments to correct several myofascial abnormalities. Common abnormalities are pain, excess muscle tension, fascial adhesions, reduced myofascial circulation, and restricted motion.

The most common myofascial abnormality is the "trigger point." These are exquisitely tender spots in myofascial tissues that respond to pressure by referring pain or other sensations. Trigger points can actively refer pain so distracting and troubling that it can disable the patient. Fortunately, trained and experienced doctors and therapists can stop trigger point pain quickly. Some medical, osteopathic, naturopathic, and chiropractic physicians, massage therapists, and physical therapists are highly skilled at stopping trigger point pain. If you can find a certified myofascial trigger point therapist in your area, you're fortunate. These therapists are specifically trained to relieve patients of symptoms caused by trigger points. (See section below titled "Certified Myofascial Trigger Point Therapists.")

We consider the use of thyroid hormone a form of myofascial therapy when it relieves myofascial abnormalities. Too little regulation of muscle cells by thyroid hormone during hypothyroidism or thyroid hormone resistance can cause chronic, excess muscle tension. The tense muscles often have pain-referring trigger points, and the points are typically resistant to physical treatments. Physical treatments may give brief, mild relief, but the points soon begin referring pain again. For these patients, only effective thyroid hormone therapy will allow the muscles to fully relax and enable physical treatments to give long-lasting relief from trigger point pain.

Just as thyroid hormone therapy can improve the state of muscle, so can a food that corrects low blood sugar. Some patients' acute pain is caused by trigger points activated by low blood sugar. We keep food (such as bananas or multi-grain bread) in the office. When low blood sugar is the cause of a patient's pain, we have her eat, and within twenty to thirty minutes, the pain subsides. After the food has reduced the pain, we're able to use physical treatments to completely stop it. For some patients, the food itself completely stops the pain without any need for physical treatment.

Some B vitamin deficiencies in some patients cause excess muscle tension and pain-referring trigger points. Physical treatments seldom effectively relieve the patients' pain. The treatments become effective, however, after the patients begin using supplemental vitamins to relieve the deficiencies.

Ultrasound

When used properly, ultrasound is highly effective in stopping pain referred by trigger points. It is especially effective when used in combination with stripping massage, stretching of the involved muscle, and moist heat.

Dr. Devin Starlanyl has explained well that fibromyalgia patients are highly prone to developing trigger points.[37][130] For these patients, ultrasound treatment is particularly helpful. It stops, at least for a time, the pain referred by their trigger points. But in addition, it has a soothing effect that can provide fibromyalgia patients with welcome relaxation.[36]

We use ultrasound rather than other forms of physical therapy for a special reason. As I (GH-L) explained in 2000 in a French medical journal[136] and at a related conference,[38] ultrasound simultaneously treats several types of soft tissue problems. Ultrasound reduces the irritability of active and latent trigger points, and it relaxes tight muscles. The ultrasound energy softens and even breaks down scar tissue. The treatment inhibits the transmission of pain impulses by type C nerve fibers. It also triggers the release of opiate-like chemicals, causing mild sedation.

When you're having ultrasound treatment, your doctor or therapist will touch a "sound head" to your skin. This is the hand-held instrument that delivers ultrasound energy to your tissues. The clinician will apply a gel substance to your skin and then slide the sound head through the gel. The gel aids the passage of ultrasound energy from the sound head into your skin. When the sound head is delivering enough ultrasound energy to your tissues, you'll feel warmth under it. The warmth should feel soothing, and the effect on you should be somewhat akin to the effects of a hot bath. The heat shouldn't be so intense that you feel you're on the verge of being burned. If you feel the heat mounting painfully, let your clinician know. If the ultrasound energy is too intense, it can cause a trigger point to refer pain. If you feel an aching sensation under the sound head, let your clinician know.

Ultrasound can soften fascial adhesions. When applied immediately before cross-friction massage, ultrasound can increase the effectiveness of this manual treatment. And by inhibiting the transmission of pain impulses, ultrasound can reduce the discomfort for which cross-friction massage is famous.

CHIROPRACTIC CARE

In a study in the mid-1980s, fibromyalgia patients ranked chiropractic care among the most effective treatments for them.[141] Another study showed that spinal manipulation and massage of the muscles along the spine increased fibromyalgia patients' sense of well-being.[143,p.45] In still another study, fibromyalgia patients preferred chiropractic care and massage therapy over other forms of treatment.[139]

Many chiropractic physicians have massage therapists on staff. This arrangement is convenient for fibromyalgia patients; they can get both forms of care in one clinic.

As yet, few researchers have studied the effects of chiropractic treatments on fibromyalgia patients.[20] The results of a few studies,[131][143] however, are consistent with our extensive and systematic clinical experience. Our experience and the studies show that fibromyalgia patients benefit most from a combination of myofascial therapy and spinal adjustments.[132][137] Other patients with poor metabolic health but different diagnoses, such as chronic fatigue syndrome, also benefit most from these particular forms of physical treatment.

Chiropractic physicians vary in the biochemical treatments they use. Most use clinical nutrition in their practices. Some also use nutrient injections and intravenous infusions, and many use over-the-counter medications.

Chiropractic physicians are also diverse in their use of physical treatments. Some limit their practices to spinal adjusting and disregard their patients' myofascial problems. Other physicians treat both their patients' spinal and myofascial problems. Some physicians treat their patients' myofascial problems only with manual techniques, such as sustained finger pressure into trigger points. Other physicians use dry needling of myofascial trigger points, and others inject substances into the points. Still others treat myofascial problems with methods similar to ours: ultrasound, manual techniques, muscle stretching, moist heat, and guiding patients in properly managing their muscles and spine.

This diversity among chiropractic physicians requires that you work to find one who meets your individual needs. At minimum, we advise you to look for a chiropractic physician who uses both spinal adjustments and myofascial therapy. Preferably, the physician will include ultrasound in his treatment of trigger points.

We strongly recommend this precaution: If you have poor metabolic health, don't limit the physical treatment you receive to spinal adjustments. Some chiropractic doctors expect too much from spinal adjustments alone. If you have fibromyalgia or other symptoms due to poor metabolic health, your muscles are most likely affected. As a result, you may have pain from excess muscle tension and from myofascial trigger points. The most expedient approach to relieving these muscle-related symptoms is direct treatment of your muscles. Unfortunately, some chiropractic doctors try to indoctrinate patients into believing that the spinal adjustment alone—especially of the upper cervical spine—is the best treatment approach. This tactic is *not* in the best interest of patients with muscle-related problems. The likely outcome of such care is the continuation and possibly worsening of symptoms. If you're seeing a chiropractic doctor who takes this limited approach, be sure you're also under the care of a massage therapist or a certified myofascial trigger point therapist (see section below). Since muscles are so often involved in poor metabolic health, the care these therapists provide is far more important than the spinal adjustments alone. I (JCL) learned from a systematic case study that spinal adjustments can reduce the irritability of some trigger points.[129] But clearly, the effectiveness of the adjustments pales in comparison with the effectiveness of direct muscle treatment. Many adjustments over several weeks may be needed only to *reduce* the irritability of trigger points. By contrast, direct muscle therapy often completely stops muscle pain almost immediately. We hastily add, however, that you should preferably receive both spinal adjustments and myofascial therapy.

Spinal Adjustments

"Spinal adjustments" are also called "spinal manipulations." No matter what you call the treatment, you may need it to reach optimal metabolic health.

Spinal adjustments are a physical treatment many clinicians use to correct a complex of problems with the spine. By tradition, chiropractic doctors have called this complex the "spinal subluxation" (see section below for explanation of the term).

Chiropractors have championed the cause of correcting subluxations as one way to improve health. Unfortunately, some unscientific and fanatical chiropractors (referred to as "straight") have promoted the correction of subluxations as an almost magical and universal way to improve health. This minority of chiropractors has understandably elicited disdain from critics of the chiropractic profession. They've also evoked scorn from many chiropractic doctors who consider them an embarrassment and an obstacle to advancement of the profession.

Equally unfortunately, many critics of the chiropractic profession have been just as unscientific and fanatical as the straight chiropractors. These critics have wrongly portrayed all chiropractic doctors as overzealous promoters of spinal adjustments. Most chiropractic doctors' practices, however, are as holistic as their legal scope of practice permits. They integrate a variety of therapies, including spinal adjustments, to provide their patients with the highest possible quality of care. We strongly recommend that each patient with poor metabolic health find and come under the care of such a chiropractic doctor.

Spinal Subluxations

The value in spinal adjustments is that they correct spinal subluxations, at least for a while. Spinal subluxations generate an excess of sensory nerve impulses that bombard the spinal cord.

These impulses then travel up to the brain stem and brain. The overflow of impulses can cause excess mental and physical arousal. The arousal can make us restless, irritable, and anxious, and it can interfere with sleep.[198][199] It's convenient to think of the excess arousal as stress.

Clinicians give patients with slow metabolism a diagnosis of "fibromyalgia" when their main symptom is chronic, widespread pain. Their widespread, persistent pain is caused mainly by too little thyroid hormone regulation of the "pain control system" in the spinal cord. Because of the inadequate thyroid hormone regulation, the system doesn't work properly.

The pain control system is a network of nerves in the spinal cord and brain stem. Chemicals normally released by these nerves reduce the flow of nerve impulses coming into the spinal cord from other parts of the body. When not regulated normally by thyroid hormone, the control system allows too many nerve impulses to reach the brain. The person then experiences chronic, widespread aches and pains.

Our studies have shown that most fibromyalgia patients' pain is lastingly relieved when they undergo metabolic rehab involving the use of the proper form and dose of thyroid hormone.[92][93][94] [135][161][162][187][188][189] Until a patient can undergo metabolic rehab, however, and while her pain control system is still impaired, it's important that she do whatever she can to reduce the flow of nerve impulses into her spinal cord, brain stem, and brain. Getting spinal adjustments is one useful way to accomplish this. The adjustments reduce the flow of impulses reaching the spinal cord from spinal subluxations, tight muscles, and myofascial trigger points.[133]

It's helpful to think of spinal subluxations as rheostats turned too high, allowing too much current to flow into the spinal cord and brain. Adjusting the spine to correct the subluxations is like turning the rheostats down and reducing the current flow to normal. This benefit of spinal adjustments accounts in part for fibromyalgia patients ranking chiropractic care (along with massage therapy) as their first choice among treatment methods.

MASSAGE

Massage therapy improves blood circulation and lymph flow, relaxes patients, increases their overall sense of well-being, and relieves muscle pain. If the world were perfect, we would all have a massage at least once a week. Like the rest of us, those with poor metabolic health get along best when they have regular massages. But massage is even more important to their well-being than to ours.

The underlying cause of fibromyalgia, of course, is impaired metabolism, and metabolic rehab is essential if patients are to recover. In the meantime, massage therapy can make patients' lives far more bearable. As we wrote above, fibromyalgia patients prefer massage therapy (along with chiropractic care) more than any other form of treatment, including medications.[139] Studies haven't been done to learn exactly which massage therapy techniques give patients the most palliative relief. So, you must try different techniques, possibly by different massage therapists, to find which works best for you.

There are many different styles of massage therapy. Some are gentle; others are more intense. Some massage therapists have worked extensively with fibromyalgia patients. As a result, they have learned how to modify their techniques so the patients get therapeutic effects without adverse reactions. Some massage therapists, however, insist on working too deeply in patients' tissues, and this may cause symptom flares (see section below titled "What Kind of Physical Treatment *Not* to Have"). Be sure to give your massage therapist feedback on your experience during massage, especially if it is too painful. A good method of feedback is to rate for your therapist from 0-to-10 how much discomfort you're experiencing. A rating of "0" would be no discomfort, and "10" would be extreme pain.

Fibromyalgia patients may fare best by finding a massage therapist who has been a fibromyalgia patient. For example, Vicky Massey, who wrote the *Foreword* to this book, became a massage therapist after recovering from her fibromyalgia through metabolic rehab. (To contact Vicky, see the link to "Vicky Massey" on the homepage of <www.drlowe.com>. Also, see the section titled "Health Care Professionals" in the *Resources* section at the end of the book.) Therapists such as Vicky are especially attuned, through personal experience, to the special needs of fibromyalgia patients.

CERTIFIED MYOFASCIAL TRIGGER POINT THERAPISTS

No discussion of myofascial trigger points is complete today without mention of certified myofascial trigger point therapists. The profession is based on the teachings of Dr. Janet Travell and Dr. David Simons. Dr. Travell, the mother of trigger point therapy, took special interest in the profession and nurtured it.

Some clinicians in other disciplines and specialties, such as chiropractic, have studied and practiced enough to have gained extraordinary expertise at diagnosing and treating myofascial trigger points. But only certified myofascial trigger point therapists make up a profession in which all members are highly-trained specialists in trigger point therapy. Most certified therapists are also massage therapists.

If certified therapists are available in your area, we encourage you to consult one for effective trigger point treatment. To find a therapist in your area, you can visit the website for the National Association of Myofascial Trigger Point Therapists. See <www.myofascialtherapy.org>. You can also visit the website of the Academy of Myofascial Trigger Point Therapists. See <www.npimall.com/amtpt>.

WHAT KIND OF PHYSICAL TREATMENT *NOT* TO HAVE

Never submit to abusively painful physical treatments. Many

patients with poor metabolic health have been abused too much already. Commonly, they've endured the unfavorable attitudes of doctors, relatives, and coworkers. Such social and psychological abuse can be hard to control. By contrast, patients can easily stop abuse in the form of painful physical treatment.

It's especially important that patients with poor metabolic health and a diagnosis of "fibromyalgia" not submit to painful physical treatment. The pain-control system in the spinal cord and brain stem of these patients is impaired. As a result, painful physical treatment is more painful to them than to other people. The painful treatment may also worsen their overall health.

Treating some physical problems, such as scar tissue, nearly always requires discomfort. Discomfort or pain, for example, is common when a doctor or therapist uses manual cross-friction massage on scar tissue. (Applying ultrasound before cross-friction massage can reduce the discomfort during the therapy. Ultrasound softens the scar tissue. It also inhibits the transmission of pain signals from the scar tissue through type C nerve fibers.) No physical problem we're aware of, however, requires that the doctor or therapist gratuitously induce severe pain. In our experience, few clinicians do this, but some definitely do. Most often, inducing severe pain in a patient during physical treatment shows a lack of sophistication in properly resolving the patient's problem.

Give your doctor or therapist verbal feedback when he's giving you physical treatment. We depend on feedback from our patients, for example, to know if we're applying too much pressure as we treat trigger points. Trust your perceptions when evaluating whether or not a particular treatment by a particular clinician is helping or harming you. If your doctor or therapist insists that physical treatment must hurt severely to be effective, we suggest you leave and don't look back.

MAKING SURE YOU'RE GETTING
EFFECTIVE PHYSICAL TREATMENT

Make sure the physical treatment you're receiving is effective. Continue it only if it's giving you satisfying results—not because the clinician suggests that it will *eventually* work for you. Some clinicians work to sell patients on going through as many treatments with them as possible. These clinicians conveniently ignore the greater potential of other forms of treatment for promptly relieving patients' symptoms. No health care discipline is exempt from this overselling of services by some of its members.

Many patients undergo long courses of drug treatment that at best only mask their pain, when physical therapies could quickly stop the pain. Tragically, thousands of people die each year from the heavy use of nonsteroidal anti-inflammatory drugs (NSAIDS). Doctors often prescribe one NSAID after another in a futile effort to find one that will relieve a patient's pain. Many patients use larger and larger doses of the drugs because smaller doses don't effectively relieve their pain. From the NSAID use, many patients sustain stomach, intestinal, and kidney damage, and die as a result. Yet physical therapies may have stopped or controlled the pain of most of these patients, eliminating any need to use NSAIDS at all.

Deciding whether spinal subluxations or myofasical trigger points are causing a patient's pain is sometimes difficult. If subluxations are the cause, spinal adjustments are the proper form of treatment. When we can't distinguish the cause, a trial of spinal adjustments may be needed. Unfortunately, many patients with trigger point pain that myofascial therapy could quickly relieve go through a series of spinal adjustments intended to relieve the pain. If a short trial of spinal adjustments doesn't work, a longer series of them isn't likely to. Undergoing more adjustments in the hope that they will eventually work can be expensive and inconvenient. In addition, getting effective treatment *quickly* is more important than many patients and clinicians realize: Delaying effective treatment may lead to chronic pain that's far more tenacious and widespread than the original pain.[138]

Chapter 14

Coffee & Caffeine

SOME RHEUMATOLOGISTS AND FIBROMYALGIA SUPPORT group leaders advise fibromyalgia patients to give up caffeine completely. The reason they give is that "caffeine worsens pain." Patients who have a diagnosis of fibromyalgia are by definition in chronic pain, and most are open to pretty much anything that will soften their pain—even stopping the use of caffeine. But for most of these patients, stopping their use of caffeine isn't likely to reduce their pain; in fact, eliminating caffeine may even worsen their pain. (See section below titled "Caffeine and Pain.")

We sympathize with the confusion some patients feel when different doctors give exactly opposite advice—in this instance, some saying caffeine can increase pain, and others like us, saying it can reduce it. As in most instances of disagreement, each point of view contains at least an element of truth. For us to be clear on what the element of truth is in each point of view, and then make practical use of the information, we must examine the available evidence and then adjust our understanding according to what the evidence tells us.

WHAT PATIENTS HAVE TAUGHT US ABOUT CAFFEINE USE

On most new patients' first visit with us, they're hesitant to admit that they use caffeine. Other health care practitioners have admonished them for using it, and they anticipate that we'll agree with the other practitioners. But when we assure them that we believe patients can enhance their health through the prudent use of caffeine, they relax and talk freely about their experiences with the substance.

The typical patient with hypothyroidism or thyroid hormone resistance tells us that a moderate amount of caffeine improves her mood, sharpens her mind, reduces her fatigue, and warms her up a bit. And the usual patient with a diagnosis of fibromyalgia tells us that caffeine either reduces her pain or makes it more tolerable for a time.

It's compelling that the majority of patients tell us they benefit from their use of caffeine. But to be sure these patients aren't just deluding themselves, we've studied the published research literature. In doing so, we've found that overall, the studies support our patients' claims.

CAFFEINE AND PAIN

Many patients who've attended fibromyalgia support groups, especially some sponsored by the Arthritis Foundation, have told us that group leaders advise them to stop all caffeine use. This advice is based on a warning from the groups' rheumatology advisors that caffeine worsens the pain of fibromyalgia. So, official opinion within these groups is that patients had best forswear caffeine, and give it up once and for all.

This opinion clashes with what our fibromyalgia patients tell us about their experiences with caffeine—that it actually reduces their pain or enables them to better tolerate it. (See section above.) It also clashes with the results of the only study we've found in which patients used caffeine as a fibromyalgia treatment. (See first paragraph in section below titled "Pain-Reducing Effects of Caffeine.")

We've often looked at the published studies on pain and caffeine. And indeed, some studies show that caffeine can initiate or worsen some people's pain. But this applies to a small percentage of people. What applies to them definitely doesn't apply to the majority of people. And it certainly doesn't justify the belief that caffeine worsens fibromyalgia patients' pain.

Caffeine Can Worsen *Some* People's Pain

We've found three instances in which caffeine may cause or

worsen pain. Let's briefly consider each.

Excess Caffeine Sensitivity. Some people develop pain, especially headaches, in response to too much caffeine. What constitutes "too much" varies among individuals. For sure, some people deluge themselves with caffeine; they consume so much that most any of us would have adverse effects from the amount.

For a few people, though, as little as 100 mg of caffeine may cause headaches. The 100 mg is equal to the caffeine in a cup of coffee, a dark chocolate bar, two cups of tea, or two tablets of the typical pain medicine containing caffeine and an analgesic.[375]

Each person who uses caffeine should learn how much is too much for her. Those who are sensitive to even small amounts of caffeine would best avoid it altogether.

Abruptly Stopping Heavy Caffeine Use. Headaches at the base of the skull for heavy caffeine users who abruptly stop using it are legend. When a heavy user decides to stop, she should gradually taper her daily dose. If the headaches occur anyway, the person can usually relieve the pain by positioning a cold pack against the base of the skull. The cold pack should be separated from the skin by some thin material such as a pillow case.

Some anti-caffeine individuals argue that the only pain that caffeine relieves is the headaches that occur when people abruptly stop using it. Too many studies to reference here have shown this argument to be false. Taking caffeine does relieve "caffeine withdrawal headaches," but it also directly and indirectly reduces other types of pain (see section below titled "Pain-Reducing Effects of Caffeine").

Breast Pain. Some women—but certainly not most—have breast pain that's associated with their caffeine use. This was reported by researchers who recently reviewed studies of breast pain published between 1975 and 2002. It's important to note the researchers' recommended solution to the breast pain. Their solution wasn't total abstinence from caffeine; instead, it was "caffeine reduction."[348]

Similarly, Dr. Michael Murray and Dr. Joseph Pizzorno, in their *Textbook of Natural Medicine* (see *Resources*), don't advise women to fully give up caffeine. They explain how caffeine contributes to the fibrocystic breast disease of some women. In their treatment recommendations, they don't write that affected women should totally and forever stop their use of caffeine. Instead, they write, "All methylxanthines [such as caffeine] should be eliminated until symptoms are alleviated. They can then be reintroduced in small amounts."[293]

Pain-Reducing Effects of Caffeine

The belief of many rheumatologists and fibromyalgia support group leaders that caffeine increases fibromyalgia patients' pain is contradicted by a Norwegian study. When patients used caffeine along with acetaminophen and the chemical in Soma, they had less pain and less feelings of sickness, and their sleep improved.[383] Of course, in this study, we can't distinguish the benefits of caffeine from those of the acetaminophen and the chemical in Soma. Other studies of caffeine and pain, however, suggest that using caffeine can benefit fibromyalgia patients.

The painkilling effect of analgesics such as aspirin or acetaminophen is enhanced by caffeine in doses of 65 mg or more. Taking caffeine with analgesics increases the percentage of people whose headaches are relieved.[378] When women use caffeine with aspirin or acetaminophen, it usually effectively relieves their acute menstrual migraine.[354] And when migraine patients use caffeine in combination with ergotamine, it usually effectively relieves their headaches.[355] And, surgeons report that intravenous caffeine effectively relieves a patient's headache caused by a lumbar spinal puncture.[380]

People with positive moods experience less pain.[349][350][351][352] Caffeine improves mood (see section below titled "Improved Mood"), and because of this, researchers speculated that improved mood from using caffeine accounts for the chemical's painkilling effect. To test this idea, they conducted a study that factored out the effect of mood on pain relief. They found that two doses of caffeine (65 mg and 130 mg) had a direct painkilling effect that wasn't caused by improved mood.[353] This finding is consistent with new information on pain mechanisms that suggests caffeine directly reduces pain by chemically interfering with nerve transmission.[379]

Caffeine reduced the pain women experienced when they were exposed to intense cold.[374] It also raised the pain threshold and pain tolerance of men and women when they were exposed to painful cold.[376]

Caffeine, then, can increase the pain of a small percentage of people, but otherwise, the chemical doesn't increase pain. This is exactly opposite from what many fibromyalgia support group leaders and rheumatologists tell patients. The truth is that using moderate amounts of caffeine usually reduces pain. It's for that very reason that many painkilling medications contain caffeine. Thus, group leaders and rheumatologists who advise all patients to abstain from using caffeine are dispensing patently bad advice. Patients will fare best by initially rejecting it. Then, they should learn through personal experimentation whether using caffeine benefits them. If it does, they should prudently use it as they see fit.

OTHER BENEFITS OF USING CAFFEINE

Using caffeine wisely can provide a wide range of health benefits. Here we'll consider a few that are relevant to people who want to improve their metabolic health.

Improved Mood

Caffeine is the most widely used mind-altering drug.[369] A few researchers seem beside themselves with scorn that people are at liberty to use caffeine to alter their moods. These researchers show their pejorative attitude by labeling caffeine a "drug of abuse"[370] and not bothering to distinguish between its harmful and helpful uses. Presumably, they'd prefer that caffeine be on the prescription list and restricted to uses dictated by doctors.

Admittedly, a small percentage of people with addictive tendencies use caffeine to their own detriment. In our experience, however, most people use the chemical responsibly to enhance their daily mental and emotional experiences. We see no problem with most people treating themselves with caffeine.

Much is to be gained in the way of mood control by the use of caffeine. Researchers have found that the use of moderate amounts of caffeine usually improves mood.[384] In women with low anxiety, for example, caffeine improved mood and reduced depression.[374]

Even small doses of caffeine leave users feeling happier, calmer, and less tense. But some studies show a progressive benefit from the consumption of larger amounts. Studies in several countries, for instance, show that nurses have a high risk for suicide. But the suicide rate is lower among those who drink more coffee. And the more they drink, the lower their suicide rate.[366][367] In fact, the association between larger consumption and lower suicide rate is *strong*.[366] Most likely, the lower suicide rate results from the improved mood induced by caffeine and similar chemicals in the nurses' coffee.

Energy and Alertness

When our Editor, Jackie Yellin, saw that we were including pro-caffeine information in this book, she commented, "The information will be an eye opener—both figuratively and literally!" Indeed, we expect that some readers are already wide-eyed from our pro-caffeine views. And, as most hypometabolic caffeine users already know, the chemical can provide the verve to open wide, eyes half closed from lethargy and lack of drive.

People usually feel more energetic after ingesting even small amounts of caffeine.[376] Researchers found that caffeine enhanced early morning alertness in men.[356] It also reduced next-day drowsiness among men who took tranquilizers the night before.[356][357]

Other researchers found that caffeine reduced "subjective sleepiness," meaning that those using it didn't feel as sleepy.[358] After being totally deprived of sleep, 200 mg of caffeine reduced sleepiness and lane-drifting when young people did mock driving for 30 minutes. For people who had five hours of sleep, 200 mg reduced sleepiness and lane-drifting for two hours. The researchers concluded that by using caffeine, drivers can reduce the high incidence of early-morning driving accidents caused by sleepiness.[359]

One research group used a variety of performance tests with people who were slightly sleep deprived. The researchers found that 300 mg of slow-release caffeine safely and efficiently enabled the people to remain vigilant and perform well.[360] Caffeine has long been considered a useful chemical for enabling soldiers to stay awake and perform well.[361]

These studies explain reports we've heard from many patients who are hypothyroid or thyroid hormone resistant. Until proper thyroid hormone therapy relieved their drowsiness and fatigue, they successfully used caffeine to remain alert. They did so at work and in other situations where they had to perform well.

Mental Ability

People have long recognized that using caffeine improves mental function. For example, Sir James MacKintosh, who died in 1862, wrote, "The powers of man's mind are directly proportional to the quality of the coffee he drinks."[365] Many modern studies uphold his opinion.

Caffeine is listed as a mild brain stimulant and "cognitive enhancer." Researchers have reported that it improved performance on tests of attention, sustained attention, semantic memory, logical reasoning, free recall, delayed recall, problem-solving, recognition tasks, mental speed-related tasks, perceptual sensitivity in visual search, reading speed, and perception of problems. Moderate amounts of caffeine can enhance mental abilities,[384][385] but even small amounts leave most users feeling more "clearheaded."[376]

And, people don't appear to develop tolerance to the performance-enhancing effects of caffeine.

Women who had a higher lifetime and current consumption of coffee scored better than other women on a variety of tests of mental function.[386] In another study, when subjects were deprived of sleep for 64 hours, 300 mg of slow-release caffeine enabled them to stay vigilant and function mentally better than subjects who didn't use caffeine.[387] In addition, caffeine improved alertness and performance on sustained attention tasks.[388]

A precaution is warranted for those considering using caffeine to enhance their mental function. The chemical appears to improve mental function by an overall activation of the brain. The activation can be overdone, and when it is, mental function may be impaired. As we've said before, it's important to experiment and find a caffeine dose that benefits you but doesn't harm you.

Athletic Performance

Caffeine enhances athletic performance so much that it's on the list of substances banned by the International Olympic Committee.[364] That's documentation enough, so we won't cite studies here.

We will point out, though, that caffeine may help hypometabolic patients engage in more exercise than they otherwise could. With comprehensive metabolic rehab, most patients' exercise tolerance will markedly improve. And, using a moderate amount of caffeine before exercise is likely to provide a slight boost that will enable you to benefit more from the activity and increase your exercise tolerance.

OUR ADVICE ON CAFFEINE USE

We could go on and on citing evidence of benefits from using moderate amounts of caffeine. Some of the benefits are fascinating. For example, caffeine is an antioxidant that provides some protection against radiation, mutations, and cancer.[362] And when used in combination with ephedrine or ephedra, caffeine is an effective fat-reducing agent.[363][377] But alas, this isn't a book on caffeine, so we'll limit our discussion of benefits to the sections above and give our advice on the proper use of caffeine.

Coffee or Caffeine Tablets

As we tell most of our patients, we advocate coffee-drinking. Drinking coffee within some twenty minutes after it's prepared provides antioxidant benefits. If you don't like coffee or it bothers your stomach, but you want the benefits of using caffeine, consider taking caffeine tablets.

With caffeine tablets, you can precisely regulate the amount of caffeine you take in. Most caffeine tablets contain 200 mg. The precise content in each tablet enables you to evaluate the effects of different doses on yourself.

Three Qualifications to
Our Advice to Use Caffeine

When we advise you to use caffeine, we do it with three qualifications. These are things you must consider in your prudent evaluation of your use of caffeine.

First, Decide Whether You Have Any Adverse Effects From Caffeine. Some people have adverse effects that can't be avoided, and they'd best not use caffeine. But most adverse effects involve an improper use of caffeine. Some people, for example, simply consume so much caffeine that it makes them anxious or nervous. Others take caffeine so close to bedtime that it causes them to have insomnia. These people can avoid these harmful effects simply by taking less caffeine and abstaining from its use too close to bedtime.

Second, Find What for You Is an Effective Dose of Caffeine That Doesn't Overstimulate You. This means finding the amount that gives you the benefits you want, but that doesn't make you anxious, restless, or irritable. Some people induce these symptoms in themselves by taking higher and higher doses of caffeine to further increase their energy level and improve their mood and cognitive function. The prudent use of caffeine, however, involves learning your effective but non-overstimulating dose. It also involves abstaining from taking a dose that experience has shown is too much for you.

Becoming anxious, restless, or irritable from too much caffeine can be counterproductive. For instance, if your purpose in taking caffeine is to improve your mental functions, anxiety, restlessness, and irritability from overstimulation will provide the opposite—poor memory, concentration, and performance at mental tasks. Also, experiencing anxiety from taking too much caffeine is a worsening of mood—the opposite from the improved mood most people experience from using small to moderate amounts of caffeine.

Third, Evaluate Your Own Attitude Toward Your Use of Caffeine. Today, an anti-caffeine prejudice predominates among health care professionals and writers of self-help literature. By "prejudice," we mean that these people have concluded, despite contrary scientific evidence, that using caffeine is always harmful. If you suspect that they're right, and while consuming caffeine you hold fearful thoughts of it harming you, you may eventually be harmed by your own thoughts rather than by the caffeine. This, of course, would be the equivalent of a disease-inducing hypnotic suggestion. If you doubt the safety of moderate caffeine use, read everything you can on the subject and form your own opinion. If you come to believe that using caffeine is harmful, you'd best give it up. But if you come to agree with us—that the anti-caffeine faction is wrong—then use caffeine prudently and without fear to enhance your health.

With these qualifications in mind, we advise you to use caffeine (assuming you have no non-correctable adverse effects from it), and to do it *judiciously*. By that, we mean that you should ignore unscientific, emotionally-driven warnings against caffeine use, find the dosage that is enough but not too much for you, and consume it shamelessly!"[15]

PRECAUTIONS

We have several precautions for your use of coffee and caffeine. Considering these may help you to avoid problems using either.

Adverse Reactions to Caffeine

If you poorly tolerate even small amounts of caffeine, you had best not use it at all. Even if you get some benefit from caffeine, if you have one of several specific health problems, it's probably best that you abstain from using it until you get the problem under control.

If you have panic attacks, caffeine may initiate or worsen them.[381] If you have a peptic or duodenal ulcer, caffeine may worsen the associated pain.[382] If small amounts of caffeine give you headaches, you might have to give it up altogether. But if caffeine causes breast pain, you'll probably have to stop using it for some time, and then find a low dose that doesn't cause the pain to recur. (See section above titled "Caffeine Can Worsen *Some* People's Pain").

If you get the jitters or an upset stomach when you use caffeine, reduce the amount you use. Keep reducing it until you know how much you can use without experiencing these effects.

If caffeine interferes with your sleep, try using it earlier in the day. For the average person, about half of a dose of caffeine is out of the body five hours after it's taken. It's probably best if you don't take caffeine for six hours before your bedtime.

Verve From the Use of Caffeine: A Social Liability for Some. In the section above titled "Energy and Alertness," we said that caffeine provides "verve." This is a French word meaning enthusiasm, vigor, and liveliness. The French term also means chatter. This particular meaning is closer to the original Latin word from which the term verve is derived: *verba*, meaning talk.

Many people talk more after they've ingested caffeine. But people are affected to different degrees. Caffeine virtually brings some usually speechless people to life; after a cup or two of coffee, they carry on conversations much like anyone else. They become enjoyable, interesting, and engaging to their companions.

Caffeine transforms a few people, however, into endless chatterers that annoy anyone they're with. They blabber on nonstop, rambling from one trivial matter to another, completely oblivious to the likelihood that others might have something to say. These people are likely to find their companions—who can't get a word in edgewise—reluctant to have coffee with them again.

Reacting to caffeine in this garrulous way can damage one's social relations. The damage exemplifies the importance of recognizing when caffeine has harmful effects on us. A reality check is in order under several circumstances: If caffeine upsets your stomach and you find yourself taking calcium-tablets to quell the upset; if caffeine makes you nervous and this sabotages successful outcomes to business and social interactions; or if you have breast pain that's worse when you use more caffeine on average.

Fortunately, such adverse reactions to caffeine are rare. Most people can use it with no harm to themselves; in fact, they can use it to enhance their health and quality of life. We encourage this majority to use caffeine, but to do so *prudently*.

Coffee and Pregnancy

Some researchers have found that many pregnant women who drank more than five cups of coffee per day had problems with their pregnancies. As a group, the women had a high incidence of impending abortion, premature labor, and fetuses small for gestational age. They also had high rates of spontaneous abortion, chromosomal abnormality, and multiple congenital abnormalities.

The researchers emphasized, however, that they didn't know if these problems with pregnancy were caused directly by the coffee. Social and economic factors might have been responsible.[368] Regardless, we feel that women should err on the side of caution and consume only small amounts of caffeine during pregnancy.

Organic Coffee

We strongly recommend that you make your coffee from organic coffee beans. By using organic beans, you'll minimize your intake of pesticides and other man-made chemical contaminants. We've explained the importance of organic foods in the section titled "Organic Foods" in *Chapter 4*.

Avoiding Oxidation of Your Coffee. We also recommend that you grind your organic coffee beans just before you make coffee. Grinding them earlier will increase the oxidation of fats in the coffee. The oxidized fats are harmful to our health.

■ For more on caffeine and its proper use, see *The Metabolic Treatment of Fibromyalgia*. Read Chapter 5.2, section titled "Caffeine," pages 969-970. Also read Chapter 5.5, pages 1035-1042.

SECTION III
OBSTACLES TO YOUR RECOVERY: GETTING PAST THEM

Chapter 15

Troubleshooting

IN THIS CHAPTER, WE PRESENT the most common obstacles to recovery for patients undergoing metabolic rehab. We also explain the ways most patients remove or get around the obstacles.

You should be able to identify most obstacles to your recovery in one of three ways:

- Find and read about the obstacles in this chapter.
- Look in the index of this book for key words related to what you suspect is the obstacle. Go to the pages in the chapters that contain information on the obstacle. Read them to decide whether you may be right about the obstacle, and to learn how to overcome it.
- Go to the webpage that contains our troubleshooting section for those of you using the program we've described in *Your Guide to Metabolic Health*. Read about what you suspect is the obstacle you're facing. Learn the suggested solution and apply it in your case. The webpage address is: <www.McDowellPublishing.com/TroubleShooting/ygmh.htm> As more and more readers of *Your Guide to Metabolic Health* communicate with us about obstacles they run into, we'll continue to update and add to our troubleshooting section.

If you use the three resources above, but you still can't figure out what's holding back your progress, we'll be happy to help as much as we can. You have three other options:

- Write to us at AskDrLowe@drlowe.com. We'll reply to your e-mail. Please be patient, though. Sometimes we're overwhelmed with requests for information. We try to answer everyone, although occasionally it takes a little time. Please note:

In the subject line of your e-mail, type "YGMH." This will let us know that we have an e-mail from someone working with *Your Guide to Metabolic Health* who has run into an obstacle. We'll give your e-mail top priority.

- Work with us through a long-distance consulting relationship. We help as many patients as we can by answering the questions they send to AskDrLowe@drlowe.com. But in some cases, we can only help by studying details of the patient's case through her medical and health history, lab test results, and exam results. In these cases, we can usually help the patient through a consulting relationship. We're able to help patients through long-distance consulting who live in most states in the United States, most provinces in Canada, and in countries as far away as the United Kingdom, Austria, Israel, South Africa, Australia, and New Zealand. To learn about our long-distance consulting services, see the following webpage: <www.drlowe. com/clincare/labtests.htm>

- Work with us at our Center for Metabolic Health in Boulder, Colorado. Some patients prefer to come to Boulder for evaluation and treatment. Other patients must come if we're to learn enough about them individually to be able to help them improve or recover. Of course, the Boulder area is one of the most beautiful places to visit in the United States. The alternative medicine community in Boulder is large, and the local citizenry is predominantly health-oriented. If you stay in a local motel, you can order delivery of organic foods from some restaurants. To learn about coming for personalized care at our Center, see the following webpage: <www.drlowe.com/ clincare/clinicpatient.htm> Also, see *Resources*.

FIRST STEP IN TROUBLESHOOTING

The first step to take in troubleshooting is to make sure you're doing all that you must to achieve or maintain metabolic health. We list these essential practices in Table 1.

Go down the list of essential practices (left-hand column). If you're doing a practice—and know you're doing it properly!—place a check mark in the "Yes" column to the right.

If you know you're not doing it, or not doing it right, place a check mark in the "No" column. If you're not sure, place a check mark in the "?" column.

A check mark in the "No" or "?" column for a practice suggests that failure to benefit from that practice is an obstacle to your full recovery. If you place a check mark in the "No" or "?" columns, you should read or reread the chapter designated in the far right column titled "Where You Can Learn More." By carefully reading the chapter related to the practice(s) you're not doing, or not sure you're doing, you should be able to learn how to get around that obstacle.

Using this table is a simplified version of the method we use to help our patients identify and get around obstacles to their recovery. It may seem too simple. Regardless, using it involves the same type of systematic analyses we do that enable us to get most of our patients well.

An Extremely Important Point: When the table directs you to a chapter, don't just read the relevant information and stop there. You must—you absolutely *must!*—put the information to practical use in your program of metabolic rehab. In *Chapter 2*, we pointed out that you must identify the factors that may be impeding your metabolism and keeping you at a low level of metabolic health. (See section titled "Metabolism-slowing Factors: What You Must Change to Improve Your Symptoms.")

TWO MAIN CATEGORIES OF OBSTACLES TO RECOVERY

Obstacles to recovery generally fall into two main categories: Those that involve lifestyle practices, and those related to the services health care practitioners provide. Some obstacles, however, fall into both categories.

Below, for example, we've classified the section titled "Troublesome Drugs" under obstacles involving professional services. In the troublesome drugs section, we've included overstimulation by caffeine and decongestants. You obviously don't have to have a prescription to use these chemicals. We included them in that professional services section only for convenience.

We also included potential problems with antidepressants in the troublesome drugs section. Patients must have prescriptions to buy antidepressants in most countries. But nowadays, patients can buy antidepressants without a prescription from foreign Internet pharmacies. The patient who gets an antidepressant this way isn't using the services of a doctor. We could class her antidepressant use under lifestyle practices rather than professional services. But the effort would be unwieldy. So, we've lumped all potentially troublesome drugs together. The point is that some obstacles overlap the two categories.

Below, we include several of the most common obstacles in the two categories. For more, see our troubleshooting webpage: <www.McDowellPublishing.com/TroubleShooting/ygmh.htm>

OBSTACLES INVOLVING LIFESTYLE PRACTICES

Patients most commonly encounter two general obstacles among lifestyle practices: failure to guide their treatment with graphs of their symptoms, and failure to engage in necessary lifestyle practices.

You Don't *Think* You've Improved at All

Occasionally a patient whom we're guiding through metabolic rehab tells us, "I'm so depressed about my treatment. It's been two months now, and I haven't improved a bit!"

When we hear this, we open the patient's file and take out her graphs. Typically, the graphs show some degree of improvement—often as much as 50%. We show the graphs to the patient and she undergoes a prompt reality adjustment, whereupon she acknowledges that she's improved remarkably so far and that she's merely having a bad day, perhaps for some reason unrelated to her metabolic health.

If you've been making lifestyle changes and perhaps using some professional services to improve your metabolic health, chances are, you've had some improvement. If you have a bad day, or several, your state of mind on those days can temporarily erase all memory of the progress you've made. And it can cause you to falsely believe you've made no progress at all. If you don't have graphs that show your progress, you've denied yourself a prompt and powerful reality adjustment tool.

Some patients who read *Your Guide to Metabolic Health* won't use graphs, despite our emphasizing the importance of doing so. At times, they'll feel disheartened at what seems to be little or no progress. Occasionally, one of these patients will contact us for help, and she'll complain that her metabolic rehab isn't working. When we ask, "What does your symptom graph show?" and she replies, "I don't have a graph," we'll simply inform her, "You haven't been doing metabolic rehab."

You're Doing Metabolic Rehab *Only* When:
1. you've selected your symptoms to eliminate
2. you've created a severity scale for each symptom
3. you've begun graphing your scores from the scales at regular intervals
4. you improve your metabolism through lifestyle changes and/or medical therapies

If you *think* you're not improving, but you don't know for sure because you've failed to properly monitor your symptoms, read carefully over *Chapter 2* and *Chapter 3*.

Not Engaging in Necessary Lifestyle Practices
Patients often consult us who are using thyroid hormone but doing few or none of the lifestyle practices essential to metabolic health. Predictably, these patients have improved little if at all. None of them have achieved their full potential for metabolic health.

A few of these patients began using thyroid hormone at the advice of another patient—one who went through metabolic rehab, but who gave up doing one or more lifestyle practices such as exercise to tolerance. This patient passed along to the others, who were new to metabolic rehab, her version of the treatment. That version didn't include exercise to tolerance. By the time we hear from one

Table 1. Are you doing each of these practices that are essential to effective metabolic rehab?				
Essential Practices	Yes	No	?	Where You Can Learn More
Keeping a list of symptoms you want to eliminate				Chapter 2
Measuring the severity of your symptoms with scales, and graphing the scores				Chapter 3
Eating a wholesome diet				Chapter 4
Taking nutritional supplements				Chapters 5 & 6
Exercising to tolerance				Chapter 10
Abstaining from taking troublesome drugs				See below, "Troublesome Drugs"
Using adequate amounts of thyroid hormone				Chapter 7
Getting needed physical treatment				Chapter 13
Avoiding chemical contaminants				Chapter 12
Being treated for other hormone deficiencies or imbalances				Chapters 8 & 9
Being treated for other medical disorders				See below, "Disorders Other than Hypometabolism"

of the people new to metabolic therapy—but who already takes thyroid hormone—she's gotten limited benefit from the hormone. When these patients, both old and new, begin exercising to tolerance and engaging in the other lifestyle practices, they markedly improve.

Patients who won't exercise, take nutritional supplements, or eat a wholesome diet usually have two "good" reasons: They don't have time to exercise or prepare wholesome foods, and they don't want to spend their money on supplements and organic foods. We often ask them, "What do you value more—saving time and money by disregarding the lifestyle practices, or being healthy and feeling good?" Before answering this question, mindful patients will consider that by disregarding the practices, they'll eventually spend the saved time and money dealing with their symptoms of poor metabolic health.

Some people simply hope they can fully neglect the lifestyle practices and get healthy with the use of thyroid hormone alone. They expect far too much from merely taking thyroid hormone. The effects on the body of the lifestyle practices are synergistic to the effects of thyroid hormone. These effects interact with one another to produce and enhance metabolic health. Because of this, if you fail to engage in the lifestyle practices—even if you're taking a high-enough dose of thyroid hormone—you won't achieve optimal metabolic health. In fact, you may not improve much at all.

(*Note:* Consider the "normal" person—one who already has enough thyroid hormone regulating her metabolism. If she doesn't exercise and eat correctly, she won't maintain good health either!)

Let the following words resound from the pages of this book— For *optimal* metabolic health, you *must* use *all* the synergistic metabolism-regulating lifestyle practices and therapies we describe in *Your Guide to Metabolic Health*!

A Conscious Choice Not to Take Advantage of the Full Treatment Protocol. Some patients consciously choose not to avail themselves of the full benefits metabolic rehab can provide.

Most often, these patients decide not to engage in lifestyle practices required for their full recovery.

Some patients choose to keep eating loads of sugary foods each day. They do so with full knowledge that the hypoglycemia the sugary foods cause makes it impossible for them to fully recover. Their episodes of low blood sugar force them to keep their thyroid hormone dose too low to benefit them. But fully recovering their health isn't worth giving up brief, sugar-induced surges of pleasure, even though the surges are followed by hours of misery.

Other patients choose not to stop taking trouble-causing drugs. We have some young female patients, for example, who opt to continue taking birth control pills when these are obviously interfering with their progress. Progestins in the pills cause symptoms by inducing insulin resistance, and the resulting energy-deficiency symptoms make it impossible for the young women to fully recover. The benefits of using the pills, however, are more important to them at their stage in life than being completely well.

If you choose not to change some lifestyle practice that's keeping you ill, we respect your personal choice. We believe, however, that it's important to be honest with yourself; in doing so, you should accept the limited improvement that your choice will impose on you.

Far too common is the patient who stays in denial about the lifestyle practices that are sabotaging her health. Refusing to see that her lifestyle choices are sustaining her symptoms, she usually undergoes expensive diagnostic tests in the hope that her doctor will find some treatable cause for her misery. If the doctor finds something to treat, this gives the patient—at least theoretically—something to blame her symptoms on. And this conveniently relieves her for a while of the need to improve her lifestyle. In the meantime, her denial helps drive health care costs further through the clouds, and it wastes the time of doctors that could be better spent helping people who're willing to work to get well.

Not Improving Enough
From Lifestyle Practices Alone

Many patients have symptoms of slow metabolism even after they've adopted the lifestyle changes that are necessary for metabolic health. They've stuck to a wholesome diet, taken nutritional supplements, exercised to tolerance, avoided metabolism-impeding drugs, and gotten needed physical treatment. Moreover, their alternative doctors may have treated them for candida[88][96] or mycoplasm infections,[87] or leaky gut syndrome. And, the doctors may have put them through several detoxification programs. But alas, the patients still have symptoms of slow metabolism.

If we've just described your personal experience, we'll assume you've rigorously used metabolic rehab as we've explained it in this book: You've engaged in the lifestyle practices. You've also monitored the severity of your symptoms at regular intervals, and you've posted your symptom scores to a line graph. Maybe your graph shows that your symptoms have improved a bit, and subjectively you feel a little better. But despite all this, you haven't improved enough.

The most likely obstacle standing in your way is the need for effective thyroid hormone therapy. We say this because no factor other than too little thyroid hormone regulation more tenaciously keeps people sick when they're doing everything else right.

Here are some important points to remember about taking thyroid hormone: Many patients "doing everything else right"—but still not improving—are already using thyroid hormone. Many are using T_4 alone, which helps precious few patients fully recover their health. Some are taking desiccated thyroid, but their dosages are too low. And some are resistant to thyroid hormone, and will recover only by using plain T_3.

If you're not yet taking thyroid hormone, to get safe and effective thyroid hormone therapy, you'll have to find an alternative doctor. Conventional thyroid hormone therapy is notoriously ineffective. (See *Chapter 7.*)

OBSTACLES RELATED TO THE SERVICES
OF HEALTH CARE PRACTITIONERS

The most common problems we've encountered with treatments by health care professionals fall into several categories. Doctors prescribing drugs to control symptoms without treating the underlying cause (as with fibromyalgia patients) is possibly the most common. The way around this problem is to switch from conventional to alternative medicine.

Another common obstacle is doctors failing to provide proper treatment with thyroid hormone. We extensively cover this subject in *Chapter 7*. We also provide a great deal of information about this problem on our troubleshooting webpage: <www.McDowellPublishing.com/TroubleShooting/ygmh.htm>

Tenacious infections can interfere with patients' progress (see <www.McDowellPublishing.com/TroubleShooting/ ygmh.htm>), though we see this far less often than some of the other problems. Also, medical disorders with symptoms that mimic those of hypometabolism can confuse a patient, leaving her not knowing what's causing the symptoms (see below, "Disorders Other than Hypometabolism").

Another of the most common obstacles to a patient's recovery is her use of troublesome drugs. We cover this in the next section.

Troublesome Drugs

The use of different drugs can be an obstacle to recovery during metabolic rehab. Various drugs can interfere in different ways. In Table 2, we've included the drugs that have most often stood in the way of our patients' recovery.

Some patients aren't able to muster the drive to exercise because of their use of medications such as Vicodin, Xanax, or Soma Compound. These drugs may have previously made life tolerable, but they can limit the benefits patients could otherwise gain from metabolic therapy.

Narcotics. Most patients with a diagnosis of fibromyalgia who use narcotics don't get the pain relief they expect. Commonly, when these patients consult us, they have pain over 100% of their bodies, and they estimate the intensity of their pain as 100%. So, their pain couldn't be worse, despite the narcotics they use.

Among hypometabolic patients, it's those whose pain leads to a diagnosis of fibromyalgia who are most likely to begin using narcotics. As we've said elsewhere in this book, we have roughly an 85% success rate with fibromyalgia patients; that is, only about 15% of patients fail to markedly improve or fully recover. Prominent among this 15% who fail to recover are patients using maintenance doses of narcotic medications.

We've found that some patients who take maintenance doses of narcotics (several doses during each day) aren't able to use doses of thyroid hormone high enough to be effective. The patients using narcotics become overstimulated by low doses of thyroid hormone before they can reach their therapeutic dose. Tachycardia (a resting heart rate of 100 or more beats per minute) is the most common symptom among these patients.

Another problem is that most of the patients taking narcotics aren't able to exercise to tolerance. And without being able to engage in this metabolism-regulating lifestyle practice, they simply aren't able to achieve metabolic health.

Of course, some patients who take maintenance doses of narcotics don't have these problems. Nor, in our experience, do patients who use narcotics on an occasional (as-needed) basis. If you must use a maintenance dose of narcotics, hopefully it won't interfere with your thyroid hormone therapy. But if you develop what seems to be thyroid hormone overstimulation at a low dose, we encourage you to discuss with your doctor a potential interaction of the narcotic with the thyroid hormone. We work with each patient as an individual, and when a patient must use a narcotic (as the rare patient must), we do everything possible to help her recover while respecting that special need. In the end, however, some patients must make a choice between continuing their narcotic use and recovering from their fibromyalgia symptoms.

We want to emphasize an important point: We know that using narcotics is a boon to many patients who live with chronic pain from which there is no available escape. We have no objection to such patients using narcotics. Most fibromyalgia patients, however, can escape their pain, although narcotic addiction often blocks the escape.

Discussing this subject openly carries a distinct risk. Many patients using narcotics promptly join campaigns of hostility toward doctors who express concern about narcotic addiction. These patients are joined in the effort by some doctors who themselves have a diagnosis of fibromyalgia, and who liberally prescribe narcotics for their patients and use narcotics themselves.

Despite this unfortunate social phenomenon, we have no choice but to be honest with patients using narcotics who inquire about treatment with us. For us not to discuss the subject forthrightly would be unethical. The patient who uses narcotics and wants to undergo metabolic rehab has two options. First, before starting rehab, she can enlist the cooperation of the doctor who prescribes her narcotics to help her stop them. Or she can commit to stopping the narcotic (again with the cooperation of the prescribing doctor) shortly after beginning metabolic rehab. If a patient chooses to continue taking maintenance doses of a narcotic, the chance of treatment failure is high. Again, we make no value judgment about a patient's choice either way, but professional ethics compel us to be honest about the issues involved.

If you use a maintenance dose of a narcotic, and you choose to stop, we strongly recommend that you enlist the help of your prescribing doctor. With his or her support, you may better tolerate the symptoms of narcotic withdrawal.

Beta-Blocking Drugs. Beta-blocking drugs impair metabolism by binding to beta-receptors. Binding of the drugs to the receptors prevents the nerve-transmitters adrenaline and noradrenaline from binding to the receptors. When these and other metabolism-driving chemicals can't bind to beta-receptors, cell metabolism slows down.

Hyperthyroid patients whose tissues are overstimulated often use beta-blockers to stop the overstimulation. The main reason hyperthyroidism causes overstimulation is that the excess thyroid hormone overly increases the density of beta-receptors on cell membranes. With so many beta-receptors on the membranes, even small amounts of adrenaline and noradrenaline cause cell metabolism to race. (The effect is much like taking too much caffeine.) Because of the way thyroid hormone works in the body, the beta-blocker is able to stop the overstimulation.

Table 2. Prescription drugs that commonly impede metabolism

Medication	Possible Effects

Tricyclic antidepressants
    amitriptyline, cyclobenzaprine
	Inhibits TSH release,
	    increases heart rate

Benzodiazepines
    Xanax, Valium, Atavan
	Reduces physical activity
	    through sedation

Beta blockers Inderal, propranolol, Atenolol	Slows metabolism

Narcotics
    OxyContin, Vicodan
	Impairs ability to exercise,
	    causes overstimulation

For some patients, however, taking large doses of beta-blockers, or taking doses several times through the day, can have adverse effects. The drugs can cause disturbed sleep, fatigue, and depression. Some patients who use beta-blockers to control mitral valve prolapse develop symptoms that lead to a diagnosis of fibromyalgia. For a few of these patients, stopping the beta-blockers completely relieves the symptoms. Other patients, however, must undergo metabolic rehab to completely recover, especially if they've used beta-blockers for years.

Many patients take beta-blockers for mild hypertension. Some of these patients' hypertension is caused by too little thyroid hormone regulation. For them, a high-enough daily dose of the proper form of thyroid hormone can reduce their blood pressure to normal.

If patients are to benefit from the use of thyroid hormone, they must stop taking beta-blockers. Otherwise, the beta-blockers will nullify the effects of the thyroid hormone on the body. To our amazement, some patients who consult us have been taking both beta-blockers and thyroid hormone for years—both prescribed by the same doctor!

Tricyclic Antidepressants. Tricyclic antidepressants (such as amitriptyline and cyclobenzaprine) may interfere with metabolic treatment. These drugs alone may cause tachycardia and ischemic heart disease.

Thyroid hormone typically increases the heart rate as it increases the density of beta-receptors (see above section titled "beta-blocking drugs") on cardiac muscle. We've observed that when some patients use both tricyclic antidepressants and thyroid hormone, they have a greater increase in heart rate than either medication causes alone. Because of this, unless patients have depression that's responsive *only* to antidepressants, we believe they should stop the tricyclic drugs before beginning to use thyroid hormone. Thyroid hormone alone relieves many patients' depression, so they don't need to use antidepressants.

For hypometabolic patients with a diagnosis of fibromyalgia or chronic fatigue syndrome, there's little point in taking tricyclic antidepressants anyway. Long-term studies have shown that other than a faint improvement in only 30% of patients during the first month of use, the drugs are no more effective than placebos.[21] [283][284] (See *Chapter 11*, section titled "Antidepressants as Sleep Aids.") Some patients report that they're not able to sleep without these drugs, but it's possible that this is a placebo effect. Most of our patients sleep well by taking 50 mg of diphenhydramine 30 minutes before bedtime if necessary. (This usually only happens during the beginning of metabolic rehab. After the therapy begins to normalize their metabolism, most patients are able to sleep without any aids). Diphenhydramine has a short half-life, and some patients must take another 50 mg after four or five hours of sleep. The drug is available over the counter in the United States.

Caffeine. Caffeine can be an obstacle to recovery. It doesn't have to be an obstacle, however. In fact, it can help optimize your metabolic health—as long as you use it prudently (see *Chapter 14*).

Caffeine can be a problem, though, when it overstimulates you. It's wise, of course, to avoid ingesting so much that it causes symptoms such as tremors, anxiety, and irritability. If you want to use caffeine to enhance your health, you should find the dose that benefits you but doesn't overstimulate. That is, find the amount that's just right for you.

Keep this important point in mind: If you begin using thyroid hormone, when you reach your effective daily dose, it will probably make you more sensitive to caffeine. When this happens, the amount of caffeine that before was right for you will instead overstimulate you. The simple solution is to test lower amounts of caffeine and find the one that's now right for you.

Patients occasionally consult us who believe the overstimulation they experience several times each day is from too high a dose of thyroid hormone. If they were taking too much thyroid hormone, symptoms of overstimulation would be more steady rather than episodic. A little questioning reveals that the episodes of overstimulation follow the patient's consumption of caffeine. When they lower the amount of caffeine they take in, the episodes of overstimulation disappear—even at the same thyroid hormone dose they thought was overstimulating them. (Episodes of overstimulation can also occur when patients take some antihistamines or decongestants, although these usually cause overstimulation for longer times. See the next section, "Cold Medicines, Decongestants, and Diet Drugs.")

Cold Medicines, Decongestants, and Diet Drugs. Some chemicals in cold medicines, decongestants, and diet drugs are stimulants. This is especially true of pseudoephedrine in cold medicines and decongestants, and ephedra in diet drugs. High enough doses of these chemicals will overstimulate almost anyone; lower doses aren't overstimulating. Thyroid hormone, however, can render one more sensitive to the chemicals. When it does, a dose of one of the chemicals that wasn't overstimulating may come to be so.

Some patients consult us who had been using the same dose of thyroid hormone with good effect for months. Then, suddenly, they developed symptoms of overstimulation. To help these patients figure out the cause of their symptoms, we always ask whether or not they've been taking a cold medicine or decongestant. When they stop the drug, or lower their dose enough, their overstimulation stops even though they continue taking the same daily dose of thyroid hormone.

Disorders Other Than Hypometabolism

We're always on alert for disorders other than impaired metabolism that can produce similar symptoms. The most common ones are rheumatoid arthritis, Lyme disease, systemic lupus erythematosus, brain stem compression due to Chiari malformation, cervical cord compression due to spinal stenosis, polymyalgia rheumatica, myopathy, and myofascial pain syndrome.

If you have one of these other disorders rather than symptoms of slow metabolism, effective treatment for the other disorder should relieve the symptoms. It's important to keep in mind, however, that you can have one of these other disorders *and* hypometabolism at the same time. Recovering from your symptoms will then require that you get effective treatment for both conditions.[90]

Chapter 16

Other Obstacles to Your Recovery

SEVERAL OBSTACLES CAN INTERFERE WITH your achieving optimal metabolic health. The most common we've seen are: lack of support from loved ones, too little knowledge of one's disorder, support groups that don't focus on recovery, and managed medical care. You can better get past any of these potential obstacles when you understand how they can interfere.

WHEN YOUR FAMILY ISN'T HELPING . . . OR WORSE

Your family may not go along with the lifestyle changes you must make to improve your metabolism and your health. Or, worse, they may give you a rough time for making the changes. Sadly, it's common for a patient's family to ridicule her. Some family members try to make the patient feel guilty for spending too much time on herself instead of constantly meeting their needs or demands.

If you insist that your family make lifestyle changes with you, they may resist just because you're demanding the changes. They may even consciously or unconsciously sabotage your efforts to improve your health. You're likely to get better results by serving as an example to them. When they see you improving, they may be inspired to make the health-inducing changes you have made. We've learned through watching some of our own loved ones that accepting them as they are—although still setting an example for them—is the most productive and peaceful choice.

Some spouses, partners, family members, or friends feel threatened when a patient begins to feel better and has more energy to pursue interests that may, or may not, include them. In such instances, the *status quo* is being upset. If you find yourself in this situation, allow time for the involved loved ones to adjust to your improving health and expanding vision of what your life can be. Hopefully, they will adapt in their own time if you're patient with them. Be sure to explore and share common interests with them as well. This may help them see that their fears aren't justified—that your recovering your health doesn't mean a loss to them.

When some patients recover from a chronic illness, their families need the help of a psychotherapist or counselor to adjust constructively to resulting changes in family dynamics. If this is the case with your family, we encourage you to view finding solutions through professional help as a sign of commitment and strength.

If your loved ones can't or won't give you support, search for a supportive recovery-oriented group—or form your own. But if you search for one, be wary: some groups can do you more harm than good (see section below titled "Support Groups and Internet News Groups").

TOO LITTLE KNOWLEDGE OF YOUR DISORDER

The Internet brought an end to the long span of time during which most patients remained ignorant of their health disorders. Patients no longer have to get by with the crumbs of information their doctors provide (often *false* information at that!).

In years past, patients were victimized because they had to depend only on what doctors told them. Accurate and scientific medical information was largely unavailable to most patients. This put them at a huge disadvantage in making decisions about their health.

Sadly, conventional doctors in the 20th century often betrayed patients' welfare by using treatments that weren't the best options. And tragically, the treatments they used often weren't the safest. The treatments conventional doctors commonly offered, many of which harmed and even killed patients, enriched the drug companies. The drug companies returned the favor, lending their wealth and influence to a perpetuation of the myth that conventional doctors were usually responsible, humane, conscientious, and scientifically-oriented. Large medical organizations, with the cooperation of many practicing doctors, did their best to misguide people about what was best for their health. I (JCL) am old enough to remember conventional doctors publicly arguing that diet, nutritional supplementation, and exercise had nothing to do with health, and all we could do was wait for sickness to overcome us, and then submit strictly to the use of drugs and surgery to save us. No one can convince me that these doctors were so ignorant that they believed such tripe.

Many of the same large medical organizations contributed further to conventional medicine's influence by using their power, partly in collusion with drug companies, to persecute whole professions that offered the public safer forms of treatment, professions such as chiropractic and naturopathy. This was truly a low point in the history of medicine.

With access to the Internet, you can set yourself free from dependence on conventional medicine's financially-driven beliefs, propaganda, and ineffective and harmful treatments. You can accomplish this by learning about the wide array of alternatives to conventional medicine. Then you can independently decide for yourself which of these will serve you best in optimizing your metabolism and recovering your health.

Consider a patient of mine (GII-L) for whom "surfing" the net was a lifesaver. She had struggled with symptoms of fibromyalgia for several years. Her symptoms became so severe that she had to quit her job teaching high school biology. She had tried self-help techniques, and when these didn't prove effective, she visited a prominent East-coast rheumatologist who was a fibromyalgia "specialist." He offered her the typical cocktail of tricyclic antidepressants, muscle relaxers, and narcotics. He told her *not* to get on the Internet. Dissatisfied with his recommendations, she defiantly went home and logged onto the 'Net. Our website was the first she located, and she promptly called to make an appointment. She worked diligently and had an excellent response to treatment in just a few months. She and her family have been very active for several years now with travel and other adventures, and her family can hardly keep up with her!

Many months after her recovery when this patient's family was moving to a new home, she ran across a journal where she had recorded her suicidal thoughts and plans prior to beginning metabolic rehab. She read her words to her teenage son, and they held each other and cried. Until then, no one in her family had known how desperate she had been before metabolic rehab. When we were discussing this incident, she told me her son had commented on the drugs—the antidepressants, relaxants, and narcotics—the rheumatologist had offered her. "Gee, Mom," he said, "you didn't need to go to that other doctor. Some of my friends at school could have done that much for you!" He was joking, of course, but the joke is a sad commentary on the conventional treatment offered to fibromyalgia patients. The treatment the rheumatologist offered this patient was bad, but even worse was his command to stay off the Internet. Defying his misguided advice, of course, led to her full recovery.

We can only admire the defiance of this particular patient and recommend that meeker patients emulate it. Many patients already have, however. Mary Shomon is the host and guide at the world's largest website on thyroid disease. We recently asked her: "You do more than most anybody else to provide people with information on thyroid disease and treatment. And you've done this for a long time. Looking back over that time, do you think patients have become more assertive and actively engaged in learning about their diseases?"

> I know that patients who are on the Internet are definitely becoming more assertive! I hear this all the time, because I hear patients tell me they walked into their doctor's office carrying a copy of my book, or printouts from my website, and the doctor says, "Oh, no, you're not bringing information from that Mary Shomon." That's music to my ears![10]

We also asked Mary: "From your central point in the buzzing world of information about thyroid disease and treatment, do you feel that the plight of patients is improving overall? Do you see any trend that allows you to predict what patients' plight will be in the near future?" She replied:

> I feel like there is a slight improvement in the plight of patients. I hear from more and more people who walk into their doctor's offices armed with Internet printouts and a copy of my book, determined to get the tests they need and not to accept the common "You're just stressed, depressed, or PMSed" writeoff from their doctors. These people are spending less time without a diagnosis, and are getting treated more quickly. I don't really know of any trends that will help predict patients' plight in the future. To be truthful, I still really feel for those who aren't online. There are millions of thyroid patients who still think that there are no options but to live their lives condemned to chronic illness simply because their doctors don't believe in optimizing their thyroid treatment.[10]

Our last question for Mary was: "What is your personal view about the advantages of using the Internet?"

> Doctors will need to be more knowledgeable about particular subjects. And hopefully, smarter patients and smarter doctors will make for faster diagnoses and better treatments![10]

SUPPORT GROUPS AND INTERNET NEWS GROUPS

We advised above that you be wary in looking for a support or Internet discussion group. We'll explain why you should be cautious.

Whether it's wise for a patient to take part in a support or Internet news group depends on what the group offers. Leaders and members of some groups focus so much on the health problem itself that they never get around to considering solutions. I (GH-L) spoke to one group whose questions after my presentation were concerned solely with referrals to disability lawyers. I explained that we focus on helping patients recover rather than get disability. This appeared to fall on deaf ears.

Leaders of some groups encourage patients not to try "alternative medicine doctors." Instead, they argue that patients should wait for conventional medical researchers to learn the cause and cure of fibromyalgia. Patients who follow this advice have a long wait.

You may not have noticed, but conventional medical researchers—especially those at the National Institutes of Health (NIH) and Centers for Disease Control (CDC)—don't discover the causes and cures of diseases. The money for *not* finding them is simply too good. Medical heretic Robert S. Mendelsohn, M.D. said in the late 1980s: "Doctors at the NIH and CDC are the Keystone Cops of modern medicine. And that's why they haven't solved a health problem in the fifty years of their existence."

It is, in fact, those "alternative medicine doctors" some group leaders caution patients to avoid who most often find the causes and cures of diseases. And they're the doctors who provide effective treatments. You'll find, however, that most support groups affiliated with national medical organizations strive to discourage patients from considering alternatives to the failed conventional medical approach. The group leaders often dictate which speakers patients get to hear and what educational materials are at hand for them to read. Essentially, these leaders usurp the patients' right to decide for themselves and function as mind control agents on behalf of the national medical organizations.

If you want to see how the traditional support group works, watch the movie, *Lorenzo's Oil* (see *Resources*). It's a true story that's fascinating and amazing. And it couldn't be more informative about the role traditional support groups serve for conventional medicine.

If you search for a support group in your hometown, or you surf the Internet for a news group, look for one that is recovery-oriented. If a group focuses on how to be a better patient, how to live with and "sooth" the symptoms of your disorder, or how to navigate the legal system to qualify for disability, we believe you'll be better off without it.

Bear in mind, however, that it may be hard to find recovered patients in a support group. Once most patients recover, they become busily engaged in their lives and have little or no motivation to attend support groups. This fact, in our view, diminishes the value of most of these groups.

MANAGED CARE

Managed care can be an obstacle in that it keeps your doctor from cooperating with you. At the same time, though, managed care has stimulated many patients to realize that they *must* take responsibility for their own health. Managed care isn't going to provide good health. At best, it helps with crisis management, although it often fails even to provide that. If you have managed care insurance, you're simply going to have to take responsibility for your own health.

Most doctors we talk with who are involved in managed care wish they weren't. They aren't allowed enough time with their patients to provide the quality of health care they feel is necessary. It's no wonder that most hypometabolic patients aren't happy with the results they get from managed care.

Holistic treatment protocols like metabolic rehab require far more time from doctors than managed care allows. This is one reason we don't participate in the managed care system, we're on no lists of preferred providers, and we're not Medicare or Medicaid providers.

Chapter 17

A Final Word:
Hope and Commitment

IF WE CAN ACCOMPLISH ONLY one thing with this book, we want to give you hope—hope that you *can* markedly improve or completely recover your metabolic health.

A tragic and perverse feature of modern mainstream medicine is that it gives millions of patients the exact opposite of hope. The best example is the widespread sense of hopelessness among hypo-thyroid patients whose doctors treat them according to the beliefs of conventional endocrinologists. Other examples are patients with diagnoses of fibromyalgia or chronic fatigue syndrome.

Mainstream doctors treat these patients with expensive, poten-tially harmful drugs—not because the drugs help, but for two other reasons: scientific incompetence and the funding of medical re-searchers and specialists by corporations that market the drugs.

Most patients with these diagnoses will continue to suffer while under mainstream medical care. But you don't have to con-tinue suffering. Our research team and others have found the un-derlying causes of most patients' poor metabolic health. Correcting these causes isn't always easy. But the fact is, most patients *can* improve or recover. The probability is high that you can too, with one critical qualification—that you first commit to getting well.

When we enter a clinical relationship with a new patient, we make a commitment. We commit to give the patient all the time and attention needed to help her improve as much as possible. To improve or recover using *Your Guide to Metabolic Health*, you must make a similar commitment on your own behalf: You must commit to doing *anything required* to get well.

If you're working with a doctor or therapist, you may not get a similar commitment from him. Today, many doctors and thera-pists can't make such commitments for reasons beyond their control—the managed care system in the United States or socialized medicine in countries such as the United Kingdom. These systems make it impossible for many clinicians working within them to abide by such commitments. They simply don't have the time or the financial inducement to cooperate with rehab of any sort. If your doctor or therapist works within managed care or socialized medicine, you may have to harden your resolve even more. You will have to do your own monitoring and graphing, and you'll have to advise your doctor or therapist of any changes needed in your treatment regimen. This approach is less than ideal, but it has worked for some patients. A sterling example is Vicky Massey, who wrote the *Foreword* to this book.

Keep in mind that a commitment to get well means this: You resolutely *refuse* to let obstacles stand in your way. You simply won't accept failure. You'll do what's needed despite inconvenience, sacrifice, and expense. Commitment means that if you don't improve enough through your own efforts, you'll enlist the help of the most cooperative, collaborative clinicians you can find. It means that if those clinical relationships don't work out, you'll find others that will. And commitment means that you'll steadfastly continue on until you improve to your satisfaction or completely recover your health.

Ultimately, as we said elsewhere in this book, commitment means that you accept and live by Yoda's rule of conduct: "There is no *try*—there is only *do*, or *do not*." It is our sincere wish that through your committed efforts, you achieve optimal metabolic health.

References

1. Lowe, J.C.: *The Metabolic Treatment of Fibromyalgia.* Boulder, McDowell Publishing Co., 2000. (Book available through www.McDowellPublishing.com)

2. Lowe, J.C., Reichman, A.J., Honeyman, G., and Yellin, J.: Thyroid status of fibromyalgia patients (abstract). *Clin. Bull. Myofascial Ther.,* 3(1):69-70, 1998.

3. Lowe, J.C.: Thyroid status of 38 fibromyalgia patients: implications for the etiology of fibromyalgia. *Clin. Bull. Myofascial Ther.,* 2(1):47-64, 1997.

4. Honeyman-Lowe, G.: Vitamin C—How Much and How Often? *A Newsletter From Dr. Gina Honeyman-Lowe.* Nov. 5, 1997, pp.1-3.

5. Pauling, L.: *How to Live Longer and Feel Better.* New York, Avon Books, 1987.

6. Lowe, J.C.: *The Purpose and Practice of Myofascial Therapy.* Accompanying manual (Audio cassette album). Houston, McDowell Publishing Co., 1989.

7. Lowe, J.C.: *Nutritional Therapy: A Desk Manual.* Houston, Gulf Coast Publishing, 1982.

8. Tepperman, J. and Tepperman, H.M.: *Metabolic and Endocrine Physiology,* 5th edition. Chicago, Year Book Medical Publishers, Inc., 1987.

9. Travell, J.G. and Simons, D.G.: *Myofascial Pain and Dysfunction: The Trigger Point Manual,* Vol. 1. Baltimore, Williams and Wilkins, 1983.

10. Shomon, M.: Personal communication. July 1, 2000.

11. Shomon, M.: *Living Well With Hypothyroidism.* New York, Avon Books, 2000. <www.thyroid-info.com/book.htm/>

12. Medi-Span, Inc.: Database Version 97.2. Data© 1997.

13. Lee, J.R., Hanley, J., and Hopkins, V.: *What Your Doctor May Not Tell You About Menopause.* New York, Warner Books, 1996.

14. Gaby, A.R.: *Preventing and Reversing Osteoporosis.* Rocklin, Prima Publishing, 1994.

15. AskDrLowe, Oct. 24, 1997. <www.drlowe.com>

16. <thyroid.about.com/library/weekly/aanewTSHrange.htm>

17. *PDR for Herbal Medicines.* Montvale, Medical Economics Co., Inc., 1998.

18. Starlanyl, D.J., Jeffrey, J.L., Roentsch, G., and Taylor-Olson, C.: The effect of transdermal T_3 (triiodothyronine) on geloid masses found in patients with both fibromyalgia and myofascial pain: double-blinded, crossover N of 1 clinical study. *Myalgies Internat.,* 2-2:8-18, 2001-2002.

19. Lowe, J.C.: Fibromyalgia: are chiropractic adjustments appropriate? *Dyn. Chiro.,* Dec., 1992, p.23.

20. Wolfe, F.: Personal communication, March 8, 1991.

21. Carette, S.: What have clinical trials taught us about the treatment of fibromyalgia? *J. Musculoskel. Pain,* 3:133-140, 1995.

22. Starlanyl, D.J. and Jeffrey, J.L.: Geloid masses in a patient with both fibromyalgia and chronic myofascial pain. *Phys. Ther. Case Rep.,* 4:22-31, 2001.

23. Teitelbaum, J.: *From Fatigued to Fantastic.* New York, Avery, 1996.

24. Rovati, L.C., et al.: A large randomized, placebo-controlled, double-blind study of glucosamine sulfate vs piroxicam and vs their assocation on the kinetics of the symptomatic effect in knee osteoarthritis. *Osteoarthritis Cartilage,*

2(Suppl.1):56, 1994.

25. Intelihealth: Health News: Release of PCBs higher than thought. Associated Press, May 22, 2000.

26. Pauling, L.: *Vitamin C, the Common Cold, and the Flu.* San Francisco, W.H. Freeman & Co., 1976.

27. Reuters Hourly News Summary, Aug. 12, 1997.

28. Morris, R.D., et al.: Chlorination, chlorination by-products, and cancer: a meta-analysis. *Am. J. Public Health*, 82(7):955-963, 1992.

29. Doyle, T.J., et al.: The association of drinking water source and chlorination by-products with cancer incidence among postmenopausal women in Iowa: a prospective cohort study. *Am. J. Public Health*, 87(7):1168-1176, 1997.

30. Escobar-Morreale, H.F., Obregón, M.J., Escobar del Rey, F., and Morreale de Escobar, G.: Replacement therapy for hypothyroidism with thyroxine alone does not ensure euthyroidism in all tissues, as studied in thyroidectomized rats. *J. Clin. Invest.*, 96:2828-2838, 1995.

31. Beech, J.A., et al.: Nitrates, chlorates and trihalomethanes in swimming pool water. *Am. J. Public Health*, 70(1):79-82, 1980.

32. Orme, J., et al.: Effects of chlorine dioxide on thyroid function in neonatal rats. *J. Toxicol. Environ. Health*, 15(2):315-322, 1985.

33. Bercz, J.P., et al.: Subchronic toxicity of chlorine dioxide and related compounds in drinking water in the nonhuman primate. *Environ. Health Perspect.*, 46:47-55, 1982.

34. Harrington, R.M., et al.: Effects of chlorine dioxide on thyroid function in the African green monkey and the rat. *J. Toxicol. Environ. Health,* 19(2):235-242, 1986.

35. Revis, N.W., et al.: Relationship of dietary iodide and drinking water disinfectants to thyroid function in experimental animals. *Environ. Health Perspect.*, 69:243-248, 1986.

36. Honeyman-Lowe, G.: Ultrasound treatment for trigger points: differences in technique for myofascial pain syndrome and fibromyalgia patients. *Lyon Méditerranée Médical: Médecine du Sud-Est.* No.2:12-15, 1999.

37. Starlanyl, D.: <www.sover.net/~devstar>

38. Honeyman-Lowe, G.: Ultrasound treatment of the fibromyalgia patient. Paper presented at the French Fibromyalgia Association of Région Rhône-Alpes, Grenoble, France, May 6, 2000.

39. Gedye, J.L.: Personal communication with John C. Lowe, Oct. 12, 1998.

40. Reichman, A.J.: Personal communication with John C. Lowe, Oct. 15, 1997.

41. Reuters, Washington, Sept. 1, 2000.

42. deVries, H.A.: Tranquilizer effect of exercise: A critical review. *Physic. Sports Med.*, Nov. 1981, pp.46-55.

43. Morgan, W.P. and Horstman, D.H.: Anxiety reduction following acute physical activity (abstract). *Med. Sci. Sports*, 8:62, 1976.

44. Sime, W.E.: A comparison of exercise and meditation in reducing physiological response to stress. *Med. Sci. Sports*, 9:55, 1977.

45. deVries, H.A., Wiswell, R.A., Bulbulian, R., and Moritani, T.: Tranquilizer effect of exercise: acute effects of moderate aerobic exercise on spinal reflex

activation level. *Am. J. Phys. Med.*, 60:57-66, 1981.

46. deVries, H.A., Simard, C., Wiswell, R.A., Heckathorne, E., and Caragetta, V.: Fusimotor system involvement in the tranquilizer effect of exercise. *Am. J. Phys. Med.*, 61:111-112, 1982.

47. Lowe, J.C.: Physical activity: a form of physiopsychotherapy. *Dig. Chiro. Econ.*, 21(2):33-37, 1978.

48. Lowe, J.C.: Psychological benefits of physical activity. *ACA J. Chiro.*, 13(1): S1-S6, 1979.

49. Tavares, V. and Branco, J.: Relation of sleep related complaints with tender points and pain intensity in fibromyalgia syndrome. *J. Musculoskel. Pain,* 3(Suppl.1):138, 1995.

50. Seers, K. and Carroll, D.: Relaxation techniques for acute pain management: a systematic review. *J. Adv. Nursing*, 27:466-475, 1998.

51. Nielson, W.R., Walker, C., and McCain, G.A.: Cognitive behavioral treatment of fibromyalgia syndrome: preliminary findings. *J. Rheumatol.*, 19:98-103, 1992.

52. Carroll, D. and Seers, K.: Relaxation for the relief of chronic pain: a systematic review. *J. Adv. Nursing*, 27:476-487, 1998.

53. Jacobson, E.: *Progressive Relaxation.* Chicago, Univ. of Chicago Press, 1938.

54. Jacobson, E.: The cultivation of physiological relaxation. *Ann. Intern. Med.,* 19:965-972, 1943.

55. Jacobson, E.: The course of relaxation of muscles of athletes. *Am. J. Psychol.,* 48:98-108, 1936.

56. Sainsbury, P. and Gibson, J.G.: Symptoms of anxiety and the accompanying physiological changes in the muscular system. *J. Neurol. Neurosurg. Psychiatry*, 17:216-224, 1954.

57. Williams, R.J.: *The Wonderful World Within You: Your Inner Nutritional Environment.* New York, Bantam Books, Inc., 1977.

58. Escobar-Morreale, H.F., del Rey, F.E., Obregón, M.J., and de Escobar, G.M.: Only the combined treatment with thyroxine and triiodothyronine ensures euthyroidism in all tissues of the thyroidectomized rat. *Endocrinology*, 137(6): 2490-2502, 1996.

59. Lowe, J.C.: Series of colon irrigations: a poor substitute for proper nutrition. *T.C.C. Review*, 4(6):17-18, 1978.

60. Lowe, J.C.: The original contingencies hypothesis. *Dig. Chir. Econ.*, 21(4):38, 1979.

61. Lowe, J.C.: Toxemia. *T.C.C. Review*, 4(7):12-13, 1979.

62. Lowe, J.C.: The nutritional management of muscular dystrophy. *Dig. Chir. Econ.*, 21(5):20, 1979.

63. Lowe, J.C.: A danger in the use of vitamin C with aspirin. *ACA J. Chir.*, 16(7): S-65-67, 1979.

64. Lowe, J.C.: A history of man's diet. *T.C.C. Review*, 5(2):22-24, 1979.

65. Lowe, J.C.: Arthritis of intestinal origin; its correction through diet. *Dig. Chir. Econ.*, 21(6):14, 1979.

66. Lowe, J.C.: Pangamic acid (vitamin B15) and joint instability due to ligamentous laxity. *Dig. Chir. Econ.*, 22(1):52-57, July-Aug., 1979.

67. Lowe, J.C.: Nutrition, ligaments, and the need for spinal manipulation. *T.C.C. Review*, 5(3):25-27, May, 1979.

68. Lowe, J.C.: Are straight chiropractors covering up a symptom of improper nutrition? *Dig. Chir. Econ.*, 22(2):56-59, 1979.

69. Lowe, J.C.: Does high protein intake lead to intestinal toxemia? *T.C.C. Review*, 5(4):20-22, Nov., 1979.

70. Lowe, J.C.: The minimum protein requirement: an answer to Immerman. *A.C.A. J. Chir.*, 1979.

71. Lowe, J.C.: Diet, nutrition, and the starting point of chiropractic care. *Today's Chir.*, 8(4):18-20, 1979.

72. Lowe, J.C.: Improper nutrition: today's foundation of biomechanical stress. *Dig. Chir. Econ.*, 22(5): 32-35, 1980.

73. Kaunitz, H.: Biological effects of transfatty acids. *Z. Ernahrungswiss*, 15(1): 26-33, 1976.

74. Mindell, E.: *Earl Mindell's Supplement Bible*. New York, Simon & Schuster,1998.

75. Mindell, E.: *Earl Mindell's Vitamin Bible*. New York, Warner Books, 1999.

76. Schneider-Helmert, D. and Spinweber, C.L.: Evaluation of L-tryptophan for treatment of insomnia: a review. *Psychopharmacology*, 89:1-7, 1986.

77. Lowe, J.C.: The nutritional treatment of arthritic diseases. *ACA J. Chir.*, XI: S-89-96, 1977.

78. Lowe, J.C.: Arthritis: can nutrition help? *Healthways Mag.*, 32(4):6-10, Nov.-Dec., 1977.

79. Lowe, J.C.: Your intestines and your health. *Altern. Mag.*, 2(8):58-61, 1978.

80. Sawin, C.T.: The development and use of thyroid preparations. In *The Thyroid Gland: A Practical Clinical Treatise*. Edited by L. Van Middlesworth, Jr., Chicago, Year Book Medical Publishers, Inc., 1986, pp.389-403.

81. Lowe, J.C.: Oral contraceptives and myofascial pain. *Dig. Chir. Econ.*, 34: 100-101, 1991.

82. Lowe, J.C.: Myofascial pain and "The Pill." *J. Nat. Assoc. Trigger Point Myother.*, 5.1:5, 1992.

83. Lowe, J.C.: Speech before Texans for Health Freedom, Dallas, Texas, Jan. 16, 1999.

84. Burke, C.W.: Adrenocortical insufficiency. *Clin. Endocrinol. Metab.*, 14(4): 947-976, 1985.

85. Pearch, C.J. and Himsworth, R.L.: Total and free thyroid hormone concentration in patients receiving maintenance replacement treatment with thyroxine. *Brit. Med. J.*, 288: 693-695, 1984.

86. Samaan, N.A.: Hypoglycemia secondary to endocrine deficiencies. *Endocrinol. Metab. Clin. North Am.*, 18(1):145-154, 1989.

87. Nicolson, G.L.: Considerations when undergoing treatment for chronic infections found in chronic fatigue syndrome, fibromyalgia syndrome and Gulf War illnesses (Part 1). Antibiotics recommended when indicated for treatment of Gulf War illness/CFIDS/FMS (Part 2). *Intern. J. Med.*, 1:115-117,123-128, 1998.

88. Crook, W.G.: *The Yeast Connection and the Woman*. Jackson, Professional

Books, Inc., 1998.

89. Hamburger, J.I.: Strategies for cost-effective thyroid function testing with modern methods. In *Diagnostic Methods in Clinical Thyroidology*. Edited by J.I. Hamburger, New York, Springer-Verlag, 1989, pp.63-109.

90. Lowe, J.C.: The Brady/Schneider proposal: a misdirected reclassification of fibromyalgia. *Dyn. Chir.*, 20(4):12,14,25, 2002.

91. Alverez, W.C.: *An Introduction to Gastro-Enterology*, 4th edition. New York, Paul B. Hoeber, Inc., 1948.

92. Lowe, J.C., Garrison, R., Reichman, A., Yellin, J., Thompson, M., and Kaufman, D.: Effectiveness and safety of T_3 therapy for euthyroid fibromyalgia: a double-blind, placebo-controlled response-driven crossover study, *Clin. Bull. Myofascial Ther.*, 2(2/3):31-57, 1997.

93. Lowe, J.C., Reichman, A., Yellin, J.: The process of change with T_3 therapy for euthyroid fibromyalgia: a double-blind placebo-controlled crossover study, *Clin. Bull. Myofascial Ther.*, 2(2/3):91-124, 1997.

94. Lowe, J.C., Garrison, R., Reichman, A., Yellin, J.: Triiodothyronine (T_3) treatment of euthyroid fibromyalgia: a small-n replication of a double-blind placebo-controlled crossover study. *Clin. Bull. Myofascial Ther.*, 2(4):71-88, 1997.

95. Dorn, J., Vena, J., Brasure, J., et al.: Lifetime physical activity and breast cancer risk in pre- and postmenopausal women. *Med. Sci. Sports Exerc.*, 35(2):278-285, 2003.

96. McNett, M.: The role of candida in fibromyalgia. From power-point presentation and personal communication with J.C. Lowe, Aug. 17, 2002.

97. Liew, L.: *The Natural Estrogen Diet*. Alameda, Hunter House, Inc., 1999.

98. Wiklund, I.K., Mattsson, L.A., Lindgren, R., et al.: Effects of a standardized ginseng extract on quality of life and physiological parameters in symptomatic postmenopausal women: a double-blind, placebo-controlled trial. *Int. J. Clin. Pharmacol. Res.*, 19(3):89-99, 1999.

99. Tode, T., Kikuchi, Y., Hirata, J., et al.: Effect of Korean red ginseng on psychological functions in patients with severe climacteric syndromes. *Int. J. Gynaecol. Obstet.*, 67(3):169-174, 1999.

100. Fujiwara, S., et al.: Mass gramentographic determination of ferulic acid in plasma after oral administration of gamma oryzanol. *Chem. Parm. Bull.*, 30: 973-979, 1982.

101. Stock, J.M., Surks, M.I., and Oppenheimer, J.H.: Replacement dosage of L-thyroxine in hypothyroidism. *N. Engl. J. Med.*, 290:529-533, 1974.

102. Evered, D., Young, E.T., Ornston, B.J., Menzies, R., Smith, P.A., and Hall, R.: Treatment of hypothyroidism: a reappraisal of thyroxine therapy. *Br. Med. J.*, iii:131-134, 1973.

103. Guyton, A.C.: *Textbook of Medical Physiology*, 8th edition. Philadelphia, W.B. Saunders Co., 1991.

104. Jefferies, W.McK.: *Safe Uses of Cortisol*, 2nd edition. Springfield, Charles C. Thomas, 1996.

105. DeGroot, L.J., Larsen, P.R., Refetoff, S., and Stanbury, J.B.: *The Thyroid and Its Diseases*, 5th edition. New York, John Wiley & Sons, Inc., 1984.

106. Jefferies, W.McK.: Glucocorticoid therapy: an overmaligned reputation with untapped potential benefits. In *Controversies in Internal Medicine*, II. Edited by F.J. Inglefinger, R.V. Ebert, M. Finland, and A.S. Relman, Philadelphia, Saunders, 1974, pp.439-445.

107. Jefferies, W.McK.: Cortisol and immunity. *Med. Hypotheses*, 34:198-208, 1991.

108. Jefferies, W.McK.: Mild adrenocortical deficiency, chronic allergies, autoimmune disorders and the chronic fatigue syndrome: a continuation of the cortisone story. *Med. Hypotheses*, 42:183-184, 1994.

109. Lowe, J.C.: What your myofascial patients should know about anti-inflammatory steroids. *Dyn. Chiro.*, June 1, 1989, pp.3-4.

110. Meyers, F.H., Jawetz, E., and Golfien, A.: *Review of Medical Pharmacology*, 4th edition, Los Altos, Lange Medical Publications, 1974.

111. Schubert, M. and Hamerman, D.: *A Primer on Connective Tissue Biochemistry*. Philadelphia, Lea and Febiger, 1968.

112. Clark, S., Tindall, E., and Bennett, R.M.: A double blind crossover trial of prednisone versus placebo in the treatment of fibrositis. *J. Rheumatol.*, 12(5): 980-983, 1985.

113. Weil, A.: *Natural Health, Natural Medicine*, Boston, Houghton Mifflin Co., 1998.

114. Bland, J.: *Nutritional Management of the Underlying Causes of Chronic Disease*. Audio cassette album., tape #6. Institute for Functional Medicine, Inc., 2000.

115. Jefferies, W.McK., Kelly, L.W., Jr., Sydnor, K.L., Levy, R.P., and Cooper, G.: Metabolic effects of a single intravenous infusion of hydrocortisone related to plasma levels in a normal versus an adrenally insufficient subject. *J. Clin. Endocrinol. Metab.*, 17:186-200, 1957.

116. Jefferies, W.McK.: Low dosage glucocorticoid therapy. *Arch. Intern. Med.*, 119:265-278, 1967.

117. Demiroglu, H. and Dundar, S.: Hyperkalaemia in acute leukaemia: a sign of adrenocortical insufficiency. *J. Intern. Med.*, 242(2):111-115, 1997.

118. Wisner, K.L. and Stowe, Z.N.: Psychobiology of postpartum mood disorders. *Semin. Reprod. Endocrinol.*, 15(1):77-89, 1997.

119. Toppozada, M.K., Ramadan, M., el-Sawi, M., Mehanna, M.T., Khamis, Y., and Marzouk, S.: Effect of Norplant implants on the pituitary-adrenal axis function and reserve capacity. *Contraception*, 55(1):7-10, 1997.

120. Davis, J. and Sheppard, M.: Acute adrenal crisis precipitated by thyroxine. *Br. Med. J.* (Clin. Res. Ed.), 292(6535):1595, 1986.

121. Fonseca, V., Brown, R., Hochhauser, D., Ginsburg, J., and Havard, C.W.: Acute adrenal crisis precipitated by thyroxine. *Br. Med. J.* (Clin Res Ed), 292 (6529):1185-1186, 1986.

122. Gilliland, P.F.: Endocrine emergencies: adrenal crisis, myxedema coma, and thyroid storm. *Postgrad. Med.*, 74(5):215-220, 225-227, 1983.

123. McDermott, M.T., Georgitis, W.J., and Asp, A.A.: Adrenal crisis in active duty service members. *Mil. Med.*, 161(10):624-626, 1996.

124. Adelman, H.M., Cacciatore, M.L., Pascual, J.F., Mike, J.M., Alberts, W.M.,

and Wallach, P.M.: Case report: Castleman disease in association with POEMS. *Am. J. Med. Sci.*, 307(2):112-114, 124, 1994.

125. Oki, Y., Iino, K., Iwabuchi, M., and Yoshimi, T.: Medical management after pituitary surgery. *Nippon Rinsho,* 51(10):2748-2753, 1993.

126. Yamamoto, M., Yoshida, K., Yonezawa, K., and Mizugaki, M.: Parenteral replacement of 1-T_4 in hypothyroid patients with esophageal stenosis and unconsciousness. *Nippon Naibunpi Gakkai Zasshi,* 69(6):588-593, 1993.

127. Vgontzas, A.N., Mastorakos, G., Bixler, E.O., Kales, A., Gold, P.W., and Chrousos, G.P.: Sleep deprivation effects on the activity of the hypothalamic-pituitary-adrenal and growth axes: potential clinical implications. *Clin. Endocrinol.* (Oxf), 51(2):205-215, 1999.

128. Ryumin, V.: His description of landing on Earth. In *The Home Planet.* Edited by K.W. Kelley, Moscow, Mir Publishers, 1988.

129. Lowe, J.C.: The effects of cervical spinal manipulation on the pressure/pain thresholds of infraspinatus trigger points: a case study. *J. Myofascial Ther.,* 1(1):25-30, 1994.

130. Starlanyl, D. and Copeland, M.E.: *Fibromyalgia & Chronic Myofascial Pain Syndrome,* 2nd edition. Oakland, New Harbinger Publications, Inc., 2001.

131. Hains, G. and Hains, F.: A combined ischemic compression and spinal manipulation in the treatment of fibromyalgia: a preliminary estimate of dose and efficacy. *J. Manipulat. Physiol. Ther*, 23(4):225-230, 2000.

132. Lowe, J.C. and Honeyman-Lowe, G.: Thyroid dysfunction and fibromyalgia. In *Fibromyalgia Syndrome: A Practitioner's Guide to Treatment.* Edited by L. Chaitow, Edinburgh, Churchill Livingston, 1999.

133. Lowe, J. C.: The subluxation and the trigger point: measuring how they interact. *Chir. J.,* Dec., 1992.

134. Derry, D.M.: Consequences of the TSH. *Brit. Med. J.,* May 29, 2000.

135. Lowe, J.C., Reichman, A., Yellin, J.: A case-control study of metabolic therapy for fibromyalgia: long-term follow-up comparison of treated and untreated patients (abstract). *Clin. Bull. Myofascial Ther.,* 3(1):23-24, 1998.

136. Honeyman-Lowe, G.: Ultrasound treatment of the fibromyalgia patient. *Lyon Méditerranée Médical: Médecine du Sud-Est.,* 36(1):30-31, 2000.

137. Lowe, J.C. and Honeyman-Lowe, G.: Facilitating the decrease in fibromyalgic pain during metabolic rehabilitation. an essential role for soft tissue therapies. *J. Bodywork Movem. Ther.,* 2(4):208-217, 1998.

138. Mense, S. and Simons, D.G.: *Muscle Pain: Understanding Its Nature, Diagnosis, and Treatment.* Philadelphia, Lippincott Williams & Wilkins Publishers, 2001.

139. Pioro-Boisset, M., Esdaile, J.M., and Fitzcharles, M.S.: Alternative medicine use in fibromyalgia syndrome. *Arthritis Care Res.,* 9:13-17, 1996.

140. Fitzcharles, M.A. and Esdaile, J.M.: Nonphysician practitioner treatments and fibromyalgia syndrome. *J. Rheumatol.,* 24(5):937-940, 1997.

141. Wolfe, F.: The clinical syndrome of fibrositis. *Am. J. Med.,* 81(Suppl.3A):7-14, 1986.

142. Murray, M. and Pizzorno, J.: *Encyclopedia of Natural Medicine,* 2nd edition. Rocklin, Prima Publishing, 1998.

143. Backstrom, G. and Rubin, B.R.: *When Muscle Pain Won't Go Away*. Dallas, Taylor Publishing Co., 1992.

144. Karzel, K. and Domenjoz, R.: Effect of hexosamine derivatives and uronic acid derivatives on glycosaminoglycan metabolism of fibroblast cultures. *Pharmacology*, 5:337-345, 1971.

145. Blonstein, J.: Control of swelling in boxing injuries. *Practitioner*, 203:206, 1960.

146. Benediktsson, R. and Edwards, C.R.: Apparent mineralocorticoid excess. *J. Hum. Hypertens.*, 8(5):371-375, 1994.

147. Nilsson, R.: Endocrine modulators in the food chain and environment. *Toxicol. Pathol.*, 28(3):420-431, 2000.

148. Stewart, P.M., Whorwood, C.B., and Walker, B.R.: Steroid hormones and hypertension: the cortisol-cortisone shuttle. *Steroids*, 58(12):614-620, 1993.

149. Gordon, C.M., Glowacki, J., and LeBoff, M.S.: DHEA and the skeleton (through the ages). *Endocrine*, 11(1):1-11, 1999.

150. Wolf, O.T. and Kirschbaum, C.: Actions of dehydroepiandrosterone and its sulfate in the central nervous system: effects on cognition and emotion in animals and humans. *Brain Res. Brain Res. Rev.*, 30(3):264-288, 1999.

151. L'Allemand, D. and Biason-Lauber, A.: Intra-adrenal regulation of androgen synthesis. *Eur. J. Clin. Invest.*, 30(S3):28-33, 2000.

152. Labrie, F., Luu-The, V., Labrie, C., and Simard, J.: DHEA and its transformation into androgens and estrogens in peripheral target tissues: intracrinology. *Front. Neuroendocrinol.*, 22(3):185-212, 2001.

153. Thurman, F.M. and Thompson, W.O.: Low basal metabolism without myxedema. *Arch. Intern. Med.*, 46:879- 897, 1930.

154. Kalimi, M. and Regelson, W.: *The Biological Role of Dehydroepiandrosterone*. De Gruyter, New York, 1990.

155. Whitaker, J.: *Dr. Whitaker's Guide to Natural Healing*. Rocklin, Prima Publishing, 1996.

156. van Rensburg, S.J., Potocnik, F.C., Kiss, T., et al.: Serum concentrations of some metals and steroids in patients with chronic fatigue syndrome with reference to neurological and cognitive abnormalities. *Brain Res. Bull.*, 55(2): 319-325, 2001.

157. Dessein, P.H., Shipton, E.A., Joffe, B.I., Hadebe, D.P., Stanwix, A.E., and Van der Merwe, B.A.: Hyposecretion of adrenal androgens and the relation of serum adrenal steroids, serotonin and insulin-like growth factor-1 to clinical features in women with fibromyalgia. *Pain*, 83(2):313-319, 1999.

158. Gerber, G.S.: Saw palmetto for the treatment of men with lower urinary tract symptoms. *J. Urol.*, 163(5):1408-1412, 2000.

159. Dagues, F. and Costa, P.: Medical treatment of disorders of the bladder sphincter. *Rev. Prat.*, 45(3):337-341, 1995.

160. Cristoni, A., Di Pierro, F., and Bombardelli, E.: Botanical derivatives for the prostate. *Fitoterapia*, 71CY: Netherlands: S21-S28, 2000.

161. Lowe, J. and Honeyman-Lowe, G.: Thyroid disease and fibromyalgia syndrome. *Lyon Méditerranée Médical: Médecine du Sud-Est.*, 36(1):15-17, 2000.

REFERENCES

162. Lowe, J.C. and Honeyman-Lowe, G.: Fibromyalgia and thyroid disease. Paper presented in Grenoble, France, May 6 (conference of the French Fibromyalgia Association of Région Rhône-Alpes) and discussed in Toulon, France on May 11 (at the Centre Hospitalier Intercommunal), 2000.

163. Hiemeyer, K., Lutz, R., and Menninger, H.: Dependence of tender points upon posture: a key to the understanding of fibromyalgia syndrome. *J. Manual Med.*, 5:169-174, 1990.

164. Ishizuki,Y., Hirooka, Y., Murata, Y., and Togashi, K.: The effects on the thyroid gland of soybeans administered experimentally in healthy subjects. *Nippon Naibunpi Gakkai Zasshi*, 67:(5)622-629, 1991.

165. Leibenson, C.: Self-treatment of the slump posture. *J. Bodywork Movem. Ther.*, 5(2):99-100, 2001.

166. Bennett, R.M., Clark, S.R., Burckhardt, C.S., and Walczyk, J.: A double-blind placebo-controlled study of growth hormone therapy in fibromyalgia. *J. Musculoskel. Pain* (abstract), 3(Suppl.1):110, 1995.

167. Harrer, G. and Schulz, V.: Clinical investigation of *hypericum*. *J. Geriatr. Psychi. Neurol.*, 7(Suppl.1):S6-S8, 1994.

168. De Smet, P.A.G. and Nolen, W.: St. John's wort as an antidepressant. *Brit. Med. J.*, 313:241-242, 1996.

169. Poldinger, W., Calanchini, B., and Schwarz, W.: A functional-dimensional approach to depression: serotonin deficiency as a target syndrome in a comparision of 5-hydroxytryptophan and fluvoxamine. *Psychopathology*, 24:53-81, 1991.

170. Van Hiele, J.J.: L-5-hydroxytryptophan in depression: the first substitution therapy in psychiatry. *Neuropsychobiology*, 6:230-240, 1980.

171. Van Praag, H.M.: Management of depression with serotonin precursors. *Biol. Psychiatry*, 16:291-310, 1981.

172. Van Praag, H.M. and Lemus, C.: Monoamine precursors in the treatment of psychiatric disorders. In *Nutrition and the Brain*, Vol. 7. Edited by R.J. Wurtman and J.J. Wurtman, New York, Raven Press, 1986, pp.89-139.

173. Singh, Y.: Kava: an overview. *J. Ethnopharmacol.*, 37:13-45, 1992.

174. Kleijnen, J. and Knipschild, P.: Ginkgo biloba for cerebral insufficiency. *Br. J. Clin. Pharmacol.*, 34:352-358, 1992.

175. Sikora, R., et al.: Ginkgo biloba extract in the therapy of erectile dysfunction. *J. Urol.*, 141:188A, 1989.

176. Saito, H., Yoshida, Y., and Takagi, K.: Effect of *Panax ginseng* root on exhaustive exercise in mice. *Jap. J. Pharmacol.*, 24:119-127, 1974.

177. Hikino, H.: Traditional remedies and modern assessment: the case of ginseng. In *The Medicinal Plant Industry*. Edited by R.O.B. Wijeskera, Boca Raton, CRC Press, 1991, pp.149-166.

178. Brekhman, I.I. and Dardymov, I.V.: New substances of plant origin which increase nonspecific resistance. *Ann. Rev. Pharmacol.*, 9:419-430, 1969.

179. Bhattacharya, S.K. and Mitra, S.K.: Anxiolytic activity of Panax ginseng roots: an experimental study. *J. Ethnopharmacol.*, 34:87-92, 1991.

180. Hallstrom, C., Fulder, S., and Carruthers, M.: Effects of ginseng on nurses on night duty. *Comp. Med. East & West*, 6:277-282, 1982.

181. Bauer, R. and Wagner, H.: Echinacea species as potential immunostimulatory drugs. *Econ. Med. Plant Res.*, 5:253-321, 1991.

182. Schoneberger, D.: the influence of immune-stimulating effects of pressed juice from Echinacea purpurea on the course and severity of colds: results of a double-blind study. *Forum Immunol.*, 8:2-12, 1992.

183. Chang, H.M. and But, P.P.H. (Editors): *Pharmacology and Applications of Chinese Materia Medica. Singapore*, World Scientific, 1987, pp.1041-1046.

184. Zhao, K.S., et al.: Enhancement of the immune response in mice by *Astragalus membranaceus. Immunopharmacol.*, 20:225-233, 1988.

185. Barnes, B.O. and Galton, L.: *Hypothyroidism: The Unsuspected Illness.* New York, Harper & Row, Publishers, 1976.

186. Yamauchi, J., et al.: Inhibition of LH secretion by gamma oryzanol in the rat. *Horm. Metabol. Res.*, 13:185, 1981.

187. Lowe, J.C.: T_3-induced recovery from fibromyalgia by a hypothyroid patient resistant to T_4 and desiccated thyroid. *J. Myofascial Ther.*, 1(4):26-31, 1995.

188. Lowe, J.C.: Results of an open trial of T_3 therapy with 77 euthyroid female fibromyalgia patients. *Clin. Bull. Myofascial Ther.*, 2(1):35-37, 1997.

189. Honeyman, G.S.: Metabolic therapy for hypothyroid and euthyroid fibromyalgia: two case reports. *Clin. Bull. Myofascial Ther.*, 2(4):19-49, 1997.

190. Meschino, J.: Gamma oryzanol: an impressive, yet underappreciated natural agent for the treatment of hot flashes in menopause. *Dyn. Chir.*, 20(20):34-35, 2002.

191. Brown, R.S., Ramirez, D.E., and Taub, J.M.: The prescription of exercise for depression. Paper read at ACSM meeting, Washington, D.C., May 24, 1978.

192. Young, R.J. and Ismael, A.H.: Relationship between anthropometric, physiological, biochemical and personality variables before and after a four-month conditioning program for middle-aged men. *J. Sports Med. Phys. Fitness*, 16:267-276, 1976.

193. Stamford, B.A., Hambacher, W., and Fallica, A.: Effects of daily physical exercise on the psychiatric state of institutionalized geriatric mental patients. *Res. Quart.*, 45:34-41, 1974.

194. deVries, H.A.: *Physiology of Exercise*, 4th edition. Dubuque, Wm. C. Brown Publishers, 1986.

195. Williams, R.J.: *Nutrition Against Disease*. New York, Bantam , 1971.

196. Teperi, J. and Rimpela, M.: Menstrual pain, health and behaviour in girls. *Soc. Sci. Med.*, 29(2):163-169, 1989.

197. Lee, J.R., Hanley, J., and Hopkins, V.: *What Your Doctor May Not Tell You About Premenopause.* New York, Warner Books, 1999.

198. Lowe, J.C.: The myofascial genesis of unpleasant thoughts and emotions: its neural basis. *Dig. Chir. Econ.*, 32:78,80-81, 1989.

199. Lowe, J.C.: The emotional effects of noxious myofascial stimulation. *Am. Chir. Mag.*, 22-24, Jan., 1989.

200. Lowe, J.C.: Calcium and magnesium deficiencies and the vertebral subluxation. *ACA J. Chiro.*, IX:S-128-129, 1975.

201. Lowe, J.C.: Calcium, magnesium, and muscle spasms. *Chir. Fam. Physician*, 3(6):18-21, Sept., 1981.

202. Laux, M. and Conrad, C.: *Natural Woman, Natural Menopause*. New York, Harper Perennial, 1998.

203. Golomb, L.M., Solidum, A.A., and Warren, M.P.: Primary dysmenorrhea and physical activity. *Med. Sci. Sports Exerc.*, 30(6):906-909, 1998.

204. Burke, B.E., Olson, R.D., and Cusack, B.J.: Randomized, controlled trial of phytoestrogen in the prophylactic treatment of menstrual migraine. *Biomed Pharmacother.*, 56(6):283-288, 2002.

205. Weetman, A.P.: Fortnightly review: Hypothyroidism: screening and subclinical disease. *Brit. Med. J.*, 314:1175, 1997.

206. Chrisstie, S. and Walker, A.F.: Vitex agnus castus: a review of its traditional and modern therapeutic use, and current use from a survey of practitioners. *Eur. J. Herb. Med.*, 3(3):29-45, 1998.

207. Bone, K.: Phytotherapy review and commentary. *Townsend Letter for Doctors & Patients*, #235:41-42, Feb/Mar, 2003.

208. Han, K.K., Soares, J.M. Jr., Haidar, M.A., et al.: Benefits of soy isoflavone therapeutic regimen on menopausal symptoms. *Obstet. Gynecol.*, 99(3):389-394, 2002.

209. Shanafelt, T.D., Barton, D.L., Adjei, A.A., et al.: Pathophysiology and treatment of hot flashes. *Mayo Clin. Proc.*, 77(11):1207-1218, 2002.

210. Lowe, J.C.: What your hypothyroid patients should know about synthroid. *Dyn. Chiro.*, 19(22):26-41, 2001.

211. <thyroid.about.com/library/news/bllowe.htm>

212. Wiersinga, W.M.: Thyroid hormone replacement therapy. *Horm. Res.*, 56 (Suppl.)S1:74-81, 2001.

213. Barton, D. Loprinzi, C., and Wahner-Roedler, D.: Hot flashes: aetiology and management. *Drugs Aging*, 18(8):597-606, 2001.

214. Farquhar, D.: Postmenopausal hormone replacement therapy for chronic disease prevention: results from the Women's Health Initiative trial. *CMAJ*, 167 (4):245, 2002.

215. Borysenko, J.: *Inner Peace for Busy People*. Carlsbad, Hay House, Inc., 2001.

216. Rossouw, J.E., Anderson, G.L., Prentice, R.L., et al.: Risks and benefits of estrogen plus progestin in healthy postmenopausal women: principal results from the Women's Health Initiative randomized controlled trial. *JAMA*, 288 (3):321-333, 2002.

217. Stephenson, J.: FDA orders estrogen safety warnings: agency offers guidance for HRT use. *JAMA*, 289(5):537-538, 2003.

218. Beral, V., Banks, E., and Reeves, G.: Evidence from randomised trials on the long-term effects of hormone replacement therapy. *Lancet*, 360(9337):942-944, 2002.

219. Durrant-Peatfield, B.: *The Great Thyroid Scandal and How to Survive It*. London, Barons Down Publishing, 2002.

220. Usala, S.J., Tennyson, G.E., Bale, A.E., et al.: A base mutation of the c-erbAβ thyroid hormone receptor in a kindred with generalized thyroid hormone resistance: molecular heterogeneity in two other kindreds. *J. Clin. Invest.*, 85:93-100, 1990.

221. Refetoff, S., Dewind, L.T., and DeGroot, L.J.: Familial syndrome combining deaf-mutism, stippled epiphyses, goiter and abnormally high PBI: possible target organ refractoriness to thyroid hormone. *J. Clin. Endocrinol. Metab.*, 27:279, 1967.

222. Official Statement of the Fibromyalgia Research Foundation: T_4 Replacement Therapy: An Obstacle to Recovery from Fibromyalgia. <www.drlowe.com/frf/england2002/full.htm>

223. Goldstein, J.A.: *Betrayal by the Brain.* New York, Haworth Medical Press, 1996.

224. Pert, C.: *Molecules of Emotion.* New York, Scribner, 1997.

225. Constant, E.L., de Volder, A.G., Ivanoiu, A., et al.: Cerebral blood flow and glucose metabolism in hypothyroidism: a positron emission tomography study. *J. Clin. Endocrinol. Metab.*, 86(8):3864-3870, 2001.

226. Kimball, L.E., Kulinskaya, E., Brown, B., Johnston, C., and Farid, N.R.: Does smoking increase relapse rates in Graves' disease? *J. Endocrinol. Invest.*, 25(2):152-157, 2002.

227. Langer, S.E. and Scheer, J.F.: *Solved: The Riddle of Illness*, 3rd edition. Lincolnwood, Keats Publilshing, 2000.

228. Kreiger, N. and Parkes, R.: Cigarette smoking and the risk of thyroid cancer. *Eur. J. Cancer*, 36(15):1969-1973, 2000.

229. Brix, T.H., Hansen, P.S., Kyvik, K.O., and Hegedus, L.: Cigarette smoking and risk of clinically overt thyroid disease: a population-based twin case-control study. *Arch. Intern. Med.*, 160(5):661-666, 2000.

230. Fisher, C.L., Mannino, D.M., Herman, W.H., and Frumkin, H.: Cigarette smoking and thyroid hormone levels in males. *Int. J. Epidemiol.*, 26(5):972-977, 1997.

231. Fukata, S., Kuma, K., and Sugawara, M.: Relationship between cigarette smoking and hypothyroidism in patients with Hashimoto's thyroiditis. *J. Endocrinol. Invest.*, 19(9):607-612, 1996.

232. Muller, B., Zulewski, H., Huber, P., Ratcliffe, J.G., and Staub, J.J.: Impaired action of thyroid hormone associated with smoking in women with hypothyroidism. *N. Engl. J. Med.*, 333(15):964-969, 1995.

233. Bertelsen, J.B.: Cigarette smoking and the thyroid gland. *Ugeskr Laeger*, 157 (28):4019-4022, 1995.

234. Green, W.L..: Extrinsic and intrinsic variables. In *Werner and Ingbar's The Thyroid: A Fundamental and Clinical Text*, 6th edition. Edited by L.E. Braverman and R.D. Utiger, New York, J.B. Lippincott Co., 1991, pp.322-335.

235. Larsen, P.R.: Salicylate-induced increases in free triiodothyronine in human serum: evidence of inhibition of triiodothyronine binding to thyroxine-binding globulin and thyroxine-binding prealbumin. *J. Clin. Invest.*, 51:1125, 1972.

236. Baranetsky, N.G., Chertow, B.S., Web, M.D., et al.: Combined phenytoin and salicylate effects on thyroid function tests. *Arch. Int. Pharmaco-dyn.* 284:166, 1986.

237. Wang, R., Nelson, J.C., and Wilcox, R.B.: Salsalate and salicylate binding to and their displacement of thyroxine from thyroxine-binding globulin,

transthyretin, and albumin. *Thyroid*, 9(4):359-364, 1999.

238. Agnew, H.W., Webb, W.B., and Williams, R.L.: Comparison of stage four and 1-REM sleep deprivation. *Percept. Mot. Skills*, 24:851-858, 1967.

239. Moldofsky, H., Scarisbrick, P., England, R., and Smythe, H.: Musculoskeletal symptoms and non-REM sleep disturbance in patients with "fibrositis syndrome" and healthy subjects. *Psychosomat. Med.* 37(4):341-351, 1975.

240. Moldofsky, H. and Scarisbrick, P.: Induction of neurasthenic musculoskeletal pain syndrome by selective sleep stage deprivation. *Psychosom. Med.*, 38:35-44, 1976.

241. Flesch, R.: *How to Write, Speak, and Think More Effectively*. New York, Signet, 1976.

242. Colborn, T., Dumanoski, D., and Myers, J.P.: *Our Stolen Future*. New York, Penguin Books USA, Inc., 1996.

243. Montagu, A.: *The Human Revolution*, New York, Bantom, 1965.

244. Campbell, B.: *Human Evolution*, 2nd edition. Chicago, Aldine Publishing Co., 1974.

245. Lee, R.B.: What hunters do for a living, or how to make out on scarce resources. In (eds), *Man the Hunter*, Chicago. Edited by R.B. Lee and I. De Vore, Chicago, Aldine Publishing Co., 1968, pp.30-48.

246. Sears, B. and Lawren, B.: *The Zone: A Dietary Road Map*. New York, Regan Books, 1995.

247. Rubio, M.A.: Implications of fiber in different pathologies. *Nutr. Hosp.*, 17 (Suppl.2):17-29, 2002.

248. Mary Shomon: *Living Well with Autoimmune Disease*. New York, Harper Collins, 2002. <www.autoimmunebook.com>

249. Reuben, D.: *The Save Your Life Diet*. New York, Ballantine Books, 1975.

250. Walker, W.A., Bellini, C.A., and Walker, W.A.: The intestinal mucosa barrier to intact antigenic protein: difference between colon and small intestine. *Am. J. Surgery*, 133:57, 1977.

251. Walker, W.A. and Isselbacher, K.J.: Uptake and transport of macromolecules by the intestine: possible role in clinical disorders. *Gastroenterology*, 67:531, 1974.

252. Ecker, R.E.: An alternative view of high-fiber diets. *Nutri. Perspect.*, 2(1): 17-21, 1979.

253. Editorial. Polyamines in psoriasis. *J. Invest. Dermatol.*, 81:385-387, 1983.

254. Editorial. Polyamines and psoriasis. *Arch. Dermatol.*, 115:943-944, 1979.

255. Proctor, M., et al.: Lowered cutaneous and urinary levels of polyamines with clinical improvement in treated psoriasis. *Arch. Dermatol.*, 115:945-949, 1979.

256. Tam, I.: Diet as a source of human exposure to polychlorinated dibenzo-P-dioxins (PCDD). *Rocz. Panstw. Zakl. Hig.*, 50(3):241-251, 1999.

257. DeVito, M.J. and Schecter, A.: Exposure assessment to dioxins from the use of tampons and diapers. *Environ. Health Perspect.*, 110(1):23-28, 2002.

258. Puntaric, D. et al.: Small countries and the dioxin scandal: how to control imported food? *Croat. Med. J.*, 41(2):150-153, 2000.

259. Nidever, J.E.: A factor analytic study of general muscular tension. Ph.D. dis-

sertation, University of California at Los Angeles, 1959.

260. Cordain, L., et al.: Fatty acid analysis of wild ruminant tissues: evolutionary implications for reducing diet-related chronic disease. *Eur. J. Clin. Nutr.*, 56 (3):181-191, 2002.

261. Burton, B.T.: *Human Nutrition.* New York, McGraw-Hill Book Co., 1976.

262. Collier, G.R. and Sinclair, A.J.: Role of N-6 and N-3 fatty acids in the dietary treatment of metabolic disorders. *Ann. N. Y. Acad. Sci.*, 683:322-330, 1993.

263. Makino, M., et al.: Effect of eicosapentaenoic acid ethyl ester on hypothyroid function. *J. Endocrinol.*, 171(2):259-265, 2001.

264. Tapiero, H., et al.: Polyunsaturated fatty acids (PUFA) and eicosanoids in human health and pathologies. *Biomed. Pharmacother.*, 56(5):215-222, 2002.

265. Ximenes da Silva, A., et al.: Glucose transport and utilization are altered in the brain of rats deficient in n-3 polyunsaturated fatty acids. *J. Neurochem.*, 81(6):1328-1337, 2002.

266. Hollingworth, H.L.: The influence of caffeine on mental and motor efficiency. *Arch. Psychol.*, 20:1-66, 1912.

267. Lininger, S.W., Gaby, A.R., Austin, A., et al.: *The Natural Pharmacy.* Rocklin, Prima Publishing, 1999.

268. Blum, I., Vered, Y., Graff, E., et al.: The influence of meal composition on plasma serotonin and norepinephrine concentrations. *Metabolism*, 41:137-140, 1992.

269. Morin, C.M., Culbert, J.P., and Schwartz, S.M.: Nonpharmacological interventions for insomnia: a meta-analysis of treatment efficacy. *Am. J. Psychiatr.*, 151:1172-1180, 1994.

270. Phillips, B.A. and Danner, F.J.: Cigarette smoking and sleep disturbance. *Arch. Intern. Med.*, 155:734-737, 1995.

271. Zhadanova, I.V., Wurtman, R.J., Lynch, H.J., et al.: Sleep-inducing effects of low doses of melatonin ingested in the evening. *Clin. Pharmacol. Ther.*, 57:552-558, 1995.

272. Singer, C., McArthur, A., Hughes, R., et al.: Melatonin and sleep in the elderly. *J. Am. Geiatr. Soc.* (abstract), 44:51, 1996.

273. Soulairac, A. and Lambinet, H.: Etudes cliniques de líaction du precurseur de la serotonine le L-5-hydroxy-tryptophane, sur les troubles du sommeil. *Schweiz. Bundschau. Med.*, 77:19-23, 1998.

274. Culligan Store Solutions. (800)487-4621, 1999.

275. Grandjean, P.: Human exposure to nickel. *IARC Sci. Publ.*, (53):469-485, 1984.

276. Denkhaus, E. and Salnikow, K.: Nickel essentiality, toxicity, and carcinogenicity. *Crit. Rev. Oncol. Hematol.*, 42(1):35-56, 2002.

277. Arnold, L.M., Keck, P.E. Jr., and Welge, J.A.: Antidepressant treatment of fibromyalgia. A meta-analysis and review. *Psychosomatics*, 41(2):104-113, 2000.

278. Isomeri, R., Mikkelsson, M., Latikka, P., and Kammonen, K.: Effects of amitriptyline and cardiovascular fitness training on pain in patients with primary fibromyalgia. *J. Musculoskel. Pain*, 1(3/4):253-265, 1993.

REFERENCES

279. Carette, S., Oakson, G., Guimont, C., and Steriade, M.: Sleep electroencephalography and the clinical response to amitriptyline in patients with fibromyalgia. *Arthritis Rheumatol.*, 38(9):1211-1217, 1995.

280. Goldenberg, D.L., Manisky, M., Mossey, C., Ruthazer, R., and Schmid, C.: The independent and combined efficacy of fluoxetine and amitriptyline in the treatment of fibromyalgia. *Arthritis Rheum.*, 38(Suppl.):S229, 1995.

281. Ginsberg, F., Mancaux, A., Joos, E., Vanhove, P., and Famaey, J-P.: A randomized placebo-controlled trial of sustained-release amitriptyline in primary fibromyalgia. *J. Musculoskel. Pain*, 4(3):37-47, 1996.

282. Fransen, J. and Russell, I.J.: *The Fibromyalgia Help Book: Practical Guide to Living Better with Fibromyalgia*. Saint Paul, Smith House Press, 1996.

283. Carette, S., Bell, M., Reynolds, et al.: A controlled trial of amitriptyline, cyclobenzaprine, and placebo in fibromyalgia. *Arthritis Rheum.*, 35(Suppl.9): 112, 1992.

284. Carette, S., Bell, M.J., et al.: Comparison of amitriptyline, cyclobenzaprine, and placebo in the treatment of fibromyalgia. *Arthritis Rheum.*, 37(1):32-40, 1994.

285. Miller, L.G.: Antidepressants and cancer: cause for concern? *J. Clin. Psycho pharmacol.*, 13(1):1-2, 1993.

286. Marx, J.: Do antidepressants promote tumors? *Science,* 257:22-23, 1992.

287. Teitelbaum, J.: *From Fatigued to Fantastic*, 2nd edition. New York, Penguin Putnam Inc., 2001.

288. Lowe, J.C. and Honeyman-Lowe, G.: Sleep disturbance and fibromyalgia. *A2Zzz: Publication of the Association of Polysomnographic Technologists.* In press, 2003

289. Moldofsky, H.: Management of sleep disorders in fibromyalgia. *Rheum. Dis. Clin. North Am.*, 28(2):353-365, 2002.

290. Wolfe, F., Smythe, H.A., Yunus, M.B., et al.: The American College of Rheumatology 1990 criteria for the classification of fibromyalgia: report of the multicenter criteria committee. *Arthritis Rheumatol.*, 33:160-172, 1990.

291. James, M.J., Gibson, R.A., and Cleland, L.G.: Dietary polyunsaturated fatty acids and inflammatory mediator production. *Am. J. Clin. Nutr.*, 71(1Suppl.): 343S-348S, 2000.

292. Seaman, D.R.: The diet-induced proinflammatory state: a cause of chronic pain and other degenerative diseases? *J. Manip. Physiol. Ther.*, 25(3):168-179, 2002.

293. Lowe, J.C. and Honeyman-Lowe, G.: Fibromyalgia syndrome. *Textbook of Natural Medicine*, 3rd edition. Edited by M. Murray and J. Pizzorno. Elsevier, in press.

294. Steiger, A., Trachsel, L., Guldner, J., et al.: Neurosteroid pregnenolone induces sleep-EEG changes in man compatible with inverse agnostic GABAA-receptor modulation. *Brain Res.*, 615:267-274, 1993.

295. Benson, H.: *The Relaxation Response*. New York, Avon, 1990.

296. Lowe, J. C.: Globalization of myofascial pain syndromes. *Dyn. Chir.*, March 14, 1990, p.18.

297. Hoffman, B.B. and Lefkowitz, R.J.: Adrenergic receptor antagonists. *Good-*

man and Gilman's The Pharmacological Basis of Therapeutics, 8th edition. New York: Pergamon Press. 1990, pp.221-243.

298. Imaki M., Hatanaka, Y., Ogawa, Y., et al.: An epidemiological study on relationship between the hours of sleep and life style factors in Japanese factory workers. J. Physiol. Anthropol. Appl. Human Sci., 21(2):115-120, 2002.

299. Dollander, M.: Etiology of adults's [sic] insomnia. Encephale, 28(6):493-502, 2002.

300. Rajput, V. and Bromley, S.M.: Chronic insomnia: a practical review. Am. Fam. Physician, 60(5):1431-1438, 1999.

301. Prusinski, A.: Insomnia and its treatment. Neurol. Neurochir. Pol., 32 (Suppl.)6:51-60, 1999.

302. Foster, J.H., Powell, J.E., Marshall, E.J., et al.: Quality of life in alcohol-dependent subjects: a review. Qual. Life Res., 8(3):255-261, 1999.

303. Shephard, R.J.: Exercise and relaxation in health promotion. Sports Med., 23 (4):211-217, 1997.

304. Stone, B.M. and Turner, C.: Promoting sleep in shiftworkers and intercontinental travelers. Chronobiol. Int., 14(2):133-143, 1997.

305. Kales, A., Heuser, G., and Jacobson, A.: All night sleep studies in hypothyroid patients, before and after treatment. J. Clin. Endocrinol., 27:1593-1599, 1967.

306. Shochat, T., Loredo, J., and Ancoli-Israel, S.: Sleep disorders in the elderly. Curr. Treat. Options Neurol., 3(1):19-36, 2001.

307. Moldofsky, H.: Sleep and fibrositis syndrome. Rheum. Dis. Clin. North Amer., 15:91-103, 1989.

308. Saskin, P., Moldofsky, H., and Salem, L.: Sleep and symptoms in psychophysiologic insomnia and fibrositis. Sleep Res., 16:421, 1987.

309. Harding, S.M.: Sleep in fibromyalgia patients: subjective and objective findings. Am. J. Med. Sci., 315(6):367-376, 1998.

310. Hemmeter, U., Kocher, R., Ladewig, D., et al.: Sleep disorders in chronic pain and generalized tendomyopathy. Schweiz. Med. Wochenschr., 125(49): 2391-2397, 1995.

311. Ramsay, I.D.: Thyroid Disease and Muscle Dysfunction. Chicago, Year Book Medical Publishers, Inc., 1974.

312. Watanakunakorn, C., Hodges, R.E., and Evans, T.C.: Myxedema: a study of 400 cases. Arch. Intern. Med., 116:183-190, 1965.

313. Hayashi, M., Saisho, S., Suzuki, H., Shimozawa, K., and Iwakawa, Y.: Sleep disturbance in children with congenital and acquired hypothyroidism. No To Hattatsu. Brain Dev., 20:294-300, 1988.

314. Maimonides, M.: Mishneh Torah. In The Book of Knowledge. Edited by M. Hyamson, Boys Town Jerusalem Publishers, 1962.

315. Semeniuk, T., Jhangri, G.S., and Le Melledo, J.M.: Neuroactive steroid levels in patients with generalized anxiety disorder. J. Neuropsychiatry Clin. Neurosci., 13(3):396-398, 2001.

316. Heydari, B. and Le Melledo, J.M.: Low pregnenolone sulphate plasma concentrations in patients with generalized social phobia. Psychol. Med., 32(5): 929-933, 2002.

REFERENCES

317. Donaldson, M.S., Speight, N., and Loomis, S.: Fibromyalgia syndrome improved using a mostly raw vegetarian diet: An observational study. *BMC Complement. Altern. Med.*, 1(1):7, 2001.

318. Bramwell, B., Ferguson, S., Scarlett, N., and Macintosh, A.: The use of ascorbigen in the treatment of fibromyalgia patients: a preliminary trial. *Altern. Med. Rev.*, 5(5):455-462, 2000.

319. Azad, K.A., Alam, M.N., Haq, S.A., et al.: Vegetarian diet in the treatment of fibromyalgia. *Bangladesh Med. Res. Counc. Bull.*, 26(2):41-47, 2000.

320. Smith, J.D., Terpening, C.M., Schmidt, S.O., et al.: Relief of fibromyalgia symptoms following discontinuation of dietary excitotoxins. *Ann. Pharmacother.*, 35(6):702-706, 2001.

321. Merchant, R.E. and Andre, C.A.: A review of recent clinical trials of the nutritional supplement Chlorella pyrenoidosa in the treatment of fibromyalgia, hypertension, and ulcerative colitis. *Altern. Ther. Health Med.*, 7(3):79-91, 2001.

322. Hanninen, K., Kaartinen, K., Rauma, A.L., et al.: Antioxidants in vegan diet and rheumatic disorders. *Toxicology*, 155(1-3):45-53, 2000.

323. Kaartinen, K., Lammi, K., Hypen, M., et al.: Vegan diet alleviates fibromyalgia symptoms. *Scand. J. Rheumatol.*, 29(5):308-313, 2000.

324. Merchant, R.E., Carmack, C.A., and Wise, C.M.: Nutritional supplementation with Chlorella pyrenoidosa for patients with fibromyalgia syndrome: a pilot study. *Phytother. Res.*, 14(3):167-173, 2000.

325. Dykman, K.D., Tone, C., Ford, C., and Dykman, R.A.: The effects of nutritional supplements on the symptoms of fibromyalgia and chronic fatigue syndrome. *Integr. Physiol. Behav. Sci.*, 33(1): 61-71, 1998.

326. Dalton, S.O., Johansen, C., Mellemkjaer, L., et al.. Antidepressant medications and risk for cancer. *Epidemiology*, 11(2):171-176, 2000.

327. Steingart, A.B. and Cotterchio, M.: Do antidepressants cause, promote, or inhibit cancers? *J. Clin. Epidemiol.*, 48(11):1407-1412, 1995.

328. Crowson, A.N. and Magro, C.M.: Antidepressant therapy. A possible cause of atypical cutaneous lymphoid hyperplasia. *Arch. Dermatol.*, 131(8):925-929, 1995.

329. Mizumaki, K. and Inoue, H.: Drug-induced arrhythmias. *Nippon Rinsho*, 60 (7):1449-1455, 2002.

330. Chong, S.A., Mythily, J., and Mahendran, R.: Cardiac effects of psychotropic drugs. *Ann. Acad. Med. Singapore*, 30(6):625-631, 2001.

331. Roose, S.P.: Considerations for the use of antidepressants in patients with cardiovascular disease. *Am. Heart J.*, 140(4 Suppl.):84-88, 2000.

332. Glassman, A.H.: Cardiovascular effects of antidepressant drugs: updated. *Int. Clin. Psychopharmacol.*, 13(Suppl.)5:S25-S30, 1998.

333. Inoue, H.: Drug-induced arrhythmias. *Nippon Rinsho*, 54(8):2220-2226, 1996.

334. Preskorn, S.H.: Fatality associated with combined fluoxetine-amitriptyline therapy. *JAMA*, 277(21), 1997.

335. Bell, D.S. and Ovalle, F.: Use of soy protein supplement and resultant need for increased dose of levothyroxine. *Endocr. Pract.*, 7(3):193-194, 2001.

336. Skibola, C.F. and Smith, M.T.: Potential health impacts of excessive flavonoid intake. *Free Radic. Biol. Med.*, 29(3-4):375-383, 2000.

337. Butchko, H.H., Stargel, W.W., Comer, C.P., et al.: Aspartame: review of safety. *Regul. Toxicol. Pharmacol.*, 35(2 Pt.2):S1-S93, 2002.

338. Garriga, M.M. and Metcalfe, D.D.: Aspartame intolerance. *Ann. Allergy*, 61 (6 Pt.2):63-69, 1988.

339. Olney, J.W.: Excitotoxic food additives--relevance of animal studies to human safety. *Neurobehav. Toxicol. Teratol.*, 6(6):455-462, 1984.

340. Reif-Lehrer, L.: Possible significance of adverse reactions to glutamate in humans. *Fed. Proc.*, 35(11):2205-2211, 1976.

341. Yang, W.H., Drouin, M.A., Herbert, M., et al.: The monosodium glutamate symptom complex: assessment in a double-blind, placebo-controlled, randomized study. *J. Allergy Clin. Immunol.*, 99:757-762, 1997.

342. <www.nacb.org/Thyroid_LMPG.html>

343. Savard, P., Merand, Y., Bedard, P., et al.: Comparative effects of neonatal hypothyroidism and euthyroidism on TRH and substance P content of lumbar spinal cord in saline and PCPA-treated rats. *Brain Res.*, 277(2):263-268, 1983.

344. Savard, P., Blanchard, L.M., Merand, Y., et al.: Influences of both thyroid and bovine growth hormones on substance P, thyrotropin-releasing hormone, serotonin and 5-hydroxyindoleacetic acid contents in the lumbar spinal cord of developing rats. *Brain Res.*, 315(1):105-110, 1984.

345. Johansen, K., Hansen, J.M., and Skovsted, L.: Myxoedema and thyrotoxicosis: relations between clinical state and concentrations of thyroxine and triiodothyronine in blood. *Acta Med. Scand.*, 204(5):361-364, 1978.

346. Morita, T. and Tokura, H.: Effects of lights of different color temperature on the nocturnal changes in core temperature and melatonin in humans. *Appl. Human Sci.*, 15(5):243-246, 1996.

347. Garcia-Borreguero, D., Larrosa, O., de la Llave, Y., et al.: Treatment of restless legs syndrome with gabapentin: a double-blind, cross-over study. *Neurology*, 59(10):1573-1579, 2002.

348. Norlock, F.E.: Benign breast pain in women: a practical approach to evaluation and treatment. *J. Am. Med. Womens Assoc.*, 57(2):85-90, Spring, 2002.

349. Kaiko, R.F., Wallensstein, S.L., Rogers, A.G., et al.: Analgesic and mood effects of heroin and morphine in cancer patients. *N. Engl. J. Med.*, 304:1501-1504, 1981.

350. Taenzer, P., Melzack, R., and Jeans, M.E.: Influence of psychological factors on postoperative pain, mood, and analgesic requirements. *Pain*, 24:331-342, 1986.

351. Ward, N., Bokan, J.A., Phillips, M., et al.: Antidepressants in concomitant chronic back pain and depression: doxepin and desipramine compared. *J. Clin. Psychiat.*, 45:54-57, 1984.

352. Ward, N., Bokan, J., Ang, J., et al.: Differential effects of fenfluramine and dextroamphetamine on acute and chronic pain. In *Advances in Pain Research and Therapy*, Vol. 9. Edited by H.L. Fields, New York, Raven Press, 1985, pp.753-760.

353. Ward, N., Whitney, C., Avery, D., and Dunner, D.: The analgesic effects of caffeine in headache. *Pain*, 44:151-155, 1991.
354. Silberstein, S.D.: Menstrual migraine. *J. Womens Health Gend. Based Med.*, 8(7):919-931, 1999.
355. Sawynok, J.: Pharmacological rationale for the clinical use of caffeine. *Drugs*, 49(1):37-50, 1995.
356. Johnson, L.C., Spinweber, C.L., and Gomez, S.A.: Benzodiazepines and caffeine: effect on daytime sleepiness, performance, and mood. *Psychopharmacology* (Berl), 101(2):160-167, 1990.
357. Roehrs, T., Zwyghuizen-Doorenbos, A., Smith, D., et al.: Reversal by caffeine of triazolam-induced impairment of waking function. *Psychopharmacol. Ser.*, 6:194-202, 1988.
358. Harrison, Y. and Horne, J.A.: Sleep loss and temporal memory. *Q. J. Exp. Psychol.*, 53(1):271-279, 2000.
359. Reyner, L.A. and Horne, J.A.: Early morning driver sleepiness: effectiveness of 200 mg caffeine. *Psychophysiology*, 37(2):251-256, 2000.
360. Lagarde, D., Batejat, D., Sicard, B., Trocherie, S., Chassard, D., Enslen, M., and Chauffard, F.: Slow-release caffeine: a new response to the effects of a limited sleep deprivation. *Sleep*, 23(5):651-661, 2000.
361. Giam, G.C.: Effects of sleep deprivation with reference to military operations. *Ann. Acad. Med. Singapore*, 26(1):88-93, 1997.
362. Devasagayam, T.P. and Kesavan, P.C.: Radioprotective and antioxidant action of caffeine: mechanistic considerations. *Indian J. Exp. Biol.*, 34(4):291-297, 1996.
363. Fillmore, C.M., Bartoli, L., Bach, R., et al.: Nutrition and dietary supplements. *Phys. Med. Rehabil. Clin. N. Am.*, 10(3):673-703, 1999
364. Clarkson, P.M.: Nutrition for improved sports performance. Current issues on ergogenic aids. *Sports Med.*, 21(6):393-401, 1996.
365. MacKintosh, J.: Quote on a plaque in the men's room in St. Louis Bakery in Tulsa, Oklahoma, 2001.
366. Kawachi, I., Willett, W.C., Colditz, G.A., et al.: A prospective study of coffee drinking and suicide in women. *Arch. Intern. Med.*, 156(5):521-525, 1996
367. Hawton, K. and Vislisel, L.: Suicide in nurses. *Suicide Life Threat Behav.*, 29(1):86-95, 1999.
368. Furuhashi, N., Sato, S., Suzuki, M., et al.: Effects of caffeine ingestion during pregnancy. *Gynecol. Obstet. Invest.*, 19(4):187-191, 1985.
369. Hadfield, M.G.: Caffeine and the olfactory bulb. *Mol. Neurobiol.*, 15(1):31-39, 1997.
370. Harlan, R.E. and Garcia, M.M.: Drugs of abuse and immediate-early genes in the forebrain. *Mol. Neurobiol.*, 16(3):221-267, 1998.
371. Plassart-Schiess, E. and Baulieu, E.E.: Neurosteroids: recent findings. *Brain Res. Brain Res. Rev.*, 37(1-3):133-140, 2001.
372. Gniot-Szulzycka, J. and Bohr, I.: Steroid modulation of GABA(A) receptors. *Postepy. Hig. Med. Dosw.*, 49(3):409-424, 1995.
373. Holsboer, F., Grasser, A., Friess, E., et al.: Steroid effects on central neurons

and implications for psychiatric and neurological disorders. *Ann. N.Y. Acad. Sci.*, 746:345-359,1994.

374. Keogh, E. and Chaloner, N.: The moderating effect of anxiety sensitivity on caffeine-induced hypoalgesia in healthy women. *Psychopharmacology* (Berl), 164(4):429-431, 2002.

375. Schonewille, W.J.: Chronic daily headaches caused by too much caffeine. *Ned. Tijdschr. Geneeskd.*, 146(40):1861-1863, 2002.

376. Keogh, E. and Witt, G.: Hypoalgesic effect of caffeine in normotensive men and women. *Psychophysiology*, 38(6):886-895, 2001.

377. Boozer, C.N., Daly, P.A., Homel, P., et al.: Herbal ephedra/caffeine for weight loss: a 6-month randomized safety and efficacy trial. *Int. J. Obes. Relat. Metab. Disord.*, 26(5):593-604, 2002.

378. Zhang, W.Y.: A benefit-risk assessment of caffeine as an analgesic adjuvant. *Drug Saf.*, 24(15):1127-1142, 2001.

379. Sawynok, J.: Adenosine receptor activation and nociception. *Eur. J. Pharmacol.*, 347(1):1-11, 1998.

380. Morewood, G.H.: A rational approach to the cause, prevention and treatment of postdural puncture headache. *CMAJ*, 149(8):1087-1093, 1993.

381. Roy-Byrne, P.P. and Uhde, T.W.: Exogenous factors in panic disorder: clinical and research implications. *J. Clin. Psychiatry*, 49(2):56-61, 1988.

382. Katz, J.: The course of peptic ulcer disease. *Med. Clin. North Am.*, 75(4): 831-840, 1991.

383. Vaeroy, H., Abrahamsen, A., Førre, O., and Kass, E.: Treatment of fibromyalgia (fibrositis syndrome): a parallel double-blind trial with carisoprodol, paracetamol and caffeine (Somadril comp) versus placebo. *Clin. Rheumatol.*, 8(2):245-250, 1989.

384. Lieberman, H.R.: The effects of ginseng, ephedrine, and caffeine on cognitive performance, mood and energy. *Nutr. Rev.*, 59(4):91-102, 2001.

385. Riedel, W.J. and Jorissen, B.L.: Nutrients, age and cognitive function. *Curr. Opin. Clin. Nutr. Metab. Care*, 1(6):579-585, 1998.

386. Johnson-Kozlow, M., Kritz-Silverstein, D., Barrett-Connor, E., et al.: Coffee consumption and cognitive function among older adults. *Am. J. Epidemiol.*, 156(9):842-850, 2002.

387. Beaumont, M., Batejat, D., Pierard, C., et al.: Slow release caffeine and prolonged (64-h) continuous wakefulness: effects on vigilance and cognitive performance. *J. Sleep Res.*, 10(4):265-276, 2001.

388. Smith, A., Maben, A., and Brockman, P.: Effects of evening meals and caffeine on cognitive performance, mood and cardiovascular functioning. *Appetite*, 22(1):57-65, 1994.

389. Shomon, M.: Qualitative survey of health status of 907 thyroid patients. Conducted by Mary Shomon, mshomon@thyroid-info.com, Jan. 15, 2003. <www.prnewswire.com> Complete survey available at <thyroid.about.com/library/weekly/aasurvey.htm>

390. Toft, A.D.: T_3/T_4 combination therapy. *Endocrine Abstracts*, 3:S40, 2002. <www.endocrine-abstracts.org/ea/0003/ea0003s40.htm>

391. Toft, A.D.: Thyroid hormone replacement: one hormone or two? *N. Engl. J.*

Med., 340(6):469-470, 1999.

392. Bunevicius, B., Kazanavicius, G., Zalinkevicius, R., and Prange, A.J. Jr.: Effects of thyroxine as compared with thyroxine plus triiodothyronine in patients with hypothyroidism. *N. Engl. J. Med.*, 340(6):424-429, 1999.

393. Toft, A.: Letter to Linda Thipthorp. Aug. 14, 2002.

394. MaryShomon's Thyroid Site:

395. Thyroid UK:

396. <www.drlowe.com>

397. Akwa, Y. and Baulieu, E.E.: Neurosteroids: behavioral aspects and physiological implications. *J. Soc. Biol.*, 193(3):293-298, 1999.

398. Northrup, C.: *Women's Bodies, Women's Wisdom.* New York, Bantam Books, 1998.

399. Salter, A.: *Conditioned Reflex Therapy.* New York, Capricorn Books, 1961.

400. Teitelbaum, J.: Highly effective treatments for pain and fatigue. *Townsend Letter for Doctors & Patients*, #234:126-127, Jan., 2003.

401. Teitelbaum, J.: Chronic fatigue syndrome and fibromyalgia. *Health Hotline* (publication of Vitamin Cottage Grocers, Colorado), Jan.-Feb, 6-7:2003.

402. Warmingham, P.: Fibromyalgia has been solved. *Fibro Focus Supporter,* 3:1-3, 2002.

403. Lowe, J.C., Eichelberger, J., Manso, G., et al.: Improvement in euthyroid fibromyalgia patients treated with T_3. *J. Myofascial Ther.*, 1(2):16-29, 1994.

404. Kraus, R.P., Phoenix, E., Edmonds, M.W., Nicholson, I.R., Chandarana, P.C., and Tokmakejian, S.: Exaggerated TSH responses to TRH in depressed patients with "normal" baseline TSH. *J. Clin. Psychiatry*, 58(6):266-270, 1997.

405. Kabadi, U.M. and Cech, R.: Normal thyroxine and elevated thyrotropin concentrations: evolving hypothyroidism or persistent euthyroidism with reset thyrostat. *J. Endocrinol. Invest.*, 20(6):319-326, 1997.

406. Fraser, W.D., Biggart, E.M., O'Reilly, D. St. J., Gray, H.W., and McKillop, J.H.: Are biochemical tests of thyroid function of any value in monitoring patients receiving thyroxine replacement? *Br. Med. J.*, 293:808-810, 1986.

Forms

Symptom Severity Scales

When you estimate the severity of your symptoms, think back over the past week, or the time since your last estimate. Then place a mark on the scale that represents the average severity of the symptom during that time.

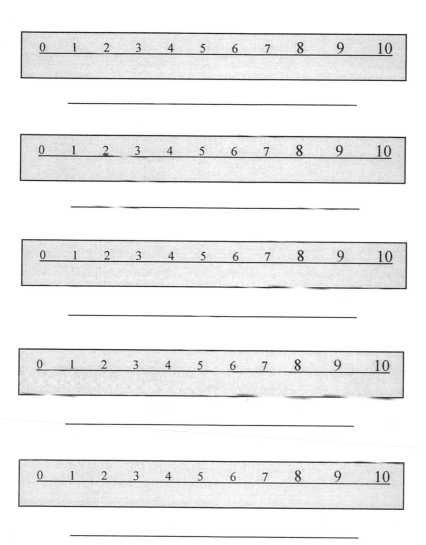

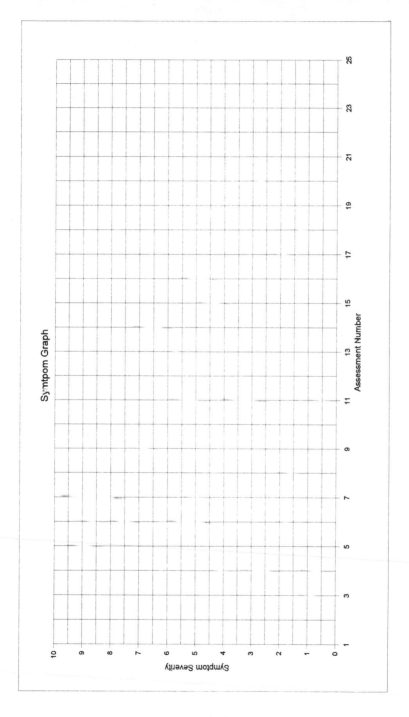

Symptom Graph

Are you overstimulated?

Name _____   Date _____

To gather information about possible overstimulation from thyroid hormone, please answer the following questions. You should fill out this form several times to get a baseline before your doctor has you begin using thyroid hormone. After your doctor starts your thyroid hormone therapy, complete the form with the others in this section at set intervals. To decide whether you're overstimulated, compare your most recent overstimulation form with those you completed prior to beginning the use of thyroid hormone. As always, share your concerns, your graphs, and your overstimulation forms with your doctor.

The thyroid hormone preparation I'm using?_____

My daily dosage?_____ My resting heart rate today?_____

Rate the intensity of any of the following symptoms you're experiencing. If you aren't experiencing the symptom, please mark "0".

Symptom											
Rapid heart rate	0	1	2	3	4	5	6	7	8	9	10
Pounding heart	0	1	2	3	4	5	6	7	8	9	10
Muscle tremors	0	1	2	3	4	5	6	7	8	9	10
Excess body heat	0	1	2	3	4	5	6	7	8	9	10
Excess perspiration	0	1	2	3	4	5	6	7	8	9	10
Diarrhea	0	1	2	3	4	5	6	7	8	9	10
Insomnia	0	1	2	3	4	5	6	7	8	9	10
Irritability	0	1	2	3	4	5	6	7	8	9	10
Restlessness	0	1	2	3	4	5	6	7	8	9	10
Anxiety	0	1	2	3	4	5	6	7	8	9	10
Fatigue	0	1	2	3	4	5	6	7	8	9	10
Weakness	0	1	2	3	4	5	6	7	8	9	10
Appetite change	0	1	2	3	4	5	6	7	8	9	10
Weight change	0	1	2	3	4	5	6	7	8	9	10
Menstrual problems	0	1	2	3	4	5	6	7	8	9	10

Resources

Dr. Gina Honeyman-Lowe
Director of Clinical Care
Center for Metabolic Health
1800 30th Street, Suite 217A
Boulder, CO 80301
(303) 413-9100
DrGHL@drlowe.com
www.drlowe.com

Dr. John C. Lowe
Board Certified: American Academy of Pain Management
Director of Research: Fibromyalgia Research Foundation
1800 30th Street, Suite 217A
Boulder, CO 80301
(303) 413-9100
DrLowe@drlowe.com
www.drlowe.com

As we've written several places in *Your Guide to Metabolic Health*, we're available for long-distance consulting or for clinical care at our clinic in Boulder, Colorado.

(**Help with troubleshooting.** When you're going through your own metabolic rehab, we hope all goes smoothly. If one or more obstacles are holding back your progress, read *Chapter 15*, Troubleshooting. If the information there doesn't help, you may find help at our troubleshooting webpage: <www.McDowellPublishing.com/TroubleShooting/ygmh.htm> If you don't find a solution to your problem there, you can write to us at AskDrLowe@drlowe.com. In the subject line of your e-mail, type "YGMH." This will tell us that we have an e-mail from someone working with *Your Guide to Metabolic Health* and having a problem.)

*   *   *   *   *

Richard Finn, C.M.T.P.T.
Certified Myofascial Trigger Point Therapist
1312 East Carson Street
Pittsburgh, PA 15203
(412) 481-2553 Fax: (412) 381-6922

www.npimall.com/amtpt
(One of the world's foremost authorities on trigger points and myofascial therapy. Director of the Pittsburgh School of Pain Management and an active clinician. Extremely knowledgeable about metabolic rehabilitation.)

Stephen E. Langer, M.D.
3031 Telegraph Avenue, Suite 230
Berkeley, CA 94705
(510) 548-7384
(Physician who specializes in hypothyroidism. Coauthor with James Scheer of the best-selling book on hypothyroidism, *Solved: The Riddle of Illness,* now in its third edition.)

Craig Liebenson, D.C.
10474 Santa Monica Blvd.
202 Los Angeles, CA 90025
(310) 470-2909 Fax: (310) 470-3286
(Chiropractic doctor, expert in neuromusculoskeletal rehabilitation, author, lecturer.)

Vicky Massey, L.M.P.
15317 Meridian E., Suite A
Puyallup, WA 98375
(253) 445-5193 Fax: (253) 537-6072
www.drlowe.com/vicky.htm
(Licensed massage practitioner, expert on fibromyalgia and metabolic rehabilitation, and member of the Board of Professional Advisors to the Fibromyalgia Research Foundation.)

Michael McNett, M.D.
The Paragon Clinic
4332 N. Elston Ave.
Chicago, IL 60641
(773) 604-5321
www.paragonclinic.com
(Internist who is expert at treating candida infections, especially in fibromyalgia patients.)

Bret R. Staley, D.C.
1170 North Moapa Valley Blvd., Suite C
Overton, NV 89040
(702) 397-2273 Fax: (702) 397-2705
(Chiropractic physician who is expert at metabolic rehabilitation.)

Linda Thipthorp
Truro, Cornwall
United Kingdom
Tel: 01872 240337
Lynthip@aol.com
(Recovered hypothyroid patient, patients' advocate, and counselor of patients with hypothyroidism and thyroid hormone resistance.)

BOOKS

Dr. John C. Lowe: *The Metabolic Treatment of Fibromyalgia.* Boulder, McDowell Publishing Co., 2000. (Order at: <www.mcdowellpublishing.com>, by phone at 303-570-7231, or by fax to 303-604-0773.)

Dr. John C. Lowe: *Speeding Up to Normal.* McDowell Publishing Co., available: summer, 2003. (Order at: <www.mcdowellpublishing.com>, by phone at 303-570-7231, or by fax to 303-604-0773.)

Dr. John C. Lowe: *Tyranny of the TSH.* McDowell Publishing Co., available: fall, 2003. (Order at: <www.mcdowellpublishing.com>, by phone at 303-570-7231, or by fax to 303-604-0773.)

* * * * *

Covert Bailey: *Fit or Fat.* Boston, Houghton Mifflin Co., 1978.

Dr. Broda O. Barnes and L. Galton: *Hypothyroidism: The Unsuspected Illness.* New York, Harper & Row, Publishers, 1976.

Dr. Leon Chaitow: *Fibromyalgia and Muscle Pain.* London, Thorsons, 2001.

Drs. Theo Colborn, D. Dumanoski, and J.P. Myers: *Our Stolen Future.* New York, Penguin Books, Inc., 1996.

Dr. Alan R. Gaby: *Preventing and Reversing Osteoporosis: Every Woman's Essential Guide.* Rocklin, Prima Publishing, 1994.

Diana Holmes: *Tears Behind Closed Doors: Failure to Diagnose an Underactive Thyroid—The Truth Behind Tragedy,* 1999. (To order, contact Vine House Distribution, telephone from USA: 0-11-44-1825-723-398 Fax: 0-11-44-1825-724-188.)

Dr. Steven E. Langer and James F. Scheer: *Solved: The Riddle of Illness,* 3rd edition. Keats Publishing, 2000.

Dr. Marcus Laux. *Natural Woman, Natural Menopause.* New York, Harper Perennial, 1998.

Dr. John R. Lee and Dr. J. Hanley: *What Your Doctor May Not Have Told You About Menopause.* New York, Warner Books, 1996.

Dr. Earl Mindell: *Earl Mindell's Supplement Bible.* New York, Fireside, 1998.

Dr. Earl Mindell: *Earl Mindell's Vitamin Bible.* New York, Simon & Schuster, 1998.

Dr. Michael Murray and Dr. Joseph Pizzorno: *Encyclopedia of Natural Medicine*, 2nd edition. Rocklin, Prima Publishing, 1998.

Dr. Michael Murray and Dr. Joseph Pizzorno: *Textbook of Natural Medicine,* 3rd edition, Elsevier, in press.

Dr. Linus Pauling: *How to Live Longer and Feel Better.* New York, Avon Books, 1987.

Dr. Linus Pauling: *Vitamin C, the Common Cold, and the Flu.* W.H. Freeman and Co., 1976.

Dr. Barry Durrant-Peatfield: *The Great Thyroid Scandal and How to Survive It.* London, Barons Down Publishing, 2002. (Order at: <www.baronsdownpublishing.com>.)

Mary Shomon: *Living Well With Autoimmune Disease.* New York, HarperCollins, 2002. (Order at: <www.autoimmunebook.com>.)

Mary Shomon: *Living Well With Hypothyroidism: What Your Doctor Doesn't Tell You . . . That You Need to Know.* Avon Books, New York, 2000. (Order at: <http://thyroid.about.com/health/thyroid/library/thyroidbook/blintro3.htm>.)

Mary Shomon: *Sticking Out Our Necks: The Thyroid Disease News Report.* Popular newsletter on thyroid disease and its treatment. (Order at: <www.thyroid-info.com> or by phone at 888-810-9471.)

Dr. Devin J. Starlanyl: *The Fibromyalgia Advocate.* Oakland, New Harbinger Publications, Inc., 1998.

Dr. Julian Whitaker: *Dr. Whitaker's Guide to Natural Healing.* Rocklin, Prima Publishing, 1996

Dr. Roger J. Williams: *Nutrition Against Disease.* New York, Bantam Books, 1971.

Dr. Roger J. Williams.: *The Wonderful World Within You: Your Inner Nutritional Environment*. Bantam Books, New York, 1977.

MOVIE

Lorenzo's Oil. Universal City Studios, 1992. Movie starring Nick Nolte, Susan Sarandon, and Peter Ustinov. We strongly recommend watching this movie. It shows how most traditional support groups disempower people with difficult-to-solve medical problems. This movie will give you an understanding of why we recommend that fibromyalgia/chronic fatigue syndrome patients be extremely cautious when looking for a support group.

ORGANIZATIONS

Fibromyalgia Research Foundation
P.O. Box 81, Lafayette, CO 80026
(303) 413-9100
www.drlowe.com/frf.htm

*   *   *   *   *

Albert Ellis Institute
45 East 65th Street, New York, NY 10021
www.rebt.org
E-mail: info@rebt.org
(Mecca of rational-emotive-behavioral therapy. Provides treatment for clients and training for health care professionals. For catalog of books, tapes, and seminars: call 800-323-4738 or 212-535-0822, or fax to 212-249-3582.)

Herb Research Foundation
1007 Pearl Street, Suite 200, Boulder, CO 80302, (800) 748-2617
www.herbs.org
Herbal Hotline: (303) 449-2265
(This organization charges a nominal, understandable fee to provide information. They have a packet specifically on herbal support for the thyroid gland.)

National Association of Myofascial Trigger Point Therapists
Referral network for certified myofascial trigger point therapists:
(800) 845-3454
www.myofascialtherapy.org
E-mail: info@myofascialtherapy.org

Pittsburgh School of Pain Management
1312 East Carson Street, Pittsburgh, PA 15203
(412) 481-2553 Fax: (412) 381-6922
www.PainSchool.com
E-mail: amtpt@stairgate.net
(Provides treatment for pain and dysfunction from myofascial trigger points and training programs for therapists. Richard Finn, C.M.T.P.T. is Director.)

Rational Recovery
Box 800, Lotus CA 95651, (530) 621-2667 or (530) 621-4374
www.rational.org
(Support group for alcoholics and drug addicts whose aim is to empty its chairs; emphasis is on *recovery*.)

WEBSITES

DrLowe.com
www.drlowe.com
(Website on metabolic health. Contains massive information on fibromyalgia, chronic fatigue syndrome, hypothyroidism, thyroid hormone resistance, myofascial pain, and related health matters. Several highly-qualified people answer readers' questions at drlowe.com.)

*　*　*　*　*

Candida-Yeast Website
www.candida-yeast.com
(Site that features the work of the main popularizer of candida treatment, Dr. William G. Crook.)

PubMed
www.ncbi.nlm.nih.gov/entrez/query.fcgi?CMD=search&DB=PubMed
(At PubMed, readers will find summaries of millions of studies on medical conditions and their treatment.)

Thyroid.About.com
http://thyroid.about.com
(Mary Shomon's popular website on thyroid disease.)

Thyroid UK
www.thyroiduk.org
(Educational articles on hypothyroidism, and referrals to doctors in the United Kingdom.)

Glossary

ACR: American College of Rheumatology.

Adrenergic receptor: A protein molecule in cell membranes that catecholamines (such as adrenaline and noradrenaline) bind with to initiate changes in cell metabolism. There are alpha and beta forms of the adrenergic receptor.

Alpha-Adrenergic receptor: A receptor that binds to adrenaline and noradrenaline (catecholamines) and inhibits cell processes.

Armour Thyroid: Tablets containing thyroid hormone produced naturally by pigs' thyroid glands. Each grain contains 38 mcg of T_4 and 9 mcg of T_3. Inactive ingredients include calcium stearate, dextrose, and mineral oil. Marketed by Forest Pharmaceuticals, Inc.

Atrial fibrillation: The atria are the two small upper chambers of the heart. They receive blood from the veins and in turn force it into the large chambers of the heart called the ventricles. Fibrillation is uncontrolled twitching or quivering of muscle fibrils. Normally, the muscles of the atria contract rhythmically. In atrial fibrillation, however, the atrial muscles twitch rapidly and irregularly. The irregular twitchings of the atria bombards the ventricles, potentially causing them, too, to contract irregularly.

Benzodiazepines: A family of minor tranquilizers. They reduce or eliminate anxiety and convulsions, and produce sedation and muscle relaxation.

Beta-Adrenergic receptor: A receptor that binds to adrenaline and noradrenaline (catecholamines) and increases cell processes.

Brain stem: The earliest evolved part of the brain, located between the spinal cord and the cerebral cortex. Brain stem centers regulate autonomic functions such as breathing and the urination reflex.

Candida albicans: A species of fungus that is a constituent of the flora of the human gastrointestinal tract. Under some conditions that cause an imbalance in the intestinal flora, such as prolonged antibiotic use, *Candida albicans* may overgrow to the degree that it becomes pathogenic.

Clinical features vary from widespread skin and mucous membrane infections to conditions that may prove fatal, such as septicemia, meningitis, or endocarditis.

Central hypothyroidism: Decreased thyroid gland production and secretion of thyroid hormone due to dysfunction of the pituitary gland or hypothalamus.

Central nervous system: The brain and spinal cord; usually abbreviated as CNS.

CFS: Chronic fatigue syndrome.

Chronic fatigue syndrome: As defined by the United States Centers for Disease Control, debilitating fatigue lasting for longer than six months.

Clinical medicine: The practice of medicine in which the clinician uses a wide range of methods to make diagnostic and treatment decisions. The clinician uses the patient's history and symptoms along with the results of physical exam procedures and technical test methods. The clinician and patient usually have a collaborative relationship. In contrast to extremist medical technocrats, the practitioner of clinical medicine trusts his judgment based on his bank of knowledge, clinical experiences, and observations and interactions with his patients. See "Clinician."

Clinician: Any health care practitioner. The term applies to medical, osteopathic, and chiropractic physicians. It also applies to bodyworkers such as massage therapists, myofascial trigger point therapists, and physical therapists. The term also applies to mental health practitioners such as psychologists, social workers, and those trainers and guides within the human potential movement.

CNS: Central nervous system.

Colon: Large intestine; the lower portion of the intestinal tract.

Cortisol: The steroid hormone most abundantly secreted by the adrenal cortex in humans. Also called hydrocortisone. Increased cortisol secretion is a part of the physiological process of stress response.

Cynomel: Brand name for synthetic T_3; sold in Mexico as an over-the-counter product.

Cytomel: Brand name for synthetic T_3; Jones Medical Industries, Inc.

Drive, motor: See "Motor drive."

ECG: See "Electrocardiogram." Also called EKG.

EEG: See "Electroencephalogram."

EKG: See "Electrocardiogram." Also called ECG.

Electrocardiogram: A recording on graph paper of the electrical currents of the heart. Also called EKG and ECG.

Electroencephalogram: A recording on graphs of the electrical activity of the brain. Also called EEG. The activity is measured and converted into graphic form by an instrument called an electroencephalograph. Brain electrical activity is measured through electrodes placed on the skull.

Enzyme: A protein that catalyzes chemical reactions to occur at rates hundreds-to-thousands of times faster than would happen in its absence. The reactions catalyzed by enzymes regulate cell metabolism, the assembly of large molecules from smaller ones (anabolism), and the breakdown of large molecules to smaller ones (catabolism). Vitamins and/or minerals that attach to enzymes are necessary to the normal function of the enzymes.

Euthyroid: Normal function of the hypothalamic-pituitary-thyroid axis. The patient has reference range levels of TSH and thyroid hormone. See "Reference range."

Fibromyalgia: A diagnostic term for patients who have chronic widespread pain and tenderness at predetermined body sites. The pain and tenderness result mainly from impairment of the CNS pain-modulating system due to under-regulation by thyroid hormone.

Free radical: An atom or molecule with an unpaired electron in its outer shell. The unpaired electron makes the atom or molecule extremely reactive and capable of undergoing rapid chain reactions that destabilize other molecules and produce many more free radicals. Antioxidants, uric acid, and some enzymes inactivate free radicals.

Goiter: Chronically enlarged thyroid gland that's not caused by a tumor.

Growth hormone: A hormone produced and secreted into the blood by the pituitary gland. Thyroid hormone powerfully regulates production of the hormone; too little thyroid hormone regulation of the pituitary reduces growth hormone production.

Hormone: A substance produced by one tissue and transported through the circulating blood to affect the biochemical and/or physiological activity of another tissue. Most hormones are either peptides or steroids.

HPA axis: Term used to refer to the hypothalamus, pituitary gland, and adrenal cortices as a function chain. In response to stressful physical, physiological, chemical, mechanical, or psychological stimuli, cells of the hypothalamus release corticotropin releasing hormone (CRH) and arginine-vasopressin (AVP). These two hormones stimulate the release of adrenocorticotropin hormone (ACTH) from the pituitary gland. In turn, ACTH stimulates cells of the adrenal cortices to release cortisol. Cortisol helps cells of the body adapt to stress. Normally, the HPA axis is most active in the morning and becomes less active through the day and night.

5-HTP: 5-hydroxytryptophan.

5-Hydroxytryptophan: A compound normally derived from the amino acid tryptophan; abbreviated as 5-HTP. It is converted to serotonin (5-hydroxytryptamine). 5-HTP is extracted from seeds of *Griffonia simplicifolia*, an African plant. The extract is available for purchase as a medication.

Hyperthyroidism: Production of abnormally large amounts of thyroid hormone by the thyroid gland. Hyperthyroidism is *not* synonymous with thyrotoxicosis. See "Thyrotoxicosis."

Hypometabolism: Literally, slow metabolism. Many times in this book, we write "symptoms of hypometabolism." We're referring to metabolism slow enough to cause cells and tissues to dysfunction and for health problems to develop.

Hypothyroidism: Abnormally low thyroid hormone production and secretion by the thyroid gland. See "Primary hypothyroidism" and "Central hypothyroidism."

Hypothyroidism, central: See "Central hypothyroidism."

Hypothyroidism, primary: See "Primary Hypothyroidism."

Hypothyroidism, subclinical: Defined as an elevated TSH level with reference range thyroid hormone levels.

Insomnia: Difficulty getting enough sleep, especially when chronic. May involve awakening too early, or difficulty falling or staying asleep.

IU: International Unit.

ME: Myalgic encephalomyelitis.

Medical technocrat: A practitioner of technocratic medicine. See "Technocratic medicine."

Metabolism: 1. The total of all chemical changes that occur in cells and thereby contribute to the overall operation of the body. Metabolism involves two classes of changes. First is anabolism: chemical changes that convert small molecules into larger ones. Second is catabolism: changes that convert large molecules into smaller ones. 2. Complete chemical processing of a compound in the body.

mg: Milligram (one-thousandth of a gram: 1/1,000 g).

Motor drive: The capability, readiness, or inclination of a person to engage in physical activity.

Myxedema; Non-pitting edema, usually localized to different skin tissue sites; associated with hypothyroidism. Myxedema was the first recognized sign assumed to represent thyroid hormone deficiency. During the early part of the 20th century, clinicians used the presence of myxedema to diagnose hypothyroidism. The mechanism of the edema is the accumulation of water-binding compounds in the ground substance of the involved connective tissue.

Neurotransmitter: A substance, such as adrenaline, that transmits nerve signals across gaps between nerves.

NSAIDS: Nonsteroidal anti-inflammatory drugs.

Orthostatic hypotension: A sudden drop in blood pressure upon assuming an erect posture. Synonymous with postural hypotension.

Palpation: Examination through touch. The clinician feels the body part being examined with his fingers, thumbs, or hands.

Peripheral resistance to thyroid hormone: A condition in which the tissues other than those of the pituitary gland have a lower-than-normal response to thyroid hormone. As a result, normal amounts of thyroid hormone fail to maintain a normal metabolic rate. The patient has slow metabolism and hypothyroid-like symptoms. But because the patient's thyroid gland is normal and her pituitary gland responds normally to thyroid hormone, her thyroid function test results are normal. These patients are often said to be "clinically hypothyroid but biochemically euthyroid."

Peripheral tissues: Used in two different senses: 1. Tissues outside the central nervous system; distinguished from central tissues. 2. Tissues other than the pituitary gland. When used in this sense, the brain and spinal cord are considered peripheral tissues.

Pharmacologic hormone dose: A dose of a hormone that is higher than the amount produced by the body of the average person.

Physiologic hormone dose: A dose of a hormone that is consistent with the amount produced in the average person.

Primary hypothyroidism: Decreased production and secretion of thyroid hormones by the thyroid gland due to some disorder of the gland. Synonymous with thyroidal hypothyroidism.

Range of normal: See "Reference range."

Receptor: A cellular molecule that binds specific substances, and as a complex with the substances, influences cell processes. Receptors are composed of one or more proteins, and they occupy either the outer cell membrane, the fluid inside cells, or sites on DNA.

Reference range: Term used to replace "range of normal." The usual range of test values for a presumably healthy population. Often defined as the range within which 95% of healthy patients' test values fall.

Replacement dose, cortisol: As defined by William McK. Jefferies,[104,p.13] a cortisol dose that maintains a person (in normal health in the unstressed state) whose adrenal cortices have been removed. The cortisol must be taken with physiologic amounts of androgenic and sodium-retaining hormones.

Replacement dose, thyroid hormone: The dose of thyroid hormone, usually T_4, that keeps the TSH and thyroid hormone levels within the reference ranges. Considered by conventional clinicians to be an amount sufficient to meet the needs of tissues for metabolic stimulation. Evidence shows, however, that replacement doses of T_4 (1) do not provide normal amounts of T_3 within the cells of many tissues, (2) do not maintain normal tissue metabolism, and (3) are a common cause of symptoms diagnosed as "new diseases" such as fibromyalgia and chronic fatigue syndrome.

Sign: A manifestation of disease or dysfunction that can be observed or measured by another person such as a clinician. Signs are objective evidence of the disease or dysfunction. Signs are distinguished from symptoms, which are subjective impressions of the patient. See "Symptom."

Slow metabolism: An alternate term for "hypometabolism." See "Hypometabolism."

Somatomedin C: A hormone produced and secreted mainly by liver cells under the influence of growth hormone and thyroid hormone. Somatomedin C stimulates the deposition of protein in injured tissues under the influence of growth hormone. By powerfully regulating production of both somatomedin C and growth hormone, thyroid hormone is indirectly responsible for normal tissue growth and repair.

Steroid hormones: Hormones made from steroids. Steroids are a large group of organic compounds that are fat-soluble. Bile acids, for example, are steroids that emulsify fats from food in the small intestine. The body makes steroid hormones from these stearoid compounds. For example, the adrenal cortex makes DHEA and cortisol. The ovaries and testicles make three steroid hormones from the compounds: estrogen, progesterone, and testosterone. Steroid hormones have specific physiological actions in most tissues of the body.

Subclinical hypothyroidism: See "Hypothyroidism, subclinical."

Subluxation: See "Vertebral subluxation."

Supplement, thyroid hormone: A thyroid hormone supplement implies less than a full replacement dose of exogenous thyroid hormone. Supplemental thyroid hormone is taken as an addition to thyroid hormone produced and secreted by the thyroid gland.

Symptom: A perception by a patient of a variation from normal structure or function that indicates dysfunction or disease.

Synthroid: Brand of synthetic T_4 (levothyroxine sodium tablets). Inactive ingredients include acacia, confectioner's sugar, lactose, starch, magnesium stearate, providone, talc, and single or different combinations of color additives that vary in tablets of different strength. Provided in tablets of eleven different dosages. Abbott Laboratories.

T_3: Triiodothyronine.

T_4: Tetraiodothyronine (thyroxine or levothyroxine).

Tachycardia: Rapid heart rate. Tachycardia is defined as a resting heart rate of 100 beats or more per minute.

Technocratic medicine: The practice of medicine based on a philosophy of medical technocracy. Medical technocracy is the advocacy of reforming medical practice so that it's conducted according to the reported findings of technologists. In this form of practice, diagnostic and treatment decisions are based almost exclusively on the outcome of objective tests. Typically, the practitioner of technocratic medicine disavows the methods of clinical medicine. He tends to devalue the patient's symptoms and signs and communication with the patient. Commonly, the practitioner has an extremist faith in the outcome of objective tests peculiar to his specialty. The technocratic practitioner's specialized knowledge usually gives rise to a sense of superiority over patients and practitioners of clinical medicine. This sense of superiority is typically reflected in a personality disorder involving arrogance and dogmatism that tend to alienate patients and practitioners of clinical medicine.

Thyroidectomy: Surgical removal of the thyroid gland. Often used as an adjective, as in "thyroidectomized rats."

GLOSSARY

Thyroid hormone products, brand names: Products are available that contain only synthetic T_4, only synthetic T_3, synthetic T_4 and T_3, and T_4 and T_3 derived from animal thyroid glands.

Thyroid hormone products by brand name and hormone content*

CONTENTS	BRAND NAME
Synthetic T_4	Levothroid, Levoxine, Levoxyl, Synthroid
Synthetic T_3	Cynomel, Cyronine, Cytomel, Euthroid, Linomel, Liothyronin, Neo-Tiroimade, Ro-Thyronine, Tertroxin, Thybon-forte, Thyrotardin, Tiromel, Tironina, Ti-Tre, Trijod.Sanabo, Trijodthyronin, Trijodthyr.50, Trijodthyr.Leo, Triostat
Synthetic T_4 & T_3	Thyrolar
Naturally-derived T_4 & T_3	Armour Thyroid, Westhroid, Naturethroid, S-P-T, Nutri-Meds

*See each manufacturer's information for more detailed descriptions.

Thyroid state: Functional status of the thyroid gland: hyperfunction (hyperthyroidism), normal function (euthyroidism), or hypofunction (hypothyroidism).

Thyroid-stimulating hormone: Abbreviated as TSH. Also called thyrotropin. One of the hormones released by the anterior pituitary gland. TSH passes through the blood to the thyroid gland and stimulates all functions of the thyroid gland. In this way, TSH increases the thyroid gland's synthesis and secretion of T_4 and T_3. See "TSH test."

Thyrolar: Product that contains synthetic T_4 and T_3. The ratio of T_4 to T_3 is 4:1. Available in five potencies. Tablets contain several inactive ingredients including dyes. Forest Pharmaceuticals, Inc.

Thyrotoxicosis: Symptoms of tissue overstimulation by thyroid hormone. Thyrotoxicosis is *not* synonymous with hyperthyroidism. See "Hyperthyroidism."

373

Thyrotropin-releasing hormone: Hormone secreted by the hypothalamus that stimulates pituitary cells to produce and secrete TSH. Abbreviated as TRH.

TRH: See "Thyrotropin-releasing hormone."

TRH-stimulation test: A lab test that identifies patients with central hypothyroidism.

TSH: Abbreviation for thyroid-stimulating hormone. See "Thyroid-stimulating hormone " and "TSH test."

TSH test: A measure of the TSH in the circulating blood. The test result shows the effect of thyroid hormone in the blood on pituitary gland cells that produce TSH. Most doctors mistakenly believe that the TSH level is a measure of the effect of thyroid hormone on the tissues of the body other than the pituitary. This is a false belief that leaves millions of patients chronically ill and accounts for the premature death of inestimable numbers of people from heart attacks, strokes, and suicide. See "Thyroid-stimulating hormone."

Vertebral subluxation: A segment of the spine having abnormal movement. Usually, motion is restricted, but it may be excessive. The part of the spinal cord and nerves associated with the spinal segment function abnormally.

Yoda: A 3000 year-old sage from the movie *Star Wars* who trained Jedi masters.

Index

Page numbers followed by (f) indicate figures; those followed by (t) indicate tables; those followed by (b) indicates boxes.